# THE DOCTRINE OF RECONCILIATION
*Karl Barth*

# THE DOCTRINE OF RECONCILIATION

Church Dogmatics

*Karl Barth*

*Translator* G. W. Bromiley

*Editors* G. W. Bromiley and T. F. Torrance

**continuum**

LONDON • NEW YORK

**Continuum**

The Tower Building
11 York Road
London SE1 7NX

15 East 26th Street
Suite 1703
New York
NY 10010

*www.continuumbooks.com*

First edition copyright © T&T Clark Ltd, 1956
First paperback edition copyright © T&T Clark International, 2004
This edition 2004

Authorised English translation of *Die Kirchliche Dogmatik IV:*
*Die Lehre von der Versöhnung 1*
copyright © Evangelischer Verlag A.G., Zollikon–Zürich

ISBN 0 8264 7792 5

British Library Cataloguing-in-Publication Data
A catalogue record for this book is available from the British Library

Typeset by RefineCatch Limited, Bungay, Suffolk
Printed and bound in Great Britain by Antony Rowe, Chippenham, Wiltshire

# Contents

# Editors' Preface

As mentioned in the Preface to I, 2, the publication of the more recent part-volume IV, I has been expedited in order that readers who so desire may keep in touch with the more recent development of the *Dogmatics*. The part-volume is of particular interest because it introduces us to the central doctrine of the Christian faith—the atonement. Barth's account of the doctrine entails three part-volumes devoted to the three forms of the doctrine corresponding to the threefold confession of Jesus Christ as very God, very Man and the God-Man. The first form—the theme of the present part-volume—starts with Christ as the God who humbled Himself as a servant to accomplish the work of reconciliation. The second is concerned with Christ as the royal man in whom man is exalted and adopted into the fellowship with God. And the third treats of Christ as the God-Man who is the Guarantor of atonement. The translation of the second part-volume will soon be in the printers' hands, but the third has yet to appear in German.

In addition to the general note on the structure and translation of the *Dogmatics* in the Preface to I, 2 (to which readers are referred), two particular observations may be made. The first concerns the word *Versöhnung*, which is given by Barth a rich content that includes both "atonement" and "reconciliation." Hence, while the latter term is preferred for the title, both are used in the body of the text according to the requirements of the context. The word "redemption," incidentally, is almost always used in connexion with the work of the Holy Spirit and with the eschatological perspective of God's saving work.

The second is in regard to the term *Stellvertretung*, which enshrines the notions both of representation and substitution, and never the one without the other. Representation by itself is particularly inadequate as a rendering, though this aspect is present, and the word is used more often perhaps than it ought to be in view of the prevailing prejudice against substitution. In most cases the latter is both fuller and truer, but, as the text discloses, it is given a sense more radical than is normally the case in English, because Barth envisages it as a total displacement of sinful man by the incarnate, crucified and risen Son; and also more comprehensive, because it is related to the whole life and work of Jesus Christ, including His heavenly intercession. The objective reality, not only of Christ's historical birth, life, death and resurrection, but also of His once-for-all work of reconciliation on our behalf and in our place, is Barth's tacit but definitive answer to the "demythologisation" crusade of Bultmann, which involves the genuinely mythologising process of reinterpreting Christ's incarnation and reconciling work in terms of existentialist decision and timeless re-enactment. The point of this answer depends on the bold and thorough-going doctrine of *Stellvertretung*.

Our thanks are again due to the Assistant Editor, the Reverend Professor J. K. S. Reid, for his careful scrutiny of the proofs and many useful corrections and emendations; and also to the publishers and printers for their unfailing patience, helpfulness and diligence.

Edinburgh, *Michaelmas* 1956.

# Foreword

Two more years have passed since the appearance of the last part-volume. For me they have been more than occupied by work on this first survey of the vast territory of the doctrine of reconciliation. I have been very conscious of the very special responsibility laid on the theologian at this centre of all Christian knowledge. To fail here is to fail everywhere. To be on the right track here makes it impossible to be completely mistaken in the whole. Week by week and even day by day I have had, and will have (in the continuation), to exercise constant vigilance to find that right track and not to lose it.

The necessary effort demands a corresponding concentration of time and energy. And it means that I must again excuse myself for refusing to perform many other tasks and legitimate claims and expectations. I am more with my contemporaries, and especially those who accompany this work, than I can make it appear to them directly. Every word or sign of sympathy expressed by them is a comfort and encouragement for which I am most grateful, even though I can say so only occasionally to a few. I must also excuse myself to those who think it necessary to attack me—either on account of the *Dogmatics* or of other actions or positions. I read their judicious (and often not so judicious) sayings and learn from them what I can: but the time when I had the liberty and desire to plunge into public or private disputations has completely passed. My "neighbours" are for the most part my students here in Basel, who in my lectures are always the first to hear the further instalments of the *Church Dogmatics*. Like their predecessors in Göttingen, Münster and Bonn, they see to it that I cannot become a "carefully preserved Jerome."

The present situation in theology and also the peculiar themes of this book mean that throughout I have found myself in an intensive, although for the most part quiet, debate with Rudolf Bultmann. His name is not mentioned often. But his subject is always present, even in those places where with his methods and results before me I have consciously ignored him. I respect the man, his mind and aim and achievements, and the zeal of his following. I only wish that I could do him greater justice. But if I have to choose between, on the one hand, accepting the rule which he has proclaimed and thus not being able to say certain things which I perceive and which I believe ought to be said, or having to say them very differently from how I perceive them, and on the other hand saying them quite freely, but making myself guilty of using what he regards as an "obscure conceptuality," then I have no option but to choose the second. His hermeneutical suggestions can become binding on me only when I am convinced that by following them I would say the same things better and more freely. For the time being, I am not so convinced.

Some casual readers may miss what I say about the division of the total material of this further main part of the whole work upon which I have now embarked, and of the reasons for it. They are now expressly reminded that what is offered in this first part-volume is only a first survey which has yet to be followed by two more (together with a chapter of ethics). Those who think that something important has been omitted must not judge before the time but wait to see if it will come up later.

I should like to take this opportunity to correct certain annoying errors committed in the earlier volumes. In III, 2, p. 338 I ascribed to Raphael a painting by Titian: how, I do not understand. In III, 4, p. 398 I translated Dr. Albert Schweitzer at a stroke from Ogowe in West Africa to the Zambesi in East Africa, a mistake I ought to have been able to spot even from my school days. A printer's error, for which I am also responsible, is that in III, 3, p. 417, l. 1, the sense was completely destroyed by the omission of a "not." Those who possess the volumes are requested to correct all this nonsense.

Students who deserve particular mention for help in the preparation of this volume are Friedrich Wilhelm Marquardt and Gerhard Bauer.

To conclude, I often think that there are few men who have cause to be so grateful to God and man as I have. I am still in good heart, and—without having to carry the dignity and responsibility of being head of a school—I can devote myself to this great task surrounded with as much consideration and loyalty. The rcsult is that although the task is a heavy one I do not have to stagger under its weight, but year in year out it carries me along with it. I now turn to it again. The way is long. But "having still time on the earth . . ."

Basel, *June* 1953.

# THE SUBJECT-MATTER AND PROBLEMS OF THE DOCTRINE OF RECONCILIATION

# The Work of God the Reconciler

The subject-matter, origin and content of the message received and proclaimed by the Christian community is at its heart the free act of the faithfulness of God in which He takes the lost cause of man, who has denied Him as Creator and in so doing ruined himself as creature, and makes it His own in Jesus Christ, carrying it through to its goal and in that way maintaining and manifesting His own glory in the world.

## 1. God With Us

We enter that sphere of Christian knowledge in which we have to do with the heart of the message received by and laid upon the Christian community and therefore with the heart of the Church's dogmatics: that is to say, with the heart of its subject-matter, origin and content. It has a circumference, the doctrine of creation and the doctrine of the last things, the redemption and consummation. But the covenant fulfilled in the atonement is its centre. From this point we can and must see a circumference. But we can see it only from this point. A mistaken or deficient perception here would mean error or deficiency everywhere: the weakening or obscuring of the message, the confession and dogmatics as such. From this point either everything is clear and true and helpful, or it is not so anywhere. This involves a high responsibility in the task which now confronts us.

It would be possible and quite correct to describe the covenant fulfilled in the work of reconciliation as the heart of the subject-matter of

Christian faith, of the origin of Christian love, of the content of Christian hope. But the faith and love and hope of the Christian community and the Christians assembled in it live by the message received by and laid upon them, not the reverse. And even if we tried to put them in the forefront, we should have to lay the emphasis upon their subject-matter, origin and content, which are not immanent to them, and which do not exhaust themselves in them. For Christian faith is faith *in*, Christian love is love *through*, and Christian hope is hope *in* God the Father, Son and Holy Spirit. There is something prior, outside, different from them which encounters them. It is God whom they encounter, from whom they have their being, whom they can lay hold of but not apprehend or exhaust. Not even the message by which faith and love and hope live, not even the confession with which the community responds to the message, not even the dogmatics in which it gives an account of the message and its own response, and finally of its faith and love and hope as such, can take the place of God. If we tried to start with faith and love and hope, we would still have to go back to that free and higher other in which they have their basis. And in the face of it we should have to say even of them that at their heart they have to do with the covenant fulfilled in the work of atonement, and that it is in their relation to this covenant that they are secure or insecure, effective or impotent, genuine or false.

Our first task will be to describe this Christian centre in a first and most general approximation. The title 'God with Us' is meant as a most general description of the whole complex of Christian understanding and doctrine which here confronts us.

At its heart the Christian message is a common statement on the part of certain men, i.e., those who are assembled in the Christian community. It includes a statement about themselves, about the individual existence of these men in their own time and situation. And it is essential to it that this should be so. But it only includes it. For primarily it is a statement about God: that it is He who is with them as God. *Only* with those who dare to make this statement, who as the recipients and bearers of the Christian message, as members of the Christian community, must dare to make it? With them, to the extent that they know that it is actually the case: God with us. They dare to make this statement because they were able to become and can constantly become again the recipients of this message. God with you, God with thee and thee, was its first form, and they are what they are to the extent that they hear this again and again. But as recipients they are also bearers of the message. And to this extent it is not only to them. They dare to make the statement, that God is the One who is with them as God, amongst men who do not yet know this. And it is to such that they address the statement. They do not specifically include them in that "us." Their aim is to show them what they do not yet know but what they can and should know. What? About themselves, and their individual existence in their own time and situation? That is certainly included. Much depends upon their coming to see that it applies to *them*. But everything depends upon their coming to see that it all has to do with God; that it is God who is with them as God. For it is this that applies to them. "God with us" as the core of the Christian message, the decisive general statement of the Christian community, can indeed be interpreted as "God with us men," but with the clear distinction, with us men who know it but are always learning it afresh—and as the word of our declaration to all others, and therefore with "us" other men who have always to learn it afresh because we do not yet know it, although we can know it. In this movement from a narrower to a wider usage the statement "God with us" is the centre of the Christian message—and always in such a way that it is primarily a statement about God and only then and for that reason a statement about us men.

That is the roughest outline of the matter. We must now look at this outline rather more closely in order that we may understand it correctly even in this basic form.

To this end it is perhaps instructive to recall that this "God with us" is the translation of the remarkable name Emmanuel which is mentioned three times in Is. $7^{14}$, $8^{8,10}$, and according to Mt. $1^{21f.}$ finds its fulfilment in the name of Jesus.

The three passages in Isaiah seem to belong to three independently transmitted oracles. In the redaction of the book of Isaiah they were all related to that remarkable period (cf. Martin Noth, *Geschichte Israels*, 1950, p. 218 f.) when Assyria began to emerge as a world-power and to encroach upon Syria and Palestine. This process was explained by the prophets, and primarily Isaiah, as something which ran quite contrary to the political and religious tradition of Israel, a change in the relationship between God and His people, not a breach between them, but the irruption of His judgment upon their unfaithfulness, the transition from the Yes of His grace to the No. The final form of that unfaithfulness is the refusal of Ahaz, King of Judah, to trust in Yahweh and therefore to be bold enough to offer resistance to the two kings Rezin of Damascus and Pekah of Samaria who, themselves a prey to illusions, try to force him into an alliance against Assyria. In face of this situation Isaiah announces (7[14f.]) the divine sign which is at once a promise and a warning, a sign of grace and a sign of judgment: a child will now be conceived and born. The old controversy whether his mother is called a young wife or a virgin does not in any way affect the real sense. What is important in the text is that when the child is born, that is in less than a year, he will be given the name Emmanuel, because God will have saved His people from the threat of Rezin and Pekah and they will again be rejoicing in His goodness. That is the one side of the sign. But the other is that before the child can distinguish between good and evil, a few years later, he will have to eat milk and honey, the food of the nomad. The true evil, that of the Assyrians, will then have supervened. Emmanuel will be present, but only in the wilderness, under the wrath of God. We are told the same (according to this other aspect of the sign) in Is. 8[6]: "Forasmuch as this people refuseth the waters of Shiloah that go softly, and rejoice in Rezin and Remaliah's son, now therefore behold, the Lord bringeth upon them the waters of the river (Euphrates), strong and many, and he shall come up over all his channels, and go over all his banks: and he shall pass through Judah; he shall overflow and go over, he shall reach even to the neck; and the stretching out of his wings shall fill the breadth of thy land, O Emmanuel." In contrast, Is. 8[9f.] looks again in the opposite direction, evidently beyond the momentarily irresistibly triumphant Assyria (though this is not perhaps a compelling reason why we should not ascribe it to Isaiah): "Rage furiously, ye people, and be afraid. Give ear, ye of far countries. Gird yourselves and be afraid, yes gird yourselves and be afraid. Take counsel together, and it shall come to nought. Resolve, and it shall not stand. For—Emmanuel."

Who is "Emmanuel"? Hardly a historical figure of the period. Perhaps a traditional name, or one selected by the prophet, to describe the expected Redemptor-King of the last day, to whom a kind of pre-existence is here ascribed. Perhaps the personification of what the remnant-Israel of Judah understood its God to be, and therefore itself, or according to the prophets ought to have done so. Perhaps both? Certainly a special key to the continual mystery of the history of this people in days of prosperity and in days of adversity, under the hand of God in blessing and in cursing. "God with us" is true when the people is at rest. It is also true when the enemy invades and devastates its land. It is always true, in spite of and in the most irresistible movements of history. It is so because and to the extent that in all these things there is revealed the gracious action of God to His people. No matter who or what is concretely envisaged in these passages, they obviously mean this: Emmanuel is the content of the recognition in which the God of Israel reveals Himself in all His acts and dispositions; He is the God who does not work and act without His people, but who is with His people as their God and therefore as their hope.

We are reminded of this remarkable name in Mt. 1[21f.]. The reference here is to a single, final and exclusive act of the God of Israel as the goal and recapitulation of all His acts. But this act, the birth and naming of Jesus, is similar to the events in the days of King Ahaz in that once again we have come to a change in the relationship between God and His people. As the Evangelist sees it, it is this time the great change compared with which what took place before was only from his point of view a prelude. And now it is the equally unexpected change from perdition to salvation, from an age-long judgment to a new and final blessing. And the Emmanuel-sign has it in common with the name of Jesus that the latter, too, although this time in the reverse direction, is a sign for both: a sign "for the fall and rising again of many in Israel" (Lk. 2³⁴), a sign both of the deepest extremity imposed by God (as in Is. 8⁶ᶠ·) and also of the uttermost preservation and salvation ordained by God (as in Is.8⁹ᶠ·). Over and in both it is Emmanuel, "God with us," and now therefore (ἵνα πληρωθῇ τὸ ῥηθὲν ὑπὸ κυρίου διὰ τοῦ προφήτου λέγοντος) Jesus, Jehoshuah, "God helps."

1. Our starting-point is that this "God with us" at the heart of the Christian message is the description of an act of God, or better, of God Himself in this act of His. It is a report, not therefore a statement of fact on the basis of general observation or consideration. God with us, or what is meant by these three words, is not an object of investigation or speculation. It is not a state, but an event. God is, of course, and that in the strictest sense originally and properly, so that everything else which is, in a way which cannot be compared at all with His being, can be so only through Him, only in relation to Him, only from Him and to Him. Now even when He is "with us," He is what He is, and in the way that He is; and all the power and truth of His being "with us" is the power and truth of His incomparable being which is proper to Him and to Him alone, His being as God. He is both in His life in eternity in Himself, and also in His life as Creator in the time of the world created by Him; by and in Himself, and also above and in this world, and therefore according to the heart of the Christian message with us men. And He is who He is, and lives as what He is, in that He does what He does. How can we know God if His being is unknown or obscure or indifferent? But how can we know God if we do not find the truth and power of His being in His life, and of His life in His act? We know about God only if we are witnesses—however distantly and modestly—of His act. And we speak about God only as we can do so—however deficiently—as those who proclaim His act. "God with us" as it occurs at the heart of the Christian message is the attestation and report of the life and act of God as the One who is.

But if it means that God is with us—and the message of the Christian community certainly implies that it does really apply to us men—then that presupposes that we men, in our own very different way, which cannot be compared with the being of God, but which on the basis of the divine being and life and act is a very real way, that we also *are*, and that we are in that we live in our time, and that we live in that we ourselves act in our own act. If the fact that God is with us is a report about the being and life and act of God, then from the very outset it stands in a relationship to our own being and life and acts. A report about ourselves is included in that report about God. We cannot therefore take cognisance of it, be more or less impressed by it, and then leave it as the report of something which has taken place in a quite different sphere in which we ourselves have no place. It tells us that we ourselves are in the sphere of God. It applies to us by telling us of a history which God wills to share with us and therefore of an invasion of our history—indeed, of the real truth about our history as a history which is by Him and from Him and to Him. The divine being and life and act takes place with ours, and it is only as the divine takes place that ours takes place. To put it in the simplest way, what unites God and us men is that He does not will to be God without us, that He creates us rather to share with us and therefore with our being and life and act His own incomparable being and life and act, that He does not allow His history to be His and ours ours, but causes them to take place as a common history. That is the special truth which the Christian message has to proclaim at its very heart.

2. We have just said, and this is what is meant in the Christian message, that we have to do with an event, with an act of God. The whole being and life of God is an activity, both in eternity and in worldly time, both in Himself as Father, Son and Holy Spirit, and in His relation to man and all creation. But what God does in Himself and as the Creator and Governor of man is all aimed at the particular act in which it has its centre and meaning. And everything that He wills has its ground and origin in what is revealed as His will in this one act. Thus it is not merely one amongst others of His works as Creator and Governor. Of course, it can and must be understood in this way, in accordance with the general will and work of God. But within this outer circle it forms an inner. The one God wills and works all things, but here He wills and works a particular thing: not one with others, but one for the sake of which He wills and works all others. As one with others this act is also the *telos* of all the acts of God; of the eternal activity in which He is both in Himself and in the history of His acts in the world created by Him. It is of this that the "God with us" speaks.

Therefore even from the standpoint of us men the "God with us" does not refer to the existence of man generally as the creaturely object of the will and work of His Lord. It does refer to it. It includes it. The being, life and act of man is always quite simply his history in relation to the being, life and act of his Creator. We can say the same of all creatures. But it is far more than this. For within and beyond this general activity, God Himself in His being, life and act as Creator wills and works a special act. All His activity has its heart and end in a single act. Within and out of the general history, which with all creatures man can have in common with God in His being, life and act, there arises this act of God and that which corresponds to it in the being, life and activity of man, as a qualified history, his true history. And if the "God with us" at the heart of the Christian message speaks of the unifying factor between God and man, it speaks of a specific conjoining of the two, not always and everywhere but in a single and particular event which has a definite importance for all time and space but which takes place once and for all in a definite *hic et nunc.*

3. From the standpoint of its meaning the particularity of this event consists in the fact that it has to do with the salvation of man, that in it the general history which is common to God and man, to God and all creation, becomes at its very heart and end a redemptive history. Salvation is more than being. Salvation is fulfilment, the supreme, sufficient, definitive and indestructible fulfilment of being. Salvation is the perfect being which is not proper to created being as such but is still future. Created being as such needs salvation, but does not have it: it can only look forward to it. To that extent salvation is its *eschaton.* Salvation, fulfilment, perfect being means —and this is what created being does not have in itself—being which has a part in the being of God, from which and to which it is: not a divinised being but a being which is hidden in God, and in that sense (distinct from God and secondary) eternal being. Since salvation is not proper to created being as such, it can only come to it, and since it consists in participation in the being of God it can come only from God. The coming of this salvation is the grace of God—using the word in its narrower and most proper sense. In the wider sense the creation, preservation and over-ruling of the world and man are already grace. For if this is not proper to created being as such, it can only come to it. Only from God as the One who is originally and properly can it come about that it also has being, that it is, and not that it is not. And by that very fact there is always held out to it the opportunity of salvation: the expectation of being in perfection in participation in the divine being. But the "God with

us" at the heart of the Christian message does not mean this general grace. It means the redemptive grace of God. It is this which constitutes, factually, the singularity of the event. It is this which marks out the event within the whole history of the togetherness of God and man. Not merely the creating, preserving and over-ruling of created being, not merely the creating of an opportunity for salvation, but the fact that it actually comes, that God gives it. God gives to created being what can only be given to it and what can be given only by Him. And He does really give it: Take what is mine—this final, supreme, insurpassable gift; take it, it is meant for you. It is because it has to do with this that the activity of God indicated by the "God with us" is singular and unique. And so, too, is the invasion of the history of our own human being, life and activity described by this "God with us." And so, too, is the whole circle of God in which we find our- selves according to this centre of the Christian message. The general grace of God in creation, preservation and over-ruling still remains. That is already grace. We recognise it distinctly as such only when we see God and ourselves in the inner and special circle of His will and work, in the light of this one, particular, redemptive act of God. It is only from this standpoint that the general grace of being and the opportunity which it offers can and do become a subject for genuine gratitude and a source of serious dedication. For here it is provided that that opportunity is not offered in vain, that it is actually taken, taken by God Himself. What concerns us here is the redemptive grace of God, and to that extent something that is more and greater.

4. In the light of this we must now try to outline this particular event with rather greater precision. According to the Christian message "God with us" means God with the man for whom salvation is intended and ordained as such, as the one who is created, preserved and over-ruled by God as man. It is not as though the expectation belonged to his created being. It is not as though he had any kind of claim to it. God cannot be forced to give us a part in His divine being. The matter might have ended quite well with that general grace of being—which even in itself is great enough. But where God is not bound and man has no claim, even more compelling is the will and plan and promise of God. It goes beyond, or rather it precedes His will and work as Creator. Therefore it has to be distinguished from it, as something prior, which precedes it. The ordaining of salvation for man and of man for salvation is the original and basic will of God, the ground and purpose of His will as Creator. It is not that He first wills and works the being of the world and man, and then ordains it to

salvation. But God creates, preserves and over-rules man for this prior end and with this prior purpose, that there may be a being distinct from Himself ordained for salvation, for perfect being, for participation in His own being, because as the One who loves in freedom He has determined to exercise redemptive grace—and that there may be an object of this His redemptive grace, a partner to receive it. A further point which we must now make in describing the event indicated by the "God with us" is this. The "God with us" has nothing to do with chance. As a redemptive happening it means the revelation and confirmation of the most primitive relationship between God and man, that which was freely determined in eternity by God Himself before there was any created being. In the very fact that man is, and that he is man, he is as such chosen by God for salvation; that *eschaton* is given him by God. Not because God owes it to him. Not in virtue of any quality or capacity of his own being. Completely without claim. What takes place between God and man in that particular redemptive history is fulfilment to this extent too, that in it God—the eternal will of God with man—is justified, the eternal righteousness of His grace is active and revealed, in and with the divine right, and so too the right which He has freely given and ascribed to man by determining this concerning him. It belongs to the character of this event and its particularity that with the end it reveals the basis and beginning of all things—the glory of God, which is that of His free love, and with it—well below, but eternally grounded upon it—the dignity of man, that dignity with which He willed to invest man although it is not proper to him.

5. But again we must go further. "God with us" in the sense of the Christian message means God with us men who have forfeited the pre-determined salvation, forfeited it with a supreme and final jeopardising even of our creaturely existence. As the way from that beginning in God to the end of man with God is revealed in this particular event, its line is not a straight one, but one which is radically and—if God Himself were not there as hope—hopelessly broken. The situation of man in this event is this. He occupies a position quite different from that which he ought to occupy according to the divine intention. He does not conduct himself as the partner God has given Himself to receive His redemptive grace. He has opposed his ordination to salvation. He has turned his back on the salvation which actually comes to him. He does not find the fulfilment of his being in participation in the being of God by the gift of God. Instead, he aims at another salvation which is to be found in the sphere of his creaturely being and attained by his own effort. His belief is that he can

and should find self-fulfilment. He has himself become an *eschaton*. This is the man with whom God is dealing in this particular redemptive history: the man who has made himself quite impossible in relation to the redemptive grace of God; and in so doing, the man who has made himself quite impossible in his created being as man, who has cut the ground from under his feet, who has lost his whole *raison d'être*. What place has he before God when he has shown himself to be so utterly unworthy of that for which he was created by God, so utterly inept, so utterly unsuitable? when he has eliminated himself? What place is there for his being, his being as man, when he has denied his goal, and therefore his beginning and meaning, and when he confronts God in this negation? Despising the dignity with which God invested him, he has obviously forfeited the right which God gave and ascribed to him as the creature of God. But it is with this lost son in a far country, with man as he has fallen and now exists in this sorry plight, that God has to do in this redeeming event. And this is what reveals the gulf. This is what shows us how it stands between God and man. This is where we see the inadequacy of the partner, the point where the relationship breaks down. At a pinch this can be overlooked if we do not think of the redeeming event as the heart and end of their interconnexion, if we conceive it abstractly as the interconnexion of Creator and creature. We may take this antithesis very seriously, but we shall always have good grounds to think of it as an antithesis which can be bridged. As such it does not contain any breach, any gulf, any enmity, either on the one side or on the other, any judgment and punishment on the part of God or suffering on the part of man. But this cannot possibly be overlooked in the redeeming event referred to in the "God with us." On the contrary, what constitutes the particularity of this event is that as a redeeming event, as the fulfilment of the gracious will of God, as the reaffirmation of His right and ours, it can be conceived only in the form of a Yet and a Nevertheless, which means that it cannot be conceived at all. If man has forfeited his salvation, what do we have to grasp in this event but the inconceivable fact that all the same it is given to him? If in so doing man has lost his creaturely being, what do we have to grasp but again the inconceivable fact that all the same he will not be lost? Is it not the case that only here, in the light of the antithesis which is here revealed and overcome, is grace really known as grace, that is, as free grace, as mercy pure and simple, as *factum purum*, having its basis only in itself, in the fact that it is posited by God? For who really knows what grace is until he has seen it at work here: as the grace which is *for* man when, because man is wholly and utterly a sinner before God, it can only be against him, and when in fact, even while it is for him, it is also a plaintiff and judge against him, showing him to be incapable of satisfying either God or himself? And looking back once again, it is the grace of God as mercy pure and simple, as a sheer Yet and Nevertheless, which reveals, and by which we have to measure, how it stands with the man to whom it is granted. It is not independent reflection on the part of man, or an abstract law, but grace which shows incontrovertibly that man has forfeited his salvation and in so doing fatally jeopardised his creaturely being—which reveals his sin and the misery which is its consequence. From the redemption which takes place here we can gather from what it is that man is redeemed; from the *factum purum* of the salvation which comes to man without and in spite of his own deserts we may know the *factum brutum* which he for his part dares to set against God. Because the "God with us" at the heart of the Christian message has to do with that *factum purum* of the divine mercy, we must not fail to recognise but acknowledge without reserve that we, and those for whom God is according to this message, are those who have nothing to bring Him but a confession of this *factum brutum*: "Father, I have sinned."

6. But if the Christian "God with us" does nevertheless speak, not of a renunciation, but of the fulfilment of the redemptive will of God in that event, then no matter how inconceivable may be that which we have to grasp in this connexion, it refers to something quite different from the blind paradox of an arbitrary act of the divine omnipotence of grace. We are confronted here by the determination of that event which reveals unequivocally its uniqueness amongst the acts of God, that it declares an absolutely unique being and attitude and activity on the part of God. "God with us" means more than God over or side by side with us, before or behind us. It means more than His divine being in even the most intimate active connexion with our human being otherwise peculiar to Him. At this point, at the heart of the Christian message and in relation to the event of which it speaks, it means that God has made Himself the One who fulfils His redemptive will. It means that He Himself in His own person—at His own cost but also on His own initiative—has become the inconceivable Yet and Nevertheless of this event, and so its clear and well-founded and legitimate, its true and holy and righteous Therefore. It means that God has become man in order as such, but in divine sovereignty, to take up our case. What takes place in this work of inconceivable mercy is, therefore, the free over-ruling of God, but it is not

an arbitrary overlooking and ignoring, not an artificial bridging, covering-over or hiding, but a real closing of the breach, gulf and abyss between God and us for which we are responsible. At the very point where we refuse and fail, offending and provoking God, making ourselves impossible before Him and in that way missing our destiny, treading under foot our dignity, forfeiting our right, losing our salvation and hopelessly compromising our creaturely being—at that very point God Himself intervenes as man. Because He is God He is able not only to be God but also to be this man. Because He is God it is necessary that He should be man in quite a different way from all other men; that He should do what we do not do and not do what we do. Because He is God He puts forth His omnipotence to be this other man, to be man quite differently, in our place and for our sake. Because He is God He has and exercises the power as this man to suffer for us the consequence of our transgression, the wrath and penalty which necessarily fall on us, and in that way to satisfy Himself in our regard. And again because He is God, He has and exercises the power as this man to be His own partner in our place, the One who in free obedience accepts the ordination of man to salvation which we resist, and in that way satisfies us, i.e., achieves that which can positively satisfy us. That is the absolutely unique being, attitude and activity of God to which the "God with us" at the heart of the Christian message refers. It speaks of the peace which God Himself in this man has made between Himself and us.

We see the seriousness and force of the divine redemptive will in the fact that it is not too little and not too much for Him to make peace between Himself and us. To that end He gives Himself. He, the Creator, does not scorn to become a creature, a man like us, in order that as such He may bear and do what must be borne and done for our salvation. On the contrary, He finds and defends and vindicates His glory in doing it. Again, we see our own perversion and corruption, we see what is our offence and plight, in the fact that God (who never does anything unnecessary) can obviously be satisfied only by this supreme act, that only His own coming as man is sufficient to make good the evil which has been done. So dark is our situation that God Himself must enter and occupy it in order that it may be light. We cannot fully understand the Christian "God with us" without the greatest astonishment at the glory of the divine grace and the greatest horror at our own plight.

But even when we understand the entry of God for us in becoming man as the making of peace between Himself and us, we have still not said the decisive thing about this action. What He effects and does and reveals by becoming man—for us—is much more than the restoration of the *status quo ante*—the obviating of the loss caused by our own transgression and our restoration to the place of promise and expectation of the salvation ordained for us. God makes Himself the means of His own redemptive will, but He is obviously more than this means. And in making peace by Himself He obviously gives us more than this peace, i.e., more than a *restitutio ad integrum*, more than the preserving and assuring to us of our creaturely being and this as our opportunity for salvation. For when God makes Himself the means of His redemptive will to us, this will and we ourselves attain our goal. What is at first only God's gracious answer to our failure, God's gracious help in our plight, and even as such great and wonderful enough, is—when God Himself is the help and answer—His participation in our being, life and activity and therefore obviously our participation in His; and therefore it is nothing more nor less than the coming of salvation itself, the presence of the *eschaton* in all its fulness. The man in whom God Himself intervenes for us, suffers and acts for us, closes the gap between Himself and us as our representative, in our name and on our behalf, this man is not merely the confirmation and guarantee of our salvation, but because He is God He is salvation, our salvation. He is not merely the redeemer of our being but as such the giver and Himself the gift of its fulfilment and therefore the goal and end of the way of God— and all that as the peacemaker and saviour. It is when this great thing takes place that there takes place the even greater. This great thing is included in the "God with us" of the Christian message in so far as this speaks of God's intervening and becoming man, but in this great thing there is also included the even greater, indeed the greatest of all.

7. From all this it is surely obvious that the "God with us" carries with it in all seriousness a "We with God": the fact that we ourselves are there in our being, life and activity.

This does not seem to be apparent at a first glance. For who are we? We have seen already that we are (1) those whose history is absorbed into the history of the acts of God, and (2) made to participate in that event which is the centre and end of all the divine acts, and (3) given a share in the grace with which God actually brings salvation to man, and (4) that we are such as those whom God has thereto ordained from all eternity, but unfortunately (5) we are those who have refused His salvation and in that way denied their own destiny and perverted and wasted and hopelessly compromised their own being, life and activity, who inevitably therefore find themselves disqualified and set aside as participants in that event, and cannot be considered in relation to it. Yet beyond that and in a sense conclusively (6) we are those whose place has been taken by another, who lives and suffers and acts for them, who for them makes good that which they have spoiled, who—for them, but also without them and even against them —is their salvation. That is what we are. And what is left to us? What place is there for us when we are like that? In what sense is the history of the acts of God at this centre and end our history? Are we not without history? Have we not become mere objects? Have we not lost all responsibility? Are we not reduced to mere spectators? Is not our being deprived of all life or activity? Or does it not lack all significance as our life and activity? "God with us"—that is something which we can easily understand even in these circumstances. But how is it to include within it a "We with God"? And if it does not, how can it really be understood as a "God with us"?

The answer is that we ourselves are directly summoned, that we are lifted up, that we are awakened to our own truest being as life and act, that we are set in motion by the fact that in that one man God has made Himself our peacemaker and the giver and gift of our salvation. By it we are made free for Him. By it we are put in the place which comes to us where our salvation (really ours) can come to us from Him (really from Him). This actualisation of His redemptive will by Himself opens up to us the one true possibility of our own being. Indeed, what remains to us of life and activity in the face of this actualisation of His redemptive will by Himself can only be one thing. This one thing does not mean the extinguishing of our humanity, but its establishment. It is not a small thing, but the greatest of all. It is not for us a passive presence as spectators, but our true and highest activation—the magnifying of His grace which has its highest and most profound greatness in the fact that God has made Himself man with us, to make our cause His own, and as His own to save it from disaster and to carry it through to success. The genuine being of man as life and activity, the "We with God," is to affirm this, to admit that God is right, to be thankful for it, to accept the promise and the command which it contains, to exist as the community, and responsibly in the community, of those who know that this is all that remains to us, but that it does remain to us and that for all men everything depends upon its coming to pass. And it is this "We with God" that is meant by the Christian message in its central "God with us," when it proclaims that God Himself has taken our place, that He Himself has made peace between Himself and us, that by Himself He has accomplished our salvation, i.e., our participation in His being.

This "We with God" enclosed in the "God with us" is Christian faith, Christian love and Christian hope. These are the magnifying of the grace of God which still remain to us—and remain to us as something specifically human, as the greatest thing of all, as action in the truest sense of the word. We do not forget that it is a matter of magnifying God out of the deeps, *e profundis*. Our magnifying of God can only be that of the transgressors and rebels that we are, those who have missed their destiny, and perverted and wasted their being, life and activity. Therefore our magnifying of God cannot seek and find and have its truth and power in itself, but only in God, and therefore in that one Man in whom God is for us, who is our peace and salvation. Our faith, therefore, can only be faith in Him, and cannot live except from Him as its object. Our love can only be by Him, and can only be strong from Him as its basis. Our hope can only be hope directed upon Him, and can only be certain hope in Him as its content. Our faith, love and hope and we ourselves—however strong may be our faith, love and hope—live only by that which we cannot create, posit, awaken or deserve. And although our believing, loving and hoping themselves and as such are in us, they are not of us, but of their object, basis and content, of God, who in that one man not only answers for us with Him but answers for Himself with us, who gives it to us in freedom that we may believe, love and hope: open eyes, ears and hearts for Himself and His work, knowledge to the foolish, obedience to the wayward, freedom to the bound, life to the victims of death; and all in such a way that the glory of our own being, life and activity is still His, and can be valued, and exalted and respected by us only as His; but all in such a way that in and with His glory we too are really exalted, because in the depths where we can only give Him the glory, we find our true and proper place. It is in this way and in this sense that the Christian community proclaims "We with God" when it proclaims "God with us."

In these seven points we have said in rough outline—many things need to be amplified, explained and made more precise—almost everything that has to be said about the "God with us" as the covenant between God and us men fulfilled in the work of atonement. But we have not yet said it with the concreteness with which it is said at the heart of the Christian message, or at the heart (in the second article) of the Creed, and with which it must also be said at the heart of dogmatics, even in the briefest survey, if we are not to speak mistakenly or falsely.

For where does the community which has to deliver the message learn to know and say this "God with us"? And to what does it point those to whom the message is addressed? How far can and must this "God with us," the report of the event which constitutes its meaning and content, be declared and received in truth? How can men come to stand where they obviously have to stand in that inner circle of the relationship between God and man—to dare to make this report as a declaration of reality? And how do other men come to hear this report in such a way that it is to them a report of reality, and they find themselves challenged and empowered to pass it on to others still? How do they come to stand in the same place as the first men, as the Christian community? In other words: How does it come about amongst men that there is a communication of this "God with us," of this report, or rather, of that which is reported? That is the question which we can answer only as we say everything once again in the concrete way in which it is said at the heart of the Christian message. Everything depends upon its concrete expression: the whole truth and reality of the report, and the whole secret of the communication of the matter.

We must realise that the Christian message does not at its heart express a concept or an idea, nor does it recount an anonymous history to be taken as truth and reality only in concepts and ideas. Certainly the history is inclusive, i.e., it is one which includes in itself the whole event of the "God with us" and to that extent the history of all those to whom the "God with us" applies. But it recounts this history and speaks of its inclusive power and significance in such a way that it declares a name, binding the history strictly and indissolubly to this name and presenting it as the story of the bearer of this name. This means that all the concepts and ideas used in this report (God, man, world, eternity, time, even salvation, grace, transgression, atonement and any others) can derive their significance only from the bearer of this name and from His history, and not the reverse. They cannot have any independent importance or role based on a quite different prior interpretation. They cannot say what has to be said with some meaning of their own or in some context of their own abstracted from this name. They can serve only to describe this name— the name of Jesus Christ.

This name is the answer to our earlier question. In the Christian "God with us" there is no question of any other source and object than that indicated by this name. Other than in this name—as on the basis of the necessity and power of its conceptual context—it cannot be truth, either on the lips of those who speak it or in the ears and hearts of those who receive it. Without this name it is left insecure and unprotected. It is exposed to the suspicion that it might be only a postulate, a pure speculation, a myth. It is truth as it derives from this name and as it points to it, and only so. Where is it that the men stand who declare this message? The answer is that they stand in the sphere of the lordship of the One who bears this name, in the light and under the impelling power of His Spirit, in the community assembled and maintained and over-ruled by Him. They have not placed themselves there but He has placed them there, and it is as they stand there by Him that their report is a report of actuality. Again, where will those others stand to whom they address their report and witness, who both receive it and then, on their own responsibility, spread it further? The answer is that they too stand in the sphere of the lordship, which has now claimed them, of the One who bears this name, of His Spirit, of the call to His community which has now come to them. They too have not placed themselves there. And those who said to them "God with us" have not brought it about. But, again, it is He Himself who bears this name that has called and led and drawn them, and it is as that happens that it is given to them, too, to pass on to others their report of actuality as such. Therefore the One who shows and persuades and convinces and reveals and communicates from man to man that it is so, "God with us," is the One who bears this name, Jesus Christ, no other, and nothing else. That is what the message of the Christian community intends when at its heart it declares this name. If it were a principle and not a name indicating a person, we should have to describe it as the epistemological principle of the message. Where between man and man there is real communication of the report of what took place in Him and through Him, He Himself is there and at work, He Himself makes Himself to be recognised and acknowledged. The Christian message about Him— and without this it is not the Christian message—is established on the certainty that He is responsible for it, that He as the truth speaks through it and is received in it, that as it serves Him He Himself is present as actuality, as His own witness. He Himself by His Spirit is its guarantor. He Himself is the one who establishes and maintains and directs the community which has received it and upon which it is laid. He Himself is the strength of its defence and its offensive. He Himself is the hope of freedom and enlightenment for the many who have not yet received and accepted it. He Himself above all is the comfort, and the restlessness, and yet also the uplifting power in the weakness of its service. In a word, the Christian message lives as such by and to the One who at its heart bears the name of Jesus Christ. It becomes weak and obscure to the extent that it thinks it ought to live on other resources. And it becomes strong and clear when it is established solely in confidence in His controlling work exercised by His Spirit; to the extent that it abandons every other conceivable support or impulse, and is content to rest on His command and commission as its strength and pledge. He, Jesus Christ, is Emmanuel, "God with us." How else can He be proclaimed except as the One who proclaims Himself? And how else can human activity and speech and hearing be effective in His service except in the prayer and expectation that He will constantly do it?

The name of Jesus Christ covers the whole power of the Christian message because it indicates the whole of its content, because at its heart, which is normative for the whole, it is a message about Him, and therefore a message about the event of that "God with us."

It means Jesus Christ when (1) with this "God with us" it describes an act of God, or rather the being of God in His life and activity. If as a statement about God it is the report of an event (not a statement of fact), the report of a history in which we have a part with our being, life and activity, which God has in common with us, which inaugurated by Him is our own history, then it is so because and in so far as it is a report about Jesus Christ as the One who actually unites the divine being, life and activity with ours.

It means Jesus Christ again when (2) it describes the "God with us" as an act of God, a particular, once and for all and unique event in the midst of events in general. It is a report of this one event and of this event alone, of its meaning and importance for all of us, for men of all times and places, because and to the extent that it is a report about Him as the person who in His existence and work is absolutely unique and therefore universal in effectiveness and significance. It means the event which unites God and man and which has been accomplished in Him and in Him alone, the event of which He alone is the subject and in which we can have a part only by Him.

It means Jesus Christ again when it describes the event of "God with us" (3) as a redemptive event; as the fulfilment of man's being by participation in the divine being which comes to him by the grace of God. It is a message of redemption, and therefore a message of the last and greatest and unsurpassable thing which man can experience from God and has in fact experienced, of the gift of eternal life which has been made to him, because and in so far as it is the message of Jesus Christ—that He is the

One who, Himself God, is also man, that He therefore was and is and will be the salvation of God for us other men, that in one person He is the God who gives salvation and the man to whom it is given and who allows it to be given by Him, that as such He is the power and witness of the *eschaton* in the human present—a human present which is itself in the *eschaton*.

But the Christian message again means Jesus Christ when (4) it looks through the redemptive event of the "God with us" as through glass to the basis and beginning of all things, of the world and of man, in God, to the original ordination of man to salvation and of salvation for man as the meaning and basis even of the divine creative will. It has the particular emphasis and the specific weight of an original Word which underlies and embraces all other words so that no other word has any independent significance, as one historical report with others, it has none of the contingence of the record of one historical fact with many others, because and in so far as it is a message about Jesus Christ: that He is the One who according to the free and gracious will of God is Himself eternal salvation, the last and also the first; our eternal yesterday in God who is the same to-day and for ever.

But it means Jesus Christ again when (5) it sees and presupposes that we men with whom God is are those who have forfeited the salvation destined for us from all eternity, letting slip the opportunity for it, and in that way fatally jeopardising their creaturely being and indeed perishing were it not that God is God and therefore their hope. It is not out of mere pessimism that it sees and understands man in this way. As a message about Jesus Christ it cannot do otherwise. This name is the real Emmanuel-sign and therefore—although in the reverse direction from Is. 7[14]—the twofold sign which speaks of both the judgment of God and the grace of God in His dealings with His people. Also and first of all the sign of judgment. The well-deserved and incontestable sentence on man, His wrath and punishment, is first introduced and revealed in Jesus Christ. And it is the utterly free and unmerited nature of the grace of God introduced by Him as *factum purum* which first reveals the true relationship with God of the man to whom it is granted in Him, the *factum brutum* with which we have to do on the part of man.

And now it is absolutely clear that the Christian message means Jesus Christ, and has to name His name and does not know of any other, when (6) it says that God has made Himself the One who fulfils His redemptive will, that He has become man for us, that in the power of His Godhead He might take up our cause in our place. Jesus Christ is the man in whom

God satisfies Himself in face of our transgression and us in face of our plight. It says Jesus Christ when it speaks of this absolutely unique being, attitude and activity of God, of the peace which has been made by Him between Himself and us. And it does so because in speaking of this peace made in this way by God as a man amongst men, in speaking of this great thing, it at once goes on to speak of a greater and of the greatest thing of all, of salvation itself, which has already come to us in and with the opportunity for salvation restored in Jesus Christ, which has already been given to us, which has already become our salvation.

To conclude: How can (7) the reverse side be possible or legitimate, how can a "We with God" be really included and enclosed in the "God with us," how can it be true or actual, if it does not have reference to Jesus Christ? It is with reference to Him that in spite of all appearances to the contrary the Christian message dares to address man too as an active subject in the event of redemption, and to its content there belong the praise which we offer to the grace of God *e profundis*, man's own faith and love and hope. We have already seen in what sense this by no means self-evident fact is true, to what extent we others who are not that One belong to the redemptive act, that is, to the extent that our human being, life and activity, in the form of the praise of God, of faith and love and hope, live by their object, basis and content, to the extent that it is given to us in that way to be able to praise and believe and love and hope. But in that way means in Jesus Christ, in the fellowship between Him and us created by His Spirit, in virtue of our being, life and activity in His, and His in ours. We other men are Christians—or prospective Christians—and therefore partakers of His being, life and activity, in so far as Jesus Christ makes us such and wills to maintain and rule us as such. There is a Christian community with its special distinction and service to the extent that Jesus Christ assembles it and is present with it by His Spirit. Therefore this final part of the content of the Christian message stands or falls with Him—its characterisation and description with the naming of His name.

A note by way of final delimitation and confirmation. Our formulation is again and again that the Christian message (in all its content) means Jesus Christ. In the declaration and development of its whole content it always has reference to Him. His name, therefore, is not incidental to it. It is not a name which has to be pronounced for the sake of completeness or adornment. It is there at the very heart of it as the central and decisive Word, the Word which is always present with every other word and to which it must always return. For in uttering His name it says that it refers to Him, and therefore to its true object.

It is not trying to say something in general, a mere this or that, but it is trying to speak of Him, to show Him, to proclaim Him, to teach Him. To do this it can and must say many things. But these many things are all His things. They can be rightly said only as they look back or look away to Him. As they are said they can only be referred to Him. The Christian message is service, and the one whom it serves is at all points Jesus Christ Himself. What it says at its heart as the doctrine of the atonement is that He Himself is and lives and rules and acts, very God and very man, and that He is peace and salvation. He Himself is the whole. And in every individual part He is the One of whom it speaks, the truth of all that it attests and proclaims as true, the actuality of all that it attests and proclaims as actual. It cannot be silent when it remembers His name and utters it. It can and must at once declare it. In and with His name it can and must at once declare His cause, but only in and with His name and therefore only as His cause. This cause of His has no existence or life or validity of its own apart from or side by side with Him. It cannot be distinguished, let alone separated from Him. Everything that is said about it is measured by whether it faithfully reflects Him, whether indirectly but distinctly it refers to Him, declares Him, portrays Him, magnifies and exalts Him. It is not, therefore, the case that properly and basically the Christian message is concerned about His own affair and introduces His name only as the One who is responsible for it. To avoid this impression we have chosen the way of climax, showing the concrete form of the Christian "God with us" to be the message of Jesus Christ, not at the outset, but at the very end. Everything moves towards and everything stands and falls by the fact that it is the message about Jesus Christ.

It is no mere battle of words whether we understand it merely as the Gospel of Jesus Christ or also—and as such—the Gospel about Jesus Christ. Obviously it is the Gospel of Jesus Christ. We have laid on this every possible emphasis. He Himself is the "epistemological principle." But we must be careful not to understand Him only in this way, for, if we do, the Christian message will at once degenerate into the self-declaration of an ecclesiastical form of redemption instituted indeed by Him but now self-resting and self-motivated, or into a devotional and ethical system taught indeed by Him but self-justified and self-sufficient, or into an illumination of existence strikingly fulfilled by Him in history but living by its own light. And when this happens, the Christian message as such will no longer have anything individual or new or substantial to say to man. What it will have to say to him will not be worth saying because in the last resort and basically he can say the same thing to himself. In one form or another it has simply become the recitation of a myth. But the Christian message does say something individual, new and substantial because it speaks concretely, not mythically, because it does not know and proclaim anything side by side with or apart from Jesus Christ, because it knows and proclaims all things only as His things. It does not know and proclaim Him, therefore, merely as the representative and exponent of something other. For it, there is no something other side by side with or apart from Him. For it, there is nothing worthy of mention that is not as such His. Everything that it knows and proclaims as worthy of mention, it does so as His.

It is not, therefore, doing Him a mere courtesy when it names the name of Jesus Christ. It does not use this name as a symbol or sign which has a certain necessity on historical grounds, and a certain purpose on psychological and pedagogic grounds, to which that which it really means and has to say may be attached, which it is desirable to expound for the sake of clarity. For it, this name is not merely a cipher, under which that which it really means and has to say leads its own life and has its own truth and actuality and would be worth proclaiming for its own sake, a cipher which can at any time be omitted without affecting that which is really meant and said, or which in other ages or climes or circumstances can be replaced by some other cipher. When it speaks concretely, when it names the name of Jesus Christ, the Christian message is not referring simply to the specific form of something general, a form which as such is interchangeable: in the phrase of Lessing, a "contingent fact of history" which is the "vehicle" of an "eternal truth of reason." The peace between God and man and the salvation which comes to us men is not something general, but the specific thing itself: that concrete thing which is indicated by the name of Jesus Christ and not by any other name. For He who bears this name is Himself the peace and salvation. The peace and salvation can be known, therefore, only in Him, and proclaimed only in His name.

So much concerning the "God with us" as the most general description of our theme.

## 2. The Covenant as the Presupposition of Reconciliation

Jesus Christ is God, God as man, and therefore "God with us" men, God in the work of reconciliation. But reconciliation is the fulfilment of the covenant between God and man.

"Reconciliation" is the restitution, the resumption of a fellowship which once existed but was then threatened by dissolution. It is the maintaining, restoring and upholding of that fellowship in face of an element which disturbs and disrupts and breaks it. It is the realisation of the original purpose which underlay and controlled it in defiance and by the removal of this obstruction. The fellowship which originally existed between God and man, which was then disturbed and jeopardised, the purpose of which is now fulfilled in Jesus Christ and in the work of reconciliation, we describe as the covenant.

Covenant, *berith*, διαθήκη, is the Old Testament term for the basic relationship between the God of Israel and His people. The etymology of the word (cf. W. Eichrodt, *Theologie des Alten Testaments*, Vol. I, 1933, p. 7, n. 5; G. Quell, *Theologisches Wörterbuch zum Neuen Test*. II, p. 106 f.) seems to be uncertain. Does it mean "circumcision" as a sacrificial ceremony, or "binding" as a binding of the will of the covenant-partner, or a "meal" as the ratification of the ceremony? Or does it come from the same root as *barah* and mean "choice?" Either way it denotes an element in a legal ritual in which two partners together accept a mutual obligation. We refer at this point to the historical reality with which the Old Testament is concerned whether it actually uses the word or not: "I will be your God, and ye shall be my people" (Jer. 7[22], 11[4], 30[22], 31[33], 32[38]; Ezek. 36[28]).

"Your God" is the almighty and gracious and holy One who reveals Himself under the name of Yahweh. He is the One according to whose will and commandment and with whose powerful assistance a group of blood-related nomadic tribes of Semitic descent consciously set out to capture and did indeed capture the land of Canaan against the unforgettable background of an act of deliverance on the border of Egypt. He is the One in whose worship they found themselves united in that land, and to whose sole recognition as God and to the honouring of whose decrees they knew themselves to be pledged.

"My people" (the people "Israel") is not simply the concept of those tribes in their interconnexion as a nation, let alone the state or one of the states in which this nation took on an external political form. It is rather the sacral federation (the Amphiktyonic league) of those tribes (only indirectly identical with the nation or state of Israel) gathered together as the twelve; the Israelitish congregation or community of tribes which as such recognised in that God their unseen founder, overlord, protector and law-giver, and which had their visible cultic centre in the ark, which perhaps represented the empty throne of Yahweh and which was preserved first in Shechem, then in Bethel, then in Shiloh, being finally brought to Jerusalem in the time of David (cf. M. Noth, *Das Gesetz im Pentateuch*, 1940, p. 63 f., 70 f.; *Geschichte Israels*, 1950, p. 74 f.). According to the formulation of G. Quell (*op. cit.* p. 111) the "covenant" between the two is the answer to that problem of man before God which is presupposed by Old Testament religion in all its forms and at all its stages. It is the relationship with God as such which is everywhere presumed in the Old Testament cultus, in the law-giving, the prophecy, the historical and poetical writings. It is "a kind of common denominator" of Israelitish religion. There is relatively little direct mention of it. It is an "eternal covenant." It embraces everything that takes place between the two partners. The basic fact indicated by the word *berith* is presupposed even where on the ground and in the sphere of the covenant there are serious, even the most serious crises: movement of disloyalty, disobedience and apostasy on the part of portions or even the whole of that "community of tribes;" and to meet them divine threatenings which seem ultimately to compromise the whole status of Israel, and indeed the almost (but not more than almost) unceasing execution of these threatenings. We can hardly agree with W. Eichrodt (*op. cit.* p. 11) that the covenant may be dissolved, that at its climax the judgment which breaks on Israel means the "setting aside" of the covenant (p. 250 f.). Does it not belong to the very nature of a *berith* even between man and man that it is "unalterable, lasting and inviolable" (G. Quell, *op. cit.*, p. 116)? Can this be less, is it not much more, the case with the *berith* between God and man? Does not the saying of Deutero-Isaiah about the covenant of peace which will not be removed (Is. 54[10]) stand over everything that takes place in the relations between Yahweh and Israel?

What is true at all events is that the Old Testament covenant is a covenant of grace. It is instituted by God Himself in the fulness of sovereignty and in the freest determination and decree. And then and for that reason it is a matter of free choice and decision on the part of "Israel." God chooses for Himself this His people: this people, the community of tribes, chooses for itself this their God. This mutual choice, which takes place in this order and sequence, we have described as the basic fact, the presupposition of Old Testament religion, the standing of man before God which is always found in it. But the Old Testament understanding and the Old Testament representation of the early history of Israel make it clear that we can speak of a fact only with the greatest caution, for what is meant shows itself to be the occurrence of a basic act, something which happened there and then, and which as such can be placed alongside earlier—and also later—events. Obviously as an act which took place it cannot lose its actuality, but bears the character of an in itself inexhaustible occurrence. The Old Testament covenant, against the background and on the presupposition of which the events between God and Israel endorsed in the Old Testament take place, is not therefore a truth which is, as it were, inherent to this God or to the existence of this people or to their relationship one with another from a certain period in time, from an event which took place there and then. It is not a truth which as such has ceased to be event, the act of God and of Israel. It can, of course, be thought of as a historical fact. And it can be represented and worked out in institutions. But it is not itself an institution. It does not cease to be actual. It cannot be something given apart from the act of God and man. When the *berith* came to be understood as a given fact and an institution, in connexion with the ultimate location of a central worship in Jerusalem, but obviously even with the earlier cultus, especially in Shiloh, then at once it came under the fire of the severest prophetic criticism. The covenant remains—and it is in this way and only in this way that it does remain—the event of a divine and human choice, just as God Himself *exists* to the very depths of His being, and is therefore a (personally) living, active, acting and speaking God, and just as His human partner, His Israel, is actual only in its history, in the doing of its good and evil deeds, in the acting and suffering of the men who compose it.

For this reason there is no single and definitive narration of the original conclusion of this convenant—as there would have to be on that other view. According to the opinion advanced by many to-day, it is in the account in Josh. 24 of the action taken by Joshua in Shechem on the completion of the conquest that we have a representation which approximates most closely to an event of this kind. The conclusion of the covenant is portrayed in a very striking and solemn manner in this passage, so that if we did not know to the contrary, we might conclude that it was necessarily the only occurrence of this nature. But according to Deut. 26–30, already at the end of Moses' life and under his leadership—not this time in Canaan but in the land of Moab—it had been preceded by a conclusion of the covenant which is described as equally unique and definitive. And both these accounts stand under the shadow of the account in Ex. 24 of a covenant mediated by the same Moses at Sinai, which became so important in tradition right up to the time of the Christian Church. And even the priority of this covenant is apparently shaken by the covenant between God and Abraham which is narrated in two versions in Gen. 15 and 17, and later recalled with particular emphasis. But according to 2 K. 13[23] this could be understood as a covenant "with Abraham, Isaac and Jacob," and in any case it was preceded by the covenant with Noah in Gen. 8 and 9. And in Neh. 8–9, at the opposite end of the historical period covered by the Old Testament narratives, we have a description of the action taken in Jerusalem under Ezra after the return from exile, which can hardly be otherwise understood than as a further conclusion of the covenant, under whose strong impress—it might be supposed—the earlier narratives could easily have lost their force for that generation. And in the light of 2 Sam. 7[5–29] are we not forced to speak of a particular covenant with David, which also represents the whole? And we ought at least to ask whether there are not many conversations reported in the Old Testament between God and various individuals who in their different ways represent the whole community of Israel, in which the word *berith* is not actually used as a description, but which in substance do belong to the same series: especially the calling and commissioning of the prophets, but also of Moses, Aaron, the Judges, Saul and David? In these encounters between God and those who had special gifts in Israel, is it not possible that we have to do with the original view of the covenant between God and His people as such? And when on festivals (like that of the enthronement) the people remembered the conclusion of the covenant, it was surely not understood as a 'jubilee" of that event, but realistically as a contemporary happening. Certainly the conclusion of the covenant in the Old Testament represents a series of many such events, and we should not be thinking in Old Testament categories if we tried to understand one of them as the original, i.e., as the basic form of all the others which is simply repeated, renewed and varied in the others, and therefore as the basic act which constitutes Old Testament history and religion. The autonomy and importance which the Old Testament literature gives to each of these many events, quite irrespective of their mutual relationship, seems to make it impossible to try to find some pragmatic, historical connexion. We have to hold together Deut. 5[2]: "The Lord our God made a covenant with us in Horeb . . . not with our fathers, but with us, even us, who are all of us here alive this day"—and Deut. 29[14]: "Neither with you only do I make this convenant and this oath, but with him that standeth here with us this day before the Lord our God, and also with him that is not here with us this day." It is enough that all the accounts are at one in this, and that even in their puzzling variety they make it clear, that the presupposition of all the Old Testament happenings has itself always to be understood as an event, the event of the mutual electing of the God of Israel and His people.

But the concept of mutuality must now be elucidated. The saying of Jeremiah: "I will be your God and you will be my people" certainly speaks of a mutuality. But it also speaks (even in those passages in which the order of the two parts of the saying is reversed) of a willing on the part of God and of a subordinate obligation, or becoming and being on the part of Israel. And it is uttered as a statement made by God and not by a human writer. We have here a negation of "the compulsory union of God with His people" (W. Eichrodt, *op. cit.* p. 11) which is found in the other religious systems of the ancient east. Further, we have a decisive proof that in this context the word "covenant" does not denote a two-sided contract between two equal partners, but a more or less one-sided decree (M. Noth, *Geschichte Israels*, p. 111, n. 1). The covenant can (and must) be thought of as a "dictation on the part of an active to a passive person" (G. Quell, *op. cit.*, p. 120). In the words of Jacques Ellul (*Die theologische Begründung des Rechts*, 1948, p. 37 f.) it is a contract of adherence (*contract d'adhésion*), i.e., a contract in which one of the parties makes the arrangements and the other simply agrees. The sense in which the LXX and the New Testament speak about the διαθήκη brings out exactly the meaning of the Old Testament *berith*. It is "in every respect the arrangement of God, the mighty declaration of the sovereign will of God in history, by which He creates the relationship between Himself and the human race in accordance with His redemptive purpose, the authoritative ordinance (institution) which brings about the order of things" (J. Behm, *Theol. Wörterbuch zum N. Test.* II, p. 137). For that reason it was rightly described by the Reformed federal theologians of the 17th century as a *foedus μονόπλευρον*. This is clear in contexts like Deut. 27[16-19], where the conclusion of the covenant is represented as an act of law, in which both partners clarify their position and engage in a mutual contract. Certainly Yahweh, too, accepts an obligation. But He does so on His own free initiative. He does not have to make a contract with Israel. And the obligation which He accepts consists only in the fact that He wills to be who He is as the God of Israel: "salvation" (*Yahweh shalom*, Jud. 6[24]) and therefore—as "our" God— "our righteousness" (*Yahweh zidqenu*, Jer. 23[6], 33[16]). Yahweh does not stand above the covenant, but in it, yet He is also not under it. It is always "my covenant." Certainly there is a parallel obligation on the part of Israel. Certainly Israel declares that it will be Yahweh's "peculiar people" (*am segullah*) and that as such it will keep His commandments. But it does not do so on its own judgment, but because it has been told by God that it is so. And its keeping of the commandments consists only in the fulfilment of its being as the people which God has made it (Ps. 100³). Certainly between the two obligations there is a correspondence which is brought out particularly by Deuteronomy. That Yahweh is the salvation and righteousness of Israel is something which is known and experienced by His people only when as such it keeps His commandments. Conversely, when this does take place on the part of Israel, it cannot fail to enjoy this knowledge and experience. But if it does not happen, if there is done in Israel what ought not to be done (Gen. 34⁷; 2 Sam. 13¹²), then the salvation of its God necessarily becomes loss and His righteousness judgment. But this correspondence, too, rests on the free ordering of God, and its fulfilment is on both sides a matter of His righteousness, judgment and control. He alone is King and Judge. The correspondence, therefore, is in no sense a relationship of *do ut des* between two equal partners, a limitation which can be imposed on the activity of God by the attitude of Israel, and the acceptance of such a condition by God. The obligation which rests on God is always one which He wills to lay upon Himself. If ever Israel takes up the attitude to God that its relationship with Him is one of *do ut des*, if ever it thinks that it can control God in the light of its own attitude, if ever it tries to assert a claim in relation to God, then it is unfaithful to its own election as His peculiar people and to its own electing of God. It has already fallen away to the worship of false gods and the transgression of all His commandments. It has already rushed headlong into the judgment of God and its own destruction. And when Israel does keep the commandments of its God, when it is faithful to His election and to its own electing of Him, it will necessarily appreciate that the knowledge and experience that He is its salvation and righteousness, and the blessing in which it stands, are God's free grace, the fulfilment of an obligation which God does not owe, but which He has Himself taken upon Himself, making the execution of it His own affair.

Now in the Old Testament the whole occurrence in and with and concerning the community of tribes which is "Israel," from its formation in the earliest period to the return of the captives from exile, is regarded as the fulfilment of this covenant, as the series of positive, critical and negative deductions which God draws from it and which this community comes to know and experience in the covenant in which it exists. Of these we cannot speak in the present context. They are the great example, the great commentary on the fulfilment of that covenant which now concerns us. But necessarily we shall be reminded of this example and commentary in our whole consideration of the doctrine of the atonement.

What we have still to consider is whether the Old Testament gives us any right or title to take over that concept of the covenant which is there shown to be the presupposition of the history of Israel and to use it as a description of the presupposition of the relationship and occurrence between God and all men— "the Jew first, but also the Greek" (Rom. 1[16])—of that free connexion between God and man, based on the free grace of God, which we always have before us when we consider the universal atonement which is an event in Jesus Christ. Does the Old Testament allow or does it even perhaps command us to give to the concept of covenant the wider sense which obviously it will have to have in this context? So far there are three aspects of the meaning of the covenant in the Old Testament which we have not brought into consideration.

1. The first is at least touched on in the mention of the Noachic covenant. The detailed account offered in Gen. 9[1-17] belongs to the priestly writing. But this is making use of an older tradition, as is proved from the immediately preceding J passage in Gen. 8[20-22]. For although this does not mention the word covenant, and is only a soliloquy of Yahweh as He smells the sweet savour of the sacrifice offered up by Noah, there is in content a decisive connexion between what Yahweh says to Himself in this passage and what He says to "Noah and his sons" in Gen. 9[1, 8]. Both passages speak of an obligation which God imposes upon Himself. In both passages we can see a corresponding obligation on the part of man. But "man" here is not the community of tribes which is Israel but the whole of humanity after Noah. If, then, as accounts of a covenant —which they are—they stand in the same series as all the other accounts from Sinai to the covenant under Ezra, they differ from all the others in that they speak of a covenant of God with the whole of humanity before and outside Abraham, and indeed, in 9[10, 12, 15f.], with all the living creatures which with Noah escaped the Flood. If we compare this with Gen. 12f. we find that in relation to the "covenant" there are indeed (cf. W. Eichrodt, *op. cit.*, p. 19) "two concentric circles" (Proksch) in which the relationship of God to man is actualised: in the Noachic covenant it is with the human race as a whole, in the covenant with Abraham only with Israel. But in its own way, according to the tradition enshrined in the texts in Gen. 8 and 9, the covenant in the outer circle is no less real and unforgettable than the other. There, too, in the general occurence in the relationship "between me and all flesh" (Gen. 9[17]) we not only have to reckon with a living and active relation between the ruling and providing Creator and His creature, but we have also a covenant: a particular act of God in which He for His part pledges Himself to the man who is under pledge to Him. Nowadays the Noachic covenant is often referred to as a covenant of preservation in contrast to the covenant with Abraham as a covenant of grace and salvation. Certainly the Noachic covenant has to do with the "preservation" of the race. But we must not forget that even in the later covenant or covenants with Israel it is still a question of preservation. And again, in Gen. 8 and 9 it is not simply and abstractly a matter of "preservation," of the

continuance of this relation between the Creator and the creature. What is attested here is not simply what we call the general control of divine providence. The very fact that the reference is only to man and to creatures subordinate to him ought in itself to warn us. What the texts say is not simply that the relation will in fact continue, but—and this is not quite so self-evident—that it will continue in face and in spite of the apostasy of man. "I will not again curse the ground any more for man's sake; for the imagination of man's heart is evil from his youth; neither will I again smite any more every living thing, as I have done"—is what Yahweh says in Gen. $8^{21}$. And "neither shall all flesh be cut off any more by the waters of a flood; neither shall there any more be a flood to destroy the earth" is what He pledges to Noah and his sons in $9^{11}$. He has once carried out the threat of destruction evoked by the sin of man, in the Flood, although even then a remnant was preserved. But He will not do it again: "He lets go displeasure, and he does not ask concerning our guilt." Certainly it means preservation when He says: "While the earth remaineth, seedtime and harvest, and cold and heat, and summer and winter, and day and night shall not cease" ($8^{22}$). And for that reason: "Be ye fruitful and multiply; bring forth abundantly in the earth, and multiply therein" ($9^7$). But in view of the wickedness of the heart of man even after the Flood, which God knows well enough, this preservation of the race is by a special activity of God, that is to say, by the exercise of His longsuffering, in which He wills that men as they are—having been shown once and for all under what threat they stand—should go forward to meet One who (as yet completely unseen) has still to come, and therefore that they should not be allowed to perish, but preserved. Therefore the Noachic covenant—in a way which remarkably is much more perceptible than in the case of the covenant or covenants with Israel—is already a covenant of grace in the twofold sense of the concept grace: the free and utterly unmerited self-obligation of God to the human race which had completely fallen away from Him, but which as such is still pledged to Him (as is shown by the sacrifice of Noah in Gen. $8^{20}$ and the divine direction in Gen. $9^{1f.}$); and as the sign of the longsuffering of God obviously also the promise of the future divine coming which will far transcend the mere preserving of the race.

It is astonishing and yet it is a fact that the Old Testament should have considered the race prior to and outside Abraham in this way, on the presupposition not merely of the general relation of Creator and creature, but of a concrete activity of God in relation to it, which is not positively His redemptive activity—the same can be said of the covenant concluded with Israel—but an activity on the basis of which the nations preserved by God cannot be excluded from His redemptive work. In this sense the race, as a whole, is in covenant. It is the outer circle of which the inner is revealed from Gen. 12 onwards as Israel. It is in covenant, not by nature, not as humanity, to whom the Creator as such is obliged to show longsuffering, but on the basis of the free divine initiative and act. And genuinely so on this basis. In the light of Israel elected and called out from them, the nations can and must be regarded under this sign: under this correspondence to the sign under which Israel itself found itself placed, and therefore as itself to some extent a great community of tribes. From this point we can well understand how the Old Testament necessarily dared to present the history of creation—without using the word *berith* in the text, but factually—in an indissoluble relation to the divine covenant. The history of creation is a great cosmic prelude and example of that history of Israel which is the proper theme of the Old Testament. Creation is the outward basis of the covenant (Gen. 1) and the covenant the inward basis of creation (Gen. 2). Cf. *C D* III 1, § 41. Finally, the story of the Fall and its consequences (Gen. 3) is a happening which, for all its fearfulness, like the later resistance of Israel and the divine judgments which came upon it in consequence, does not take place outside but within a special relationship of the affirmation of man by God, of God's faithfulness to man, which is self-evidently presupposed to be unshakable. We can also understand how it is that, for all the exclusiveness with which the Old Testament speaks of the election and call of Israel, it never has any hesitation in allowing figures from outside, from the nations, time and again and sometimes with the very highest authority and function to enter the inner circle: Melchizedek, King of Salem, who in Gen. 14[18] is called "a priest of the Most High God," Jethro the Midianite, the father-in-law of Moses (Ex. 18[1f.]), Balaam, the prophet of Moab (Num. 22–24) who is forced to bless Israel against his will, the harlot Rahab of Canaan (Josh. 2) who saves the spies, Ruth the Moabitess who is the ancestress of David, the Philistine Ittai (2 Sam. 15[19]) who is one of the loyal few who pass over Kedron with David, the Syrian general Naaman (2 K. 5[1f.]), to mention only a few out of a list which is remarkably continued in the New Testament. We can also understand the respect, the sympathy, even the granting of equality, which is so often enjoined upon Israel in the Law in relation to the "stranger," and the petition in which the stranger is expressly accepted in Solomon's prayer of dedication in 1 K. 8[41f.] (seeing that strangers could sometimes be found in the temple at Jerusalem). Those who come from outside do not come from a vacuum, but from the sphere of a relationship of God to man which is also in its own way effective—not generally and naturally, but historically, in virtue of a particular divine act.

2. A second important qualification of the Old Testament concept of the covenant arises from the conception of the final mission of Israel to the nations which we find particularly in the latter part but also in the earlier portions of the book of Isaiah. Why did God separate and take to Himself and address this people? In the older tradition this question was left unanswered. But now in the light of the future an answer is given. It is given in the form of a prophecy which arises out of the situation of Israel at the end of its historical independence, but which absolutely transcends every historical consideration,

possibility or probability. In the last days it will be wonderfully shown that the covenant of Yahweh with Israel was not an end in itself, but that it had a provisional and a provisionally representative significance. Israel had and has a mission—that is the meaning of the covenant with it. In Israel—this is what will be revealed in the last days—there is to be set up a sign and a witness to all peoples. The redemptive will of God is to be declared to all humanity. That is what we are told in the particularly important saying to the Ebed Yahweh in Is. 49[6]: "It is a light thing that thou shouldest be my servant to raise up the tribes of Jacob, and to restore the preserved of Israel: I will also give thee for a light to the Gentiles, that thou mayest be my salvation unto the end of the earth." The prophetic portrayal of this future event is not unitary. In Is. 2[2-4]—which is ascribed to Isaiah, the son of Amoz, although it is found word for word in Mic. 4[1-4]—we are told: "And it shall come to pass in the last days, that the mountain of the Lord's house shall be established in the top of the mountains, and shall be exalted above the hills; and all nations shall flow unto it. And many people shall go and say, Come ye, and let us go up to the mountain of the Lord, to the house of the God of Jacob; and he will teach us of his ways, and we will walk in his paths for out of Zion shall go forth the law, and the word of the Lord from Jerusalem. And he shall judge among the nations, and shall rebuke many people: and they shall beat their swords into ploughshares, and their spears into pruninghooks: nation shall not lift up sword against nation, neither shall they learn war any more." Zion is also referred to in Is. 25[6-8], but this time in relation to a redemptive happening of universal significance which does not go and, as it were, spread out from it, but which takes place within it: "And in this mountain shall the Lord of hosts make unto all people a feast of fat things, a feast of wines on the lees, of fat things full of marrow, of wines on the lees well refined. And he will destroy in this mountain the face of the covering cast over all people, and the vail that is spread over all nations. He will swallow up death in victory; and the Lord God will wipe away tears from off all faces; and the rebuke of his people shall be taken away from off all the earth: for the Lord hath spoken it." Different again is the picture unfolded in Is. 19[18-25]. In the most concrete possible way the presentation of a historical situation—which seems to be very like that of the time of Isaiah himself—is merged into a vision of events in the last days: "In that day shall five cities in the land of Egypt speak the language of Canaan and swear to the Lord of hosts. . . . In that day there shall be an altar to the Lord in the midst of the land of Egypt, and a pillar at the border thereof to the Lord. And it shall be for a sign and for a witness to the Lord of hosts in the land of Egypt. . . . And the Lord shall be known to Egypt, and the Egyptians shall know the Lord in that day, and shall do sacrifice and oblation; yea, they shall vow a vow unto the Lord, and perform it. . . . In that day shall there be a highway out of Egypt to Assyria, and the Assyrian shall come into Egypt, and the Egyptian into Assyria, and the Egyptians shall serve with the Assyrians. In that day shall Israel be the third with Egypt and with

Assyria, even a blessing in the midst of the land: whom the Lord of hosts shall bless, saying, Blessed be Egypt my people, and Assyria the work of my hands, and Israel mine inheritance."

In the texts so far quoted we may wonder whether the eschatological event described is not conceived too much as the onesided arrangement and miraculous operation of Yahweh. But in the Ebed-Yahweh songs of Deutero-Isaiah the emphasis is unmistakably on the active co-operation of the human partner of Yahweh. The question whether this partner, the servant of the Lord, is meant as collective Israel or as a single person—and if so, which? a historical? or an eschatological?—can never be settled, because probably it does not have to be answered either the one way or the other. Thus figure may well be both an individual and also the people, and both of them in a historical and also an eschatological form. What is certain is that in and with this servant of the Lord Israel as such is at any rate introduced also as the partner of Yahweh. And in a whole series of passages it is introduced as the partner of Yahweh in an eschatological encounter with the nations, the powerful witness of Yahweh in the midst of the heathen. It is, therefore, in the light of a service which Israel has to perform that the actualisation of the prophecy of salvation is now understood. Is. 42[1-4]: "Behold my servant, whom I uphold; mine elect, in whom my soul delighteth; I have put my spirit upon him; he shall bring forth judgment (*mishpat*) to the Gentiles. He shall not cry, nor lift up, nor cause his voice to be heard in the street. A bruised reed shall he not break, and the smoking flax shall he not quench: he shall bring forth judgment unto truth. He shall not fail nor be discouraged, till he have set judgment in the earth; and the isles shall wait for his law." And Is. 42[5-8]: "Thus saith God the Lord, he that created the heavens, and stretched them out; he that spread forth the earth, and that which cometh out of it; he that giveth breath unto the people upon it, and spirit to them that walk therein: I the Lord have called thee in righteousness (*b'zedeq*), and will hold thine hand, and will keep thee, and give thee for a *berith am* (this remarkable expression recurs in Is. 49[8]: the Zurich Bible paraphrases: "a mediator of the covenant on behalf of the race"), for a light of the Gentiles; to open the blind eyes, to bring out the prisoners from the prison, and them that sit in darkness out of the prisonhouse. I am the Lord, that is my name: and my glory will I not give to another, neither my praise to graven images."

The saying in Is. 49[6] has already been mentioned. But above all there is what is rightly the best known of all the Servant Songs, Is. 52[13]–53[12], which, however we understand the one of whom it speaks, definitely belongs to this context. It is now the nations themselves—once again we have the eschatological event—who acknowledge that they have at last understood the meaning of the existence of Israel amongst them—its historical role as a mediator and the message which it has addressed to them: "Behold, my servant shall prosper, he shall be exalted and extolled, and be very high. As many were astonished at thee; his visage was so marred more than any man, and his form more than the sons of men: So shall he astonish many nations; the kings shall shut their mouths at him: for that which had not been told them shall they see; and that which they had not heard shall they consider" (Is. 52$^{13-15}$. The historical background and outlook of the song is a time and situation of the last and deepest and most hopeless abasement of the people of the covenant, or of its (kingly? or prophetic?) representative. But according to this song, in the last days the nations will recognise and acknowledge that his mission, and the universally valid word and universally effective work of God, is present even in this utter hiddenness of the historical form of His witness: "Who hath believed our report? and to whom is the arm of the Lord revealed? For he shall grow up before him as a tender plant, and as a root out of a dry ground: he hath no form nor comeliness; and when we shall see him, there is no beauty that we should desire him. He is despised and rejected of men; a man of sorrows, and acquainted with grief: and we hid, as it were, our faces from him; he was despised, and we esteemed him not" (53$^{1-3}$). "He was cut off out of the land of the living" (v. 8). "He made his grave with the wicked, and with the rich in his death" (v. 9). "Who shall declare his generation?" (v. 8). And then the great confession of the nations at the end of the age, which does not deny but confirms and even lights up this appearance: "Surely he hath borne our griefs, and carried our sorrows" (v. 4). "But he was wounded for our transgressions, he was bruised for our iniquities: the chastisement of our peace was upon him; and with his stripes we are healed. All we like sheep have gone astray; we have turned every one to his own way; and the Lord hath laid on him the iniquity of us all" (vv. 5–6). And all this means: "He shall see his seed, he shall prolong his days, and the cause of the Lord shall prosper in his hand," because he made himself "an offering for sin" (v. 10). Just as the passage begins with a soliloquy of Yahweh, so it also ends, accepting and confirming this confession of the Gentiles: "He shall see of the travail of his soul, and shall be satisfied: by his knowledge shall my righteous servant justify many; for he shall bear their iniquities. Therefore will I divide him a portion with the great, and he shall divide the spoil with the strong; because he hath poured out his soul unto death: and he was numbered with the transgressors; and he bare the sin of many, and made intercession for the transgressors" (vv. 11–12).

Seen and understood eschatologically, this is the meaning and function of the particular covenant of God with Israel. The word *berith* occurs only once in the passages quoted, in the obscure *berith am* of Is. 42$^8$. But, in fact, it forces itself upon us, for it is the covenant of people which lives and cries and suffers here, which is hemmed in and oppressed and threatened, which is more than threatened, actually overthrown and given up to destruction (and all according to the will and disposing of its God). The relatively short time of its modest existence in the sphere of world-history or of contemporary middle-eastern politics draws quickly to its close—in pain and grief and shame. What is it that the covenant-God is saying in all this? What is it that He wills by this work of His—He who has from the first and again and again shown and attested Himself as the One who is in covenant with His people? The prophets evidently associated the happenings primarily with the message that Israel had to see in it that judgment for its unfaithfulness to the Lord of the covenant which had been held before it from the very first. When that judgment began to fall—first on Samaria, then on Jerusalem—at every stage they warned and admonished and pleaded and threatened, like swimmers struggling against the twofold stream of human disobedience and the consequent wrath of God, which they tried to arrest with their call to repentance, but which by reason of its ineffectiveness they could not arrest, and therefore did not try to do so any longer but could only affirm it to be holy and just and necessary. But quite apart from the vain and empty confidence held out by the false prophets, even the true and authentic spokesmen for the covenant-God spoke always of His unchangeable faithfulness in contrast to the unfaithfulness of Israel, of the inflexibility of His purpose for His people, and therefore of the positive meaning of its history including its end. It is in this context that there arises the prophecy of the redemptive future of Israel in the last days. It presupposes the dark state of things at the present. It views it with pitiless clarity. And it does not overlay this view with the mere promise of better times to come. It does not offer by way of comfort the prospect of later historical developments. Its nerve and centre is the reference to an event which will terminate all history and all times, a history of the end. It is in this—and from this point of view the necessary destruction of Israel is only "a moment of wrath" (Is. 54[7f.]; Ps. 30[5])—that the Yes which Yahweh has spoken to His people in and with the conclusion of the covenant will be revealed and expressed as a Yes. The last time, the day of Yahweh, will indeed be the day of final judgment—the prophets of a false confidence must make no mistake about that. But as such it will also be the day of Israel's redemption—the day when the covenant which Yahweh has made with it finds its positive fulfilment.

And it is particularly the teaching of the book of Isaiah which makes it clear that as such the last day which is the day of redemption for Israel will also be the day of redemption for the nations—the day of judgment, too, but, as the day of the last judgment, the day of redemption. It will then be revealed to the nations that it is not in vain and not for its own sake that Israel was and is, that its divine election and calling and all the history which followed in its brighter or darker aspects was no mere episode but an epoch, was not accidental but necessary, that its purpose was not a particular one, but the universal purpose of its mission, that its existence was the existence of a light for all men, a light which was once overlooked, but which then shone out unmistakably in the gross darkness which covered the earth (Is. 60[1f.]—we may also recall the four rivers of Paradise in Gen. 2[10f.], and the river which flows out of the temple in Ezek. 47[1-12]). It will then be the case actually and visibly that "salvation is of the

Jews" (Jn. $4^{22}$). All the texts quoted speak of this in their varied eschatological imagery. They make it plain that the race as a whole is not forgotten in the importance of those shattering events between Yahweh and Israel which are the main subject of the Old Testament testimony. They do not speak only of the judgments which necessarily fall on the nations in relation to that which overtakes Israel. They also connect the salvation which is the final goal of the history of Israel with the salvation of the Assyrians and the Egyptians and all nations, and in such a way that the special existence of Israel is an instrument by which God finally manifests and accomplishes salvation for the nations. They speak, in fact, of a concrete presupposition which underlies the dealings of God as Lord of the world and the nations, and which for all its dissimilarity is similar to that of the history of Israel, and indeed identical with it, in that it has as its aim the grace which is to come upon them. The line which reveals this eschatological aspect of the Old Testament is not a broad one. It is only a kind of border to the true narrative and message of the Old Testament. But it belongs to it quite unmistakably. It is like the reference to that corresponding event in the earlier history, the covenant of God with the human race before Abraham, which is also a narrow line marking the earlier border of the true narrative and message of the Old Testament. But that narrative and message do have their beginning at the one point and their end at the other, the one in primal history, and the other in the corresponding eschatological history. They have this aspect even as the narrative and message of the happenings which take place on the basis of the covenant. And how could they be understood as a unity unless they had this aspect? By these strangely complementary aspects on the borders of the Old Testament we are not merely enabled but summoned to take even the most exclusive thing of which it speaks, the covenant relationship between Yahweh and Israel, which is the presupposition of everything that takes place in the relations between these two partners, and, without denying its exclusiveness, to understand it inclusively, as that which points to a covenant which was there at the beginning and which will be there at the end, the covenant of God with all men.

3. We come finally to a third strand which we cannot overlook in an intensive amplification of the Old Testament covenant concept. Even in itself and as such the covenant with Israel is capable of a radical change in structure which it will actually undergo in the last days, as we learn from Jer. $31^{31f.}$ and $32^{38f.}$. "Behold, the days come, saith the Lord, that I will make a new covenant with the house of Israel, and with the house of Judah" ($31^{31}$). "I will make an ever-lasting covenant with them" ($32^{40}$). The elements are exactly the same as in that covenant with Abraham, Moses and Joshua which is normative for the Old Testament as a whole. The formula "I will be your God, and ye shall be my people" is emphatically endorsed in both these passages and in the parallel passage in Ezek. $11^{20}$. We cannot therefore speak of a "replacement" of the first covenant by this "new" and "eternal" covenant of the last days except in a

positive sense. Even in the verses Jer. 31[35-37] which immediately follow the main passage 31[31-34], there is a most definite stress on the imperishable nature of the covenant with Israel: neither here nor elsewhere can there be any question of its interruption or cessation. What happens to this covenant with the conclusion of a new and eternal covenant is rather—and the wider context of the passage points generally in this direction—that it is upheld, that is, lifted up to its true level, that it is given its proper form, and that far from being destroyed it is maintained and confirmed. There is no question of a dissolution but rather of a revelation of the real purpose and nature of that first covenant. The relationship of God with Israel, which is the substance of the covenant, is not held up,* that is to say, arrested, and set aside and destroyed, even on the New Testament understanding of the passage. What is done away (Calvin) is only its "economy," the form in which it is revealed and active in the events of the Old Testament this side of the last days. In accordance with the completely changed conditions of the last time this form will certainly be altered, and so radically that it will no longer be recognisable in that form, and to that extent a new covenant will actually have been concluded. The form in which it was revealed and active in all the events from the exodus from Egypt to the destruction of Israel and Judah was such that in it the faithfulness and power of Yahweh seemed always to be matched and limited by the perpetually virulent and active disobedience and apostasy of the covenanted people. The prophecy says that this will end in the last days. The new and eternal covenant will not be "according to the covenant that I made with their fathers when I took them by the hand to bring them out of the land of Egypt; which my covenant they brake, although I was a Lord unto them" (31[32]). It is this that God will no longer tolerate in the last days, but will repeal and remove: "But this shall be the covenant that I shall make with the house of Israel; After those days, saith the Lord, I will put my law in their inward parts, and write it in their hearts; and will be their God, and they shall be my people" (31[33]). "And I will give them one heart, and one way, that they may fear me for ever, for the good of them, and of their children after them" (32[39f.]). Ezek. 11[19f.] (cf. 36[26f.]) is even clearer: "And I will . . . put a new spirit within you; and I will take the stony heart out of their flesh, and will give them an heart of flesh; that they may walk in my statutes, and keep mine ordinances, and do them: and they shall be my people, and I will be their God." Similarly in Deut. 30[6] we are told about a circumcision of the heart of the people which God Himself will accomplish: "to love the Lord thy God with all thine heart, and with all thy soul, that thou mayest live." All this clearly means that the circle of the covenant which in its earlier form is open on man's side will in its new form be closed: not because

---

*Note: There is a play here on the German word *aufheben*, which positively means to "raise up," but negatively means to "repeal" or "set aside."—Trans.

men will be better, but because God will deal with the same men in a completely different way, laying His hand, as it were, upon them from behind, because He Himself will turn them to Himself. To His faithfulness—He himself will see to it—there will then correspond the complementary faithfulness of His people. The covenant—God Himself will make it so—will then be one which is mutually kept, and to that extent a *foedus δίπλευρον*.

The strange but necessary consequence will then be: "And they shall teach no more every man his neighbour, and every man his brother, saying, Know the Lord: for they shall all know me, from the least of them unto the greatest of them, saith the Lord" (31[34]). But if the new and eternal form of the covenant means the ending of the fatal controversy between God and man it also means the ending of the corresponding necessity (the redemptive necessity) for that human antithesis or opposition between wise and foolish, prophets and people, teachers and scholars, the *ecclesia docens* and the *ecclesia audiens*, which even at its very best indicates a lack and encloses a judgment. It is at this point that Paul comes in (2 Cor. 3[6f.]) with his doctrine of the old and the new διαθήκη, the one of the prescriptive letter, the other of the liberating spirit which leads to obedience. In the light of this he expounds the covering on the face of Moses (Ex. 34[35f.]) as that of the temporal nature of his ministry, and he finds the same covering on the hearts of the Jews who hear Moses read without perceiving that his ministry (i.e., the ministry of the prescriptive letter) does in fact belong to the past (2 Cor. 3[15f.]). He then goes on to proclaim: "Now the Lord is that Spirit: and where the Spirit of the Lord is, there is liberty" (2 Cor. 3[17]). He then contrasts the Jew who is one only outwardly with the Jew who is one inwardly and in truth: "by the circumcision that is of the heart, in the spirit, and not in the letter" (Rom. 2[29])—that is to say, the Gentiles who have come to faith in Jesus Christ, who apart from the Law do by nature the works of the Law, who are a law to themselves in that they reveal that the Law is written in their hearts (Rom. 2[14f.]). He then can and must say with reference to the Christian community (cf. also Rom. 15[14]; Phil. 1[9f.]) that although prophecy, tongues and knowledge will fade away, love can never fail (1 Cor. 13[8]).

And now we come to the most remarkable thing of all: What is the basis and possibility of this complete change in the form of the covenant which is to take place in the last days and therefore beyond the history of Israel considered in the Old Testament? A conclusive answer is given in Jer. 31[34b]: "For I will forgive their iniquity, and I will remember their sin no more." I would not say with G. Quell (*op. cit.*, p. 126) that a covenant which has this basis is obviously no longer a covenant. I would say rather that in this way and on this basis it becomes a perfect covenant. For in this way and on this basis God will break the opposition of His people, creating and giving a new heart to the men of His people, putting His Spirit in their inward parts, making the observance of His commandments self-evident to them (Paul in Rom. 2[14] uses the word φύσις in relation to Gentile Christians), and in that way completing the circle of the covenant. In this way and on this basis the Israelitish history in the old form of the covenant—in so far as it stood under the sign of the sin of Israel and the divine reaction against it—will come to an end, together with that earlier form, to give way to the new and proper form. This ending and new beginning will be posited in the fact that God not only exercises patience as in the Noachic covenant, but that He remits guilt, that He does not remember sin, and that in this way and on this basis He not only allows an unmerited continuation of life, again as in the Noachic covenant, but reduces to order, and in a sense compulsorily places in the freedom of obedience which we owe Him as His covenant partners. This sovereign act of God which fulfils His will and plan and in which He vindicates at one and the same time His own right and that of man, is the subject of the prophecy in Jeremiah: the new basis of the new covenant. This covenant will be the covenant of the free but effective grace of God.

We must remember, however, that this conclusion of the covenant in the last days, like the Noachic covenant of the first days, is in the same series as those which were made first with Abraham and finally with Ezra. As we have seen, the prophecy of it does not mean to discredit or invalidate these others, or the covenant with Israel as such. It denies what had so far taken place on the basis of the presupposition to which those conclusions of the covenant point: the breaking of the covenant on the part of the people, and ensuing judgments on the part of God. But it does not deny the presupposition as such. It negates—or rather according to this prophecy God Himself negates—the unfaithfulness of Israel, but not the faithfulness of God Himself, nor His covenant will in relation to His people. What God will do in accordance with this prophecy will be a revelation and confirmation of what He had always willed and indeed done in the covenant with Israel. And for all the antithesis between the faithfulness of God and unfaithfulness of man, and the divine judgments which follow this antithesis, in everything that takes place in the Old Testament do we not find something of the forgiveness of the guilt and the gracious forgetting of the sin of His people, which belong to the last days, and which in fact obviously answer to the deepest being of the covenant, however out of place they may seem to be outwardly? And on this basis were there not always in this people new and fleshly and circumcised hearts, and the Spirit and freedom, and even a simple and genuine keeping of the commandments? How could there ever have been prophets, how could there have been that remnant in Israel, how could there have been penitence and prayer and also the bright and joyful worship of God in the Psalms, if not on the basis which Jer. 31 describes as the new basis of the new covenant? This basis was not simply absent in the "old" covenant—or in the one covenant in its old form (as though this had had some other basis!). It was only hidden: hidden under the form of a relationship in which, viewed as a whole, the human lack of grace was bound to be revealed side by side with the divine grace, in which therefore even grace itself, viewed as a whole, was bound to have the form of judgment. Jer. 31 is the final word in matters of the divine covenant with Israel. In the light of the last days it describes it as the covenant of the free but effective grace of God. But at the same time it is also the first word in these matters. And this description is an indication of what the divine covenant with Israel had been in substance from the very first.

What, then, we gather from the Noachic covenant, and everything that belongs to this strand, is that according to the Old Testament conception itself the special divine covenant made with Israel does not exclude the human race as a whole from the gracious will of God towards it. What we find in Isaiah's view of the status of Israel as a representative and messenger to the nations is that the covenant made with Israel has a meaning and purpose which reaches out beyond the existence of Israel. And now, from the prophecy in Jeremiah of a new covenant of forgiveness and of the Spirit and of free obedience on the part of man, we learn that the Old Testament looks beyond the past and present to a form of the relationship between God and Israel in which the covenant broken by Israel will again be set up, that the Israelite, for whom ultimately God has nothing but forgiveness, but does have it actually and effectively, must now take his place directly alongside his Gentile fellows, and that if at all he can hope for the grace and salvation of God only on this presupposition. In the light of this passage in Jer. 31 we are indeed enabled and summoned to give to the concept of the covenant the universal meaning which it acquired in the form which it manifestly assumed in Jesus Christ.

Jesus Christ is the atonement. But that means that He is the maintaining and accomplishing and fulfilling of the divine covenant as executed by God Himself. He is the eschatological realisation of the will of God for Israel and therefore for the whole race. And as such He is also the revelation of this divine will and therefore of the covenant. He is the One for whose sake and towards whom all men from the very beginning are preserved from their youth up by the longsuffering of God, notwithstanding their evil heart. And in this capacity He reveals that the particular covenant with Israel was concluded for their sake too, that in that wider circle it also encloses them. He is the servant of God who stands before God as the representative of all nations and stands amongst the nations as the representative of God, bearing the judgments of God, living and testifying by the grace of God—Himself the Israel elected and called to the covenant and to be the mediator of the covenant. And in that capacity He reveals that this covenant with Israel is made and avails for the whole race. In His own person He is the eschatological sovereign act of God who renews men and summons them to obedience by forgiving their sins. And in that capacity He reveals that the meaning and power of the covenant with Israel for the whole race is that it is a covenant of free and therefore effective grace.

The work of God in Jesus Christ is also the Word of God—the Word in which He makes known His will even as it is done to those who can hear it. And this will of God which is done begins with the institution and establishment of His covenant with man. It is done in acts of grace and mercy, of judgment and punishment, and in His Word as Gospel and Law, as comfort, admonishment and counsel. It is done primarily and basically as His will to be the God of man, to let man be His man. The whole actualisation of the will of God has its source there, in the "kindness of God toward man" (Tit. 3⁴). This is the presupposition of all the works and words of God. The whole plan and law and meaning of them derives from this source, that God the Creator wanted to make and did in fact make Himself the covenant partner of man and man the covenant partner of God. The whole doing of the will of God is the doing of His covenant will. As this covenant will it strives and conquers against the sin of man and its consequences in the atonement accomplished in Jesus Christ. But primarily, in face of the sin of man, and God's striving with it and conquering of it and of its consequences, it is His covenant will. It remains His covenant will in this antithesis, conflict and victory. It is through those that it finds its fulfilment. And the antithesis, conflict and fulfilment reveal it for what it is. They also show its origin—that it was first of all His covenant will.

It is in Jesus Christ that that antithesis is met and overcome. It is Jesus Christ who accomplishes and fulfils the will of God in face of human sin and its consequences. It is not something provisional but final that takes place in the atonement accomplished by Him. In Him God Himself enters in, and becomes man, a man amongst men, in order that He Himself in this man may carry out His will. God Himself lives and acts and speaks and suffers and triumphs for all men as this one man. When this takes place, atonement takes place. But the final thing which takes place here—just as it cannot be something provisional—cannot be a second or later thing. It can only reveal the first thing. What takes place here is the accomplishment and therefore the revelation of the original and basic will of God, as a result of which all the other works and words of God take place. What breaks out at this point is the source of all that God wills and does.

This, then, is the actualisation of the will of God in this matter, in the overcoming of this antithesis. The will of God is done in Jesus Christ, in God's own being and acting and speaking as man. But if this is so, then this actualisation, the overcoming of this antithesis, is characterised as an act of faithfulness, of constancy, of self-affirmation on the part of God, as the consequence of a presupposition already laid down by Him, as the fulfilment of a decision which underlies and therefore precedes that actualisation, an "earlier" divine decision, as the successful continuation of an act which God had already begun, from the very beginning. He becomes and is man in Jesus Christ, and as such He acts and speaks to reconcile the world to Himself, because He has bound Himself to man by the creation of heaven and earth and all things, because He cannot tolerate that this covenant should be broken, because He wills to uphold and fulfil it even though it is broken. The work of atonement in Jesus Christ is the fulfilment of the communion of Himself with man and of man with Himself which He willed and created at the very first. Even in face of man's transgression He cannot allow it to be destroyed. He does not permit that that which He willed as Creator—the inner meaning and purpose and basis of the creation—should be perverted or arrested by the transgression of man. He honours it and finally fulfils it in this conflict with the transgression and overcoming of it. The transgression can and must be understood as an episode and its overcoming in Jesus Christ as the contingent reaction of God in face of this episode. But the reaction as such takes place along the line of that action determined from the very first in the will of God and already initiated. It is only the particular form of that action in face of this episode. And in this particular form, in the fact that God becomes man for our sake, to set aside our sin and its consequences, we see both the fact and also the manner in which it is determined from the very first and already initiated. It is not only a reaction, but a work of the faithfulness of God. And the faithfulness of God has reference to the covenant between Himself and men. Even in this particular form it is the accomplishment of His covenant will. Even more, it is the affirmation and consummation of the institution of the covenant between Himself and man which took place in and with the creation. It is this covenant will which is carried out in Jesus Christ. It is this institution of the covenant which is fulfilled in Him. He does it in face of human sin, as the One who overcomes it, as the Mediator between God and man. He does it, therefore, in fulfilment of the divine reaction in face of that episode. But primarily it is the action of God, disturbed but not broken by that episode, which is now consummated. He therefore fulfils and reveals the original and basic will of God, the first act of God, His original covenant with man. It is of this, the presupposition of the atonement, that we must first speak.

What is revealed in the work of atonement in Jesus Christ, as its presupposition, is that God does not at first occupy a position of neutrality in relation to man. He is not simply distant from him and high above him. He is not merely God in His own divine sphere allowing man to be man in his sphere. He does not merely know about him and view him as a spectator. This is excluded from the outset by the fact that He is the living Creator and Lord of man, and therefore the One who actively guarantees and accompanies and controls his existence. This might, of course, imply a certain neutrality, for He is the Creator and Lord of heaven and earth and all creatures, the living One who preserves and accompanies and controls them all, so that He is for man only what He is for all other things. But in becoming man for the sake of man in the work of atonement, He reveals an attitude and purpose in respect of man which goes beyond His attitude and purpose as Creator and Lord in respect of all things. He is disposed towards man in a special way which could not be said of any other creature, and which is not only that of the Creator and Lord of man. He remains his Creator and Lord. With all other creatures, and in a special way amongst other creatures, He lavishes upon him all the riches of His goodness as Creator—why should we not say, of His grace as Creator? He gives and preserves to this human creature his human life in all the plenitude and with all the limitations of its particular possibilities. He is to him a faithful and watchful Father. He does not leave him without counsel and commandment. But that is not all. And all that, His general acting and working and speaking as Creator, has in relation to man a particular meaning and purpose: not only because it has to do with the particular creature which is man, but because from the very first His relationship with this creature is of itself a particular one and has a particular goal. The fatherly faithfulness and provision shown to him by God has a different meaning and purpose from that which is undoubtedly exercised in respect of other creatures. And so, too, the counsels and commandments which are given him by the Creator have a different meaning and purpose from the ordinances under which all other creatures undoubtedly have their being according to His will.

What God does to man and for man even as Creator has its origin in the fact that among all the creatures He has linked and bound and pledged Himself originally to man, choosing and determining and making Himself the God of man. The distinguishing mark of Israel is the fact that there is said to Israel and heard by Israel that which at the end of the history of Israel becomes an event in Jesus Christ : "I will be your God and ye shall be my people." And this is a revelation of the divine choice and decision, the divine word and the divine act, in which, in and with creation, it became truth and actuality that God made Himself the God of man : that in willing man God willed to be God for him, with him, in relation to him, acting for him, concerned with him, for his sake. God: and therefore nothing other than what He was and is and always will be in Himself as Father, Son and Holy Spirit; and all that, not for Himself alone, but for man, in his favour, in a true and actual interest in his existence, with a view to what he is to become, and therefore in a participation in what he is and lives and does and experiences; just that, nothing more but also nothing less, in fellowship with man. "I will be your God": that is the original emergence of God from any neutrality, but also His emergence from what is certainly a gracious being and working as Creator and Lord in relation to man. That is more than the creation, more than the preservation, accompaniment and overruling of His creatures. That is the covenant of God with man, from which He has bound and pledged Himself always to begin, and in virtue of which He has constituted Himself his God.

And that is the presupposition of the atonement as revealed in its actualisation in Jesus Christ: the presupposition whose consequences are deduced in the atonement; the presupposition which in the atonement is fulfilled in spite of the opposition of man. We do not postulate it. We do not grope for it in the void. We find it in that which has actually taken place in Jesus Christ. But we cannot refuse to find it in that which has actually taken place in Jesus Christ. If the final thing is true, that in Him God has become man for us men, then we cannot escape the first thing, that it is the original will of God active already in and with creation that He should be God for us men. If for us men God Himself has become man, we can, we must look into the heart of God—He Himself has opened His heart to us—to accept His saying as a first as well as a final saying: "I will be your God." We cannot, therefore, think of Him except as the One who has concluded and set up this covenant with us. We would be mistaking Him, we would obviously be making ourselves guilty of transgression, of sin, if we were to try to think of Him otherwise, if we were to try to reckon with another God, if we were to try to know and fear and love any other God but Him—the One who from the very first, from the creation of heaven and earth, has made Himself the covenant God of man, our covenant God. For according to the Word which He Himself has spoken in His supreme and final work, there is no other God. All other gods, all gods which are hostile to man, are false gods. Even though we bring the deepest reverence or the highest love, even though we bring the greatest zeal or sincerity, if they are offered to other gods, to gods that are hostile to man, we are simply beating the air, where there is no God, where God is not God. "I will be your God": not only for Israel, but, according to the revelation accomplished in Jesus Christ at the end of the history of Israel, for all men of all times and places, this was and is the critical point of all faith in God and knowledge of God and service of God. This God, or none at all. Faith in this God, the knowledge and service of this God, or godlessness. He Himself has decided this in revealing Himself as the One who was and is and is to come—God for us, our God, the God who has concluded and set up the covenant.

It is simply a matter of analysis when we go on to say that the covenant is a covenant of grace. This concept implies three things.

The first is the freedom in which it is determined and established by God, and therefore the undeservedness with which man can receive and respond to the fact that God has chosen and determined and made Himself his God. In the atonement in which the presupposition is revealed, "I will be your God," this is clear beyond any possible doubt. By his transgression man has prevented God from affirming it and holding any further fellowship with him. Man is not in a position to atone for his transgression, to reconcile himself with God. Man cannot bring forward a Jesus Christ in which his atonement with God can take place. If it is to take place, it must be from God, in the freedom of God and not of man, in the freedom of the grace of God, to which we have no claim, which would necessarily judge and condemn us, because we have sinned against it and always will sin against it, because we have shown ourselves unworthy of it. Atonement is free grace. Even the fact that God wills to be our God and to act and speak with us as such is free grace on God's side and something entirely undeserved on ours. We have only to think—God for us men, God in His majesty, God the Father, Son and Holy Spirit, God in all the fulness of His divine being, God in His holiness, power, wisdom, eternity and glory, God, who is completely self-sufficient, who does not need a fellow in order to be loved, or a companion in order to be complete: God for us men. If that is what He is, if that is what He is as the true and real and living and only God—as the One who Himself willed to become man, and in so doing proved and revealed that He cares for man, and that He does so originally and properly and intensely, if He is this God, the *Deus pro nobis*, the covenant-God, then He is so, not as limited and conditioned by our freedom, but in the exalted freedom of His grace. That is what free grace, the overflowing of His love, was and is, that He willed to be our Creator and Lord, and how much more the One who says: "I will be your God." Why among all creatures does He will to be our God? Why the God of man? Because of the preculiarities and qualities of human creatureliness? But other creatures have theirs too, and how are we to say that those of men are greater? And even if they were, it would by no means follow that man would have a claim that God must be God for man, that He should enter into covenant with us, that there should be this divine Yes originally addressed only to us. The covenant of God with man is a fact which, since it is a fact according to His revelation in Jesus Christ, we cannot deny as such. But according to the prophetic warnings God entered into covenant with other peoples as well as Israel. Why then (if He willed to contract such a relationship with creatures at all) should He not also have done so with some quite different creature as well? Why not to His greater honour with some creature which is supposed to be or actually is lower or more lowly? The fact of the covenant of God with man is obviously a fact of His free choice, the choice of His grace. There is no complementary claim of man to such a distinction. We can only accept and affirm this choice as true and actual. We can only cling to it as a fact which He has chosen and posited. We can only recognise and honour it as completely undeserved. That is the first sense in which we have to say that the covenant as the presupposition of all God does and says in relation to us men is a covenant of grace.

The second thing implied in the concept is the beneficent character proper to this presupposition of the atonement. Positively, grace means the giving of something good and redemptive and helpful. Grace is a powerful Yes spoken to the one to whom it is addressed. This, too, can be perceived at once in the atonement in which it is revealed. Atonement means the redemption of man, the fact that he is prevented from falling into the abyss into which he ought to fall as a transgressor, as the one who has interrupted the divine purpose, as the enemy of grace. And consisting as it does in the fellowship of temporal man with Jesus Christ and therefore with God, it means further that he is placed in the certain expectation of eternal salvation, which has become a temporal present and a living promise in Jesus Christ. But in this sense, too, it is simply a matter of grace to grace. For the divine benefit is simply the first thing in consequence of which the second took place. We think again—God for us men. God who in His triune being, in the fulness of His Godhead, is Himself the essence of all favour, the source and stream and sea of everything that is good, of all light and life and joy. To say God is to say eternal benefit. Now the work of His creation, and His control as the One who preserves and accompanies and rules the creature and therefore man, is certainly a favour out of His fulness. But in the covenant with man, as his God, He does not merely give out of His fulness. In His fulness He gives Himself to be with man and for man. As the benefit which He is in Himself, He makes Himself the companion of man. He does not merely give him something, however great. He gives Himself, and in so doing gives him all things. It is only of God that what man comes to experience in covenant with Him is favour. It is not always so, not by a long way in all the supposed or actual experience of man. Even in his experience of what comes to him from God, man can be blind or half-blind, and can therefore make mistakes, and can find terror and destruction in what God has allotted and given as a supreme benefit. And necessarily the benefit offered him by God can in fact and objectively become terror and destruction if he flees from God and opposes Him. Even the divine favour will then take on the aspect of wrath. God's Yes will then become a No and His grace judgment. The light itself will blind him and plunge him in darkness. Life will be to him death. But this does not mean that God will not keep His covenant, or that this will cease to be the covenant of grace, or that its meaning and purpose will cease to be the favour shown to man. How can Yahweh cease to be salvation? What it does mean is that in certain situations of its execution and history the true character must be hidden under another form— which may later be put off and (whether it is recognised by man or not, or properly recognised or not) give place again to its true form. In this form, in itself, by virtue of its meaning and purpose, and just as surely as that God is always sovereign in it, the covenant is always a relationship in which there is the conferring and receiving of a benefit, not the opposite, not a relationship of wrath and perdition, not even when it does (necessarily) appear to men like that (as it did to Job), not even when the merciful but just and holy God Himself can and will maintain and execute it in that other form (as He did so often in the history of Israel). In this positive sense, too, in its proper form and by virtue of its origin it is always the covenant of grace.

The third thing which we maintain when we describe the covenant as the covenant of grace is that the covenant engages man as the partner of God only, but actually and necessarily, to gratitude. On the side of God it is only a matter of free grace and this in the form of benefit. For the other partner in the covenant to whom God turns in this grace, the only proper thing, but the thing which is unconditionally and inescapably demanded, is that he should be thankful. How can anything more or different be asked of man? The only answer to χάρις is εὐχαριστία. But how can it be doubted for a moment that this is in fact asked of him? χάρις always demands the answer of εὐχαριστία. Grace and gratitude belong together like heaven and earth. Grace evokes gratitude like the voice an echo. Gratitude follows grace like thunder lightning. Not by virtue of any necessity of the concepts as such. But we are speaking of the grace of the God who is God for man, and of the gratitude of man as his response to this grace. Here, at any rate, the two belong together, so that only gratitude can correspond to grace, and this correspondence cannot fail. Its failure, ingratitude, is sin, transgression. Radically and basically all sin is simply ingratitude—man's refusal of the one but necessary thing which is proper to and is required of him with whom God has graciously entered into covenant. As far as man is concerned there can be no question of anything but gratitude; but gratitude is the complement which man must necessarily fulfil.

This leads us to a further point which is revealed in the atoning work accomplished in Jesus Christ, and as the presupposition of that work, that man cannot first be neutral towards God. Man is not simply distant from God and far beneath Him. He cannot let Him be God in His sphere in order in his own sphere to try to be man *in abstracto* and on his own account. He cannot simply know about God, or believe "in a God." We may say that such neutrality is excluded already by the fact that man is the living creature of God, and that as such in all his movements—whether he knows it or not—he is thrown back entirely upon God, he is dependent upon Him and bound up with Him. But there is more to it than that, for he is bound to all other creatures in that way, and all other creatures are similarly bound. When God Himself becomes man for men in the work of atonement, then quite apart from the general and in a sense external being of men under and with God this means that as creatures preserved, accompanied and over-ruled by God men have a character, we can call it a *character indelibilis*, which transcends their creatureliness as such. When God reveals in Jesus Christ that from the very first He willed to be God for man, the God of man, He also reveals that from the very first man is His man, man belongs to Him, is bound and pledged to Him. The man for whose sake God Himself became man cannot be basically neutral. He can only be a partner in His activity. For as in Jesus Christ there breaks out as truth the original thing about God: "I will be your God," so in Jesus Christ there breaks out as truth the original thing about man, "Ye shall be my people." That was and is the distinctive mark of Israel, which at the end of the history of Israel became event in Jesus Christ and in that event is revelation, the divine revelation of the destiny of man, of all men, as their determination for Him. According to this revelation, from the very first God was and is God for man, inclined to him, caring for him, his God. But so, too, according to this revelation of God from the very first man was and is man for God, subordinated and referred to Him. "Ye shall be my people" means that it is proper to you and required of you in your being, life and activity to correspond to the fact that in My being, life and activity for you I am your God.

And if the essence of God as the God of man is His grace, then the essence of men as His people, that which is proper to and demanded of them in covenant with God, is simply their thanks. But this is actually and necessarily proper to and demanded of them. Thanks is the one all-embracing, but as such valid and inescapable, content of the law of the covenant imposed upon man. It is the one and necessary thing which has to take place on the part of man. All the laws of Israel and all the concrete demands addressed by God to individual men in Israel are simply developments and specific forms of this one law, demands not to withhold from the God of the covenant the thanks which is His due, but to render it with a whole heart. The grace of God calls for this modest but active return. It is for this reason and on this basis that in the Old Testament even the detailed commands are always urged so forcefully and earnestly and emphatically, that which God wills of man being unconditionally pressed irrespective of the apparent greatness or littleness of the thing which is demanded. What is divinely required in the Old Testament has this irresistible force, the force of an either-or, which is a matter of life and death, because the thanks is demanded which cannot possibly fail to follow grace. Obedience to the commands of other gods, false gods, is usually a matter of the free inclination and judgment of man. But where the One who commands is the *Deus pro nobis*, obedience is not something which is in our hands, but the self-evident human complement and response. It is only here in the existence of man in the covenant which as such is the covenant of grace that we see the true horror of disobedience, of sin. That he should be thankful is the righteousness which is demanded of him before God. And if he is not thankful, that is his unrighteousness.

This is the basic determination of the relationship between God and man which is revealed as applicable to all men from the very first in the atonement which took place in Jesus Christ and in which the history of Israel attained its goal. This is the last thing which is revealed as the first thing for man too. When (in Jesus Christ) we look into the heart of God—for in Him He has revealed to us: "I will be your God"—we are permitted, indeed we are constrained, to look at ourselves, that what is proper to and is required of us is: "Ye shall be my people." As God is gracious to us, we may—and this "may" is the seriousness and force of every "ought"—on that account be thankful. By deciding for us God has decided concerning us. We are therefore prevented from thinking otherwise about ourselves, from seeing or understanding or explaining man in any other way, than as the being engaged and covenanted to God, and therefore simply but strictly engaged and covenanted to thanks. Just as there is no God but the God of the covenant, there is no man but the man of the covenant: the man who as such is destined and called to give thanks. And it is again transgression, sin, if even for a moment we ignore this man who is true man, trying to imagine and construct a man in himself, and to regard his destiny to give thanks to God as something which is in his own power, a matter of his own freedom of choice. The real freedom of man is decided by the fact that God is his God. In freedom he can only choose to be the man of God, i.e., to be thankful to God. With any other choice he would simply be groping in the void, betraying and destroying his true humanity. Instead of choosing in freedom, he would be choosing enslavement. By revealing Himself in Jesus Christ as from the very first the gracious God, God has decided that man can only be grateful man, the man who takes up and maintains his place in the covenant with Him, the gracious God.

It can only be by way of analysis and emphasis that we maintain that grace is not only the basis and essence, the ontological substance of the original relationship between God and man which we have described as the covenant between them willed and instituted and controlled by God. The recognition of this original covenant is also grace and therefore a free divine favour. We have described the covenant as from every point of view the presupposition of the atonement which is revealed and therefore can be recognised only in the atonement. We now need to emphasise: only in the atonement, and therefore only in Jesus Christ. Concerning the covenant fulfilled as God became man in Jesus Christ, concerning the covenant will of God executed and accomplished in Jesus Christ, concerning God's institution of the covenant as the first and basic divine act continued and completed in the action fulfilled in Jesus Christ—concerning all these things we have no other source of knowledge than through the One who is the one Word of God "whom we must hear, and trust and obey in life and in death." In all that we have said about the original place and status of God and man in their relationship one with another, we have tried never to look past Jesus Christ, but always to consider it as seen through Him and with a steadfast regard fixed on Him, "as it was in the beginning."

> We have tried to make the movement to which we are summoned by the fact that in the New Testament we are told both directly (e.g., Jn. 1[3,10]; Col. 1[16]; Heb. 1[3]) and also indirectly that the creation of God took place in Him, i.e., that it was willed and planned and completed with a view to Him as the *telos* of all things and all events, and that He is "the first-born of all creation" (Col. 1[15]). We have tried to paraphrase and give the sense of Eph. 1[4-6]: "According as he hath chosen us in him before the foundation of the world ($\pi\rho\dot{o}\ \kappa\alpha\tau\alpha\beta o\lambda\hat{\eta}\varsigma$ $\kappa\acute{o}\sigma\mu o\upsilon$), that we should be holy and without blame before him in love: having predestinated us ($\pi\rho oo\rho\acute{\iota}\sigma\alpha\varsigma\ \dot{\eta}\mu\hat{\alpha}\varsigma$) unto the adoption of children by Jesus Christ to himself, according to the good pleasure of his will, to the praise of the glory of his grace." We have understood the atonement as "predestinated according to the purpose ($\kappa\alpha\tau\dot{\alpha}\ \pi\rho\acute{o}\theta\epsilon\sigma\iota\nu$) of him who worketh all things according to the counsel of his own will" (Eph. 1[11]), as accomplished "according to the eternal purpose ($\kappa\alpha\tau\dot{\alpha}\ \pi\rho\acute{o}\theta\epsilon\sigma\iota\nu\ \tau\hat{\omega}\nu\ \alpha\grave{\iota}\acute{\omega}\nu\omega\nu$) which he purposed (or: already fulfilled as such? $\hat{\eta}\nu\ \dot{\epsilon}\pi o\acute{\iota}\eta\sigma\epsilon\nu$) in Christ Jesus our Lord" (Eph. 3[11]).

From that which in Jesus Christ took place in time according to the will of God we have tried to gather what was and is and will be the will of God at the beginning of all time, and in relation to the whole content of time. By the perception of grace at the end of the ways of God we have been led to the perception of grace at their beginning, as the presupposition of all His ways. We are certainly not in any position, nor are we constrained, to recognise this presupposition of all the ways of God, and finally of the atonement accomplished in Jesus Christ, as the covenant of grace, if we look to any other source, if we follow any other supposed Word of God than that which is spoken in Jesus Christ and in His work. When we spoke of the original and basic will of God, of His "first act" fulfilled in and with creation but transcending creation, we did not speak of an "original revelation" which we must differentiate from Jesus Christ because it is in fact different from Him. We did not speak in the light of the results of any self-knowledge or self-estimate of human reason or existence. We did not speak with reference to any observations and conclusions in respect of the laws and ordinances which rule in nature and human history. We certainly did not speak in relation to any religious disposition which is supposed to be or actually is proper to man. There is only one revelation. That revelation is the revelation of the covenant, of the original and basic will of God. How else could this be revealed to us? The concept of an "original revelation" which must be differentiated from the revelation in Jesus Christ because it is actually different from it is a purely empty concept, or one that can be filled only by illusions.

In a word, the covenant of grace which is from the beginning, the presupposition of the atonement, is not a discovery and conclusion of "natural theology." Apart from and without Jesus Christ we can say nothing at all about God and man and their relationship one with another. Least of all can we say that their relationship can be presupposed as that of a covenant of grace. Just because it is a covenant of grace, it cannot be discovered by man, nor can it be demonstrated by man. As the covenant of grace it is not amenable to any kind of human reflection or to any questions asked by man concerning the meaning and basis of the cosmos or history. Grace is inaccessible to us: how else can it be grace? Grace can only make itself accessible. Grace can never be recalled. To remember grace is itself the work of grace. The perception of grace is itself grace. Therefore if the covenant of grace is the first thing which we have to recognise and say about God and man in their relationship one with another, it is something which we can see only as it makes itself to be seen, only as it fulfils itself—which is what happened in Jesus Christ—and therefore reveals itself as true and actual. From all eternity God elected and determined that He Himself would become man for us men. From all eternity He determined that men would be those for whom He is God: His fellow-men. In willing this, in willing Jesus Christ, He wills to be our God and He wills that we should be His people. Ontologically, therefore, the covenant of grace is already included and grounded in Jesus Christ, in the human form and human content which God willed to give His Word from all eternity. The order of cognition cannot be disobedient to, but must follow, the actual order of things. If we are to know God and man and their basic and unalterable relationship one with the other, we have to hear the Word of God only in the form and with the content which God Himself has given to it, and by which He willed to lay down His own place and status, and ours, from the very first. It is only by this Word, which is Jesus Christ, and which is itself in this form and with this content the basis and meaning of the covenant, that we can learn about the covenant. This Word is not only the basis and meaning of the covenant. As a revealed Word it is also the instruction concerning it which we have to receive.

What is involved in this knowledge of the covenant, the covenant of grace which is the presupposition of the atonement fulfilled and revealed in the atonement? It is important that we should be clear about this point. For we are not in fact dealing with a theologumenon which is no doubt permissible and may be introduced in passing, but which is in any event dispensable and may in the last resort be regarded as superfluous.

In this knowledge or recognition we make the right distinction between the atonement accomplished in Jesus Christ, which is the centre and the proper subject of the Christian message and the Christian faith, and all events which are purely contingent, which have only a relative significance, which concern certain men but not all men, which may not even be necessary *rebus aliter stantibus*. Or, to put it positively, in this recognition we make a proper acknowledgment of the unconditional, eternal and divine validity and scope of the atonement accomplished in Jesus Christ, of the general and inescapable and definitive claim of that which took place in it. It is in this recognition that we are committed to a genuine regard for this centre of the Christian message and the Christian faith. Without it we cannot attain to the joy or certainty or freedom to which we are summoned by this event.

The atonement accomplished in Jesus Christ is God's retort to the sin of man and its consequences. And the sin of man is an episode. It is the original of all episodes, the essence of everything that is unnecessary, disorderly, contrary to plan and purpose. It has not escaped the knowledge and control of God. But it is not a work of His creation and not a disposition of His providence. It really comes about and is only as that which God did not will and does not will and never will will. It has its being only in the fact that it is non-being, that which from the point of view of God is unintelligible and intolerable. It takes place only as the powerful but, of course, before God absolutely powerless irruption of that which is not into the fulfilment of His will. It takes place, therefore, only under the original, radical, definitive and therefore finally triumphant No of God. It is not a limitation of His positive will. Rather it exists as it is completely conditioned by His non-will. It is alive and active in all its fearfulness only on the left hand of God.

But the atonement accomplished in Jesus Christ, like creation and the providential rule of God, is a work on the right hand of God, a work of His positive will. It is so in the highest possible sense, in a way which gives it priority and precedence over creation and providence. In Jesus Christ God comes to grips with that episode. Jesus Christ is in fact God's retort to the sin of man. This does not mean even remotely that it, too, is only an episode. Even from the point of view of God's antithesis to the sin of man, what took place in it is rather the execution, that is, the sealing and revelation, the original fact of the positive will of God in His relationship with man, and therefore of His whole will in creation and preservation. It is not simply to combat the interruption of that will, it is not merely to assert and purify polemically and yet also irenically His relationship with man, and therefore with the whole world as it was created by Him, in face of the breaking out and in of human sin, that God willed to become man and did in fact do so. He willed to do it and did it first and foremost for this positive end, to give concrete reality and actuality to the promise "I will be your God" and the command "Ye shall be my people" within the human race which could not say this of itself, but was to hear it as His Word and to live by this Word to His glory. He willed to do it and did it in order to fulfil both the promise and the command in divine truth and power, in order not only to make it possible for us men to receive them, but actually to make them heard by us (in an act which is at once one of utter condescension and supreme majesty), in order to set them amongst us and therefore to make them effective for us. What takes place in Jesus Christ, in the historical event of the atonement accomplished by Him in time, is not simply one history amongst others and not simply the reaction of God against human sin. It stands at the heart of the Christian message and the Christian faith because here God maintains and fulfils His Word as it was spoken at the very first. He affirms to us and sets among us His original promise and His original command in the concrete reality and actuality of His own being as man. He maintains and fulfils it in His conflict with our sin, vindicating His own glory and accomplishing our salvation. But He maintains and fulfils it first and foremost in affirmation and execution of the original purpose of His relationship with us men: *propter nos homines* and therefore *propter nostram salutem (Nic. Const.)*. The atonement in Jesus Christ takes place as a wrestling with and an overcoming of human sin. But at the same time and primarily it is the great act of God's faithfulness to Himself and therefore to us—His faithfulness in the execution of the plan and purpose which He had from the very first as the Creator of all things and the Lord of all events, and which He wills to accomplish in all circumstances. For this reason in Jesus Christ we are not merely dealing with one of many beings in the sphere of the created world and the world of men. He is this, too. Because He is this, because He is a being like us and with us, He enables us actually to hear the Word of God and the promise and commandment of God, and the execution of the divine purpose is fulfilled for us and as such revealed to us. As such He is born in time, at His own time. But in Jesus Christ we are not merely dealing with the author of our justification and sanctification as the sinners that we are. We are not merely dealing with the One who has saved us from death, with the Lord and Head of His Church. As such, as the One who fulfils this divine work in the world, which would be lost without Him, He is born in time, at His own time. But at the same time and beyond all that—and the power of His saving work as the Mediator is rooted and grounded in this—He is "the first-born of all creation" (Col. $1^{16}$)—the first and eternal Word of God delivered and fulfilled in time. As very God and very man He is the concrete reality and actuality of the divine command and the divine promise, the content of the will of God which exists prior to its fulfilment, the basis of the whole project and actualisation of creation and the whole process of divine providence from which all created being and becoming derives. Certainly the sin of man contradicts this first and eternal Word of God. But in the first and eternal Word of God the sin of man is already met, refuted and removed from all eternity. And in delivering and fulfilling this first and eternal Word in spite of human sin and its consequences, as He would in fact have delivered and fulfilled it quite apart from human sin, sin is also met, refuted and removed in time.

In this sense the atonement accomplished in Jesus Christ is a necessary happening. This is its unconditional validity and scope and binding force. This is why it commands the reverence due to it as the heart of the Christian message (a reverence which is the basis of all the joy and certainty and freedom of faith). For in Jesus Christ we do not have to do with a second, and subsequent, but with the first and original content of the will of God, before and above which there is no other will—either hidden or revealed in some other way—in the light of which we might have to understand and fear and love God and interpret man very differently from how they are both represented in Jesus Christ. We do not need to look beyond Jesus Christ. We do not need to consider whether it may be obligatory or legitimate to look beyond Him. When we look at Him we have all conceivable clarity and certainty. We only need to look at Him. We only need to hear the word of His historical existence and we shall hear the Word of God and look into the basis and essence of God and man and all things. The covenant between God and man, the promise and command of God, which Jesus Christ announces to us as their unity, is therefore the final thing to which we can and should and must cling, because Jesus Christ as their unity is also the first thing, because the covenant is by promise and commandment eternally grounded in Him, in the unity of God and man accomplished in Him. The recognition that this covenant is the presupposition of the atonement is therefore nothing more or less than a recognition of the sure basis of the Christian message and the Christian faith. Quite apart from the fact that it is true and necessary in itself, it would be quite out of place to ignore it.

In this recognition it is a matter of the basis of a right distinction, a right acknowledgment and a right regard for the act of atonement. Therefore once again—and from two angles—we must be quite clear with what we have to do in the presupposition which it confirms and reveals. It consists in this, that Jesus Christ, very God and very man, born and living and acting and suffering and conquering in time, is as such the one eternal Word of God at the beginning of all things.

This means at once that as the beginning of all things the presupposition of the atonement is a single, self-sufficient, independent free work of God in itself, which is not identical with the divine work in creation or with the divine creative will realised in this work. The achievement of atonement and therefore the historical actuality of Jesus Christ is not the highest *divine interruption* evolutionary continuation, the crown and completion of the positing which God has willed and accomplished of a reality of the world and man which is distinct from Himself. It is not the immanent *telos* of such a reality.

Here again we part company with Schleiermacher. To do him justice, he was in his own way concerned about the eternal basis and necessity of the appearance of Jesus Christ and therefore of the atonement as the overcoming of human sin. But this was how he conceived of the connexion and made the required reference and regress to the beginning of all things. The fulfilling of time in Jesus Christ meant for him that at the end of their historical development man, and in man finite being as such, attained in Jesus Christ that form to which they had always been potentially inclined and endowed in the relationship of complete dependence on God as infinite being. God's eternal will is done in Jesus Christ in such a way that in Him—in the undisturbed unity of His man-consciousness with His God-consciousness—man attains to the perfection ordained and necessary to him as man.

In this conception (as so often in Schleiermacher) there is a strange mixture of truth and error. Truth, because the New Testament itself indicates quite clearly, in the light of what is revealed in Jesus Christ, that we cannot understand too intimately or emphasise too strongly the relationship of the being of man and the world in their creatureliness with the being of Jesus Christ. Error, because everything is plainly topsy-turvy if we picture this relationship in such a way that the being of Jesus Christ is deduced and interpreted from the being of man and the world instead of the other way round, if we derive the atonement from creation instead of creation from the atonement, if we describe as the first and eternal Word of God that which we think we can recognise, i.e., postulate and maintain as the final word on the evolutionary process of finite being and development. No ideas or pronouncements on a supposedly attainable or attained *telos* of the immanent development of creaturely being can do justice to the *telos*, and therefore the beginning, revealed in Jesus Christ. We cannot overlook the fact that in relation to Jesus Christ the New Testament speaks of a new creation (Gal. 6[15]; 2 Cor. 5[17]), of a new man created by God (Eph. 4[24]), not of a continuation of man but of a "new birth" (Jn. 3[3]), and indeed of a new heaven and a new earth (Rev. 21[1]; 2 Pet. 3[13]). And Jesus Christ is not regarded as the fulfilment and highest form of the first Adam, but in sharp antithesis He is described as the last Adam ("The first man is of the earth, earthy, the second man is the Lord from heaven," I Cor. 15[44f.]).

The right distinction of the atonement from every purely contingent event, the right acknowledgment of its validity and scope, the right regard for that which God has said and done in it, and therefore the right recognition of the covenant which is its presupposition and which is revealed in it, the right recognition, then, of the sure basis of the Christian message and Christian faith—all these things depend on the insight that in Jesus Christ we really have to do with the first and eternal Word of God at the beginning of all things. With the beginning of all things in God, in His will and purpose and resolve, which does not follow or derive from but underlies and precedes all that reality which is distinct from Himself, the existence and history of the world and man, and therefore creation. Jesus Christ is in truth the first, i.e., the content and subject of that first divine will and purpose and resolve which underlies the beginning of the creaturely world and is therefore superior to it. This is what makes Him so new in relation to all that precedes Him in the creaturely world. He is the other, the second and last Adam as opposed to the first, just because He was before him. This is what marks Him out and distinguishes Him from Adam and from everything else that is, happens, becomes, comes and goes before and after and beside Him. He cannot, therefore, be deduced from

that which is other than Himself, from that which was before Him. He is
not a product—not even the most perfect—of the created world as such
He is in it. He belongs to it. He exists and works and reveals Himself in its
history. But He does not derive from it: it derives from Him. He is in it but
He is also quite different from it. He stands over against it as the One who
was from the beginning—its beginning—with God. He is the content and
form of the divine thought of grace, will of grace and decree of grace in
relation to the created world, before the created world was. He is the One
for whose sake God willed it and created it. He is the meaning and purpose
which it has because God willed to give it to it and did in fact give it to it.
The creation, too, and the preservation and direction of the world and
man, must be described as pure acts of divine grace. But even here we
must think strictly of Jesus Christ in whom these acts had and have their
meaning and purpose. The existence and work of Jesus Christ do not
follow from the gracious act of creation or the gracious act of divine
providence. It is for the sake of Jesus Christ that creation takes place and
God rules as the preserver and controller of world-events. These things
are all acts of divine grace only because they take place for His sake.

For in Jesus Christ we have to do with something that is new and
special in relation to creation as such—the fact that God has elected
and determined Himself as the fellow and friend of man, and elected and
determined man as His own friend and fellow. This is the divine thought
of grace and will of grace and decree of grace in relation to the world
before the world was. This is the meaning and purpose which He had in
creating it. How can this derive from the world itself? How can it be its
product or *telos*? How can it be deduced from it or explained by it? Man
has his real being in the fact that his existence was willed and is actual in
this meaning and purpose. Man is—and he is what he is as the creature of
God and by divine providence—only as and because, before he himself
was, there was in the will and purpose and decree of God this grace
towards him. He is in virtue of this eternal Word of God, which is free
in relation to himself and the whole world, which has already made
disposition concerning himself and the whole world. He is in virtue of the
covenant already concluded with God. This is the presupposition of the
atonement revealed in it and fulfilled in history by the fact that God
became man. But this covenant of God with man is grace. It is not given in
and with the nature of the creature. It is not the product or goal of that
nature, although that nature itself is from God. God did not and does not
owe it to the creature, not even to man, to elect and determine Himself for

him, and him for Himself, to will and posit his existence and essence according to this meaning and purpose. Man has no right or claim as man—because he is created man for this purpose—to stand in covenant with God. The fact that he is created for it is something beyond the grace of his created nature. It is the free covenant grace of God which is especially for him. He can perceive and accept it only in the first eternal Word of God as spoken to him in the atonement accomplished in time, in Jesus Christ. It is not in an act of spontaneous self-knowledge, but in the hearing of this first and eternal Word of God, that he can know that he does actually stand on this ground, that he is actually placed in this sphere and atmosphere, in the sphere of the covenant as the being with whom God has associated Himself and whom God has associated with Himself. But that this grace is truth, the first and final truth behind which there is concealed no other or different truth, that he can be and live absolutely by this truth, is something which he can and must perceive and accept in the first and eternal Word of God as it is spoken to him in time. This is the presupposition of the atonement revealed in the atonement. And in the recognition of this presupposition he comes to a right distinction, acknowledgment and regard.

But we must now add, or emphasise and underline a second point. The first and eternal Word of God, which underlies and precedes the creative will and work as the beginning of all things in God, means in fact Jesus Christ. It is identical with the One who, very God and very man, born and living and acting and suffering and conquering in time, accomplishes the atonement. It is He alone who is the content and form of the gracious thought and will and resolve of God in relation to the world and man before ever these were and as God willed and created them.

In this context we must not refer to the second "person" of the Trinity as such, to the eternal Son or the eternal Word of God *in abstracto*, and therefore to the so-called λόγος ἄσαρκος. What is the point of a regress to Him as the supposed basis of the being and knowledge of all things? In any case, how can we make such a regress? The second "person" of the Godhead in Himself and as such is not God the Reconciler. In Himself and as such He is not revealed to us. In Himself and as such He is not *Deus pro nobis*, either ontologically or epistemologically. He is the content of a necessary and important concept in trinitarian doctrine when we have to understand the revelation and dealings of God in the light of their free basis in the inner being and essence of God. But since we are now concerned with the revelation and dealings of God, and particularly with the atonement, with the person and work of the Mediator, it is pointless, as it is impermissible, to return to the inner being and essence of God and especially to the second person of the Trinity as such, in such a way that we ascribe to this person another form than that which God Himself has given in willing to reveal Himself and to act outwards. If it is true that God became man, then in this we have to recognise and respect His eternal will and purpose and resolve—His free and gracious will which He did not owe it either to Himself or to the world to have, by which He did not need to come to the decision to which He has in fact come, and behind which, in these circumstances, we cannot go, behind which we do not have to reckon with any Son of God in Himself, with any *λόγος ἄσαρκος*, with any other Word of God than that which was made flesh. According to the free and gracious will of God the eternal Son of God is Jesus Christ as He lived and died and rose again in time, and none other. He is the decision of God in time, and yet according to what took place in time the decision which was made from all eternity. This decision was made freely and graciously and undeservedly in an overflowing of the divine goodness. Yet—for us to whom it refers and for whose sake it was taken—it was also made bindingly, inescapably and irrevocably. We cannot, therefore, go back on it. We must not ignore it and imagine a "Logos in itself" which does not have this content and form, which is the eternal Word of God without this form and content. We could only imagine such a Logos. Like Godhead abstracted from its revelation and acts, it would necessarily be an empty concept which we would then, of course, feel obliged to fill with all kinds of contents of our own arbitrary invention. Under the title of a *λόγος ἄσαρκος* we pay homage to a *Deus absconditus* and therefore to some image of God which we have made for ourselves. And if we were to deal with a figure of this kind, we should be dangerously susceptible to the temptation, indeed we could hardly escape it, of asking whether the revelation and activity of this "Logos in itself" can altogether and always be confined to this phenomenon, the incarnation in Jesus Christ. If this is not as such the content of the eternal will of God, if Jesus Christ is not the one Word of God from all eternity, why are we not free, or even perhaps obliged, to reckon with other manifestations of the eternal Word of God, and to look at Him in the light of such manifestations? But how can we really, as it were, bracket that which God has actually done and therefore willed in Jesus Christ, not taking it seriously as His eternal will, not holding to it as the beginning of all things which in His free grace God willed to posit and has in fact posited, to which therefore we must hold? How can we look away past and beyond Him? Is it real faith and obedience which concerns itself with this regress to a pre-temporal being of the Word of God which is not His incarnate being, the being of the *Deus pro nobis*? Is it real faith and obedience which tries to set itself on the throne of God and there to construct the content and form of His will and Word which He Himself has not chosen, although He might perhaps have chosen it? We are told that it is inconceivable that all men, "even those who lived thousands of years before

*could it have been otherwise?*

*yes*

*is it?*

*no*

Jesus," should have their being in the history of Jesus, that the history of human existence should derive from that of the man Jesus (Brunner, *ZThK* 1951, p. 98). But is it so inconceivable, does it need such a great imagination to realise, is it not the simplest thing in the world, that if the history of Jesus is the event of atonement, if the atonement is real and effective because God Himself became man to be the subject of this event, if this is not concealed but revealed, if it is the factor which calls us irresistibly to faith and obedience, then how can it be otherwise than that in this factor, and therefore in the history of Jesus, we have to do with the reality which underlies and precedes all other reality as the first and eternal Word of God, that in this history we have actually to do with the ground and sphere, the atmosphere of the being of every man, whether they lived thousands of years before or after Jesus? Does not this question, this protest against the incarnate Word as the content of the eternal will of God, involve a retrogression even behind Schleiermacher, who with his doctrine of the fulfilment of creation accomplished in Jesus Christ could at least in his own way do justice to the necessary connexion between the totality of the human race and the particular history of Jesus? What is there to protest against if we simply accept that act of the greatest divine condescension and supreme divine majesty, the incarnation of His Word in Jesus Christ in the work of atonement, thus taking it in all earnest and not merely half in earnest.

But if Jesus Christ is the content and form of the first and eternal Word of God, then that means further that the beginning of all things, of the being of all men and of the whole world, even the divine willing of creation, is preceded by God's covenant with man as its basis and purpose: His promise, in which He binds and pledges Himself to man, and His command by which He pledges and binds man to Himself. At the beginning of all things in God there is the Gospel and the Law, the gracious address of God and the gracious claim of God, both directed to man, both the one Word of the *Deus pro nobis* who is the one God and beside whom there is no other. For Jesus Christ—not an empty *Logos*, but Jesus Christ the incarnate Word, the baby born in Bethlehem, the man put to death at Golgotha and raised again in the garden of Joseph of Arimathea, the man whose history this is—is the unity of the two. He is both at one and the same time. He is the promise and the command, the Gospel and the Law, the address of God to man and the claim of God upon man. That He is both as the Word of God spoken in His work, as the Word of God which has become work, is something which belongs to Himself as the eternal Son of God for Himself and prior to us. In this He is the pre-existent *Deus pro nobis*. He alone is at once and altogether very God and very man. To that extent He alone is there at the beginning of all things. As the basis and purpose of the covenant He and He alone is the content of the eternal will of God which precedes the whole being of man and of the world. But that which He is for Himself and prior to us He is with a view to us. He is, therefore, the concrete reality and actuality of the promise and command of God, the fulfilment of both, very God and very man, in one person amongst us, as a fellow-man. This first and eternal Word of God is not spoken in the void, but addressed to us. Therefore the event of the atonement is clearly His being for our sake, for our salvation, for the restoration of our relationship with God interrupted by sin. It is, therefore, this relationship with God, grounded on God's relationship with us, which in His person, that is so different and yet directed to us and in its humanity so near to us because perfectly identical with us, is revealed as the basis of the atonement and made effective for us—the pre-existent *Deus pro nobis*.

He and He alone is very God and very man in a temporal fulfilment of God's eternal will to be the true God of man and to let the man who belongs to Him become and be true man. Ultimately, therefore, Jesus Christ alone is the content of the eternal will of God, the eternal covenant between God and man. He is this as the Word of God to us and the work of God for us, and therefore in a way quite different from and not to be compared with anything we may become as hearers of this Word and those for whose sake this work is done. Yet in this difference, in the majesty with which He confronts us, but does confront us, He is the Word and work of the eternal covenant. In the truth and power of this eternal Word and work He speaks the Word and accomplishes the work of atonement in its temporal occurrence. And as we look at this Word and work, and trust in it and build upon it, we can be assured of the atonement which in it has been made in time. And since Jesus Christ is not only the subject but also the eternal and primary basis of this act of atonement, this act is definitively distinguished from all others. It demands our unconditional recognition. It lays claim to our regard. And we can have the certainty and the joy and the freedom of the faith that in spite of our sin and to take away our sin and all its consequences it has taken place once and for all. All this depends on a right recognition of the presupposition of the atonement in the counsel of God, and especially on the fact that we perceive and maintain the content and form of the eternal divine counsel exactly as it is fulfilled and revealed in time.

It is now time, and it will serve as an illustration of what we have just said, to consider a development in the history of theology to which we have so far only alluded. In the older Reformed Church there was a theology in which the concept of the covenant played so decisive a role that it came to be known as the Federal theology. It is usually connected with the name of John Coccejus (1603–1669, and Prof. in Bremen, Franeker and Leiden) in whose *Summa doctrinae de foedere et testamento Dei* (1648) it did indeed find classical and systematic form. But even before Coccejus the concept *foedus* had with varying emphasis been given prominence in a variety of conceptions, expositions and applications by quite a number of writers of whom only the best-known will be mentioned. The immediate predecessors of Coccejus were his own teachers, the theologians of the Herborn school (with whom we must also reckon the then Count John the Elder of Nassau-Dillenburg): Matthias Martini, Ludwig Crocius, W. Amesius, J. Cloppenburg. But these in turn were preceded by the Basel writers Polanus and Wolleb and the Dutch Gomarus, and we can then work back to Z. Ursinus (who was not uninfluenced by Melanchthon) and K. Olevian in Heidelberg, Andreas Hyperius in Marburg, Wolfgang Musculus in Berne, P. Boquin in France, Stephan Szegedin in Hungary, and ultimately the Reformers themselves, Zwingli, Bullinger and Calvin. And the Federal Theology continued to develop even after Coccejus, making headway in spite of the opposition of the older aristotelian-scholastic schools. In Holland it made alliance with Cartesian philosophy and found well-equipped and independent champions in Abraham Heidan and Franz Burmann, also Heinrich Heidegger in Zurich. We can say indeed that in the second half of the 17th century it was the ruling orthodoxy of the Reformed Church. Certainly what H. Heppe in the 19th century represented as the theology of the Reformed Evangelical Church corresponds to it. It even had an influence on political and juridical theory in the person of J. Althusius, a jurist of the Herborn school which preceded Coccejus. The Bremen theologian, F. A. Lampe, then secured its acceptance amongst the Pietists, who developed and applied it in many different ways. At the beginning of the 18th century it also had an occasional influence amongst Lutherans, and if the Lutheran historian G. Schrenk is right (*Gottesreich und Bund im älteren Protestantismus*, 1923) the earlier form of the "redemption-history" school of Erlangen and especially J. C. K. von Hofmann would have been quite unthinkable without it, and indirectly it had a certain exemplary significance for the philosophy of history of German Idealism, and in this way even for the Marxist view of history. This is not the place for a historical or systematic exposition and estimate of a development which was certainly remarkable in its own way. But from the standpoint which we have ourselves reached we must make certain distinctions in relation to what was and was not said in the course of this doctrinal tradition of the older Reformed Church.

1. The Federal theology was an advance on mediæval scholasticism, and the Protestant scholasticism which preceded and surrounded it, in that (true to the

century of the *baroque*) it tried to understand the work and Word of God attested in Holy Scripture dynamically and not statically, as an event and not as a system of objective and self-contained truths. When we read Coccejus—even as compared with Polan, Wolleb and the Leidner Synopsis—we cannot escape the impression that the traditional dogmatics had started to move like a frozen stream of lava. The "Loci" are no longer "Loci," common places, to which this and that must be related either not at all or on the basis of a presupposed concept, as abstract doctrine and truth revealed in and for itself. They are now different stages in a series of events, the individual moments in a movement. This movement is now understood as such to be Christian truth, and Christian doctrine is the description of this movement. This theology is concerned with the bold review of a history of God and man which unfolds itself from creation to the day of judgment. In relation to the two partners it is concerned with the history of the covenant (a history which is naturally initiated and controlled and guided to its proper end by God)—or what in the 19th century came to be called the history of redemption. We find something of the living dynamic of this history in the famous chapters in which Calvin himself (*Instit.* II, 9–11) had tried to apprehend the relationship between the Old and the New Testament under the concept of the one covenant.

But the more embracing and central and exact this apprehension becomes in the main period of the Federal theology, the more insistently the question imposes itself from what standpoint this occurrence is really regarded and represented as such. What happens when the work, the Word of God, is first isolated and then reconnected, according to the teaching of pragmatic theology, with a whole series of events which are purposefully strung out but which belong together? Does this really correspond to the state of affairs as it is prescribed for theology in Scripture? Can we historicise the activity and revelation of God? The Federal theologians were the first really to try to do this in principle, just as they were the first to read the Bible as a divinely inspired source-book by the study of which the attentive and faithful reader can gain an insight and perspective into the whole drama of the relationship between God and man, act by act, as by the help of some other source-book he might do in any other historical field. They saw excellently that the Bible tells us about an event. But they did not see that in all its forms this narrative has the character of testimony, proclamation, evangel, and that it has as its content and subject only a single event, which in every form of the attestation, although they all relate to a whole, is the single and complete decision on the part of God which as such calls for a single and complete decision on the part of man. They overlooked the fact that in all the forms of its attestation this single and complete event is a special event which has to be understood in a special way. Because of the difference of the attestation it cannot be broken up into a series of different covenant acts, or acts of redemption, which follow one another step by step, and then reassembled into a single whole. The Federal theologians did not notice that for all the exclusiveness with which they read the Scriptures, in this analysis and synthesis of the occurrence between God and man they were going beyond Scripture and missing its real content. If we think that we can handle the work and Word of God in this manner, then in our dynamic way we go beyond or fall short of Scripture and its content no less than did the older orthodoxy with its predominantly static terminology. As becomes increasingly plain in the sketches of the Federal theologians, the atonement accomplished in Jesus Christ ceases to be the history of the covenant, to which (in all the different forms of expectation and recollection) the whole Bible bears witness and in face of which theology must take up and maintain its standpoint, and it becomes a biblical history, a stage in the greater context of world-history, before which, and after which, there are other similar stages. In the case of the Federal theologians the standpoint directly in face of the witness to this one event changed its character and became a higher vantage-point from which they could see it together with all the other stages, from which they thought that they could and should make it their business to portray these stages in their variety and inter-relationship. They brought the whole under the concept of the covenant, but they did not read the concept out of this one event. Instead, they imported the concept into this one event like all the others, as the supposed essence of the varied occurrence at every stage. The Federal theology was a theological historicism to the extent that it did not allow itself to be bound to Scripture and confined to the event attested in Scripture in accordance with its reformation inheritance. And with its analysis and synthesis was it not more autonomous in relation to Scripture than it would admit to itself and gave impression to others—for it was here that what is still called "biblicism" had its origin? Could it be long before there would be a necessary demand for a wider outlook from that vantage-point, and a transition to a philosophy of general religious history, the perception and portrayal of a gradual "education of the human race"? It is clear that we cannot follow this theology even in its first and formal statement.

2. We will now look in a different direction. There was a very remarkable reason for the first introduction of the covenant concept by Zwingli (cf. G. Schrenk, *op. cit.* p. 36 f.). He used it purely and simply for the defence of infant baptism. The Anabaptists in Switzerland and elsewhere liked to describe themselves as "covenant-members," and their believers' baptism as a covenant, the sign of the true covenant, the covenant of grace, in contrast to the Abrahamic covenant of circumcision—the covenant which in a wild misunderstanding of the name Pontius* in the Apostles' Creed they described as the covenant of Pilate under which Christ suffered. In his writings *De peccato*

---

*The misunderstanding derives from the superficial resemblance between the Swiss-German *"puntnus"* (covenant) and Pontius.—Trans.

*originali* (1526) and *In catabaptistarum strophas elenchus* (1527)—his practical concern was to defend the national Church—Zwingli used against them the following argument. God first made a covenant with Adam, then with Noah, for the whole human race. He then made a covenant with Abraham for the people of Israel. But it was always the one covenant valid from the foundation of the world to its end, providing for human sin with the determination of Jesus as Mediator and Redeemer. Therefore we heathen who believe in Jesus are one in faith with Abraham, and therefore one people, one Church, with the people of Israel, heirs of the one testament, the only difference being that now that Christ has appeared in accordance with the original determination it is proclaimed and delivered to all nations, the ceremonies of the covenant with Israel are done away, and the light which lightened the fathers has shone out all the more brightly on us. The drift of the argument is this. If the children of Israel were as such, before they believed, included in the Abrahamic covenant, why should the same not be true of our children? If they received the covenant sign of circumcision, are ours not placed at an intolerable disadvantage if they do not receive baptism? But—apart from the christological content—the real point of interest in Zwingli's conception is the universal meaning and purpose which he tried to give to the covenant concept, his insistence on the covenant with Noah and even a covenant with Adam, in relation to which, and in the light of its limitations done away at the appearance of Christ, the Abrahamic covenant would almost appear to be an episode were it not that by virtue of its aiming at Christ it is already so complete that everything *post Christum natum* is seen to be only the carrying out of it and is measured by it as its standard. For Bullinger, too—who had the same practical concern about infant baptism—the new covenant is the fulfilment of the covenant with Abraham, and as such it is also the ratification of the *fœdus Dei æternum* with the whole human race, which did not cease to be a covenant of grace, or to apply to all men, because of the intervention of the law of the covenant with Israel. If it can be said that these two Zurich reformers already had a Federal theology, this universalism is its most remarkable feature. As they see it, the covenant consists in the primitive institution and revelation of a promise and of the command of faith in that promise, and of the corresponding obedience. The people or Church of the covenant is not identical with the whole race. But from the very first the covenant is open to the whole race. It is not a private concern either of Israel or of pious Christians. If the covenant is understood as the presupposition of the atonement accomplished in Jesus Christ as it is revealed in that event, then necessarily the concept does have this universal orientation: not in the sense that all men are members as such and without further ado—if that were the case it would no longer be a covenant of the free grace of God—but in the sense that as the promise and command of God it does seriously apply to all men and is made for all men, that it is the destiny of all men to become and to be members of this covenant. In this way it is the living work and Word of God in contrast to a truth concerning the being of all men as such, a metaphysical concept necessarily implicated in the being of man—or in contrast to a truth concerning the being of some men but not of others. The scheme was not altogether satisfactory as a basis for infant baptism, but in its actual content it stood for something which cannot be surrendered, the character of the covenant as the true light which lighteth every man (Jn. 1⁹) and for which, therefore, every man is claimed.

Unfortunately in the later development of the Federal theology this universalism in the thought of the covenant was quickly obscured if not obliterated, as we can see from its classical form in Coccejus. The reason was that these "modern" theologians, and it is remarkable that it was the "moderns," tried to maintain the grim doctrine (which does logically follow from Calvin's conception of predestination) that Christ did not die for all men but only for the elect. It was deduced that the covenant, at any rate the covenant of grace (beside which they now believed they could discern another covenant) is from all eternity and in its temporal fulfilment a kind of separate arrangement between God and these particular men, the *electi*, which means in practice the true adherents of the true Israelitish-Christian religion. A theology of biblical history was now replaced by a theology of biblical histories. In the recognition of the covenant the atonement made in Jesus Christ was no longer accepted as the revelation of it. Scripture was not understood as the witness to this one event. It was not read as a witness at all, but as a historical record of a pragmatico-theological character. In these circumstances the outcome was inevitable. The most significant thing in these histories and the *telos* of all of them was that they offered examples in which certain men as distinct from others emerged as genuine hearers of the Word of God and partners in His work. They, and others like them, must obviously be regarded as the covenant-partners of God, and only they. In this way the conception of the covenant led into a blind alley in which it could not embrace and apply to all but only to some: those who could be regarded as the elect in virtue of their personal relationship with God as determined one way or another—as though this is not necessarily contradicted by the calling and attitude of all genuine hearers of the Word of God and partners in His work; as though in relation to the God active and revealed in Jesus Christ we cannot, and must not, see that all other men are under the sign of the covenant set up by Him, so that far from any particularism we have to look on them with hope. But if we do not look exclusively to Jesus Christ and therefore to God we lose the capacity on this basis to think inclusively. Historicism in theology always involves psychologism, and with those who try to be serious Christians in spite of their historicism it will be of a gloomy and pessimistic and unfriendly type; although at any moment, and this is what happened in the 18th century, it can transform itself without difficulty into its very opposite, a cheap universalism. Clearly we cannot follow the Federal theology when it takes this path, in opposition to its own earlier, from a historical standpoint, very remarkable form.

3. What is the meaning and character of the covenant according to this theology? We have seen that Zwingli and Bullinger regarded it quite unequivocally as a covenant of grace. So, too, does Calvin in those two chapters of the *Institutes*, II, 9–11, which the shadow of his doctrine of an eternal double predestination has hardly touched. As he sees it, the covenant made with the fathers was already the *foedus evangelii*, of which Christ was not only the fulfilment but the eternal basis. The distinctions between the fathers and us do not any of them relate to the substance of the covenant, which was and is the same, but only to the *modus administrationis*. It is only its *accidentia, annexa accessoria*, which have been abrogated and made obsolete by the appearance of Christ. We live with them, and they lived with us, by the same promises, under the same command, by the same grace. The only difference is that for us they are incomparably more sure and certain, and that whereas for them the covenant meant servitude for us it means freedom. Similarly—and here Calvin was writing against the Anabaptists and in favour of the national Church—the sacraments of the Old Testament have changed only in form, but in substance they are identical with those of the New. In Calvin there can be no question of the Law destroying the character of the covenant as a covenant of grace, nor can we find any combination of the covenant concept with a primitive *lex naturae*. This idea came in as a result of the influence which Melanchthon came to exercise on Reformed theology—in his old age he for his part was accused of a leaning to Calvinism. In this respect we first find it in W. Musculus and S. Szegedin. Here, in contrast to Zwingli, Bullinger and Calvin, the concept of the *foedus* is suddenly divided into that of a *foedus generale*, the temporal covenant of God with the universe, the earth and man as part of creation, and the eternal *foedus speciale*, which embraces all the elect from the beginning of the world as the true seed of Abraham, and which is split up into three periods, *ante legem, sub lege, post legem*. Notice the part allotted already to the Law as a principle of order. Notice, too, that here the *foedus speciale* is the eternal covenant while the *foedus generale* is only a temporal. The introduction of what later became the dominant twofold concept must be attributed to Ursinus (*S. Theol*, 1584, *qu*. 36, cf. 10 and 30 f.). There is a *foedus naturae* which was contracted with man at creation and is therefore known to man by nature. It promises eternal life to those who obey, but threatens eternal punishment to those who disobey. In contrast there is a *foedus gratiae* which is not known to man by nature. This is the fulfilling of the Law accomplished by Christ, our restoration by His Spirit, the free promise of the gift of eternal life to those who believe in Him. Nature and grace are both on the same historical level, and confront one another as the principles of individual covenants. We hear the voice of Calvin again and find traces of a different spirit in Olevian's work, *De substantia foederis gratuiti* (1585), in which, following Jer. 31, the covenant is

again described uniformly, unequivocally and exclusively as the covenant of grace. But although Coccejus thought of Olevian with particular gratitude as his predecessor, in this important respect the later development followed the lead of Ursinus. In Franz Gomarus (*Oratio de foedere Dei*, 1594), who was clearly inclined to a certain unity of outlook—he was a strict Supralapsarian—we find the peculiar doctrine of two covenants which are founded at the same time and run concurrently and everywhere merge into each other. The first is a *foedus naturale*, which demands perfect obedience, concluded with the first parents and in them with the whole of the human race after creation, and repeated by Moses the Lawgiver. The second is a *foedus supernaturale*, in which Christ is made over to those who believe in Him and repent, not by the power of nature, but by grace. But the rivalry of the two principles cannot be overcome. Polan (in whom the covenant played only an incidental role) seems to have rendered the doubtful service of replacing the concept *foedus naturale* by what was regarded as a better description *foedus operum*, and occasionally at any rate Wolleb followed his example.

We can ignore the variations of the Herborn school in their presentation of what had now become an established dualism (given confessional status for the first time in Art. 7 of the *Westminster Confession*). Instead we will turn at once to Coccejus himself. He begins with the covenant of works, which is for him the ruling principle. This covenant is based on the Law with its promise and threats. The Law was written on the heart of Adam and is still attested by conscience. It was pronounced as the Word of God in the prohibition concerning the tree of knowledge of good and evil in Paradise, and in content it agrees with the Mosaic decalogue. The tree of life is the symbol and sacrament of the eternal life promised to the perfectly obedient man and accruing to him as a reward. The divine likeness of Adam, which is taken to mean the wisdom of his understanding, the right disposition of his will and the innocence of his spirit and affections, meant that he was fully equipped (and with him the human race covenanted with God in his person) to keep the command and therefore to participate in the promise. But his will was not unalterable and it had not yet become established in obedience. According to Coccejus everything else follows as a series of abrogations (*abrogationes, antiquationes*) of this covenant of works.

The first abrogation is by sin. Consciously and voluntarily, and with God's permission, Adam does that which is forbidden. In so doing, he and all his descendants forfeit their friendship with God, their divine likeness and the status of promise, falling under the divine curse and judgment.

The second is related to the first and consists in the institution of the covenant of grace. Man as mercifully preserved by God is bound to Him by the law of nature and the mercy of God, but He is incapable of fulfilling his obligation. Therefore God creates an effective instrument to restore man, an instrument which answers at once both to His goodness and also to His righteousness. He adopts man into a new agreement by which He wills to give man a Mediator and therefore in this just person new fellowship and peace with Himself and the promised eternal life—not now as a reward which has been earned but as a free gift. The only response demanded of sinful man is that of faith. This third step, and therefore the second abrogation of the covenant of works —we will return to this later—is understood by Coccejus as the unfolding of a pre-temporal occurrence, an eternal and free contract (*pactum*) made between God the Father and God the Son, in which the Father represents the righteousness and the Son the mercy of God, the latter adopting the function of a Mediator and pledge in the place of men.

In the third abrogation of the covenant of works as Coccejus sees it, we return to the earth and history. It is the announcing of the covenant of grace in the economy of the Old Testament prefigured in the proto-Gospel of Gen. 3[15f]. This is a form of the relationship between God and man which has the covenant of grace as its hidden basis, but a basis which is occasionally revealed. In this form as we are told in Rom. 3, there is a πάρεσις, an overlooking and ignoring of human sin, but not its ἄφεσις, its real forgiveness, and therefore the justification of sinners. It is all still a matter of type and instruction. The righteous are still intermingled with the wicked. Bondage still rules, and with it the fear of death. But all the same the Law, with its demand for righteousness and its types and shadows, is a witness to the promise. Circumcision and the passover already point to the atoning death of Christ. Everything is still a matter of expectation. It is only the Old Testament. But it is a sure expectation of the covenant of grace and therefore of the New Testament. And to that extent it is an abrogation of the first, of the covenant of works. This is revealed in the benefits of the New Testament: in the demonstration of our perfect righteousness in the obedience of the Son of God fulfilling the whole Law; in the revelation of the name of God; in the writing of the Law on our human hearts by the Spirit; in the freeing of consciences by that ἄφεσις τῶν ἁμαρτιῶν which now replaces the mere πάρεσις; in the liberation from the fear of death and the planting of the Church among the Gentiles.

The fourth abrogation of the covenant of works Coccejus calls the death of the body, i.e., the sanctification which in the work of Christ goes hand in hand with justification, sanctification as purification, as the destruction of the works of the devil and the darkness of the intellect and the badness of the human will. The Law is now a weapon in the warfare of the spirit against the flesh. The tribulations which still remain, including death, are instruments for the testing of faith and the taming of sin, opportunities for the exercise of love. That this conflict takes place distinguishes the regenerate from the unregenerate. The regenerate will not commit wilful sin, and from those that remain he will always seek refuge in the grace of God, earnest self-examination, and prayer for a pure heart.

The fifth and final abrogation of the covenant of works is what Coccejus calls the reawakening of the body. He is thinking here of the eschatological redemption and consummation. With this the validity of the covenant of works ceases altogether—that is, for the righteous. Nothing remains but the operation of the mediatorship of the guarantor of the covenant of grace and its obedience, and this operation is eternal life and salvation by the resurrection from the dead in virtue of His merit, in which the souls of the pious participate directly at death.

We relate our question concerning the essence and character of the covenant to this sketch of Coccejus because for all his individuality in relation to his predecessors and successors Coccejus represents the Federal theology in a form which is not only the most perfect, but also the ripest and strongest and most impressive.

There was one point in which the successors of Coccejus at once departed from his scheme, and it has been the subject of most of the objections against him right up to the presentations given in the dogmatic history of our own day. This is his at first sight exclusively negative estimate and presentation of the whole history of the covenant in relation to its beginning, as a gradual abrogation of the covenant of works. And in this respect two discordant features have to be noted. First, the second and obviously decisive abrogation as distinct from all the others is not a temporal event, but—like a scene in heaven in the religious plays of the Middle Ages—an eternal happening between the Father and the Son. And second, the New Testament economy has no autonomous place among these temporal events, but is mentioned only in contrast with that of the Old. In my estimation the main strength of the thinking of Coccejus is at the very point where formally the main objection is made against him, and at the point where these two discordant features are to be found within the order selected by him. Certainly, he took over from his predecessors that idea of a covenant of nature or works which was alien to the Reformers. But—and it was because of this that he felt so strong an affinity with Olevian—he had such a strong sense of the uniqueness of the divine covenant as a covenant of grace that, although he could begin his narration with the covenant of works, he could understand everything that followed only in antithesis to it, as its increasing abrogation. The doctrine of the covenant of grace was developed in relation, but only in this negative relation, to a covenant of works. The fact that he did try to bring the two together, but could do so only in the antithetical form of the abrogation of the one by the other, was obviously even to himself a disquieting reminder that his attitude to the second—if it really was the second—would have to be quite different from his attitude to the first. That is how we have to judge the scene in heaven which so singularly interrupts the series of temporal events to form the second stage. Coccejus could find no similar eternal pact between God the Father and God the Son to correspond to the covenant of nature or works. In presenting the institution of the covenant of grace in this way, did he not contradict his own historicism and say that in this covenant we have to do with a *Prius* and not a *Posterius* in relation to that which he and his predecessors had sought to characterise and describe as a special and supposedly first *foedus naturale* or *legale* or *operum*? In spite of the inconsistency in his own scheme, was he not faithful here to what he saw very well to be the real logic of the matter? And is not the same true of his other architectonic failure—that he did not try to understand and explain the particular subject of the New Testament witness, the historical incarnation of the Son of God, and the atonement made in Him, as a particular stage in this series of events, but "only" as the fulfilling or replacing of the Old Testament economy? How is it that he could and necessarily did look at it in that way? For one thing, because obviously—and this must be said in his favour—he did not want to give to the historical difference between the two economies, which he perceived and emphasised very strongly (much more strongly than Calvin), the character of a theological antithesis, but aimed rather to present the Old Testament as the witness to the promise of Jesus Christ and the New as the witness to its fulfilment. And then most of all because everything that can be said of the New Testament economy as such is already included and stated in and with what has been said in relation to that abrogation of the covenant of works which has already taken place in the bosom of the Godhead. For him the new thing in the New Testament is the oldest thing of all, that which goes back to the very beginning. And this original thing he found revealed and active as the first thing (not as a second economy following that of the Old Testament) in the New Testament economy which dissolved that of the Old Testament.

The questions which we can answer only with difficulty if at all in respect of Coccejus do not begin until we have done him justice in these matters. The meaning and character of the covenant as a covenant of grace impressed itself upon him forcefully in this way. And in his outline (even in the very things which might formally be objected against him) he has emphasised this in a remarkable manner. How was it, then, that he came to put first the covenant of nature or works or Law, negatively at least taking his direction from it, as though the covenant of grace were a covenant of grace only in antithesis to it,  and ultimately therefore only in its fulfilment and confirmation? The same question may be asked of his predecessors from Ursinus onwards. Granted that we can seriously speak of a *lex naturae*, how does it come to be connected with the divine likeness of man, his status before the Fall, the Word of God to Adam, the tree of life in Paradise, and the decalogue? And in this connexion, within the series of main theological concepts, how does it attain to the dignity of a first and special divine covenant, which then becomes the schema within which (antithetically in Coccejus) the covenant of grace is set up and its history gradually fulfilled? The more so as men who knew the Scripture as Coccejus and his fellows undoubtedly did could never speak of any institution of this second covenant in God Himself (as Coccejus did in relation to the covenant of grace)! But it is still this covenant which becomes the first and is as such the framework and standard of reference for the covenant of grace. There is only one historical explanation for this innovation, the introduction of this first stage in the history for which the Federal theology thought that it had biblical reference. This is that biblical exegesis had been invaded by a mode of thought in which this history, however extraordinary the course it took, could only unfold itself and therefore only begin as the history of man and his works, man who is good by nature and who is therefore in covenant with God—a God who is pledged to him by virtue of his goodness. To this mode of thinking it became more and more foreign to think of the history as conversely the history of God and His works, the God who originally turns to man in grace, and therefore as

from the very first the history of the covenant of grace. We have seen that Coccejus did try (with Calvin and Olevian and all the older tradition) to think this second thought which was becoming so foreign to his generation. But in face of the increasing pressure to a mode of thought which started exclusively with man (for his contemporaries had come to terms with the Cartesians), he no longer had sufficient freedom to make the leap which he really ought to have made in accordance with the biblical control of his thinking. Formally, at any rate, the thought which was becoming so foreign to the new thinking of his generation, but to which he wanted to do justice, and in his own way did do justice, could have only a secondary authority even in his writings. The first place is taken by the strange spectacle of man in Paradise to whom eternal life is promised as a reward which he has earned, whose works can perfectly fulfil the command of God (even if his obedience is not yet secure), to whom God is just as much bound by this fulfilment as he is to God, between whom and God the relationship is clearly that of a *do ut des*. And this relationship is supposed to be the original form of the covenant. In this original form it breaks down in that series of abrogations. And it does not break down first by reason of the divine covenant of grace, but by reason of human sin. Characteristically, and necessarily in view of that pressure, the second most pressing problem is not that of God's grace but that of man's sin. Through all the abrogations of the covenant of nature and works, what sin is—even as it will finally disappear—is measured by the Law of this first covenant. And it will be the decisive gift of the covenant of grace, and the function of the Mediator as the second Adam, to fulfil in our place the Law of the covenant of nature and works which was transgressed by Adam and all of us, and in that way to become our guarantor with God. And far from the first covenant being really superseded by the intervention of the Mediator, the gifted righteousness of Law (which is promised and certain to faith in Him) is necessarily followed by that further abrogation of the Law, distinguished under the concept of sanctification, which Coccejus calls the "death of the body," the battle of spirit against the flesh in the regenerate, in which the decisive weapon is once again the Law, while grace is the place to which the regenerate must always flee in view of the imperfection of his fulfilment of the Law. The first covenant and its Law loses its relevance only in that *eschaton* which is the fifth and final stage of the whole development. In spite of all assurances to the contrary, this side of the *eschaton*, in time, there is no effective abrogation of the covenant of nature and works, either in the Old Testament economy or consequently in the New. For the New Testament freedom is only freedom from the Law of the Old Testament—impressively maintained by Coccejus, e.g., in relation to the Sabbath—but the validity of the Law of that first covenant is the guiding thread which runs through the whole development, indeed it controls that development. Grace itself, whether as justification or sanctification, is always the fulfilling of that Law (perfect in Christ, imperfect in us). There is no escape from the relationship of *do ut des*, no liberation from the insecurity of the whole connexion between man and God, the fear of punishment and the expectation of reward, no radical cessation of the unfortunate preoccupation of man with himself and his works and of the even more unfortunate control of God to which this inevitably gives rise. This is impossible even in the covenant of grace connected with the covenant of works and orientated by it. This covenant of grace could not be clearly and convincingly portrayed as such. Where it was portrayed as such in the proclamation of the older Reformed Church, this was not because but in spite of its starting-point, in virtue of those elements which were foreign and ran contrary to it, and made it innocuous. Unfortunately they did not always make it innocuous.

4. We have seen that Coccejus solemnly distinguished the covenant of grace, his second abrogation of the covenant of works, by describing it as a pretemporal and intertrinitarian happening, a pact between God the Father and God the Son. It is grounded, not in the proclamation of the proto-Gospel, or in the Noachic or Abrahamic covenants, not between God and man at all, but in eternity before all worlds, in the bosom of the Godhead itself. We can ignore the rather difficult juristic details of the conception in Coccejus and his predecessors and successors. What is essential is that: God forgives sinful man and gives him a new righteousness on the one condition of faith and repentance. Ultimately this rests on the free disposing of God the Father, by virtue of which He has once and for all ascribed to a chosen portion of sinful humanity righteousness and eternal life in His Son. There is a corresponding disposing of the Son of God in virtue of which He for His part has undertaken once and for all the cause of those sinful men who are elected to sonship. The two together result in the covenant: the *pactum mutuum inter Patrem et Filium, quo Pater Filium dat ut λυτρώτην et caput populi praecogniti et Filius vicissim se sistit ad ἀπολύτρωσιν hanc peragendam* (F. Burmann, *Syn. Theol.*, 1671, II, 15, 2). The whole christologico-soteriological happening of the atonement is simply the historical execution of the engagements freely accepted by, but strictly binding on, the two divine partners, i.e., God with God. The older Reformed theology

*decree replaced by covenant*

had spoken more simply of an eternal divine "decree," as an *opus Dei internum ad extra*, and its temporal fulfilment. And in content this decree could only be the eternal divine election of grace. Coccejus and those who shared his view could also understand that which they described as the *testamentum aeternum* or the *sponsio aeterna* between the Father and the Son as an aspect of the decree of predestination (in so far as this has positive reference to election to salvation in Christ). We will have to return to this in a fifth and final point. The question we must now ask as it arises from the third point is as follows. When this supreme basis was ascribed to the covenant of grace, how was it thought possible that another covenant, the *foedus naturae* or *operum*, could be placed alongside it and even given precedence over it?—a covenant which had already been superseded and rendered superfluous by this eternal basis of the covenant of grace? which could at once be broken by the sin of man? which could then be destroyed and abrogated and made obsolete by the historical promise and fulfilment of the covenant of grace? which would completely disappear in the *eschaton*? but which, as we have seen, still constitutes the guiding thread which actually runs through the whole occurrence of salvation and by which it is measured right up to the very end? Although this covenant and its Law are plainly opposed to the covenant of grace! Although it is not possible to try to *God changed his mind!* explain it by a divine decree, an eternal and intertrinitarian decision and agreement! If the covenant of grace alone was seen to be grounded in God, did not this mean that any dualism in the concept of the covenant was at once negated? Even where it was thought necessary to speak of a first covenant of nature or works, was it really possible to see anything but the one covenant of grace, which had been instituted in eternity, which had come into force, therefore, in and with the beginning of human history, which at once embraced man and claimed him, which man had, of course, broken, but which God in faithfulness to Himself and His partner had not abrogated but maintained and ratified? Why was it thought necessary to see man in any other light than that of the pledge which God Himself had made for him in His Son even before he ever existed? Why was it thought necessary to see him in any other way than the one who in the eternal will of God was predestinated to be the brother of this Son and therefore to divine sonship? Why is there ascribed to him a status in which he did not need the Mediator and which, if it had lasted, would have made superfluous the appearance of the Mediator and therefore the fulfilment of the eternal (!) covenant of grace? Why was sin robbed of its true and frightful seriousness as a transgression of the law given to man as the predestinated brother of the Son and child of the Father, as a falling away from the special grace which the Creator had shown him from all eternity? Why instead was the grace of God made a second or a third thing, a wretched expedient of God in face of the obvious failure of a plan in relation to man which had orginally had quite a different intention and form? Why, again, was it not possible completely to banish all thought of this other plan in relation to the historical

*backup plan!*

promise and fulfilment, the Old and New Testament economy? Why had the history of the covenant of grace to be presented as though it had to do only with the execution of that original plan?—of that plan concerning whose divine meaning and basis there was nothing that could be said because nothing was or could be known of it from the Gospel they were trying to expound? Why on this side of the *eschaton* is everything always measured by a form of the relationship between God and man which had been maintained as the beginning of all things only with a *sic volo sic iubeo*? How was that even possible? How was it possible to know of the eternal basis of the covenant of grace and then not to think exclusively in the light of it, to understand and present it as the one covenant of God, as though there were some other eternity in God or elsewhere, an eternity of human nature and its connexion with God and its law and the works of this law?

5. The riddle posed by the older Federal theology at this its strongest point appears to be insoluble. But perhaps we shall find the solution if we examine rather more closely how it understood that eternal basis of the covenant of grace. As we have seen, it was taken to consist in an intertrinitarian decision, in a freely accepted but legally binding mutual obligation between God the Father and God the Son. Now there are three doubtful features in this conception.

For God to be gracious to sinful man, was there any need of a special decree to establish the unity of the righteousness and mercy of God in relation to man, of a special intertrinitarian arrangement and contract which can be distinguished from the being of God? If there was need of such a decree, then the question arises at once of a form of the will of God in which this arrangement has not yet been made and is not yet valid. We have to reckon with the existence of a God who is righteous *in abstracto* and not free to be gracious from the very first, who has to bind to the fulfilment of His promise the fulfilment of certain conditions by man, and punish their non-fulfilment. It is only with the conclusion of this contract with Himself that He ceases to be a righteous God *in abstracto* and becomes the God who in His righteousness is also merciful and therefore able to exercise grace. In this case it is not impossible or illegitimate to believe that properly, in some inner depth of His being behind the covenant of grace, He might not be able to do this. It is only on the historical level that the theologumenon of the *foedus naturae* or *operum* can be explained by the compact of the Federal theology with contemporary humanism. In fact it derives from anxiety lest there might be an essence in God in which, in spite of that contract, His righteousness and His mercy are secretly and at bottom two separate things. And this anxiety derives from the fact that the thought of that intertrinitarian contract obviously cannot have any binding and therefore consoling and assuring force. This anxiety and therefore this proposition of a covenant of works could obviously never have arisen if there had been a loyal hearing of the Gospel and a strict looking to Jesus Christ as the full and final revelation of the being of God. In the eternal decree of God revealed in Jesus

Christ the being of God would have been seen as righteous mercy and merciful righteousness from the very first. It would have been quite impossible therefore to conceive of any special plan of a God who is righteous *in abstracto*, and the whole idea of an original covenant of works would have fallen to the ground.

The conception of this intertrinitarian pact as a contract between the persons of the Father and the Son is also open to criticism. Can we really think of the first and second persons of the triune Godhead as two divine subjects and therefore as two legal subjects who can have dealings and enter into obligations one with another? This is mythology, for which there is no place in a right understanding of the doctrine of the Trinity as the doctrine of the three modes of being of the one God, which is how it was understood and presented in Reformed orthodoxy itself. God is one God. If He is thought of as the supreme and finally the only subject, He is the one subject. And if, in relation to that which He obviously does amongst us, we speak of His eternal resolves or decrees, even if we describe them as a contract, then we do not regard the divine persons of the Father and the Son as partners in this contract, but the one God—Father, Son and Holy Spirit—as the one partner, and the reality of man as distinct from God as the other. When the covenant of grace was based on a pact between two divine persons, a wider dualism was introduced into the Godhead—again in defiance of the Gospel as the revelation of the Father by the Son and of the Son by the Father, which took place in Jesus Christ. The result was an uncertainty which necessarily relativised the unconditional validity of the covenant of grace, making it doubtful whether in the revelation of this covenant we really had to do with the one will of the one God. If in God there are not merely different and fundamentally contradictory qualities, but also different subjects, who are indeed united in this matter, but had first of all to come to an agreement, how can the will of God seen in the history of the covenant of grace be known to be binding and unequivocal, the first and final Word of God? The way is then opened up on this side too for considering the possibility of some other form of His will. The question is necessarily and seriously raised of a will of God the Father which originally and basically is different from the will of God the Son. And this naturally carried with it the hypothesis of a covenant of quite a different structure and purpose preceding and underlying the covenant of grace, the hypothesis of a law in the relationship of God to man which is not the Law of His grace and which in default of a special revelation of the Father can be pictured at once according to the analogy of human ordinances. And how is the will of the eternal Son or Word of God in Himself and as such, in His pure Godhead, to become so clear and certain that we can and must cling to it alone as the revealed eternal and therefore unequivocal and binding will of God as the basis of the covenant of grace? Even the thought of the eternal divine Logos is not in itself and as such necessarily a defence against the thought of a law which is different from the Law of grace.

And this leads us to the third and decisive point. The thought of a purely intertrinitarian decision as the eternal basis of the covenant of grace may be found both sublime and uplifting. But it is definitely much too uplifting and sublime to be a Christian thought. What we have to do with it is not a relationship of God with Himself but the basis of a relationship between God and man. How can even the most perfect decision in the bosom of the Godhead, if the Godhead remains alone, be the origin of the covenant, if it is made in the absence of the one who must be present as the second partner at the institution of the covenant to make it a real covenant, that is, man? To unite God in His attitude to man—whether in respect of His properties, or as Father, Son and Holy Spirit—there is no need of any particular pact or decree. God would not be God if He were not God in this unity. And a covenant with man is not grounded merely in this unity of God in and with Himself. It is not self-evident but a new thing that in His unity with Himself from all eternity God wills to be the God of man and to make and have man as His man. This is the content of a  particular act of will which has its basis neither in the essence of God nor in that of man, and which God does not owe either to Himself or to any other being, and least of all to man. This is what we can call a decree, an *opus Dei internum ad extra*, and therefore a pact: God's free election of grace, in which even in His eternity before all time and the foundation of the world, He is no longer alone by Himself, He does not rest content with Himself, He will not restrict Himself to the wealth of His perfections and His own inner life as Father, Son and Holy Spirit. In this free act of the election of grace there is already present, and presumed, and assumed into unity with His own existence as God, the existence of the man whom He intends and loves from the very first and in whom He intends and loves all other men, of the man in whom He wills to bind Himself with all other men and all other man with Himself. In this free act of the election of grace the Son of the Father is no longer just the eternal Logos, but as such, as very God from all eternity He is also the very God and very man He will become in time. In the divine act of predestination there pre-exists the Jesus Christ who as the Son of the eternal Father and the child of the Virgin Mary will become and be the Mediator of the covenant between God and man, the One who accomplishes the act of atonement. He in whom the covenant of grace is fulfilled and revealed in history is also its eternal basis. He who in Scripture is attested to be very God and very man is also the eternal *testamentum*, the eternal *sponsio*, the eternal *pactum*, between God and man. This is the point which Coccejus and the Federal theology before and after Coccejus missed. Their doctrine of a purely intertrinitarian pact did not enable them to give an unequivocal or binding answer to the question of the form of the eternal divine decree as the beginning of all things. The result was that for all their loyalty to Scripture they inherited the notion that the covenant of grace fulfilled and revealed in history in Jesus Christ was perhaps only a secondary and subsequent divine arrangment (the foundation and history of a religion?) and not the beginning of all the ways of God. Their view of the covenant became dualistic. The idea of a basic and always determinative and concurrent covenant of nature or works was superimposed on their conception of the covenant of grace. Yet this could have been avoided—even though as children of their time they were exposed to the temptation of humanism—if they could have determined to know the eternal and therefore the only basis of the divine work in the work itself, in its temporal occurrence, to know the eternal divine Logos in His incarnation. And on this basis they might well have overcome the other weaknesses in their doctrine: the abandonment of an original universalism in the conception of the covenant; and finally the radical historicism of their understanding of Scripture.

## 3. The Fulfilment of the Broken Covenant

From the concept of the covenant as the presupposition of the reconciliation which took place in Jesus Christ we will now turn to the reconciliation itself and therefore to the fulfilment of the covenant. It consists in the fact that God realises His eternal will with man, that He makes the covenant true and actual within human history. It consists in the historical proclamation attested in the Old Testament, and the historical existence attested in the New, of the Mediator, that is, of the eternal Word of God and therefore of God Himself in His historical identity with the man Jesus of Nazareth: in the coming of His kingdom on earth, that is, in the coming and being and living and speaking and acting of this man, in the establishing and maintaining and revealing in Him of the sole supremacy of His grace in the world of men, and of the subordination of that world to this supremacy. It consists in the fact that He causes the promise and command of the covenant: "I will be your God and ye shall be my people," to become historical event in the person of Jesus Christ. It consists, therefore, in the fact that God keeps faith in time with Himself and with man, with all men in this one man.

But this fulfilment of the covenant has the character of atonement. The concept speaks of the confirmation or restoration of a fellowship which did exist but had been threatened with disruption and dissolution. Atonement does have its eternal and unshakable basis in the covenant between God and man which God willed and set up before the foundation of the world. But the covenant is successfully fulfilled by the overcoming of an obstruction which if the basis had not been unshakable would inevitably have made that fulfilment doubtful or impossible. In face of that obstruction the fulfilment can be regarded only as a divine protest effectively and redemptively made with the power of that eternal basis. And in relation to man it can be regarded only as an inconceivable overflowing of the grace of God to him.

This history of man from the very first—and the same is true of the history of every individual man—consisted, not in the keeping but the breaking of the covenant, not in the receiving but the rejecting of the promise, not in the fulfilling but the transgressing of the command, not in the gratitude which corresponds to the grace of God but in a senseless and purposeless rebellion against it, a rebellion which at bottom is quite negative, but terribly real even in this negativity. It was revealed from the very first, and it is revealed daily in small things as well as big, in the disposition as well as the acts of man, that the eternal grace of God is not merely undeserved by man, but was and is given to him as one who does not deserve it. He does not recognise it. He does not want it. At bottom he hates it. He does not see that this and this alone is life in freedom. He chafes for another freedom which can only be bondage. He does not accept the fact that he can be a member of the people of God. Therefore he does not accept the fact that God is the Lord of His people. He finds and chooses other lords and gods, and lives as though he belonged to their people. And so the grace of God to him seems to be in the void. The man to whom it comes fails to receive it. As far as he is concerned he is without grace, and therefore he fails even as a creature. Therefore it seems that although God elected man to a covenant with Himself, and created heaven and earth and man himself for the sake of this covenant, He will finally be left by Himself: God above, but not God—which is surely impossible—in these dark depths; God in heaven, but not God on an earth which is the scene of this nonsensical history; God in His own inner glory, but without that attestation of the creature for which He designed and made it and which is not merely the capacity but the destiny of its nature as He made it; God with His covenant will, but without the execution of that will, the execution of it hindered by the one whom He honoured and singled out and exalted in this will from all eternity.

This is the enormous incident of sin which openly opposes the fulfilment of the covenant and in face of which that fulfilment, if it is to come about at all, can have only the character of an atonement. And this atonement can come only from God. In face of human ingratitude, it can consist only in an overflowing of His grace and therefore in the overcoming and removing of that obstruction. There is nothing that man can contribute to it as the one who has denied his relationship with God and failed as God's partner. He cannot accomplish or expect or explain and comprehend it for himself. If it takes place, he can only accept it as a fact, whose validity and effectiveness, as the enemy of God that he is and must recognise and acknowledge himself to be, he can believe only because God does in fact show Himself and make Himself known as the one who is the master of man and his sin.

God's faithfulness cannot be mistaken, nor can it be mocked. What is the unfaithfulness of man in relation to it, and what can it accomplish? The grace of God triumphs over man and his sin—that is the fulfilment of the covenant which takes place in Jesus Christ. But it assumes and has the character of a "Yet" and a "Notwithstanding." It triumphs now—in face of human opposition—miraculously, unilaterally and autocratically—to its own self-glory.

Can we say: all the more gloriously? Is it only now that it acts and reveals itself as free grace? Is it only now that there is disclosed and operative the sovereign divine resolve which is its basis? We can and must say: "Where sin abounded, grace did much more abound" (Rom. 5²⁰). It is true that the nature and power of the grace of God is finally and unmistakably revealed only where it shows itself and acts as His free grace to the undeserving, as grace for lost sinners.

But, all the same, when the Early Church dared to sing: *O felix culpa quae tantum et talem meruit habere salvatorem*, it went too far with the *meruit habere*. For there can be no more question of man "deserving" and achieving and winning that overflowing of the grace of God by his sin than there can in any other way. It can only be recognised and acknowledged and reverenced as a fact that this depth of the love of God is revealed and active in relation to human sin in a way which is so inconceivably profound, in all the power and mystery of eternity. How can we ever ascribe this fact to ourselves? The recognition of this fact carries within it the deepest and most comforting but also the most terrifying abasement of man: that as the transgressor he is he can live only by that which he does not do himself, which it is impossible even to ask of him, which, in fact, he denies and resists; by the atonement which God has made—and all because the grace of God makes against him and the opposition he has stirred up that triumphant, effective and redemptive protest. Even the association of the words *felix* and *culpa* cannot really stand. This divine protest is effective and redemptive, but it is in bitter earnest. The grace of God does not abandon us, but only because it makes good what we have spoiled, and therefore only in that humiliation of us which brings us help and comfort, but which is inescapable in this wealth of help and comfort. Therefore—unless we do not recognise and accept this humiliation as such—we cannot possibly speak of a "happy fault." To be at fault before God is unhappiness even where the grace of God overflows in answer to and in favour of the guilty, even where the faithfulness of God is first active and revealed as such in face of man's unfaithfulness. If we cannot boast of any happy sufficiency of our being and work, we certainly cannot do so of our "happy fault," which is far more than an insufficiency, which stands indeed in opposition to and conflict with the gracious will of God.

No praise can be too high for the mighty and triumphant grace of God in the atonement as the fulfilment of the covenant. But this praise must not be spoiled by any undertone which directly or indirectly minimises or even approves the incident in virtue of which the fulfilment of the covenant necessarily has the character of an atonement. It must not be made misleading or harmful to those who hear it, or unacceptable to God. The wisdom of God which allows this episode in order to make, not the episode itself, but the overcoming of it an occasion to magnify His grace and to reveal and actualise it—we have to say for the first time—as free grace in it, in accordance with His eternal will and purpose: that wisdom is one thing. But quite a different thing is the human pseudo-wisdom which tries to pretend that this episode is in some sense necessary, and in that way to excuse or exculpate the man who is responsible for it, or even to hide from him the full danger and fatality of his action. The sin which abounds is indeed sin. As the opposition of man to the God who is in covenant with Him it is inexcusable. As the self-opposition of the man who is in covenant with God it is fatal. And the fact that grace much more abounds does not alter or limit or weaken this fact. It is a fact which must be included in our praise of the grace of God. Our praise cannot be genuine except as the praise of faith. But faith flees and clings and reclines and trusts on the God who in His free grace leads us to judgment. Faith finds its comfort and praise in His grace. But it knows that this grace is "dear" and not "cheap" (Dietrich Bonhoeffer). Therefore it does not lessen our accusation and sentence. If we live, we do not live because the confession of our sin and guilt laid on our hearts and lips by the grace of God has been weakened or embellished, but because the forgiveness of our sin has been accomplished by God in the event of the atonement. Therefore the praise of faith cannot be a denial of the truth but rather a confirmation of it: first and primarily in respect of the inconceivable glory of that which is said and given to man; but then and consequently in respect of the unutterable unworthiness of man as the recipient. Where this is not clear, with all that it entails, there is no faith. What are thought to be believing thought and speech do not revolve around the more abundant free grace of God present in the atonement made in Jesus Christ. They are in fact speculation about a myth current under the name of Jesus Christ. There is no knowledge and proclamation of what has actually been done by God under this name. We must pay attention to the warning which there is here. There is no doctrine more dangerous than the Christian doctrine of the atonement, it does indeed make "wild and careless folk" (*Heid. Cat., qu.* 64), if we do not consider it with this warning in view. The fact that it speaks of God making good what we have spoiled does not mean that we can call evil good (unless we would also call good evil). All our thinking and all that we say on this matter must be disciplined by an observance of this limit, and a refusal to transgress it in any circumstances, sense or direction.

We will now give a very general outline of what is meant by reconciliation as the fulfilment of the covenant. For this purpose we will take and expound two of the New Testament sayings which in a classic way encompass the whole of this field.

Precedence must be given to Jn. 3[16]: "For God so loved the world, that he gave his only begotten Son, that whosoever believeth on him should not perish, but have everlasting life."

ἠγάπησεν tells a definite story, gives news of a unique event: the event of God's loving. This event did not take place in heaven but on earth. It did not take place in secret, but it can be known (i.e., not as a purely spiritual process, but as something which, according to I Jn. I[1], can be heard and seen with our eyes and touched, yes, handled with our hands). This being the case, it became, it made itself the content of the message proclaimed by the Christian community. Now the object of the divine loving was the κόσμος, which means (for what follows, cf. R. Bultmann, *Das Evangelium Johannes*, 1950) the human world as a single subject in hostile antithesis to God. Not from the very first. Not because it is bad in itself. For the world was made by God (Jn. 1[10]). Not because it is posited against God in itself. Not because it is authorised or empowered to stand in this position of hostility to God. It is His possession (Jn. I[11]). Not because God has left it to itself. Not because He has given it cause for this hostility. The true light, the light of the covenant promising life, was and is present: and bright enough for every man (Jn. 1[9]). But the world knew it not

(Jn. 1¹⁰). In contrast to it the world is σκοτία, darkness (Jn. 1⁵). It does not understand God—either in itself as His creature or as illuminated by that light. But with all these characteristics it is the object of the divine loving. For with all these characteristics it is the cosmos. Created by God and illuminated by Him from the beginning, not recognising Him and therefore dark, it is still the object of His loving. This event takes place absolutely. It has this in common with the creation of the world, and the illumination which comes to it from God by creation (the covenant with God from which man always derives as from his creation), that God does not owe it to the world to love it. The world is not, as Philo and others imagined, the son of God. It is not begotten by Him. It does not share His nature, so that He is bound to it by nature, essentially. It is the free will and the free act of God that He willed to be the basis of its existence and its light. The meaning of this event is from the very first a free loving. And in its relation to that loving and in every other respect the cosmos is darkness. It has disqualified itself. Even as the world created and illuminated by Him it has ceased to be worthy of His love. But God did not in fact cease to love it. Only now did He begin genuinely and supremely to love it. Only now did this event take place and irresistibly as the event of His own pure free love, a love grounded in Himself and not in the object, a love turned toward the object only for His own sake. There can be no question of any claim of the cosmos to be loved, or consequently of any mitigation of its character as darkness, which is only revealed in all its impossibility in this event, and for which it will now be plainly accused and judged and sentenced. But this does not take place because God rejects it, but because He loves it. And His love is not merely a disposition but an act, an active measure in relation to it. Jn. 3¹⁶ describes the fulfilment and scope of this measure.

The οὕτως in relation with the later ὥστε means more than "in such a way," *hoc modo*. It does not refer only to the divine *procedere* as such, although I have often expounded it in this narrower sense in the *C.D.* It implies this *hoc modo*, but it has the force of "so much." It indicates (as Luther intended when he translated it *also*) the extraordinary nature of this loving. It is not self-evident that there should be a divine loving of the cosmos in any case. It is even less so that the divine act of love should take this form. God loves the cosmos so much, with such inconceivable strength and depth, "that (ὥστε) He gave his only begotten son." God has a Son. This Son is not the cosmos but the One whom He gave in loving the cosmos. Can we interpret the "Son" here as the "Revealer"? He is that (although not only that) when God gives Him. The fact that He is—that He declares the grace and truth of God which no man has seen (Jn. 1¹⁸)—presupposes that He was πρὸς τὸν θεόν and that He Himself was θεός (Jn. 1¹), that He was "in the bosom of the Father" (Jn. 1¹⁸), the beloved Other in relation to whom God is called and is love in Himself, in His inward life (1 Jn. 4⁸), the One who knows God as Himself and Himself as God, who does the will of God as His own will and His own will as the will of God, the One without whom—and we cannot say this of the cosmos—God would not only not be revealed but would not be God, whose existence $\pi\rho\grave{o}\varsigma\ \tau\grave{o}\nu\ \theta\varepsilon\acute{o}\nu$ and as $\theta\varepsilon\acute{o}\varsigma$ is a constituent part of the existence of God. Therefore, $\upsilon\acute{\iota}o\varsigma\ \mu o\nu o\gamma\varepsilon\nu\acute{\eta}\varsigma$, the only one of His kind? or the only-begotten, and therefore the One beside whom God has no other son, no one who is His equal, or who corresponds to Him, no other who is in Himself the object of His love, a constituent part of His divine being? In both senses: as this eternally Other in God Himself the only One who as such is able to fulfil all that God wills and does.

But it is not self-evident that in loving the world God should "give" this one. $\check{\varepsilon}\delta\omega\kappa\varepsilon\nu$ in the first instance means "gifted" Him. He did not merely gift a highest and best, a power of life and light which would help the cosmos, perhaps an endowment of the creation, perhaps a strengthening of the light of His covenant. No: He gifted to the cosmos His only Son and therefore nothing more or less than Himself. And in this context $\check{\varepsilon}\delta\omega\kappa\varepsilon\nu$ has the same force as $\pi\alpha\rho\acute{\varepsilon}\delta\omega\kappa\varepsilon\nu$: He surrendered Him, He gave Him up, He offered Him. He sends Him into the cosmos which is actually darkness as the light (Jn. 1[5]) which is to shine in the darkness but which will not be apprehended or grasped, which cannot be apprehended or grasped by the darkness. In giving Him—and giving Himself— He exposes Him—and Himself—to the greatest danger. He sets at stake His own existence as God. "He came unto His own, and His own (that is, those who are His possession) received him not" (Jn. 1[11]). He did it. But what result is possible when in relation to Him the world is irremediable darkness? What will it mean for God? Well, in this act God loved the world so much, so profoundly, that it did in fact consist in the venture of His own self-offering, in this hazarding of His own existence as God. It is His self-revelation and self-realisation (in and for the world) as a gift, and *rebus sic stantibus* that can mean only as the offering of that without which He cannot be God, and therefore of the greatest possible danger for Himself. "God so loved the world." The Christian message is the message of this act of God, of the atonement which was made in this way, of God's pledging of Himself for His creature, for His partner in the covenant, for the man who has opposed Him as an enemy. It consists in the fact that God has given Himself up into the hands of this enemy. It is in this radical sense that according to the Christian message God has loved first ($\pi\rho\tilde{\omega}\tau o\varsigma$, 1 Jn. 4[19]), not merely before we loved Him, but while we were yet sinners, while we were yet enemies (Rom. 5[8, 10]).

And now the clause introduced by ἵνα (an ἵνα which is both *finale* and *consecutivum*) speaks of the effect, the result of this offering of the Son and self-offering of God, and therefore of the purpose and the actual scope of this so perfect act of love. Those who believe in Him will not perish but have everlasting life. To understand this we do well to remember the opening and controlling part of the sentence: "For God so loved the world." What happens to those who believe on the Son is the effect of the love with which in that event God has loved not only them but the world. In the person of believers, therefore, it happens indirectly, with a view, and as a witness, to the world. We also do well to follow the hint in the commentary of E. Hoskyns (*The Fourth Gospel*, 1947, p. 218), and especially to notice what it is that is here described as happening to believers: "the divine purpose in the sending of Jesus Christ is redemption and not judgment, eternal life and not destruction and perdition." It is a matter primarily of salvation from perishing. This is the reverse side of the darkness in which the world opposes God, ranging itself against God, contradicting and withstanding Him. It has fallen a victim to destruction and perdition. In so  doing it has forfeited its right to exist as the creature of God. It cannot continue but can only be delivered up to the nothingness to which it has itself turned. The divine loving in the form of the sending of the Son is the will of God not to allow the destruction and perdition of the world. This will is His redemptive will in relation to the creature—His will not to let it perish, to maintain His creation and not to cause it to perish, not even because of the opposition of the creature, especially not because of it. But that is not all. Eternal life as the continuance of man in fellowship with God Himself, in the *consortium divinitatis*, is not in any way assured to man simply because he is the creature of God. It is rather the particular promise of that light which lighteth every man from the beginning, the light of the covenant which God has made with man. When he denies this light, when he is therefore darkness, when he does not know God, he excludes himself from the sphere of this promise. When he is lost as a creature, how can he participate in eternal life? If he breaks the covenant, he is lost as a creature, and if he is lost as a creature, the promise of the covenant cannot hold good for him. But the divine loving in the form of the sending of the Son is the confirmation of the will of God not to acquiesce in this but to cause man to have the eternal life which he has forfeited with his right to exist as a creature. It is His will not merely to rescue, but to save. He not only wills the creature to continue, but to continue in eternal fellowship with Himself. And He does not allow Himself to be foiled even in this far-reaching purpose for man by the opposition of man.

This loving Yet and Notwithstanding of God (proclaimed in the sending and therefore in the offering of the Son, in the divine self-offering) is what actually happens within this world to those who believe on the Son. Those who believe on the Son are the members of the cosmos who, while they necessarily participate as such in its opposition, and are therefore subject to perishing and have forfeited eternal life, in the sending of the Son and therefore in the self-offering of God can and must recognise God as God, and His will as a will of love, a will to rescue and to save, being ready to accept its validity and application against themselves and therefore for themselves. Those who believe on the Son are those in the cosmos who in face of the work and revelation of God, because in the giving of the Son it includes within itself God's own presence, are free but also constrained to justify God (even against themselves as members of the cosmos, and therefore against the whole cosmos). They are those who without being in any way different from others are under the forceful permission and command to affirm God and the will of God as it has been revealed to them. This is not because, as distinct from others, they are disposed and able of themselves, but because God is too strong for them. Their freedom and constraint cannot be explained by the men themselves. It can be explained only by the presence of God, His glory in the flesh (Jn. 1[14]). Only then is it genuine and strong and lasting. That is why the New Testament describes it as discipleship, the result of an act of majesty on the part of Jesus. And it is this that constitutes faith. And just as the Son on whom they believe is not of this world (ἐκ τοῦ κόσμου), so it is with believers (Jn. 17[14, 16]), although they are undoubtedly in the world (Jn. 17[11]). They are not of the world, or, to put it positively—in believing in the Son, in seeing His glory in the flesh—they are "born from above" (Jn. 3[3]). It is in this way that there takes place in them what is the purpose of the divine loving of the cosmos and therefore of the giving of the Son. As those who believe on the Son they do not perish with the world but they are rescued; they do not lose eternal life but have it. That this is the case with believers is the scope of that event and its promise for the whole world. What happens to them, and as such is only theirs, applies to the whole world, as we see from the verse which immediately follows, and is connected to v. 16 by a γάρ: "For God sent not his Son into the world to condemn the world, but that the world through him might be saved" (v. 17). Within the world, and therefore as a witness directed and appointed to it, there are men who belong to it, yet who do not perish but have everlasting life. In the setting up of this witness within the world the atonement is shown to be an atonement which is made for the world.

We will now turn to the parallel saying of Paul in 2 Cor. 5[19]: "God was in Christ reconciling the world unto himself, not imputing their trespasses unto them; and hath committed unto us the word of reconciliation."

We are taking this sentence out of its context, and even out of its (in any case loose) syntactical connexion with the preceding verse. It is the main verse in the passage, enclosing and bringing together in a pregnant way all the decisive elements in the surrounding verses. It, too, speaks of that fulfilling of the covenant which is our concern here—its execution and its scope—and in doing so it makes express use of the concept of atonement (cf. for what follows the article καταλλάσσειν, etc., by F. Büchsel, in THWB 3.N.T., 1, p. 254 f.).

Again in the main part of the sentence a story is recounted. And it is obviously the same as that which we found in Jn. 3[16]. θεός is again the acting subject and κόσμος the object of His activity. The narrative serves as a basis for the preceding verse where Paul had said that his being as καινὴ κτίσις, a man for whom old things have passed away and all things have become new (v. 17), is the work of God (ἐκ τοῦ θεοῦ) who has reconciled him to Himself in Christ and committed to him the ministry of reconciliation. In verse 19 this is repeated with a wider reference, the particular being made universal and basic.

Instead of the apostle being reconciled by God to Himself in Christ, it is now the world which is reconciled by God to Himself in Christ. The apostolic ἡμεῖς in v. 18 and the κόσμος in v. 19 are not contrasted, but in a remarkable way the apostolic "we" is a kind of particle of the world (almost the world *in nuce*, a microcosm) and the "world" is only the supreme form, the widest reference of the apostolic "we." In this way the saying about God's reconciling of the world can in fact be the basis of the preceding saying about His reconciling of the apostle. Naturally, this does not exclude the fact that for the apostle the knowledge of the reconciling of the world is grounded in the knowledge of his own reconciliation. The context makes it quite certain that the two cannot be separated.

We must insist at once that the initiative and the decisive action in the happening described as atonement are both with God (as in Jn. 3[16]). This is not to say that man's part is only passive; we will see later that there is a proper place for his activity, and what this activity is. But atonement is not "mutual in the sense of both parties becoming friends instead of enemies. Rather, in every respect the transcendence of God over man is safeguarded in the atonement" (Büchsel). We must put this even more strongly. Atonement is altogether the work of God and not of man; καταλλάσσειν is said only of God, and καταλλαγῆναι only of man. Compared with Jn. 3[16], the statement of this divine reconciling is striking in its compactness. It does not say that God loved the world in what He did, but it simply describes the act itself. And nothing is said about the "giving of the Son" or the sending of Christ. All the more impressive, therefore, is the way in which the decisive point of Jn. 3[16] is made in the participle construction, "God was in Christ reconciling . . .": it is God Himself who intervened to act and work and reveal. The apostle and the world came to have dealings with God Himself. In Paul the concept "world" is not so all-embracing but in most passages it has the same negative force as in John, and certainly in this context. Atonement takes place only where there has been strife. According to Rom. 5[6f.], those who are reconciled with God are such as were formerly weak and godless, sinners and enemies. That is how Paul judged his own case, and it is in the light of this that he usually understands and uses the concept κόσμος. Neither here nor in Rom. 5 does he speak of an enmity of God against man which is removed by the atonement. According to Rom. 5[1], the peace established by the atonement is our peace, πρὸς τὸν θεόν, not the reverse. And his subject here is the reconciling of Paul and the world made by God with Himself, not the reconciling of God with Paul and the world. The hurt which has to be made good is on our side. Notice that in Rom. 1[18] the presentation of the ὀργὴ θεοῦ consists solely in a description of the corruption of man to which God has given him up. God does not need reconciliation with men, but men need reconciliation with Him, and this verse tells us that God has made this reconciliation, and how He has made it. We are clearly taught the aim of His reconciling activity in Rom. 5[5]: "The love of God is shed abroad in our hearts by the Holy Ghost which is given unto us." It is remarkable enough that if that is the goal there has to be a reconciling of the world, and this has already taken place. But that there is a reconciling activity of God in relation to the world may be read in Rom. 11[15] and Col. 1[20]. And the goal is undoubtedly this complete conversion of the world to Him. That is how Paul had clearly experienced and known it as God's activity in his own life. But he sees this activity in his own life in the context of God's activity in the world—according to the common denominator of the event of God's intervening in Christ to reconcile the world, and His actual reconciling of the world to Himself. We cannot overlook the scope of this thought in this verse any more (and even less) than we can in Jn. 3[16].

But what does "reconciling" mean? How does God accomplish this conversion of the world to Himself? Here Paul agrees with John: By His own active presence in Jesus Christ, by His special presence and activity under this name and in this form, as distinct from His being in Himself as God and within His activity as Creator and Lord of the world. With his $\mathring{\eta}\nu\ \kappa\alpha\tau\alpha\lambda\lambda\acute{\alpha}\sigma\sigma\omega\nu$ he, too, recounts the concrete and unique story of Christ. What took place in this story? I do not see how in this context we can avoid going back to the basic meaning of $\kappa\alpha\tau\alpha\lambda\lambda\acute{\alpha}\sigma\sigma\varepsilon\iota\nu$. The conversion of the world to Himself took place in the form of an exchange, a substitution, which God has proposed between the world and Himself present and active in the person of Jesus Christ. That is what is expressly stated in the verse (21) with which the passage closes.

On the one side, the exchange: "He hath made him to be sin for us (in our place and for our sake), who knew no sin (God Himself being present and active in Him)." Here we have it in the simplest possible form. He has set Him there and revealed Him and caused Him to act and Himself acted as one who was weak and godless, a sinner and an enemy like ourselves. Here we see what is involved in that sending, that offering of the Son, that self-offering and self-hazarding of God for the sake of the world, of which we read in Jn. 3[16]. It means that in being present and active in the world in Christ, God takes part in its history. He does not affirm or participate in its culpable nature, its enmity against Himself, but He does take it upon Himself, making His own the situation into which it has fallen. Present and active in Christ, He enters into it. Indeed, it is His divine will—naturally without sinning Himself—to accept a complete solidarity with sinners, to be one with us.

And on the other side, the exchange: He does it, He takes our place in Christ, "that we (again in the simplest possible form) might be made the righteousness of God ($\delta\iota\kappa\alpha\iota\sigma\sigma\acute{\nu}\nu\eta\ \theta\varepsilon\sigma\hat{\nu}$) in Him." It does not say simply that He was made sin and we the righteousness of God. The first is obviously the means or the way to the second. But here, too, the $\mathring{\iota}\nu\alpha$ is both final and consecutive. God willed the second with the first, and brought it about by means of it. There is an exchange on this side, too. In Christ we are made the righteousness of God as Christ was made sin for us. To be made the righteousness of God means (as the positive complement to Christ's being made sin) being put in a place or status in which we are right with God, in which we are pleasing and acceptable to Him, in which we have already been received by Him, in which we are no more and no less right than God Himself is right. And all this in utter contrast to our place and status as the enemies of God, in which we cannot possibly be right with Him, in which we break His covenant with us as far as in us lies. To be made the righteousness of God means to become covenant-partners with God who keep the covenant just as faithfully as He Himself does. To make us that, God made Christ sin. And because He made Christ sin, we have in fact become that. For because He in whom God was present and active, He who knew no sin took our place and status, caused our situation to be His, accepted solidarity with us sinners, in so doing He made our place and status as sinners quite impossible. For in so doing He has finally judged sin in our place and status (ἐν σαρκί, Rom. 8³), i.e., He has done away with it as our human possibility. Where are we as sinners when our sin has been done away in Him? Where can we stand when our former place and status has been made impossible as such? There is obviously no other place or status than that of the One who expatriated us by becoming ours: the place and status of the faithful covenant-partner who is pleasing and acceptable to God and who has been accepted by Him; the place and status of Christ Himself, yes, of the God present and active in Him. In that He took our place, and was made sin for us, we are made the righteousness of God in Him, because we are put in His place.

This exchange is what happened in Christ, according to v. 21. And of the happening in Christ understood in this way Paul says in v. 19 that it is the atonement, or reconciliation—we can now return to the more obvious meaning of the concept—of the world with God which has taken place in Him. The conversion of the world to God has therefore taken place in Christ with the making of this exchange. There, then, in Christ, the weakness and godlessness and sin and enmity of the world are shown to be a lie and objectively removed once and for all. And there, too, in Christ, the peace of the world with God, the turning of man to Him, his friendship with Him, is shown to be the truth and objectively confirmed once and for all. That is the history which Paul has to narrate. As such it is the history of God with Himself, as he has already said in v. 18. But now it is also the history of God with the world, as we are told in v. 19. And notice that in this respect too (and the two cannot be separated) it has taken place once and for all, the history of a decision which has been taken and which cannot be reversed or superseded. That is how He was in Christ—we might say with Jn. 3¹⁶ that is how He loved the world—and it is so, it is in force, and must and will be, whether there are few or many who know the fact, and whatever attitude the world may take to it. The world is God's. Whatever else we may have to say about it (e.g., that it perishes) we must also remember that it is God's—not merely because it is His creature, not merely because God has sworn to be faithful to man, but because God has kept His oath, because He has taken the world from a false position in relation to Himself, because He has put it in that place which belongs to it in relationship with Himself. The reconciliation of the world with God has taken place in Christ. And because it has taken place, and taken place in Christ, we cannot go back on it. The sphere behind it has, in a sense, become hollow and empty a sphere which we cannot enter. The old has passed away, everything has become new. The new is conversion to God. In v. 18 Paul said that this had happened to him personally in Christ. In v. 19, and as the basis of the former verse, he says that it has happened to the world in Christ. It was a definitive and self-contained event.

Against this understanding of the statement we cannot appeal to v. 20 of the same passage, in which Paul singles out as the content of his activity in the "ministry of reconciliation" the entreaty: "Be ye reconciled to God." This does not refer to an extension of the atonement in the form of something which man himself can decide. We recall that in Jn. $3^{16}$ there is a corresponding mention of faith in the Son gifted, or offered up by God. The Pauline concept of faith is perhaps too narrow to permit us to equate the "Be ye reconciled to God" with a call for faith. But it does point in this direction. We can put it generally in this way. It is a request for the openness, the attention and the obedience which are needed to acknowledge that what has happened in Christ has really happened, to enter the only sphere which is now left to man, that of the new, that of the conversion to God which has taken place in Christ. The ministry of reconciliation which consists in this entreaty is not of itself self-contained, but it begins only with this self-contained and completed event. This ministry is its first concrete result. The world (the Jew first but also the Gentile) needs this ministry. The community in the world also needs it in order to be and to remain and continually to become a community. But reconciliation in itself and as such is not a process which has to be kept in motion towards some goal which is still far distant. It does not need to be repeated or extended or perfected. It is a unique history, but as such—because God in Christ was its subject—it is present in all its fulness in every age. It is also the immediate future in every age. And finally, it is the future which brings every age to an end. It rules and controls all the dimensions of time in whose limits the world and the human race exist. It is that turning from the lie to the truth, i.e., from the unfaithfulness of man to his faithfulness, and therefore from death to life, which is the basis of all world occurrence, and in a hidden but supremely true sense the purpose and measure of all contemporary occurrence, and also its goal, enclosing it on every side in order to direct it and set it right. As this completed and perfectly completed turning, reconciliation makes necessary the ministry of reconciliation, giving to it a weight and a power to arouse and edify which no other ministry and indeed no other human activity can ever emulate.

The second participle-clause in v. 19 is as follows: "not imputing their trespasses unto them" (i.e., to men in the world). It indicates the presupposition of this ministry. God took the trespasses of men quite seriously. But He did it, as we are told in v. 21, by accepting solidarity, oneness, with those who committed them. And by taking them seriously in this way, He did something total and definitive against human trespasses. He took them out of the world by removing in that exchange their very root, the man who commits them. They cannot continue, just as a plant or tree cannot live on without its root. They can still be committed, but they can no longer count, they can no longer be entered up—like items in a well-kept statement or account. What counts now, what is reckoned to men, is the righteousness of God which they are made in Jesus Christ. That and that alone is their true yesterday and to-day and tomorrow. It is on this basis that Paul takes himself and the world seriously. And it is on this basis that the world must take itself seriously, not on the basis of its trespasses which are written off in Jesus Christ, but on the basis of the righteousness of God which is reckoned to it in Jesus Christ. To call the world to the very different accounting which is only possible in Jesus Christ, that is the task and goal of the ministry of reconciliation, in which Paul finds himself placed as one who has experienced and known it.

This is what we are told in the third participle-clause in v. 19: "and hath committed unto us (the person of the apostle) the word of reconciliation." Between the apostle and the rest of the world there is the decisive difference that he has eyes and ears for the atonement which has been made, and therefore for the conversion of the world to God, for the new thing which has come and therefore for the passing away of the old, whereas the world is still blind and deaf to it. The world still lives as though the old had not yet passed away and the new come. Not recognising the truth, it still regards the lie as the truth. It still believes that it can and must maintain itself in that sphere which is hollow and empty and in which we cannot live. It is still self-deceived. And Paul sees it dreadfully held by this deception and doomed to its consequences. But it is not this difference, and the tension of it, and the dynamic of this tension, which makes him an apostle. What moves him in this difference, what prevents him from evading the tension as a kind of private person reconciled with God, what forces him to make it his own, to bear it in his own person, is the fact that what has come about for him in Christ as his reconciliation with God has come about for him for the sake of the world. His conversion as such was his calling to be an apostle, his placing in this ministry of reconciliation, or, as it is expressed here, the committing of the "word of reconciliation" to the existence of his person. The "word of reconciliation" is the indicating and making known of reconciliation in the world to which it is still unknown and which is still in the grip of the most profound and tragic self-deception. As Paul is given by Christ eyes and ears for Christ, as the atonement made in Christ becomes his, the God to whom he owes this makes him a mouthpiece to speak of this atonement to those who are still blind and deaf, who are not yet aware of the valid and effective atonement which has been made for them, who therefore lived in opposition to this fact as those who are still unreconciled, as strangers to Christ and therefore to God, and for that reason in the most painful sense of the word, strangers also to the world and to themselves. As one who has been made to see and hear, Paul cannot be silent. Called to this office by God, he has to be the mouthpiece of reconciliation. And that is what makes him an apostle. That is what constrains him. And it is the concrete reach of the turning made in Christ that where it is experienced and known it evokes this movement, underlying the community and its ministry of attestation in the world and against the world and yet also for the world.

We concluded our consideration of Jn. 3[16] with a reference to the ministry of those who, believing on the Son of God, do not perish but have everlasting life. It is not there explicitly in the text. We can only say that the verse can be logically understood only when we find in it this reference. But in 2 Cor. 5[19] both the context and the wording make it the point of the whole verse. Where the atonement made in Jesus Christ is experienced and known, it necessarily evokes this witness. In this case, therefore, we have even better justification for concluding with the judgment that reconciliation manifests itself in the establishment and the actual bearing of a witness to it as the reconciliation of the world.

# The Doctrine of Reconciliation (Survey)

The content of the doctrine of reconciliation is the knowledge of Jesus Christ who is (1) very God, that is, the God who humbles Himself, and therefore the reconciling God, (2) very man, that is, man exalted and therefore reconciled by God, and (3) in the unity of the two the guarantor and witness of our atonement.    *Humanity of God*

This threefold knowledge of Jesus Christ includes the knowledge of the sin of man: (1) his pride, (2) his sloth and (3) his falsehood—the knowledge of the event in which reconciliation is made: (1) his justification, (2) his sanctification and (3) his calling—and the knowledge of the work of the Holy Spirit in (1) the gathering, (2) the upbuilding and (3) the sending of the community, and of the being of Christians in Jesus Christ (1) in faith, (2) in love and (3) in hope.

## 1. The Grace of God in Jesus Christ

In order to be able to survey the whole, we will first select from the many things that we have to consider and explain in greater detail one primary thing, that in reconciliation as the fulfilment of the covenant of grace, as in the covenant of grace itself, we have to do with a free act of the grace of God. God re-establishes the covenant, or, rather, He maintains and continues it, in order to lead to his goal the man whom He has brought into covenant with Him. Whatever connexions there may be before or behind, they do not alter the fact that in so doing God makes a completely new start as the freest possible subject. No one who really knows Him in this activity will ever be able to think of Him as bound by these connexions or committed to this activity.

He acts to maintain and defend His own glory. But no one and nothing outside Himself could ordain for Him that this should be a matter of His glory. He acts with a view to the goal to which He wills to bring man, but there is not really any necessity which constrains Him to do this. He acts as a Creator to a creature, but sin is the self-surrender of the creature to nothingness. If this is what man wanted, God might easily have allowed man to fall and perish. He had and has plenty of other creatures in whose presence man would not necessarily be missed. He acts with the faithfulness of a covenant-Lord, but He would not have been unfaithful to Himself if He had regarded the covenant which man had broken as invalidated and destroyed. He loved the world of men, but He did not need to continue to love the sinful world of men. We can only say that He has actually done so, and that this decision and act invalidate all questions whether He might not have acted otherwise. He did make it His glory not to allow this creature to perish, not to punish the covenant-breaker by abolishing the covenant, to love sinful man in spite of and even by reason of his sin, to bring him to his goal and not to set any limits to His own faithfulness. He chose this for Himself in spite of everything. And since this was and is His choice and decision and act, those who recognise and value them as His sovereign act will not regard them as fortuitous but will find in the temporal happening of atonement God's eternal covenant with man, His eternal choice of this creature, His eternal faithfulness to Himself and to it. They will see the connexions and in them they will find the constancy of God, the divine will which is preconceived and unalterable and which is therefore necessary and triumphant in this happening. But in the light of this fulfilment of His will they will see that its eternity and inflexibility are those of His free grace, and that the glory which He willed to maintain and defend is that of His mercy—His covenant a covenant of grace and His election an election of grace; so that conversely the atonement made in Jesus Christ will be seen to be wholly an act of the grace of God and therefore an act of sovereignty which cannot be understood in all its profundity except from the fact that God is this God and a God of this kind.

The Christian dialectic of covenant, sin and reconciliation cannot therefore be subjugated at any point to the Hegelian dialectic of thesis, antithesis and synthesis. To understand it according to this formula is utterly to misunder-

*Christian dialectic NOT Hegelian*

stand it. Sin does not follow from creation and the covenant. It is already negated and excluded by the will of God active in creation. The covenant established by the free will of God is for the very purpose of safeguarding man against it. Again, sin itself is far from having reconciliation as its necessary consequence. The only necessary consequence of sin is that man should be damned and lost. Again, reconciliation is anything but a synthesis of creation and the covenant on the one hand and sin on the other. Between these there is no higher third thing in which they can be peacefully united. And reconciliation is not a higher unity, but in it God contends one-sidedly for His work in creation and the covenant and therefore one-sidedly against sin. In it the antithesis of sin is, for the first time, sharp and clear-cut. It also differs from the Hegelian synthesis in the fact that as the definitive and self-contained work of God it points beyond itself, not, of course, to a new decline into thesis and antithesis, but forward to the *eschaton* of the resurrection and eternal life, in which it has its goal and every antithesis fades. Speculators of every kind are therefore warned. But it is only the knowledge of the God who speaks and acts in the whole process in free grace which makes all speculation radically impossible.

If the atonement is an act of divine sovereignty, we are forbidden to try to deduce it from anything else or to deduce anything else from it. But, above all, we are commanded to accept and acknowledge it in all its inconceivability as something that has happened, taking it strictly as it is without thinking round it or over it. This is the place and the only place from which as Christians we can think forwards and backwards, from which a Christian knowledge of both God and man is possible. And this is the only place from which we can see and judge from the Christian standpoint what sin is. It is here that Christian preaching and instruction and pastoral care and dogmatics and ethics can begin with their own Yes and No, their *pro* and *contra*. We cannot come to them by any other way or from any higher vantage point. It is here that all natural theology perishes even before it has drawn its first breath. Why? Because this is the Word in which God Himself has set the beginning of knowledge in the vacuum where there is no beginning for man as estranged from God and himself. It is the possibility of life in general. It is also the possibility of knowledge. And beside it there is no other. This means that basically our knowledge can never get beyond it. As a knowledge of God as well as man, as a looking back to God's election, creation and covenant, and a looking forward to His coming eternal kingdom, it converges upon it from every side. Only here and not elsewhere can it try to see and clarify its presuppositions and deductions. It is therefore true that Christ is the mystery of God, that all the treasures of wisdom and knowledge are hidden in Him and not elsewhere, and that they are to be acquired in Him and not elsewhere (Col. 2³). Why? Because He who has been appointed by God the beginning of all knowledge is also the One who decides its total compass. It is, therefore, only at the risk of immediate and total blindness that we separate ourselves from It, trying to escape by discovering other depths and heights in other spheres.

Yet it is not the prohibitions that are decisive, but the command—to realise fearlessly and indefatigably in all its aspects the possibility of life and knowledge given us with the atonement made in Jesus Christ. From this source we draw our knowledge of God and man and of eternity behind and above and before us. For individuals, for the whole Church and for each succeeding generation in the Church it is an inexhaustible source. And the knowledge we draw from it is always sure and useful and necessary. It does not need to fear the suspicion that it is perhaps only an uncertain and unpractical and idle play of human thought. On the contrary, it is something which has to be brought out and thought and expressed. Why? Because God has not posited that beginning of all knowledge in vain, but as the light which does indeed lighten our way and which we have to follow confidently and obediently, with steps which may be great or small but will in any case be unfaltering. In the atonement we are dealing with a sovereign act of God. Therefore we are faced with a command which must direct all our knowing and be fulfilled in our knowing.

This sovereign act is the act of God's grace. The grace of God in the atonement is God's triumph in the antithesis, in the opposition of man to Himself. It is the lordship of His goodness *in medio inimicorum* —original, unilateral, glorious and truly divine—in which He acts quite alone, doing miracle after miracle, in which, therefore, He alone is worthy of honour and praise and glory and worship and thanksgiving. In this activity He cannot be understood except as the One who constantly surpasses Himself in His constancy and faithfulness, and yet who never compromises Himself, who does a new thing and yet does everything in order, who could not be more powerfully holy and righteous than when by His Word and in His Son He calls us who are His enemies His children, when He causes us to be His children, because in His freedom to do that He is truly the Lord. Reconciliation is God's crossing the frontier to man: supremely legitimate and yet supremely inconceivable—or conceivable only in the fact of His act of power and love.

We are reminded of the remarkable verbs used by Paul to indicate the reality of grace when he came to speak of it *expressis verbis*: πλεονάζειν (to grow, to increase, Rom. 6[1, 2], 2 Cor. 4[15]), ὑπερπλεονάζειν (to be present in fulness, 1 Tim. 1[14]), ὑπερβάλλειν (to surpass, to exceed, to excel, 2 Cor. 9[14]), ὑπερπερισσεύειν (to overflow, to superabound, Rom. 5[20]). We find a kind of boundless astonishment on the part of the apostle at the divine intervention acknowledged in the concept grace (or love).

The frontier is a real one. On the one side there is God in His glory as Creator and Lord, and also in the majesty of His holiness and righteousness. And on the other side there is man, not merely the creature, but the sinner, the one who exists in the flesh and who in the flesh is in opposition to Him. It is not merely a frontier, but a yawning abyss. Yet this abyss is crossed, not by man, not by both God and man, but only by God. It happens that God the Creator and the Lord, the Holy and the Righteous, the One who can only hide His face from what man is and does, emerges from the impenetrable mystery of His Godhead, which has become so dreadful to the sin of man, and gives Himself to man and to be known by man, to the one who has the faculties to receive and know Him, but has no will or capacity to use these faculties. He gives Himself to him as his God, as the One who did not and will not cease to be his God, the God of sinful and wholly carnal man. This man does not even know how it comes about or happens to him ("Depart from me, for I am a sinful man, O Lord," Lk. 5[8]). Even afterwards he cannot explain what has happened by any point of contact which God has found in him. But it does in fact happen that by God's intervention this man finds himself accused and humbled and judged by his God, but also and primarily received by Him and reclaimed as His possession and hidden in Him and sustained by Him and addressed and treated as His friend and indeed His child.

So, then, man can have "peace with God" (Rom. 5[1]). But how and on what basis? We can only answer: by the Word of God, in Jesus Christ, by faith in Him, by the Holy Spirit who awakens faith. But all that (and especially the naming of the name of Jesus Christ) simply points us to a riddle which confronts every human How? or On what basis?, because it is the grace of God, the coming of God to man which is grounded only in itself and can be known only by itself, the taking place of the atonement willed and accomplished by Him, the sovereign act which God did not owe to Himself or the world or any man, on which no one could bank, yet which has in fact taken place and been made manifest. It is only as willed and accomplished by God that it can be true and known to be true that that peace is given to man, that he can have it, because the covenant broken by us has been kept and fulfilled by God and is therefore in being, that in spite of ourselves, and therefore in a way which at bottom is inconceivable to us, we who are gainsayers and rebels are genuinely converted to God and are His people in the same sense that He is our God. That is the insoluble mystery of the grace of God enclosed in the name of Jesus Christ before which we stand at this point.

As His act, it is the most actual thing in heaven or earth. Effective by Him, it is effective as nothing else is effective. Revealed in Him, as His revelation it is brighter and clearer and more certain than the light of the sun or the light of any other knowledge. Already in this preliminary survey we can and must state that the righteousness with which man finds himself in some sense clothed is His righteousness and therefore new and strange, the holiness is His holiness and therefore new and strange, the truth His truth and therefore new and strange: "crowned with mercy and loving-kindness" (Ps. 103[4], cf. Ps. 5[12]). Because of this everything depends absolutely on His blessing, everything on His Word which is itself the reconciling act, everything on God Himself in the uniqueness of His action in Jesus Christ for each and every man, which as such is also the mystery of the present and future of each and every man. Everything depends on Him who is above, and therefore on what comes to man from Him and therefore from above. It does not depend at all on what man had or has or will have to contribute from below. When man is asked concerning his righteousness or holiness or truth, he can only point to his utter lack of all these things and then at once point away from himself to his clothing or crowning with all these things, that is, to Jesus Christ. The event of atonement and the actuality of man reconciled with God can be described by those who know it only in the words of Lk. 15[2]: "This man receiveth sinners, and eateth with them." It is the Holy Spirit who lays this self-knowledge upon their hearts and this confession upon their lips. It is faith and love and hope which know and speak in this way. Christian obedience consists in this, and its joy and certainty rest and renew themselves on this: that by the grace of God this is the relationship of God with man. For what the Christian community can have specially as knowledge and experience of the atonement made in Jesus Christ, for the power, therefore, of its witness to the world, everything depends on the simplicity of heart which is ready to let the grace of God be exclusively His grace, His sovereign act, His free turning to man as new and strange every morning, so that it does not know anything higher or better or more intimate or real than the fact that quite apart from anything that he can contribute to God or become and be in contrast to Him, unreservedly therefore and undeservedly, man can hold fast to God and live by and in this holding fast to Him.

In this introductory survey we must also state that unfortunately the paths of Evangelical and Roman Catholic understanding have diverged widely at this point. In the light of the latest doctrine in relation to the Virgin Mary (1950), the proclamation of which has shed a new and garish light on the situation, we can only say that, humanly speaking, they have diverged hopelessly. The heart and guiding principle of the Romanist doctrine of grace is the negation of the unity of grace as always God's grace to man, as His sovereign act which is everywhere new and strange and free. It is the negation of the unity of grace as His grace in Jesus Christ. It is the division of grace by which it is first of all His, but then—and this is where the emphasis falls—effected and empowered by His grace, it is also our grace. Against this view we must at once and quite definitely set our face (for what follows, cf. the survey given in B. Bartmann, *Dogm. Handb.* vol. 2, 1929, 113).

In the Romanist teaching a distinction is made between *gratia increata*, which is God Himself, who is the divine will of love and therefore the ground of all grace, and *gratia creata*, which is the "finite product" of the former, "but which is essentially different from God Himself, a created good." We ask: What is this created good when it is a matter of peace between man and the Creator who has been offended by him? How and in what sense can he rely on this "finite product"? How can it be essentially different from God and yet be His grace which reconciles us with Himself?

In the Romanist teaching there is a *gratia externa* which works on us only from without in the form of teaching and example. "We have to do here with the life and death of Christ, His Gospel, His miracles, providence, personal experiences, the effectiveness of the Church, the exemplary conversation of the saints. This influence is moral." For the most part it is, of course, connected with the *gratia interna*. It aims ultimately at inward effects. But it does not produce them of itself. It simply prepares the way. It makes the soul receptive. In contrast, the inward grace "effects the soul and its basic faculties, raising it to a new order of being. Its influence is physical." It adheres to the soul as a new form. We ask: How can the life and death of Christ and the Gospel (mentioned in the same breath as the effectiveness of the Church and the exemplary conversation of the saints and other good things) be described as "only" an external grace and as such obviously impotent and defective? What is this "physical" influence compared with which that of the Gospel is "only" moral?—as though the outward moral grace were not the most inward and physical. And what is this form of the soul in a higher order of being in which we are not referred absolutely and exclusively to that *gratia externa* which has only moral significance but can find comfort and be reconciled with God physically, in and by ourselves?

Within the decisive *gratia interna* there is a personal grace of sanctification (*gratia gratiam faciens*) and a grace of office (*gratia gratis data*), the charismatic endowment "which is for the most part firmly linked with the priestly *ordo*" and which reveals itself in the official power of the priesthood. We ask: Is there a personal sanctification, or a charismatic, or shall we say a priestly endowment which can be wrested even for a moment from the hand of the God who shows His grace to sinful man, and made a possession of the man who receives it, so that it does not have to be sought and received every morning afresh from God? If either the one or the other or both are really effective, how can they be so except from the very first in the event of their giving and receiving?

A further distinction is then made between *gratia actualis* and *gratia habitualis*. Both of these are subdivisions of the grace of sanctification. The first is a *motio divina* "which is given only for a time to do one or more acts." It serves to prepare the way for the reception of habitual grace, and to maintain it when it has been received, increasing it and enabling it to bring forth fruit. Habitual grace itself is constant, creating in man a kind of state of grace. We ask: Can a *motio divina* really be only a preparation for something higher and better, a means only to maintain and prosper it? Not an awakening of faith and obedience, but the *conditio sine qua non* of a real grace which consists in a human competence? And what kind of a competence is this? And what place is there for it in face of the actuality—not of human acts, but of the being and action of the gracious God? Is there a human *habitus* which deserves to be called a *habitus* of grace in itself, and as such is opposed to the actual grace of God?

There is a further distinction between *gratia medicinalis* and *gratia elevans*. Once again, the first is simply a preparation for the second, the capacitating of men for acts of the supernatural life, by the healing of his nature from the wounds of original sin and the removal of human ignorance and concupiscence. As against this, *gratia elevans*, which is the substance of *gratia interna*, as its very name indicates, accomplishes the lifting up of the faculties of the soul to another order of being, making men capable of purely supernatural activities. We ask: Is then the work of Christ as a Healer only preparatory? Does He not in this way lift us up to the supernatural life? Does He only prepare us in this way for a true being in grace, in which we will no longer need Him as a Healer, in which we are no longer the sick folk that He came to heal?

Again, there is a distinction between *gratia praeveniens* and *gratia concomitans*. The first precedes our free decision, stirring up the will to do good. The other accompanies and supports and gives stability to the activity of man as he is already free. We ask: In relation to the free will of sinful man, is grace only a stirring up of that will to do good, and then the accompanying and supporting and continual strengthening of its activity? Is there then no new creation? No awakening from the dead? Of what two partners are we really speaking then? If we are speaking of the gracious God and sinful man, how can we ever cease at any point to understand the grace which comes from God to man wholly and utterly and exclusively as *gratia praeveniens*? Can it really be understood, will it be understood, except as the grace which heals us and for that very reason lifts us up?

A further distinction is made between *gratia operans* and *gratia cooperans*. The first is active in us alone and without any co-operation on our part (*in nobis sine nobis*). Again, this is thought of as only preparatory to our own good actions: "It sets in motion those pious thoughts and stimulations of the will which always precede the free decision." As against that, *gratia cooperans* always works together with the free will (*in nobis cum nobis*). We ask: On what basis is there ever a *cooperari* in the relationship between the gracious God and sinful man which is not also and as such a pure *operari*? How do the work of God and the work of man ever come to stand on the same level, so that they can mutually limit and condition each other? How can the "above" of God which renews, and the "below" of man which stands in need of renewal, ever be placed side by side? How can the "below" of man, even when it has in fact been renewed, ever come to imagine that its renewal is a result of co-operation between the renewing "above" of God and itself?

Again, there is a distinction between *gratia sufficiens* and *gratia efficax*. The one is a grace which merely reaches out and is sufficient, but is not in itself and as such accompanied by any result. It is a grace which has to be completed by the free decision of the human will or by *gratia efficax* (a grace maintained by the Thomists in their controversy with the Molinists). This latter grace is added to the former and lends it the necessary force. We ask: Is grace as such ever *sufficiens* without being *efficax*? Is it ever effective objectively without being effective subjectively? Is grace ever a pre-condition for something else, a pre-condition which can come into force only by the free will of man or the addition of a further grace? Does the fact that man believes he can evade or resist it mean that we can speak of a grace which is not effective? Is not the really dreadful thing about human resistance to it the fact that in itself and as such, as an act of divine sovereignty, it is not merely a condition proposed to man but the absolutely binding and effective determination of his existence, which he contradicts by his resistance?

Finally, there is a distinction (the most remarkable of all) between *gratia Christi* and *gratia Dei*, or *gratia supernaturalis* and *gratia naturalis*. Since all the graces so far mentioned are extended in virtue of the merits of Christ, "they are all called the grace of Christ." Over against, or rather preceding them, there is a special "grace of God," *gratia sanitatis*, granted to man in Paradise when he was at any rate not positively unworthy of it. This grace became his own, and it is evident that it was not simply removed even from sinful man, but still remains as *gratia naturalis*. We ask: Is the concept "grace of Christ" only a kind of generic name for all the other graces? Are they merely called the grace of Christ, or are they all really His one grace? And if they are called this because they really are, is it enough to say that they are because the merits of Christ constitute the possibility and condition of their distribution? Does not this mean that at bottom the grace of Christ is restricted to those graces which are distinguished by the special concepts of *gratia externa, praeveniens, operans, sufficiens*, whereas the true graces, *gratia interna, habitualis, cooperans, efficax*, being only prepared and made possible by it, will necessarily bear another name because they derive from another source? Can we say "the grace of Christ" and mean less than the whole reality of the grace of God, the grace which cannot be exceeded by any other or higher grace, which cannot precede a true grace because it is itself the only true grace and all that grace? "The Catholic conception understands the essence of grace to be that which mediates between the will of God and the will of man" (Bartmann, p. 17). If we accept this as our "conception," how then in this mediatorial capacity can it be anything other than the grace of Christ and therefore the one grace of God—as though there were other mediators or mediations which we have to distinguish from the one Mediator? But if it is the one grace of God, how does it come about that before or alongside it there is a special *gratia Dei*, a *gratia sanitatis* or *naturalis* extended to our first parents or to man in his creaturely nature? At what point in his history or in what depth of his creaturely nature can the grace of God come to man except as the grace of Christ? Is it that we are dealing with another God than the One who is Father, Son and Holy Spirit, and who has elected from all eternity to be the God of man in Jesus Christ—so that naturally we are dealing with the other grace of this other God? But what other God can be the God of man, and what other grace can there be as a *gratia sanitatis*? But again, if the grace of Christ is the one grace of God, what place is there for these distinctions, which all have the one result, of distinguishing and indeed separating a grace in itself from a grace for us, a grace which is objectively indispensable from a grace which is subjectively effective, a grace which is merely stimulative and preparatory from a grace which co-operates with us, e.g., a *gratia operans* which, as a pure act of God, is enclosed in itself as in a glass-case from a *gratia co-operans* which lays claim upon us, or a grace which merely cleanses us from a grace which lifts us up, in short a grace which is manifestly incomplete from a grace which is perfect and complete? How dare we split up the grace of Christ and the grace of God in this way? Is it not the case that as outward grace, for example (that which is described as the grace of the life and death of Christ, of the Gospel, etc.), it is wholly inward and proper to man, and conversely, that as inward grace which is proper to us it is altogether outward, the grace of the life and death of Christ and the grace of the Gospel? Similarly, is it not the case that actual grace is habitual, and habitual actual? That *gratia praeveniens* is *concomitans*, and *sufficiens efficax*, and *vice versa*? How can that which is described as the second and perfect be perfect except in the power of the first, which is regarded as so meagre and impotent as a purely enabling and preparatory grace? How can the first not have already in itself the perfection of the second? If there is one God, and one Mediator between God and man, and therefore one grace—what place is there for all these abstractions? These are the questions which crowd in upon us as we face the final Roman Catholic distinction.

But the Romanist doctrine of grace insists on these abstractions. Naturally it also maintains—rather more emphatically on the Thomist side and rather less emphatically on the Jesuit—that in the last resort there is only one grace. But it merely says this: it does not make any use of it. It simply commemorates the fact. It says it as a precaution, e.g., to ward off the kind of questions that we have been putting. When left to itself and following its own inclination it says something very different; it talks about the division of grace. It says the first thing as a bracket in which to say the second: but it does not abolish the parenthesis in order to say it.

For, if it did, the fact would be revealed which is plainly enough proclaimed by all these characterisations and emphases, that it is definitely much more interested in the *gratia interna* than the *gratia externa*, in habitual grace than actual, in the grace which uplifts than the grace which heals, in *gratia cooperans* than *gratia operans*, in other words in the state and life and activity of grace in man than in Christ as the One who accomplishes the sovereign act of God and what man is in and by Him, in Mary than the Son of Mary, in the sacraments as the supposed means of grace than the Word and Spirit of God who reveals and attests and in that way really mediates it, in the Church as the form of grace, in the priesthood and its authority than the Lord of the community which lives by the Word and Spirit of God and therefore in His service. This is the system of fatal preferences which would be revealed if the theology of Rome were to speak of the unity of grace instead of its division, and it is to be feared that the unity which it would choose would necessarily be that of man in grace, of Mary, of the sacraments, of the Church ruled and directed by the priesthood.

Alternatively, the revelation of this strange preference might cause it to take fright and to abandon it. It would then have to decide to become a real doctrine of the grace of Christ. It would have to notice that the subjective side to which it has everywhere addressed itself in the sphere of those twofold concepts is utterly dependent upon and can be known and determined only by the objective, which it has commemorated but then abandoned it as though it were only a *conditio sine qua non*. It would have to learn to trust that the genuinely subjective is already included in the true objective, and will be found in it and not elsewhere. But in this case the Romanist theology would have to become Evangelical. And in view of its authoritative pronouncements it seems less likely to happen to-day than at any time.

What is certain is that we have to take warning at this point. If it is a matter of the grace of the one God and the one Christ, there can be only one grace. We cannot, therefore, split it up into an objective grace which is not as such strong and effective for man but simply comes before him as a possibility, and a subjective grace which, occasioned and prepared by the former, is the corresponding reality as it actually comes to man. But the grace of the one God and the one Christ, and therefore the objective grace which never comes to man except from God, must always be understood as the one complete grace, which is subjectively strong and effective in its divine objectivity, the grace which does actually reconcile man with God. And the test of this understanding of grace must be that the state of man in relation to it—apart from what we can positively say concerning him in the light of it—is clearly and unequivocally described as one of absolute need: a state in which—with all that this involves—he is and remains always a recipient, a state in which he not only does not cease but can never do more than begin (and he will always be a beginner) to beg and to reach out for it in his poverty, in order that in that poverty he may be rich. The Romanist doctrine of grace cannot survive this test. It ascribes to man in grace an *exousia* in which he can look back to the grace of Christ as such as to an indispensable but preliminary stage which he has already passed. It furnishes him with a wealth in which he is no longer poor and needy and hungry and sick, in which, therefore, he cannot be the recipient of the one complete grace of God and of Christ. At the point where its true interest emerges, it definitely does not describe him as the being which has known and experienced and acknowledged the atonement as the sovereign act of God. As reflected in its description of man in grace, God has ceased to be the free subject of the atonement, the grace of the atonement has ceased to be His grace. And since this is so, there can be no peace between this and the Evangelical doctrine of grace.

But we must not omit an irenical and ecumenical word at the conclusion of this confessional polemic. There is a very deep peace (beyond any understanding) between us Evangelical Christians and our Catholic fellow-Christians who are badly instructed in this doctrine. We cannot believe that they do in fact live by the grace which is so dreadfully divided in their dogmatics. Rather, we have to believe, and it is comforting to believe, that they as well as we—if only we did it better—do live by the one undivided grace of Jesus Christ. We have badly misunderstood what we have had to say in clear opposition to their teaching if we do not believe and therefore confess this. We wish that they would abandon both their teaching and many—very many—things in their practice which correspond so closely to it. We wish that they would give God the glory which their dogmatics (and not only their dogmatics) obviously does not give, so that we could then stand with them in a genuine *communio in sacris*. But we trust in that *communio in sacris* which—not made with hands—has already been achieved by the sovereign act of the God who reconciles us men with Himself and therefore with one another: on the far side of the Church's doctrine and practice, which even at its best (whether Evangelical or Catholic) can only be a witness made with the best of human understanding and conscience to the God who is greater than us all.

It is fitting that at this point we ourselves should now look very carefully in this other direction—at the man to whom this sovereign act applies, the man who is reconciled with God on the basis of this sovereign act. God has acted in His grace (which is always His). He has acted, therefore, without us and against us and for us, as a free subject in Jesus Christ. He has by Himself posited a new beginning. But He has really acted. What He has done is not just something which applies to us and is intended for us, a proffered opportunity and possibility. In it He has actually taken us, embraced us, as it were surrounded us, seized us from behind and turned us back again to Himself. We are dealing with the fulfilment of the covenant. God has always kept it but man has broken it. It is this breach which is healed in the sovereign act of reconciliation. God was not ready to acquiesce in the fact that while He was for us we were against Him. That had to be altered, and in Jesus Christ it has in fact been altered once and for all. That is the original and unilateral and sovereign triumph of God. That is the meaning of the crossing of the frontier or abyss from God's side as it took place in the existence of the man Jesus. The offence offered to God by the unfaithfulness of His covenant-partner, and the misery of that partner, are both removed in Him. In Him man keeps and maintains the same faithfulness to God that God had never ceased to maintain and keep to him. God keeps and maintains His faithfulness by looking and going away past the transgression of man and Himself entering in and providing for the faithfulness of man and therefore for the fulfilment of the covenant, even on the side of man. In this way God takes care for His own glory. And He does it by bringing man to glory. That is His sovereign act in the atonement. That is the grace of Jesus Christ.

It is apparent at once that the formula "God everything and man nothing" as a description of grace is not merely a "shocking simplification" but complete nonsense. Man is nothing, i.e., he has fallen a prey to nothingness, without the grace of God, as the transgressor who has delivered himself up to death, as the covenant breaker he has shown himself to be in relation to God. In the giving of His Son, however, in reconciling the world to Himself in Christ, God is indeed everything but only in order that man may not be nothing, in order that he may be His man, in order that as such he, too, may be everything in his own place, on his own level and within his own limits. The meaning and purpose of the atonement made in Jesus Christ is that man should not cease to be a subject in relation to God but that he should be maintained as such, or rather—seeing that he has himself surrendered himself as such—that he should be newly created and grounded as such, from above. This creating and grounding of a human subject which is new in relation to God and therefore in itself is, in fact, the event of the atonement made in Jesus Christ. This is what was altered in Him. This is what was accomplished by the grace of God effective and revealed in Him. In Him a new human subject was introduced, the true man beside and outside whom God does not know any other, beside and outside whom there is no other, beside and outside whom the other being of man, that old being which still continues to break the covenant, can only be a lie, an absurd self-deception, a shadow moving on the wall—the being of that man who has been long since superseded and replaced and who can only imagine that he is man, while in reality he is absolutely nothing. Yes, the atonement is the filling of this abyss of nothing, of human perdition. And it is by the abyss of the divine mercy that that other abyss is filled. It is this pure divine mercy which fills the abyss, the mercy which we have to recognise and adore in this act of God, the mercy which we have to seek afresh every morning, the mercy for which we can only ask and reach out as beggars, the mercy in relation to which we can only be recipients. By the grace of God, therefore, man is not nothing. He is God's man. He is accepted by God. He is recognised as himself a free subject, a subject who has been made free once and for all by his restoration as the faithful covenant partner of God. This is something which we must not conceal. It is something which we must definitely proclaim in our Evangelical under-standing of grace. We cannot say and demand and expect too much or too great things of man when we see him as He really is in virtue of the giving of the Son of God, of the fact that God has reconciled the world to Himself in Christ.

We underline the fact that it is a matter of a being of man. We can and must experience and know this—that is what makes a Christian a Chris-tian. But first of all, and in itself, and as the object of this experience and knowledge it is a being. Being reconciled is not a matter of the mere hoping or thinking or feeling or experience or even conviction of man. It cannot in any sense be interpreted as a matter of hypothesis (with all the "uncertainty" to which this necessarily gives rise). Its force does not depend upon the intensity with which it is hazarded, while all the time its truth is in the last resort a matter for doubt. No, the old has indeed passed away, all things are become new, God was in Christ reconciling the world to Himself, and those who believe in Him do not perish but have everlasting life. The new man who keeps the covenant has been born and is alive and revealed. Therefore we have peace with God—without any uncertainty. This alteration in the human situation has already taken place. This being is self-contained. It does not have to be reached or created. It has already come and cannot be removed. It is indestructible, it can never be superseded, it is in force, it is directly present. This is the mystery of the man reconciled to God in Jesus Christ. This is what is experienced and known in Christian knowledge and experience. And if in describing this knowledge and experience as such we have to mention all kinds of human hopes and thoughts and feelings and experiences and convictions and hypotheses and "uncertainties"—and why should not this be the case, why is it not necessarily the case in this connexion?—it is always clear that if we are really dealing with Christian knowledge and experience all these things are only comparable with the foam of a waterfall plunging down from the highest mountain tops. They derive necessarily from that being. Any truth and power that they have can come only from that in itself enduring being. Human experience and knowledge cannot of themselves attain to the being of reconciled man. They have no power to rise from appearance to being. The being is there first, and in the power of it it is then followed by everything which may happen as a more or less clear and certain acknowledgment on the part of man. Notice that we are not talking *in abstracto* of the being of God or the reality and power of the divine act of sovereignty. We are now looking at man. We are speaking of the being of man reconciled to God in Jesus Christ. For it is the meaning and reach of the atonement made in Jesus Christ, the power of the divine act of sovereignty in grace, that God willed not to keep to Himself His own true being, but to make it as such our human being and in that way to turn us back to Himself, to create the new man, to provide for the keeping of the covenant by us, to give us peace with Himself. In the atonement it is a matter of God and His being and activity for us and to us. And that means an alteration of the human situation, the result of which is an altered being of man, a being of man divinely altered. It is on this basis that as Christians we cannot think or demand or expect too much or too high things of man. He is reconciled to God in Jesus Christ. If he is to be understood aright, he can and should be understood in the light of this fact. This is the denominator by which we have to view everything that he is and does and everything that we can think and say concerning him. He can still rebel and lie and fear, but only in conflict, in impotent conflict, with his own most proper being. He can and necessarily will be judged but his own most proper being will be his judge. All his mistakes and confusions and sins are only like waves beating against the immovable rock of his own most proper being and to his sorrow necessarily breaking and dashing themselves to pieces against this rock. But human obedience, too, human constancy and virtue, useful human knowledge, human faith and love and hope, all these are only a standing and walking on the rock which bears him up, the rock of the new being given to him as his own. An Evangelical doctrine of the grace of God—if it is not to give offence and to lay itself open to the objections of its Romanist opponents—will not be guilty of a nominalism which compromises or even negates this being of the man reconciled to God in Jesus Christ. This being is the first and basic thing which we must seriously and definitively ascribe to the man reconciled to God in Jesus Christ. It is something that we have to expound and understand. We cannot go back a single step behind this being of the reconciled man. Whatever we have to think and say of man, and not only of the Christian but of man in general, at every point we have to think and say it of his being as man reconciled in Jesus Christ.

We speak of man reconciled in Jesus Christ and therefore of the being which is that of man in Him. In so doing we will characterise and describe it in its concrete reality, its individuality and power. The grace of God in which it comes and is made over to us is the grace of Jesus Christ, that is, the grace in which God from all eternity has chosen man (all men) in this One, in which He has bound Himself to man—before man even existed—in this One. He, Jesus Christ, is the One who accomplishes the sovereign act in which God has made true and actual in time the decree of His election by making atonement, in which He has introduced the new being of all men. Notice that it is those that know this new being as their own who can openly and confidently and joyfully hail it as such. It is Christians therefore who, when they have spoken of it relevantly, seriously and authoritatively, have always characterised and described it as the being which has met them as their own in Jesus Christ, which they sought and found, and found again in Him, on which they cannot pride themselves, and by which they can live only because they found it exclusively in Him.

Those who believe in Jesus Christ will never forget for a single moment that the true and actual being of reconciled man has its place in that Other who is strange and different from them, and that that is why they can participate in it with a fulness and clarity the knowledge of which would only be broken if they were to look aside to any other place. They will know that they can speak about the being of the new man only in the light of this One, and that they can never speak about it definitely enough in the light of this One. It is the being of the new man reconciled with God which in Him has truly and actually been appropriated to them and to all men.

## 2. The Being of Man in Jesus Christ

We cannot speak of the being of man except from the standpoint of the Christian and in the light of the particular being of man in Jesus Christ. To the Christian it is a matter of experience and knowledge. He knows about Jesus Christ, and the reconciliation of the world to God made in Him, and therefore the new being of man in Him. He can give an account and testify to himself and others how this new being originates. God has given it to all men in Jesus Christ. But we cannot expect that all men will be in a position to know and to give an account of Him and therefore of their true and actual being as it is hidden and enclosed and laid up for them in Him. Yet we must remember that what we can say primarily only of the Christian has a general application in the sense that we could at once say it of all men if they came to know of Jesus Christ and of what they are in Him. Christians exist in Him. In practice this is the only thing that we can call their peculiar being. But they do so only as examples, as the representatives and predecessors of all other men, of whom so long as their ears and eyes and hearts are not opened we can only say definitely that the same being in Jesus Christ is granted to them and belongs to them in Him. But Christians know and can declare what it is that belongs to them and all other men in Jesus Christ. And by the existence of the Christian we can make this clear. The being of man reconciled with God in Jesus Christ is reflected in the existence of the Christian. That is something we cannot say of others. It is not that they lack Jesus Christ and in Him the being of man reconciled to God. What they lack is obedience to His Holy Spirit, eyes and ears and hearts which are open to Him, experience and knowledge of the conversion of man to God which took place in Him, the new direction which must correspond to the new being given to them in Him, life in and with His community, a part in its ministry, the confession of

Him and witness to Him as its Lord and as the Head of all men. For that reason the being of man reconciled to God in Jesus Christ is not—yet—reflected in them. To understand and describe it, therefore, we must confine ourselves to Christians and the Christian community. The being of man reconciled to God in Jesus Christ has three aspects which are clearly different. We will first of all describe these under the three concepts of faith and love and hope. We will then see how the being of the new man described in this way has its root and basis in Jesus Christ Himself, His person and mission and work, how it is in fact hidden and enclosed and laid up in Him. But in the faith and love and hope of the Christian that which is hidden in Jesus Christ is known, that which is enclosed is opened, that which is laid up is distributed and shared. Yet they know, and they keep to this strictly, that it is known to them only as that which is hidden in Him, it is opened only as that which is enclosed in Him, it is shared only as that which is laid up in Him. They are put in this relationship to Him by the presence and operation of the Holy Spirit. It is this relationship which is described by the concepts of faith and love and hope. We will now try to follow the lines indicated by these three concepts.

The conversion of man to God in Jesus Christ takes place (1) in the fulfilment and revelation of a verdict of God on man. The being of the new man in the form of faith is man's recognition, acknowledgment and acceptance of this verdict, the making of his own subjection to this verdict. That man does accept and bow to this verdict is the work of the Holy Spirit which makes him a Christian. The verdict of God to which faith subjects itself is two-sided. It has both a negative and also a positive meaning and content.

On the one side it is a verdict which disowns and renounces. With all the truth and validity and force of a sentence which has not only been pronounced but executed, and therefore pronounced once and for all, it declares that man is no longer the transgressor, the sinner, the covenant-breaker that God has found him and he must confess himself to be, that as such he has died and perished from the earth, that he cannot be dealt with as such, that as such he has no future. Jesus Christ has taken his place as a malefactor. In his place Jesus Christ has suffered the death of a malefactor. The sentence on him as a sinner has been carried out. It cannot be reversed. It does not need to be repeated. It has fallen instead on Jesus Christ. In and with the man who was taken down dead on Golgotha man the covenant-breaker is buried and destroyed. He has ceased to be. The wrath of God which is the fire of His love has taken him away and all his transgressions and offences and errors and follies and lies and faults and crimes against God and his fellowmen and himself, just as a whole burnt offering is consumed on the altar with the flesh and skin and bones and hoofs and horns, rising up as fire to heaven and disappearing. That is how God has dealt with the man who broke covenant with Himself. God has vindicated Himself in relation to this man, as He did as Creator in relation to chaos. He could not, and would not, use this man. He could not, and would not, tolerate and have him any longer. He could and would only do away with him. He could and would only disown and renounce his existence. And that is what He has done, not merely in the form of a protest and contradiction, which would clarify but not alter the situation between them, but in the form of his destruction. This event is the divine verdict, the Word in which Christian faith believes. In virtue of this Word, i.e., in the power of this event, the existence of man as a sinner and all his transgressions are now behind him. Whatever else he may be, he will no longer be this man, the transgressor. Most definitely not, as the man who is placed under this Word. The word "forgiveness" speaks of a judicial act in which God has maintained His glory in relation to man. But it does not speak of a new purpose or disposition or attitude on the part of God. And least of all does it speak of any mitigation of the severity with which sinful man is rejected by God. Rather it speaks of the fulfilment of that rejection. The being of the new man reconciled with God in Jesus Christ is one in which man has no more future as sinful man. And in the form of Christian faith it is a being in subjection to this verdict, and in that way and to that extent a being in "the forgiveness of sins."

But the verdict of God on man in which the conversion of man to God is fulfilled has also a positive meaning and content. It is a verdict which recognises and accepts. With all the truth and validity and force of a sentence which has not only been pronounced but executed and therefore pronounced once and for all, it declares that God receives man, and that man in accordance with his election and institution as a covenant-partner—can confess himself a faithful servant of God, His recognised friend and well-loved child. In that event and verdict and Word God willed to snuff out and kill and destroy. He has done so. But He did it to secure freedom for the man in whom He delights, the man who is not merely innocent but positively righteous, the man who fulfils His will. This man alone is man's future. For it was as such that Jesus Christ took his place. And in his place Jesus Christ rendered that obedience which is required of the covenant partner of God, and in that way found His good pleasure. He did it by taking to Himself the sins of all men, by suffering at His death the death to which they had fallen a prey, by freely offering Himself as the sacrifice which had to be made when God vindicated Himself in relation to man, by choosing to suffer the wrath of God in His own body and the fire of His love in His own soul. It was in that way that He was obedient. It was in that way that He was the righteous One. It was in that way that He was recognised by God—and since He took the place of all, all men in Him. Even on this side, as the positive justification of man, the judgment of God was executed, and can never be reversed and does not need to be repeated. The resurrection of Jesus Christ from the dead is at once the fulfilment and the proclamation of this positive sentence of God. Man is a suitable human partner for the divine partner. He is the one in whom God delights. He is a faithful servant and a friend and a dear child of God. This man was brought in with the resurrection of Jesus Christ from the grave, and with just the same energy with which the old man of contradiction and opposition was done away in the death of Jesus Christ. With the creation of the new man God has vindicated Himself to us, pronouncing His verdict upon us. He willed this man. And what He willed took place. This man came, the man who is righteous for us all, who is our righteousness before God. There is no room for any fears that in the justification of man we are dealing only with a verbal action, with a kind of bracketed "as if," as though what is pronounced were not the whole truth about man. Certainly we have to do with a declaring righteous, but it is a declaration about man which is fulfilled and therefore effective in this event, which corresponds to actuality because it creates and therefore reveals the actuality. It is a declaring righteous which without any reserve can be called a making righteous. Christian faith does not believe in a sentence which is ineffective, or only partly effective. As faith in Jesus Christ who is risen from the dead it believes in a sentence which is absolutely effective, so that man is not merely called righteous before God, but is righteous before God. He believes that God has vindicated Himself in relation to man, not partly but wholly, not negatively only but positively, replacing the old man by a new and obedient man. He believes that by calling that One His own dear Son in whom He is well pleased, God has set up not a provisional but a definitive order in the relationship between Himself and man. He believes in the freedom of the children of God which is not merely demonstrated but given and made over in the resurrection of Jesus Christ from the dead. He believes in the fulfilment of the divine election actualised in this event, and therefore in the revelation and demonstration of it given in this event. As faith it lives by the divine Word of power spoken in this event. The being of the new man reconciled with God in Jesus Christ is one in which man has a future only as the righteous one that he is before God in Jesus Christ. In Christian faith man subjects himself to the judgment by which eternal life is already— effectively—ascribed and promised to him, a judgment beside which he is not able to see before him any other.

We have been speaking of what is usually comprised under the concept of justification. Justification definitely means the sentence executed and revealed in Jesus Christ and His death and resurrection, the No and the Yes with which God vindicates Himself in relation to covenant-breaking man, with which He converts him to Himself and therefore reconciles him with Himself. He does it by the destruction of the old and the creation of a new man.

But we can understand the concept justification (the justification of the sinner) in all its truth and individual force only when we see that basically and inclusively it stands for God's acting and speaking in His own cause, in fulfilment of His eternal will with man. Only then and on that basis does it stand for the grace and goodness and mercy of God as they come to man. These inconceivable benefits do, of course, come to man. It is the eternal will of God to let them do so. But Christian faith finds all its comfort and joy in the fact, and it clings to it, that this gracious and good and merciful judgment of God on man is primarily God's own cause, that in this judgment the cause of man is safeguarded—and with a sovereign assurance— by the fact that God has made it His own cause, and that as such, quite apart from anything that we can do about it. He carried it through to a successful conclusion. In the light of this Christian faith itself, as man's subjection to this verdict, can be understood as a form of the being of the new man. It is in faith that man can find and know that he is justified with an ultimate confidence and assurance. For His own honour and glory, acting solely in His own cause, God has denied and renounced his being in unrighteousness. That is the force of this verdict on the negative side. That is the meaning of it in all circumstances. That is why the believer will not perish. That is why his sins are forgiven. Again, for His own honour and glory, acting solely in His own cause, God has recognised and accepted a being in righteousness. That is the force of the verdict on the positive side. And in all circumstances man can and should hold to the fact that this verdict is in force and that he is the servant and friend and child of God. In virtue of this verdict he has eternal life. The truth and power of faith depend on the fact that it is not a work of human arbitrariness, not even the arbitrariness of a supreme need and longing for redemption, but man's subjection to the divine verdict in which it is a matter of God's own honour and glory—and as such a subjection an act of pure obedience. As this act of obedience faith is a work of the Holy Spirit, and as true faith, and only as such, it is justifying faith.

Why is it so necessary to be clear about this? There are other forms of the new man besides faith and therefore subjection to God's sentence of negative and positive pardon. But in the conversion of man to God we have to do with this basic thing. The being of the new man is a being in the truth and force of this twofold pardon. To that extent faith is the only form of this new being. Before God, i.e., in relationship to God, we are not unrighteous and rejected but righteous and accepted only by faith, not by love and hope. And we are this by faith in so far as faith is that act of obedience, that subjection to the will of God acting and speaking in His own cause and therefore in sovereign power, that acknowledgment of the honour and glory of God in relation to man. It cannot, therefore, be an arbitrary human act. Even if it is a knowledge and acceptance of what has taken place negatively and positively for all men in Jesus Christ, it is not enough—if it is really to be justifying faith and the form of the new being of man—that it should simply know this and accept it. Even if it is the heart's confidence of this or that man that what took place for all men in Jesus Christ took place and is true and actual and applies in his case, too, it is still not enough—however great may be the depth and sincerity of this confidence—if faith is to justify him and in faith he is to be a new man. It is not enough because that twofold divine pardon was pronounced in Jesus Christ, that destruction of the unrighteous and creation of the righteous being took place—and this is why it is true and actual—in Him. It was for man, but it was for man in Him, in the One who is another, a stranger, confronting even man with his sincere acceptance and heart's confidence, in the One to whom man can only cling as to the high-priest who officiates and speaks and acts for him, that is to say, in faith in Him. Not in faith in himself.

To put it even more clearly and pointedly—only with a lack of faith in himself. The great gulf between the believer and the One in whom he believes carries with it the fact that he cannot receive that pardon and experience his liberation from unrighteousness and to righteousness

without having to become aware and recognise and confess that in himself he is altogether unworthy of it, that although he is liberated in very
truth by Jesus Christ, yet in himself, in his daily and even hourly thoughts
and words and works, he is not liberated at all. His own being contradicts
his being in Jesus Christ. Confronted with that being, in the clear light of
that being, he finds that in his own being the old man is not yet dead or
the new created. In his own being—contrary to the divine judgment—he
will again and again find that he is a covenant-breaker, a sinner, a transgressor. In his own being—contrary to the divine verdict—he will never
find the faithful servant and friend and dear child of God. In his own being
he will never with his own eyes see himself as in any respect justified, but
always in supreme need of justification by God. And all this in faith itself
and as such. How then is he going to find himself sinless, and even
positively righteous? Certainly not by the sincerity and depth of his faith,
or the fineness of it as a theological virtue. For where would be the virtue
of this faith if as a believer he saw himself in the light and under the
judgment of the One in whom he believes? As a being and work liberated
from the unrighteousness of the old man and filled with the righteousness
of the new he cannot plead before Him his faith—let alone anything else.
And remarkably enough, the more sincere and deep our faith actually is,
the less we will find in our faith as in all our other being and activity, the
more strange and impossible will be the thought that we can please God
with this one work of faith, the more we will try to cling to the fact that we
have died as the old man in Jesus Christ, and that we are created and alive
as a new man in Jesus Christ, and that we have not to produce our own
confirmation of this righteousness before God in our life and being, not
our own Christian righteousness, not our own righteousness of faith as a
product and achievement and state of our own heart and mind in which
we can lay hold of the truth and power of the divine verdict. In faith the
Christian will find himself justified because believing in this divine
sentence fulfilled and revealed in Jesus Christ he dashes himself against
the rock of that work of God which God has willed and done, certainly
on behalf of man, but primarily for His own sake, to assert His honour
and to maintain His glory against him. Believing in Jesus Christ he will
encounter the divine decision which is basically the self-affirmation of
God against the creature and therefore the decision of grace in his favour,
thus making quite impossible and irrelevant any counter-question concerning that which might correspond to it in the way of human work or
life or faith. Because seriously and ultimately the justifying sentence of

God is the self-affirmation of God worked out and revealed in this way, it will have incontrovertible truth and an unconditional force against everything that man either is of himself or does of himself, the truth and force of the divinity with which God intervened against man and therefore for him, and which cannot be limited by anything that may or may not correspond on the part of man. Christian faith will cling to and find its confidence and support in this divinity of the justifying sentence, without concerning itself about anything—indeed in face and spite of anything— that the believer may find and will necessarily bewail as his own being and essence. This divine judgment will demand a subjection and sheer obedience (and find them in faith) in which man must resolutely turn his back on his own being, in which he finds the old man still there and the new man not yet present, and sets his face equally resolutely to his being in Jesus Christ in which the former is dead and the latter lives. In faith there will be no place for looking back to our own righteousness or unrighteousness; for conclusions as to the freedom reached or not reached by us, for reflections concerning the worthiness or unworthiness of our response to the divine verdict. Faith can and must be faith only in the truth and actuality of the work of God done and revealed in Jesus Christ, faith in the transcendent and victorious nature of this work, based upon the honour and glory of God which are so clearly asserted in face of all human opposition that however dark and malicious this may be it can never be more than a shadow dispersing before the light, and can be regarded and treated only as such. Both before and behind man will dare to live only by his faith. When faith is like this, it is the faith which justifies a man in spite of his sin. For then it is his genuine conversion from himself as a covenant-breaker and transgressor to the gracious and mighty God— a conversion in which he ceases to be unrighteous and begins to be the righteous man he is, pleasing to God and God's dear child. Faith of this kind is the work of the Holy Spirit which makes man a Christian.

But this is not the only form of the conversion of man to God accomplished in Jesus Christ. It is the first form: negative and positive justification by the true and mighty sentence of God, and therefore the form of faith. But there is also another form, (2) the placing of man under the divine direction. We might also speak of the law, commandment, ordinance, demand or claim of God. The being of man in the form of Christian love consists in the fact that he accepts the divine direction. That he does this is another form of the work of the Holy Spirit which makes him a Christian.

God's justifying sentence is His all-powerful decision what man really is and is not. In Jesus Christ he is not a rebel but a servant, not an enemy but a friend, not lost to God but a child in the Father's house. God's direction is also an all-powerful decision, His own divine act of lordship. By this means, too, God vindicates His honour and maintains His glory. By this means, too, He exercises authority. But in God's direction it is plain how He exercises authority, how His divine authority is constituted as opposed to all other authorities, what it means radically and finally to stand under the divine lordship. God's direction is the directing of man into the freedom of His children. It is this which has taken place in Jesus Christ no less uniquely than the once-for-all fulfilment of the divine sentence on man. In suffering in our stead the death of the old man, and bringing in by His resurrection the life of the new, He has made room for the being of all men at peace with God. On the basis of what man is and is not by virtue of the divine sentence passed and revealed in Jesus Christ, in face of that twofold pardon, he has no other place but this—the kingdom in which God can be at peace with him and he at peace with God. Jesus Christ —and this is the second element in His work and ministry as the Reconciler between God and us—is the all-powerful direction of God to us to occupy this place, to live in this kingdom. If we are told in Him who we are and are not, we are also told in Him where we belong, where we have to be and live. Only told? Only directed? Only informed? Is it only an invitation or a demand to enter? All that and more. Jesus Christ is God's mighty command to open our eyes and to realise that this place is all around us, that we are already in this kingdom, that we have no alternative but to adjust ourselves to it, that we have our being and continuance here and nowhere else. In Him we are already there, we already belong to it. To enter at His command is to realise that in Him we are already inside. To follow His invitation and demand is to find ourselves in the situation already created in Him and in Him already our own situation. That is man's reconciliation with God in the form of the issuing and receiving of the divine direction.

Words like law, commandment, ordinance, etc., although they are quite possible and relevant, do not quite suffice to indicate what is meant, because they so easily give the impression of something which has not been already done, which has still to be done by the decision and act which are demanded of man himself. The decision and act of man are, of course, required by the direction given and revealed in Jesus Christ. But the requirement of the divine direction is based on the fact that in Jesus Christ man has already been put in the place and kingdom of peace with

God. His decision and act, therefore, can consist only in obedience to the fact that he begins and does not cease to breathe in this place and kingdom, that he follows the decision already made and the act already accomplished by God, confirming them in his own human decision and act; that he, for his part, chooses what has already been chosen and actualised for him. That is why we use the word direction   we might almost say the advice or hint. It is not a loud and stern and foreign thing, but the quiet and gentle and intimate awakening of children in the Father's house to life in that house. That is how God exercises authority. All divine authority has ultimately and basically this character. At its heart all God's ruling and ordering and demanding is like this. But it is in the direction given and revealed in Jesus Christ that the character of divine authority and lordship is unmistakably perceived.

What is it, then, that we are dealing with? What is this place and kingdom in which God's direction summons man to awaken and remain and act? We have already mentioned the decisive concept: it is a matter of man's direction into the freedom for which he is made free in Jesus Christ (in that twofold pardon), in peace with God. It is the place and kingdom which already surrounds him, in which he is already placed, in which he has only to find himself. God's direction is the direction to do this, to make use of his freedom. He has not won his freedom himself. He has not come to this place in his own power or worth, by reason of his own virtue or skill. He does not control it. The kingdom of freedom is not one in which he can act as lord. It is not for him to try to act in it according to his own judgment. If he did, he would certainly not be free, he would secretly have left that place. It is the house of his Father, and he needs the Father's guidance to act in it and therefore to be free. But he receives and has this. And it is the essence of the freedom for which he is freed in Jesus Christ that he is not alone, that he is not left to himself, that he is not directed to his own judgment, that he must not be his own lord and master, or exist in himself imprisoned in his own arbitrariness and self-sufficiency. In every form this would be bondage—the unfreedom of the lost rebel and enemy from which he has been loosed. Freedom means being in a spontaneous and therefore willing agreement with the sovereign freedom of God. This freedom is the being of man, not in himself but in Jesus Christ, in the place and kingdom which have been opened up to us in Him and which already surround us in Him. Because it is not in ourselves but in Jesus Christ that we are free, that we are the covenant-partners and children of God, we need His direction and lordship and therefore the direction and lordship that come to us in Him. And because it is in Him that we are really free, He is Himself our direction, our guiding into freedom, our awakening to life in that freedom, our guidance to make use of it, our Lord and King, and therefore in this sense too our reconciliation with God, the One who fulfils our conversion to Him.

As distinct from justification, and as its necessary consequence, this subjection of man to the divine direction is usually called sanctification. It is nothing other than the basic presupposition of all Christian ethics. Sanctification is the claiming of all human life and being and activity by the will of God for the active fulfilment of that will.

We must note first that this subjection of man under God's direction and therefore his sanctification is a form of the atonement, of the conversion of man to God accomplished and revealed in Jesus Christ. It is an element in His activity as man's reconciliation with God. Sanctification cannot then be separated from justification, as though it has to do with man's contribution to his reconciliation with God. Sanctification does not mean our self-sanctifying as the filling out of the justification which comes to man by God. It is sanctification by and in Jesus Christ, who, according to 1 Cor. $1^{30}$, is made unto us both justification and sanctification. Certainly we have to do with the work of man, what he does and what he leaves undone. But it is his work in a peace with God which he himself has not made, and in which he cannot of himself take a single step that is a work in which he really shows himself a faithful and adequate covenant-partner of God and God's dear child. The fact that he does take these steps, that he does good works, is something which takes place only in the truth and power of the divine direction. It is just as much a matter of God's free grace as is the decision who and what he is and is not before God. In Christian ethics, therefore, the atonement made in Jesus Christ cannot simply be a presupposition which has been left far behind. Ethics, too, must testify directly to the atonement which man himself does not make, but which God has made in him as His own work, by giving him direction in Jesus Christ.

And equally clearly we must then say that sanctification consists in the fact that in and through Jesus Christ man is called by God into freedom; summoned to use the freedom in which he has already been put in Jesus Christ. God's direction and man's subjection to it has no other meaning and purpose than this. Everything that it means concretely, all the individual directions which have to be unfolded in Christian ethics, can only be concretions of the one necessary direction to the freedom given to man. The placing of man under this direction must not be understood as his subjection to any other law. On the contrary, all the legislation and commanding of God that we meet with in the Old and New Testaments has to be understood as a call to the awakening to that freedom, as a direction to make use of that freedom which is given us once and for all in Jesus Christ, and which we can never abandon on any pretext if our action is obedience. It is a matter of learning to breathe and to live in that freedom, of taking it with all seriousness.

As Christian faith is the human response to God's justifying sentence, so Christian love is the human response to His direction. The reconciliation of the world with God, i.e., man's conversion to God in Jesus Christ, his being as liberated both negatively and positively—this is something which is experienced and known and acknowledged in Him. And when this is the case, then in the truth and power of the one Holy Spirit God's direction or guidance or hint is also received: in Jesus Christ man is directed by God to awakening and life in the freedom for which He has made him free. If it is given to us to know Jesus Christ as the priestly Representative of all men, that is, as the One in whom in the name of all, and therefore for us, the human covenant-breaker was put to death and the faithful servant and intimate friend and dear child of God is brought into being, then it is ordained and given that we should accept Him as the King and Lord of all men and therefore as our Lord. The obedience of faith is followed by the obedience of love—in practice, of course, it may sometimes precede, but it always accompanies it as a second form of the particular being of the Christian in Jesus Christ, which cannot be separated from the first but is quite distinct from it. Sanctification is the second aspect of the reconciliation of man with God willed and accomplished and revealed by God. It comes after and together with the redemption of man from the power of darkness. It consists in his placing into "the kingdom of the son of his love" (Col. $1^{13}$). God Himself is love and revealed Himself as such by sending His only Son into the world in order that we might live through Him (1 Jn. $4^{8f.}$). In Jesus Christ God has created a final and indestructible fellowship between Himself and all men, between all men and Himself, a fellowship which is final and indestructible because it is based upon His own interposition and guaranteed by it. That is the actualisation and revelation of His love which is as such the direction to which man is subjected and the Christian love which receives it responds. It consists simply in the affirmation of the existence of this fellowship as such, just as faith consists in the affirmation of its foundation. In Jesus Christ God has demonstrated, He has made it visible and audible and perceptible, that He loved the world, that He did not will to be God without it, without all men, without each individual man in particular. And in the same Jesus Christ He has demonstrated, He has made it visible and audible and perceptible, that the world and all men and each individual man in particular cannot be without Him. The demonstration that He belongs to the world and the world to Him is the choice and work of His love in Jesus Christ, "the kingdom of the son of his love." In general terms Christian love is the active human recognition of this proof of the love of God. It recognises it by following it, imitating it, modelling itself upon it. It is the attitude in which man gives himself to reflect the divine attitude. That he can do this, that he can love, is his sanctification, his breathing and living in the place and atmosphere of freedom, his keeping of the covenant as a faithful partner. That he can love is the work of the Holy Spirit which makes man a Christian. And now we must distinguish two separate elements, or, better, dimensions, in Christian love.

The love of God in Jesus Christ is decisively, fundamentally and comprehensively His coming together with all men and their coming together with Him. This coming together is not deserved by man, but forfeited. Yet it has been accomplished by God in His free grace, defying and overcoming the sin of man. As this coming together the love of God active and revealed in Jesus Christ is the fulfilling of the covenant by Him. It embraces *realiter* both the world and the community, non-Christians and Christians. But the knowledge and proclamation of it is a matter only for the Christian community. Those who know it are marked off from all other men as Christians. But this coming together of God and man cannot be known to be fulfilled except as it is actively worked out. God has conjoined Himself with man, existing in his own activity, and He has conjoined man existing in his own activity with Himself. God is not idle but active. For good or evil, therefore, man must be active too. Therefore the recognition of this coming together as such is not merely a conscious but an active being of man in God. And this active being consists in the fact that man for his part in answer to that divine activity not merely knows himself to be brought together but does actively come together with God in thought and word and work: within the limits, of course, of his human capacity, and humbly seeking the One who has already found him in His own free grace, but within those limits with all his heart and soul and mind and strength (Mk. 12$^{29f.}$). This active coming together of man with God will be the realising of all the possibilities of his active being beside which, in the knowledge of the communion achieved by God and therefore of the love of God, he cannot see any other possibilities. In this way it will be an activity which is at bottom voluntary, which excludes the fear of any other forces but God, which claims him wholly and utterly. It will be accomplished as an act of pure gratitude, which does not make any claim and which is therefore complete. And in all this it will be a kind of silhouette of the elective, free and total activity of God Himself to whom he makes a human response. To that extent it will be a following and imitation of that activity, the love to God which is the response to the love of God. In accordance with what He did and revealed in Jesus Christ, God willed from all eternity not to be without man. And now, recognising this will of God, man wills not to be without God. His activity is therefore characterised by the will to seek God and to find Him, that is, to enquire concerning His commandment, to be guided by His decisions and attitudes, and to follow His direction. Existence without love has now been left behind as an error and a lie. Therefore he no longer needs to have any fear. He no longer takes pleasure in being self-sufficient and self-responsible, his own lord and master because his own owner. That is the delusion which he has left behind in the knowledge of his coming together with God as God willed and accomplished it. He cannot live in it any longer. He still knows it. It still presses in upon him. But because of that knowledge it has no more power over him. He now lives by suppressing it wherever it arises. He now lives as one who seeks God in his activity. Poetically and rhetorically we might describe the Christian life in much stronger terms. But we will be careful to remember that the substance of anything we might say will always be this, that we are dealing with a fact which is not at all self-evident—that man for his part will seek the God who in Jesus Christ has already sought and found him that was lost, corresponding to the divine action, realising on his side the fellowship which has been set up by God. And above all we will be careful not to separate the concept of this love for God and therefore of this seeking of God from the human activity conditioned by it. We need not be fanatically anti-mystical. As one element in the activity which puts the love to God into effect, there may be a place for a feeling of enjoyable contemplation of God. But it cannot take the place of that activity. Man's being reconciled with God, his conversion to God, is from this second standpoint of sanctification his active being. It is in this being as such that God is either loved or not loved.

But this carries with it the fact that there can be no question of a justification of man by his love to God—perhaps as a continuation or actual-isation of his justification by faith. Certainly the divine direction, the direction into love to God, can never be lacking in the man who has subjected himself to the divine sentence in the knowledge of it. But it is the pardoning sentence of God alone which is the basis of fellowship between God and man, and which therefore justifies man. And the fact that he is justified is something which he finds to be true and actual only in faith. That he can love, i.e., seek God is his freedom to live in that fellowship on the basis which has been laid down by God and God alone. But because we are here dealing with human activity, with the sum of the Christian *ethos* and its always doubtful fulfilment, it can as little contribute to the setting up of that fellowship and therefore to justification as can faith itself as the human recognition that it has been set up.

It amounts to this, that in love man is occupied with something else, and he ought always to be so. It would completely destroy the essential character of Christian love as the freedom given to man and to be kept by man if we tried to burden it with the, in itself, impossible and superfluous task of accomplishing or actualising or even completing the justification of man. No one can and will love God who does not believe. No one can and will love God except in the grounding of his being in the fellowship with God realised in that divine judgment. If we are to be justified by faith, in faith we will not look either at our works or our sins. Similarly in love—in the works of our love to God —we will not consider the possibility of trying subsequently to fulfil or to complete of ourselves that grounding of our being. Christian love does not will anything from God. It starts from the point that there is nothing to will which has not already been given. It does not will anything from the One who is everything to it. It wills only God Himself because He is God, because He is this God. It wills simply to love Him, as the man who is reconciled with Him on the basis of His sentence fulfilled and revealed in Jesus Christ can love Him immediately and unquestioningly and unreservedly, but as also he must love Him. The love in which man thinks that he can justify himself before God is not as such a love which derives from faith. It is not a free and pure love which loves God for His own sake, because He is God. It is rather a work of the old mercenary spirit, of the man who at bottom hates the grace of God instead of praising and honouring it. It is therefore a return to the state of sin, of covenant-breaking. Christian love to God is a free and pure love which honours and praises unreservedly the grace of God. For Christian ethics everything depends on the fact that it should be understood as an independent form of the conversion of man to God (and therefore of His reconciliation with Him) and not otherwise. The erroneous teaching of the Council of Trent involves a false understanding both of justification by faith and also of sanctification in love.

But Christian love has a second dimension inseparably connected with the first. The love of God in Jesus Christ brings together Himself with all men and all men with Himself. But at the same time it is obviously the coming together of all men one with another. And as that communion is known it is at once and necessarily evident that there is a solidarity of all men in the fellowship with God in which they have all been placed in Jesus Christ, and a special solidarity of those who are aware of the fact, the fellowship of those who believe in Him, the Christian community. In this horizontal dimension Christian love is love to the neighbour or the brother. This must be distinguished from love to God which is Christian love in the vertical dimension. It will not take place without love to God. And there would be no love to God if it did not take place. But while it can only follow, and must follow, this prior love, it is an autonomous loving, for God in heaven and the neighbour on earth are two and not one. Love to others cannot exhaust itself in love to God, nor can love to God exhaust itself in love to others. The one cannot be replaced and made unnecessary by the other. But love to God—to the God who reconciles the world to Himself in Jesus Christ—evokes love to the neighbour and the brother. And love to the man who is made a neighbour and a brother in Jesus Christ follows love to God. The following of the divine loving in Christian love would be incomplete, indeed it would fail altogether—and we must remember the very sharp warnings on this point in the first Epistle of John—if it did not take this twofold form, the one having priority as the great commandment of Mk. $12^{29f.}$ and the other being subordinate to it as the second commandment. Within the great reflection of the love of God in Christian love as such and generally, love to the neighbour and the brother must again reflect the Christian love to God. Jesus Christ alone is made unto us sanctification. He is the King who is appointed the ruler and lawgiver and judge of every man. But with His known people this King has also a much larger unknown people, which, according to Heb. $2^{11}$, He, the only Son of the Father, is not ashamed to call His brethren even down to the most lowly members. And according to Mt. $25^{31f.}$ the criterion at His judgment will be the question what we have done or not done to Him in the person of the least of His brethren. They are not identical with Him, but they are witnesses which we must not overlook or ignore, witnesses of the poverty which He accepted to establish that fellowship between God and man which is given to the world and gives light to the Christian community, witnesses of the wealth which in Him is given secretly to the world and openly to the Christian community in that fellowship. In their person they represent Him as the neighbour, as the one who fell among thieves, and as the Good Samaritan who took him and poured oil into his wounds and brought him to the inn at his own expense. They are not identical with Him. But He cannot be had without them. And that means that God cannot be had without them, nor can reconciliation with Him nor conversion to Him. He cannot be had without gratitude for their witness and a willingness to be witnesses to them, without love to them, without their indispensability to each one whom God loves, without that one seriously setting out and never ceasing to seek and to find them, both in the community and therefore in the world as well, Christian and also non-Christian neighbours. Christian love is at one and the same time love to God and love to the neighbour—and it is love to the neighbour because it is love to God. This is the test whether it is the response to God's own love, whether it is the work of the Holy Spirit. If it stands this test, then *mutatis mutandis* but substantially everything that can be said of love to God can be said of love to the neighbour. It is a coming together on the horizontal level, of man and man. As such it is not merely conscious, but ready and indeed voluntary. It is a total coming together which excludes all other possible relationships to the neighbour and claims a man wholly and utterly. To that extent it is a perfect counterpart to the vertical coming together of man with God. And it cannot be exhausted by mere feelings, or a mere outlook, let alone mere words. It is an active being.

But it does not on that account contribute anything at all to the justification of man. And it is the glory of it that it cannot even think of trying to do so, because it derives from the justification of man, from the divine sentence of pardon, and therefore it lives by the faith in which we cannot look away to anything else—either our good works or bad—but must be content to be what we are by God's sentence fulfilled and revealed in Jesus Christ without any co-operation on our part. Even neighbourly love cannot look away to anything that might be won or attained from God by means of it. Just as love to God can envisage and seek and love only God, and for His own sake, so love to the neighbour can envisage and seek and love only the neighbour, and for his own sake. As in the vertical, so in the horizontal dimension, it is free and pure love. There is no question of any gain accruing to the one who loves, either in time or in eternity. There is no ulterior thought of another end, even if this were the highest and most necessary end for man. The neighbour will notice the fact, and he will not find himself loved even in the most fervent and zealous works of Christian charity, if this love is one which looks away, and not a pure act of obedience—as faith also is in its own way. Christian love as the complement of love to God is real neighbourly and brotherly love to the extent that it is exercised without any ulterior thought or question, being shown freely and purely to the neighbour as a neighbour and the brother as a brother, being shown only because in his Christian and also in his non-Christian form he is a member of the people of which Jesus Christ is the King, because this King wills that those who recognise Him should recognise Him again in the members of His people in the narrower and wider sense, because the coming together of God and man accomplished in Him carries with it unconditionally and without reserve and therefore with genuine force the work of bringing together man and man.

Where love exists in both dimensions without any ulterior motive, where it is grounded in itself and does not try to be anything but a necessary response to the love of God, it is that "fulfilling of the law" of which we read in Mk. $12^{29f.}$ and Rom. $13^{10}$. It is obedience to God's direction, the keeping of convenant faithfulness by man, the meaning of the whole *ethos* of the man reconciled and converted to God in Jesus Christ.

The conversion of man to God which took place in Jesus Christ has another form as well as these two, and it will now be our task to characterise and briefly to describe this final form. It consists (3) in the positing and equipping of man as the bearer of the divine promise. In the fact that he participates in this promise and lives in the light of it the being of man consists in Christian hope. And in this third form the work of the Holy Spirit which makes man a Christian is that man—for this is hope—is obedient to the promise as Abraham was, that he is ready to participate in it and to live in the light of it.

God's judgment and direction, and therefore man's justification and sanctification, and therefore faith and love do not embrace the whole of that act of atonement accomplished and revealed in Jesus Christ which reconstitutes the being of man, and therefore they do not embrace the whole of the specifically Christian being established and formed by the knowledge of Jesus Christ. In our presentation so far there is lacking any consideration of what we might call the teleological determination of the being of man and of the Christian in Jesus Christ.

In that section of dogmatics which is specifically known as soteriology, i.e., the doctrine of the salvation which comes to man in Jesus Christ, it has been customary since the Reformation to think in the main only in the two categories so far mentioned. The doctrine of Luther centred upon the contrast and complementarity of faith and works, that is, love, or, conversely, the Law and the Gospel. And Calvin returned constantly to the dialectic of justification and sanctification. These were the two concepts which dominated the Reformed theology which succeeded Calvin. But they are also the iron basis and core of what the Lutheran orthodox thought it possible to describe as the *ordo salutis*. And in line with the general Protestant tradition Schleiermacher in this context treated first of regeneration (conversion and justification) and then of sanctification. Our consideration of the two spheres described in this or some similar way has certainly convinced us of the correctness and importance—an importance which cannot be over-estimated—of these two aspects, and their indispensability as the basic description of the man reconciled in Jesus Christ and especially of the Christian who knows Jesus Christ. The Reformers did well to concentrate on them as they wrestled with the problems of their own day. In the controversy with Roman Catholicism their exact treatment will always play a decisive part. Even in relation to the subject-matter as presented for our consideration by the biblical witness, there can be no question that here in justification and sanctification, or faith and love, or at an even higher level God's verdict and direction, we find ourselves at what is from this standpoint, the being of man reconciled to God in Jesus Christ, the very heart and centre of the Christian message. There can be no escaping the questions: How can I lay hold of a gracious God? and, How can I live in accordance with the fact that I have a gracious God? And these questions must always be rightly answered with all the actuality which they can never lose. But we must not overlook the fact that as we take note of the witness of the New Testament at this very heart and centre of the matter there is a third moment which we have to treat independently and as true in and for itself. It is of this that we must now speak, the moment of the promise given to man in Jesus Christ, and therefore Christian hope, and therefore the calling of man side by side with his justification and sanctification.

It was not enough—that is, it did not correspond to the fulness of the New Testament witness and a comprehensive investigation of the point at issue—when under the title *De vocatione* the Protestant tradition tried to speak only in an introductory and comprehensive way about the subjective *applicatio salutis*, i.e., man's entry into the sphere of justification and sanctification, of faith and love, his regeneration and conversion as his entry into a state of grace, the basic activity of the Holy Spirit in general and the rise of faith in particular. In a treatment of this kind it necessarily seems that the sphere of justification and sanctification, of faith and love, is marked off from behind as that which is properly sacred—although not without some reference to its limitation by what has to be said separately in the doctrine of the last things. We must admit that Calvin did see very clearly the problem of the teleological determination and direction of the whole being and status of man as changed in Christ and shaped for conversion to God. He felt the problem, and he treated it in a lasting and impressive way in his conception of the *promissio* as the basis of faith and his presentation of the *vita christiana* as directed to the *vita futura*. But for him the *spes* seems to be only an essential and indeed the properly compulsive element in *fides*. It is this in the New Testament. But in the New Testament it is more than this. And in the New Testament the calling of God is never simply as it was described in Protestant orthodoxy, the basis of the entry into the specific state of grace, or Christianity. This state never has the character of a being which is included and exhausted in the form of faith and love, a being which will then be superseded by and merged into the, as it were, quite different being in eternal glory to which it moves. In the New Testament the being of man in Jesus Christ is rather a being under and with the promise, as it is also a being under the verdict and direction, of God. It is a being which in its totality is teleologically directed, an eschatological being. Calling speaks of more than calling into a state of justification and sanctification. As such and with independent truth and power calling is man's forward direction to God as his future, his new creation as a being which not only derives from the sentence of God in faith and is placed under His present direction in love but beyond that receives and embraces His promise in hope, looking forward therefore and moving forward to Him. The Protestant tradition was, of course, helped and corrected by the fact that it never neglected to consider the last things. Inevitably, too, something of this had to be brought out indirectly in the discussion of justification and sanctification, of faith and love. But it is still only too true that in that tradition the being of man in Jesus Christ has as such a very this-worldly, immanentist, even middle-class appearance. The older Protestant soteriology with its classical and in its way magnificent pre-occupation with the two first points did not make it sufficiently clear that this being as such is a being under the promise, that the reality of the salvation given to man is as such the gift of this promise, that the Christian affirmation and appropriation of the divine gift is as such hope based upon and directed to this promise. In Evangelical dogmatics we must not neglect the two first points. But we must bring out no less emphatically the prophetic element of the being of man reconciled with God in Jesus Christ.

The restoration, renewal and fulfilment of the covenant between God and man in the atonement made and revealed in Jesus Christ is complete as man's justification as a covenant-partner and his sanctification to be a covenant-partner, as the establishment and formation of the fellowship between himself and God, just as God's creation was perfect as the beginning of all His ways with the created order. But, like creation, it is not an end but a beginning—complete in itself and as such, but still a beginning. It is not, therefore, an end in itself. Nor is it simply conditioned by what might happen further between God and man on quite different presuppositions, just as the (in itself) perfect creation of God was not simply conditioned by the subsequent history of the convenant, but took place for the sake of the covenant and to that extent was itself the beginning of the covenant. So, too, reconciliation, the being of man converted to God in Jesus Christ, is as such a beginning. It is not merely a *restitutio ad integrum*. It is not merely the creation of a final and stable relationship in which the disturbance of the balance between God and the world has been corrected, and, with the re-establishment of the normal order of superiority demanded by their conjunction, God and the world can co-exist quietly and contentedly: God having pronounced His verdict and giving His direction, man in faith in Him and in love to Him and his neighbour. It is not the restoration of a parallelism and equipoise in which God and the world, God and man, will now continue to live together happily. This is—slightly caricatured—the this-worldly, immanentist and middle-class understanding of the being in Jesus Christ given by God to the world and known and experienced by Christians. In contrast to all such ideas, this being in all its completeness is only a beginning—a being in which man looks eagerly forward to the activity of God and his own fellowship with Him, just as in faith he looks back to it and in love he sees it as present. It is a being which is still open for God, open for that which has not yet happened in the restoration of the covenant as such, for that which has yet to happen on the basis of that restoration. It is not only under the verdict and direction of God but also under the promise of God, in which we have to do with this future event, with this still expected being of God for man, with yet another form of the fellowship between God and man. The justification and sanctification of man have a purpose and goal.

It is not self-evident that they should have, that apart from what he may be under God's verdict and direction man as reconciled with God should also be given by this same God a future, a *telos*. Those limited ideas might well correspond to the reality. For what man may be under God's verdict and direction, in faith and love, is certainly complete enough in itself. But, in fact, they do not correspond to the reality. In fact the perfection of the being in Jesus Christ (without anything lacking in the first two forms) has a further extension. The justification and sanctification of man

THE DOCTRINE OF RECONCILIATION

do in fact include a purpose and goal. This is not self-evident. It is only as a further proof of the overflowing goodness of God that it is in fact the case that the being of man in Jesus Christ is a being not merely in possession and action but also in expectation. And for this reason the calling of man is obviously a thing apart and additional to his justification and sanctification, as is also Christian hope In relation to Christian faith and Christian love. For it is a thing apart, it is the grace of God in a new and particular form, that He not only wills to make man His servant and friend and child, His faithful covenant-partner, to have him as such and to cause him to walk before Him as such, but also that beyond and in all this (as is shown in a type in the figure of Abraham) He wills to make something of him, He has for him a purpose, an end. According to the promise given him in Jesus Christ, God has in fact a purpose for man in all this. And in the knowledge of the promise given in Jesus Christ man is, in fact, called to give to God not merely the response of the obedience of faith and the obedience of love, but also the response of the obedience of hope. We must therefore regard the calling of man as the third aspect of the reconciliation of man with God which God Himself has willed and accomplished and revealed.

What does the promise of God mean? It means that the being of man acquires a direction, because it acquires a destiny and a perspective. This is something which the verdict and direction of God do not mean taken and understood by themselves, even though they are as such the perfect Word of God. The end of man's justified and sanctified being, of Christian faith and Christian love, belongs to the conversion of man to God. Man cannot take this to himself. But God gives it to him in reconciling him to Himself in Jesus Christ. He gives him His pledge—already redeemed and operative in Jesus Christ —that is the strong sense of the word promise. And now he can and must live as the one who has this pledge, and therefore with the forward direction and destiny given by it and perspective opened up by it: forward to what he will be according to this pledge. In the fulfilment of the covenant he receives this pledge and accepts this call to advance.

But to what does it point him? In a very general way, to the actualisation and preservation of the fellowship between God and himself established in the fulfilment of the covenant. God's promise shows him that this fellowship is not simply a—two-dimensional—connexion, not simply a relationship, but that it has a depth in which at first it is alien and unknown to man, yet in which it is to be confided and made known to him, that there is something common to both God and man upon which man cannot lay his hand but which God promises to lay in his hand.

For a proper understanding everything depends upon our giving the right name to what is shown and pledged to man by the divine promise. In the New Testament it is briefly and very well described as "eternal life" (cf. Jn. 3[16]). This brings out with a clarity which can hardly be excelled the fact that it is a being in a depth of fellowship with God which has yet to be disclosed. Only God lives an "eternal life." If man is to have it, it can only be on the ground that God wills to live in fellowship with him. But if God wills that, it can be said and promised by Him to man living in his present only as a thing which is new to him in his present. It is, then, to his actual future with God that he moves forward in the possession of this promise. But what is meant by "eternal life" if it is promised to man as his future with God, if, therefore, in eternal life he is not to cease to be a man, a creature and as such identical with himself, the one he now is? if in that depth of fellowship with God he is not to be merged into God or changed into some quite different being?—which would necessarily mean that it was not really a matter of his future, that the promise did not concern and apply to him, man, as such, that it had nothing whatever to do with his present.

How can eternal life be promised to him, man? How can it be his future with God in this present? In this connexion we usually speak of man's future resting in God or his future supreme bliss before God, or of a contemplation and adoration of God which in its permanence constitutes his future beatitude. And, rightly understood, all this must not be rejected. But if we describe the content of the promise in this way, we must be careful not to form pagan conceptions of God and the eternal life that He lives and the eternal life that He promises to man, as though at bottom God was a supreme being with neither life, nor activity, nor history, in a neutrality which can never be moved or affected by anything, a being with which man can ultimately be united only in rest or in some kind of passive enjoyment or adoring contemplation. The God who is Father, Son and Holy Spirit, active and revealed to us as the eternally living God in Jesus Christ, is not in any sense this supposedly "supreme" being. And  unless we say something very much more, rest and enjoyment and contemplation are not the right words to describe a being in the depth of fellowship with Him. According to the witness of Holy Scripture—in correspondence with His triune being, and as indicated by the biblical concept of eternity—God is historical even in Himself, and much more so in His relationship to the reality which is distinct from Himself. He is the Lord of His kingdom, deciding, acting, ruling, doing good, creating peace, judging, giving joy, living in His will and acts. And that kingdom is not merely a kingdom which He possesses in the cosmos created by Him. It is the kingdom which He sets up in the course of a historical movement which has a beginning, a middle and an end. It is the kingdom which comes from heaven to earth. And that is how He encounters us and reveals Himself to us in Jesus Christ, for He is still the active ruler when He combats the sin and misery of the world, when in the work of atonement He converts it to Himself in this One. If it is the case that man is given a promise for his own future in this as yet unrevealed depth of fellowship with God, it cannot be otherwise than that the content of the promise should correspond to the being of God. The fellowship of man with God is completed and completes itself as it enters this depth. And this complete fellowship, the "eternal" life of man, must consist in a future being of man with God as this active ruler. And it is hard to see how we can better describe it in summary form than by calling it a being which is in the words of Lk. 20[36] like that of the angels in that it is a being in the service of God. Luther showed a perception amounting to genius—for in some way he transcended himself—when in his exposition of the second article in the *Shorter Catechism* he described the end of the redemption of man accomplished in Jesus Christ in the following way: "in order that I may be His, and live under Him in His kingdom, and serve Him in eternal right-eousness and virtue and blessedness, as He is risen from the dead and lives and reigns in eternity." To live under Him in His kingdom and to serve Him: it is here that all rest and joy and contemplation and adoration in the eternal life promised to man have their meaning and basis. It is the calling to this which is the *telos* of justification and sanctification. The future of man in covenant with God (in the position and function which he will have in relation to that of God) is to be the partner of God and to live as such. We are, in fact, dealing with what synergism of every age and type has tried to ascribe to man at a place where it does not—yet—belong to him, and has confused and falsified everything by trying to ascribe it to him at that place, that is, in his status under the verdict and direction of God. The fact that he is subjected to the divine verdict and can believe in the knowledge of it, the fact that he is placed under the divine direction and can love in the knowledge of it, does not in any sense include within itself a co-operation of man with God, but in faith and love man responds, he corresponds, to what is simply the work of God for him and to him, the

Word of God spoken to him and concerning him. Of course, the same is true in hope. As a recipient and bearer of the divine promise he stands in relation to God as one who can only respond or correspond.

But here we are speaking of the content of the promise, not of his status in hope, but of what he hopes for as he receives the promise and knows it as such. And of this, of the future of man as indicated and pledged in the divine promise, we have to say that it is a being in a co-operation of service with God. This being is in His kingdom, and therefore under Him. But its form now is not simply one of response and correspondence. It is not simply in the distinctness and antithesis which even in the status of hope must be our attitude. To be sure, the creatureliness and identity of man will certainly not be destroyed. Therefore the distinctness and antithesis in relation to God will also remain. But this being will be a being by the side of God, the participation of man in the being and life of God, a willing of what He wills and a doing of what He does. It will be a being not only as object, but as an active subject in the fellowship of God with the created world and man, a being in a partnership with God which is actively undertaken and maintained, a being in man's own free responsibility with God for the cause of God. That is the inconceivable height which is promised to man when he is reconciled with God, converted to God, justified and sanctified. That is the honour, the dignity, the glory of eternal life which God has pledged. That is how man will come to eternal rest and enter into eternal joy and really contemplate God and adore Him. He will serve God, for that is what God has ordained for him and for the race, that is what He has appointed ultimately for the whole non-human cosmos. God does not regard man as too lowly or incapable or unworthy to consider him for this or to promise that this is what he will be. And He does not regard Himself as too exalted to will to set him beside Him and to make use of his service like that of the angels. It is obviously because everything depends on man being set there and used in that way, on his being called to service at His side, it is obviously for that reason—and we can only wonder afresh when we consider the fact—that He let it cost Him the offering of His Son and therefore His own interposition to convert man to Himself.

And the men of the Christian community are those who hear the promise given to the world of men, just as they are those who hear the verdict pronounced on it and the direction given to it. They are those who see the light as it shines before man, as it has already shone most definitely into and for the present being of man. They are those who can therefore walk with open eyes in this light given to the world. They are those who know that everything and all things—including themselves, and they are the ones who grasp it—are appointed and set up for this purpose. They are those who have the perspective that they will "live under Him in His kingdom, and serve Him." Christians, therefore, are those who are able not only to believe and love but also to hope—to hope for the future of the world with God and therefore for their own future with Him. Christians are those who are able to accept and consciously to apprehend not only the justification and sanctification of man, but also his calling in Jesus Christ to eternal life.

This calling took place in what was done for man and the world in the atonement made in Jesus Christ. The atonement accomplished in Him is not only the fulfilment of the sentence and the disclosure of the direction but also the effective proclamation of the promise or pledge of God. It is the divine call to advance under which man is placed by the fulfilment of the covenant and his conversion to God. It alone! We have to do here again only with the grace of God. How can man—even the man who believes and loves—ever come to the point of calling himself to advance, of promising himself the inconceivable height of eternal life with God in His service? As the content of his hope he could perhaps imagine either "immortality" in another life decked out with various characteristics, or all kinds of significant possibilities in this life. Let him beware lest he be deluded and disillusioned in the one respect no less than the other. But no man can imagine of himself his future with God, his service of God as his future being (in this life as in that which is to come). No man can take and ascribe it to himself, anticipating it as his eternal or even his temporal future, that he will render to God a service which he himself offers and God accepts, a service which is complete and real both objectively and subjectively. Not even the pious Christian can do this, any more than he can take and ascribe to himself his justification and sanctification. He can and should live under the promise. He is so placed and equipped that he can have this future and move towards it in the present. But only because the promise and the pledge of it are given him by God, just as he can only accept the verdict and direction of God and therefore his justification and sanctification. The more clearly we see that in the content of this pledge we have to do with nothing less than the acceptance of what synergism falsely believes can be ascribed to man, the more clearly we will see that the pledge that he will serve God can only be given to man and can never be the arrogant postulate of man. Here, as everywhere in the event of atonement, such a postulate is quite superfluous. For in Jesus Christ the promise or pledge of God—which cannot be compared with anything we might promise ourselves—is already given to us. It is actually made to the world. So then (without having to create illusions about itself) the world is no longer a world without hope. As it stands under the verdict and direction of God, so too it stands under the promise of God. It is the world set in the light of its future with God. Hence man is the being which exists in this direction, under this determination, with this perspective. And the Christian is the man who for himself and others can know this and therefore hope. His hope derives from Jesus Christ, for Jesus Christ is Himself the divine pledge as such. And He hopes in Jesus Christ, for Jesus Christ is also the content of the divine pledge. That is what we have now briefly to explain.

Jesus Christ is the divine pledge as such—its effective and authentic proclamation. In Him that to which it refers has already taken place. It is already present. He is the man who lives not only under the verdict and direction of God but also in the truth of His promise. He is not merely righteous and well-pleasing to God and the object of His love, but beyond that He is taken and used by Him, standing in His service and at His side, working with Him, living eternal life, clothed with His honour and dignity and glory. He Himself as the eternally living God is also the eternally living man. The world is reconciled and converted to God in Him in the fact that He is this man, not merely in distinctness and antithesis in relation to God, but also in participation in His being and work, not merely in responsibility to Him, but with a responsibility for His cause, not merely as His servant and friend and child, but as a ruler in His kingdom. No one beside Him is man in this way, just as no one beside Him is as man the same divine Son of the Father. For that reason He (alone) is for all of us (only) the pledge of what we ourselves will be, we who are and will be only men and not God. For that reason in His present (alone) we have to do (only) with our future with God. For that reason the future allotted to us in Him cannot be that of rulers, but only of servants of the one God who alone is King. Our present emphasis, however, must not be upon the qualifications but upon the positive truth that the reconciliation of the world with God consists in the fact that a promise is given it by God Himself and therefore absolutely, that in Him its own future is already present, that in Him even in its present life it is already seized and determined by its future being. Because God has made Himself one with it in Jesus Christ, because He Himself was and is present in it, it has the divine pledge of its future life. Therefore whether it knows it or not, it is not a world without hope, just as on the same ground it cannot be simply a lost world or a completely loveless and unsanctified world. In Him it has become a world in which the divine call to advance has been heard once and for all and is now regulative. In Him it has been constituted in the fact and appointed to it, it exists in the perspective, that it belongs to God, and that while it will not be divinised in some way and made identical with Him, it will find the essence of all creaturely glory in serving Him, actively siding with Him and helping Him and in this way—for all its unlikeness like Jesus Christ—being clothed with all the honour and also with all the joy and peace of eternal life. When the Christian knows Jesus Christ as the One in whom this has taken place for the world, he not only believes and loves, but also hopes. And his hope derives from Jesus Christ, i.e., as he hears and understands the pledge which God has given in Him, making it his own, letting his life be shaped by this promise and opened up for the future.

But Jesus Christ is also the content of the divine pledge, the One in whom the Christian is summoned to hope. It is a terrible thing if at this point, at the last moment, we ignore Him as though He were only a means or instrument or channel, and look to something different from Him, some general gift mediated by Him, regarding this as the object of Christian hope, the future posited for the world and man. The question of the future of the being of man and its direction to that future is such an important and burning question that everything hinges upon whether we answer it rightly or wrongly. If we look aside here, trying to understand the awaited and expected being of man and all creation in the service of God only as the manifestation of a general idea of man or of being, we shall betray the fact that for all our recalling and appealing to the name of Jesus Christ earlier—indeed from the very first in our discussion of the being of reconciled man—we have not really been thinking or answering in relation to Him, but have been developing an anthropological concept which we have found elsewhere and to which we have simply given a christological superscription. In its own way this might or might not have value. But it does not belong to the Christian message or to the heart of that message. The great truth which is proper to what we have to see at this point does not shine out from a concept like that, nor can we expect from it that comfort in living and dying which we need to find at this point. This can be expected, and the divine promise can be understood in its kerygmatic and pneumatic force, only when it is continually seen and understood that, like the divine verdict and the divine direction, the divine promise of the future of the being of man is not only revealed but is actual, an event, only in Jesus Christ, that it is therefore in every way, not only noetically but ontically, enclosed in Him and indeed identical with Him. If we abide by the witness of the New Testament, it will keep us at this point from the mistake of separating the promise itself from that which is promised, and therefore from a new uncertainty. By that witness we are compellingly summoned to regard Jesus Christ not only as the revelation and form of the divine promise but also as its fulfilment and content. The future promised to the world and man, and awaited by the uplifted head of the Christian, is in the New Testament concentrated and comprehended in the one event of the coming of Jesus Christ Himself. He is the eternally living man who as such is the future of the world and of every man, and the hope of the Christian. By His coming to His disciples after His resurrection in the revelation of the forty days He pointed to Himself as their hope and future. In so doing He showed them and the whole community that their own hope and future and that of the world are to be found in His own coming as revealed in a way which none will fail to see and recognise. His own coming is the end to which in its supreme consummation, in its form as God's promise, the covenant fulfilled by Him, the reconciliation of the world with God accomplished by Him, can only move and point as to something beyond itself. As He is the meaning and basis of creation, so He is the bearer and substance of the redemption and consummation which closes the time of the creature, human time. Therefore the calling to expect and hasten towards this end and goal and new beginning, the divine call to advance which opens up the way for man, is the summons to look and to move forward to the One who not only was—before all time and in His own time—who not only is, as the centre of all time, but who also comes as the end of all time, as the Judge of all things which have lived and will live at any time, and therefore as the beginning of the being of the world and man the beginning of their eternal being on the right hand or the left. The calling of man is related to Him no less totally than his justification and sanctification. In hope no less than faith and love we have to do with Him, with the revelation and operation of the grace of God shown to the world and man in Him. And according to what we have already said, this means that in Him man is taken up into that dimension of depth of his being in fellowship with God which is still concealed, which is still only indicated to him. The fact that man can serve God, like the fact that he is justified and sanctified before God, is His affair. It is true for us in Him. The eternal life of man will be found in Him. In Him it will be true, and it will remain true and always be true afresh in eternity as the time of God, that man "may live under Him in His kingdom, and serve Him." In Him he will show himself accepted by God, worthy and capable and usable, able to be with Him to will what He wills, to do what He does, to support His cause. In Him all this will be his rest and joy in God, his eternal contemplation and adoration of God. In Him he will be clothed with the glory of his own eternal life with God. In eternal life, in the glory of the service of God promised to man, it is not a question of a future which is peculiar to man as such and in general. It is a question of His future, the future of Jesus Christ, and of the future of humanity and each individual man in Him.

In Him alone! The exclusiveness of the promise as of the sentence and direction of God, of the calling as of the justification and sanctification of man—the fact that everything is enclosed in Jesus Christ alone—inevitably carries with it the judgment of the world to which each individual moves. For if everything is in Him alone, there is nothing outside of Him. Who does not have to fear this "outside of Him," since none of us can take and ascribe it to himself that he will be found in Him and that he will therefore live under Him and serve Him in His kingdom? But how can our fear be anxious, how can it be anything but a joyful awe even in respect of all men, when the exclusiveness of this future is known as His, when He is known as the Judge who will come to judge the quick and the dead? And when He is not known? Then He must be believed and loved and hoped for as the eternally living One, and the future of the whole world, by those who do know Him. The last word in the matter, both in theory and in practice, is that it is their concern, their task, their responsibility to shine as light in the darkness, to proclaim Him to others as the eternally living One, even to those who do not seem to know Him as such. It is one thing to be unreservedly in earnest to-day about the possibility of eternal damnation for some, and to rejoice equally unreservedly to-morrow at that of eternal reconciliation for all. But it is quite another (and this is the task of the Christian community) to know that one is responsible for attesting with the Christian word and the Christian existence (and the existence no less clearly than the word) Jesus Christ not only as the Lord but also as the Saviour of the world and therefore its future. Christians will never find that they are called to anything other than hope—for themselves and the world. If they were, they would find that they were called to look and to move forward to someone or something other than their Saviour. But then *eo ipso* they would no longer be Christians.

We have still to say a few words about the hope of Christians as such. Let us say first that in their own case they hope for the eternal life in the service of God which comes to them in Jesus Christ. The fact that they can be obedient to the divine calling, recognising and understanding the divine promise as such, includes the fact that as these men amongst others they are themselves reached and approached by that promise, that they can relate themselves to it in person. Jesus Christ and their future in Him is their own personal hope, the hope of their own personal redemption and consummation. They await their own personal being at the end to which they are pointed by the covenant fulfilled in Jesus Christ. But if this is their affair it is not their private affair. Called by God, they are called with their hope of their own future, without asking what will be the outcome, to be the first representatives of all those who so far do not have this hope either for themselves or at all, just as faith and love are so far alien to them, because Jesus Christ Himself is not known to them, because they do not yet know of the atonement made in Him. The relation of Christians to others is that they can hope for them. The one thing is the measure of the other. The more earnestly they hope for themselves, the more earnestly they will do so as (scattered and isolated) witnesses to the promise given to the whole world in their by no means easy status as representatives of others. And the more serious they are in their hoping for others—however isolated and scattered—the more seriously they will be able to hope for themselves, the more compellingly they will have to ask themselves whether they really do hope for themselves.

But what does it mean to hope? We have said concerning the divine promise that, like the divine verdict and the divine direction in the atonement made in Jesus Christ, it has come down, as it were, from above, from God into the world of men loved by God, that it has in a sense been incorporated or implanted into their status and being and non-being, so that objectively they cannot be without it, objectively they have their goal and future in Jesus Christ and therefore in the service of God. In the light of this we can and must understand Christian hope as the coming alive of the promise incorporated in the world of men, or as the taking root of the promise implanted in it. From this standpoint the coming alive or taking root of the promise in the world of men is the work of the Holy Spirit which makes man a Christian. And that means that in the act of Christian hope the objective becomes subjective. It is affirmed. In the person of the Christian the world of men strives after and seizes the goal and future given to it in Jesus Christ. It waits for it, it hastens towards it, it reaches out for it. In the act of Christian hope that which is promised (as promised and therefore future) is already present. Jesus Christ as the (promised and coming) eternally living One is already present. Not merely virtually and effectively, but actually and actively in the person of the Christian. In the act of Christian hope man lives not merely in the factuality of the decision made by God concerning his whole being, but also in the factuality of his own corresponding thoughts and words and works in relation to the service of God, conditioned for and directed towards that service, and in the perspective of that goal. This particular factuality constitutes the particularity of Christian being in hope which is revealed only in the particularity of Christian perception. Christians do not merely see things differently from others. From God's point of view they are different from others, just as they are different from others in relation to the divine verdict and direction when the Holy Spirit awakens them to faith and love. They do not merely live under the promise, which could be said of all men. They live in and with and by the promise. They seize it. They apprehend it. They conform themselves to it. And therefore in their present life they live as those who belong to the future. That which is promised and He who is promised are seen and heard by them in all their futurity. Here and now in their hearts and minds and senses He unsettles and consoles them, moves and compels them, carries and upholds them (judging and establishing and directing). Within their present life and that of the world they are arrested by this future One and pledged and committed to Him. This particularity of their present being distinguishes Christians from other men, and it is in this very particularity that they are the representatives of other men. And to hope means to be different from other men and to act for them in this particularity.

But at this point we must take note of an important distinction. Christian hope is a present being in and with and by the promise of the future. But in the one hope there will always be inseparably the great hope and also a small hope. All through temporal life there will be the expectation of eternal life. But there will also be its expectation in this temporal life. There will be confidence in the One who comes as the end and new beginning of all things. There will also be confidence in His appearing within the ordinary course of things as they still move towards that end and new beginning. There is a joy in anticipation of the perfect service of God which awaits man when God is all in all. But in this joy there is also a joy and zest for the service which to-day or to-morrow can be our trans-itory future. The promise and therefore our calling are in two dimensions.

They refer to the last and ultimate things, but also to the penultimate and provisional. They refer to the whole, but also concretely to the details, to the one in all, but also to the all in one. The promised future is not only that of the day of the Lord at the end of all days, but because it is the end and goal of all days it is also to-day and to-morrow. In Christian hope there is no division in this respect, but again the one is the measure of the other.

Hope seizes, or rather is seized by, the promise of the future. To that extent it is the great hope, the expectation of the eternal life which has still to be manifested and given to us, confidence in the coming Jesus Christ as the end and new beginning of all things, the joy in anticipation of the perfect being of man and all creatures in the service of God which is pledged because it is already actualised in Him. As it seizes the promise of the future it is in every respect—not only hope which derives from Him but also hope in Him as the eternally living One. He, the content of the promise and the object of hope, cannot be replaced by any other. If there is also a small hope for to-day and to-morrow, if there are also temporal, penultimate, provisional and detailed hopes for the immediate future, it is only because He is the future One who shows Himself in every future; it is only in the framework and setting, in the power and the patience of the great and comprehensive hope which is present to man in Him. It is He alone in His futurity, and to that extent as the One who is beyond, who gives hope to the present, the life of man in this world, where otherwise there is no hope. The small hopes are only for the sake of the great hope from which they derive. The provisional promise is only in the light and power of the final promise. If the latter is weak, the former cannot possibly be strong. If the latter perishes, the former will perish with it. If man does not seriously wait for Jesus Christ, at bottom he will not wait for anything else. Daily hope can persist only where in basis and essence it is itself eternal hope.

But the converse must also be perceived and stated. Christian hope is a present being in and with and by the promise of the future, a being which is seized by the promise of God and called. If a man does not seize this hope, apprehend it, conform himself to it here and now as a man who belongs to the future, he is not one who has Christian hope. Rather, it will be revealed that he does not genuinely hope for the perfection and wholeness of His being in the service of God, for eternal life in its futurity, that he does not wait for Jesus Christ as the coming One. If he waits for Him here and now, then the here and now cease to be futureless. He looks for Him, the coming One, to-day and to-morrow, that is, in the decisions in which he has to live to-day and to-morrow as long as time and space are given him. He does not make them without direction or into a future which is empty, but in obedience to his calling, towards that future promised him by God by which the future of to-day and to-morrow is surrounded and lit up, in the light of which every temporal, provisional, penultimate, detailed future necessarily becomes a sign and summons, a detailed and therefore a concrete call to advance which he can only observe and obey. Where there is the great hope, necessarily there are small hopes for the immediate future. These hopes have their basis and strength only in the great hope. They are small, relative and conditioned. In their detailed content they may be mistaken and open to correction. But within these limits they are genuine hopes. And it is certainly in these many little hopes that the Christian lives from day to day if he really lives in the great hope. And perhaps he is most clearly distinguished from the non-Christian by the fact that, directed to the great hope, and without any illusions, he does not fail and is never weary to live daily in these little hopes. But this necessarily means that he is daily willing and ready for the small and provisional and imperfect service of God which the immediate future will demand of him because a great and final and perfect being in the service of God is the future of the world and all men, and therefore his future also.

### 3. Jesus Christ the Mediator

To get a complete view of the event of the reconciliation of man with God as the fulfilment of the covenant we have so far looked in two directions: first upwards, to God who loves the world, and then downwards, to the world which is loved by God; first to the divine and sovereign act of reconciling grace, then to the being of man reconciled with God in this act. We must now look at a third aspect, between the reconciling God above and reconciled man below. Even when we looked in those two first directions we had continually to bear in mind that there is a middle point between them. And more than a middle point, there is one thing which both differentiates and comprehends the reconciling God above and reconciled man below, one thing in which there is actualised and revealed both in themselves and in their inseparable connexion, indeed identity, the reconciling God as such in the sovereign act of His grace, and reconciled man as such in his being grounded in that divine act, the turning of God to man, and based upon it the conversion of man to God. The atonement as the fulfilment of the covenant is neither grace in itself as the being of the gracious God, nor is it the work of grace in itself and as such, the being of the man to whom God is gracious. Nor is it the sum of the two nor their mutual relationship. It is rather the middle point, the one thing from which neither the God who turns to man nor man converted to God can be abstracted, in which and by which both are what they are, in which and to which they stand in that mutual relationship. It is only from this middle point that we have been able to look upwards and downwards, and as we tried always to find and name something concrete we had all the more necessarily to come back to it again and again. But that one thing in the middle is one person, Jesus Christ. He is the atonement as the fulfilment of the covenant. In Him that turning of God to man and conversion of man to God is actuality in the appointed order of the mutual inter-relationship, and therefore in such a way that the former aims at the latter and the latter is grounded in the former. In Him both are in this order the one whole of the event of reconciliation. Our third task —in our present order of thinking—is obviously to understand Him as this one whole.

We have already been on our guard against the possibility of regarding and treating the name of Jesus Christ in a purely "nominalistic" way, as a formal historical or symbolical sign of the event of atonement. This event is not merely outward but inward. It corresponds not only to cognition but to being. It is not in any sense accidentally but necessarily enclosed in Him, as it also took place in Him. It looks both to the reconciling God and reconciled man, and it is found in its unity and completeness in His existence. For that reason He who bears this name, and His existence, must really be regarded as the middle point which embraces the whole and includes it within itself, the middle point in which the sovereign act of the reconciling God and the being of reconciled man are one.

We spoke about a third task, but this third task is simply to show the basis and aim of the answers we gave to the first two, to name and describe the truth in all answers to the question of the gracious God and the man who participates in His grace. Jesus Christ cannot be a third theme which we can separate from the two first. He is the one theme expounded in the two first. If we could speak of the reconciling God and reconciled man only by looking upwards and downwards from Jesus Christ, and constantly looking back to Him, we can speak of Jesus Christ only as we consistently keep before us the one whole of the covenant between God and man fulfilled by Him, and therefore of both the above and the below. He exists as the Mediator between God and man in the sense that in Him God's reconciling of man and man's reconciliation with God are event. He exists in the sense that in this event God encounters and is revealed to all men as the gracious God and in this event again all men are placed under the consequence and outworking of this encounter and revelation. He exists in this action of God for and with all men and in that which happens to all men in the course of it. He exists in the totality of his being and work as the Mediator—He alone as the Mediator, but living and active in His mediatorial office. When we come to speak of Jesus Christ, therefore, it is necessary that what we have to say about Him particularly should for all its particularity be shown to be that which gathers together all that we said in relation to both the above and the below.

But at this point we have to make an important decision in relation to the form and method of the Christian doctrine of the atonement.

It was and is customary to have a single complete and self-contained chapter on Jesus Christ, the so-called "Christology," as the climax in the whole presentation. This includes (1) a special doctrine of the "person" of Christ, i.e., the incarnation of the Word of God, and also His Godhead and manhood in their relationship the one to the other, (2) a special doctrine of His work (following the *munus triplex* arrangement of the Reformation period), and usually (3) a special doctrine of the two "states" of Christ, His humiliation and exaltation. It is then customary to leave the Christology and to develop a special doctrine of the subjective application and appropriation of the salvation objectively accomplished by Jesus Christ, and finally a doctrine of the Church and the means of grace as the mediation between Christ and the Christian. It is also part of the traditional form of the doctrine, just to mention it in passing, that this whole complex is preceded by a doctrine of sin as its negative presupposition and the *terminus a quo* for the whole.

For the moment our question is simply this, whether it is actually the case that what we have to say concerning Jesus Christ can be gathered together in the one section on Christology, over against which there is a completely different section which includes what we have to say concerning man and the Church. This schematism seems logically very illuminating, and didactically useful. At a first glance it may even seem unavoidable from this standpoint. Yet it is not really calculated to enable us to expound the actual subject-matter. In the New Testament there are many christological statements both direct and indirect. But where do we find a special Christology?—a Christ in Himself, abstracted from what He is amongst the men of Israel and His disciples and the world, from what He is on their behalf? Does He ever exist except in this relationship? Certainly He is the absolutely dominating figure, the absolutely unique One in this environment. Certainly He is the determinative and creative subject of everything that takes place in it. But how and in what sense can He be separated from it and considered apart? Where and how else can He be seen and heard and grasped except as their revelation and grace and judgment and liberation and calling and promise, as the One who is absolutely with and for these men? And at what point do the New Testament writers leave their Christology behind? At what point does it not constantly advance in the form of new insights concerning both God and man?

We have said that Jesus Christ exists in the totality of His work as the Mediator. He alone is the One who fulfils it, but He does completely fulfil it, so that in and with what we have to say about Him in particular we necessarily speak about that comprehensive whole which constitutes its particularity.

But we shall do this either obscurely or not at all if we think that we can crystallise the necessary statements concerning Jesus Christ Himself and as such into a self-contained Christology, in which what He is and means and does and accomplishes for man is not yet revealed or revealed only in the far distance, which must be completed by a special presentation of the relevance of His existence for us, by a related but relatively autonomous soteriology and ecclesiology. The necessary result which this separation has always had is twofold. On the one hand Christology takes on the appearance of an ontology and dramatics arbitrarily constructed from Scripture and tradition. The bearing of it may or may not be seen, but in any case it can never emerge from the half-light of the contingency or non-necessity of a purely historical record or even the recitation of a myth. On the other hand, soteriology and ecclesiology either as a doctrine of the grace and justification and sanctification which comes to us or simply as a doctrine of Christian piety can never escape the tendency to commend itself in relation to Christology, and ultimately to free itself from it, as that which is true and essential, as that which is of practical importance and necessity, as that which is "existentially relevant." And at a pinch can we not omit and dispense with Christology altogether as a doctrine of the being and work of Christ as such? In the last resort, even if we do away with the christological preliminaries, can we not still succeed in working out either a doctrine of grace, of sanctification or justification, or a practical individual or congregational life as such—especially in relation to the non-Christian world? Is not the Christology ultimately only so much ballast which can be jettisoned without loss?—especially when this appears to be desirable on historico-critical and philosophical grounds? On two sides the traditional order has given too much occasion for this kind of division and abstraction for us not to have to ask seriously whether we ought still to follow it. What is said about Jesus Christ Himself, the christological propositions as such are constitutive, essential, necessary and central in the Christian doctrine of reconciliation. In them we have to do with that one whole. They cannot, therefore, bear that respectful isolation with which they have been and are so often treated. They cannot and will not stand alone and be true alone, with all the other statements about God and man and sin and grace and justification and the Church true alongside them. Rather they must be represented and thought of as the statement from which all truth derives, which control the whole nexus, which themselves constitute and reveal this nexus. Self-evidently they have to be made, they cannot simply disappear, their own content must not be dissolved, they cannot be transposed into purely interpretative subordinate statements descriptive of the grace actual and active in Jesus Christ. Otherwise we would be well on the way to asserting the autonomy of the event of atonement in relation to the One who must be regarded and understood as the subject, executor and Lord.

To all appearances Franz Hermann Reinhold Frank has not escaped this tendency, although of all modern dogmaticians he is of special interest in that he felt strongly, as I see it, the problematical nature of the traditional order and made the most determined efforts to overcome it. The whole doctrine of the atonement (which he calls "regeneration") is brought by him (*Syst. der Chr. Wahrheit*, 2, 2, 1886) under the one concept of the "evolving humanity of God with its centre in the divine-human redeemer." He then describes how this "humanity of God" evolved in fallen humanity and especially in Israel for the sake of the God-man, how it was posited in the person of the God-man in order to grow out of the God-man: objectively by the Holy Spirit and the means of grace in word and sacrament; subjectively in the *ordo salutis* of justifying and renewing faith; objectively-subjectively in the existence of the Church. Here we have a powerful concern—in its own way it amounts to what we can only call a genius—to see together what traditional dogmatics had always separated, the God-man and the humanity of God. And in its own way it is very impressive. But we have to ask whether in spite of his fine "for the sake of" and "in" and "out of" Frank has not (in an excess of good intention) slipped speculatively into a view which alters ever so slightly the Christian message. His main theme is the regenerate "humanity of God." The God-man is rightly described as the centre, but He is pictured only in this function, being made subservient to the evolving and positing and growing of the humanity of God. But while it is true that He does serve this end, does this exhaust what He is for it and in relation to it? Ontologically is it not a matter of Him first, and only then and in Him of the "humanity of God"?

On the one side, then, our task is so to present the doctrine of reconciliation that it is always clear that it has to do wholly and utterly with Jesus Christ, that He is the active subject (and not simply a means or predicate of its happening). This means that we have to develop and present the doctrine of reconciliation in the light of definite christological perceptions and propositions, focussing attention upon Jesus Christ as the beginning and the middle and the end. And it is clear that to do this we must introduce what we have to say particularly about Jesus Christ in all its particularity into the basis of every individual thought-sequence. For in its particularity it includes within itself the whole. But, on the other hand, it is our task not to separate what we have to say particularly about Jesus Christ but to bring it into immediate connexion with what He is not for Himself but for us, what He is as the One who makes reconciliation, as the One who fulfils the covenant, as the One in whom the world and man have been and are converted to God. This means that we have to indicate the fact and the extent to which He does in fact establish and control this happening, to which He is its beginning and middle and end. It is clear, then, that what we have to say particularly about Jesus Christ can only be the culminating sentence in every thought-sequence, the sentence which controls the whole, and in the light of which we can apply ourselves seriously to the problems of soteriology and ecclesiology, of the application and appropriation of the salvation which appeared in Him and was given to man, the problem, therefore, of the existence of the community.

But who is He, the One who is the middle point, the Mediator between the reconciling action of God and the reconciled being of man, in whom both at once are actual and revealed? If we have rightly grasped and described the event of reconciliation in these two main points, then we shall not be mistaken if in relation to the Mediator Jesus Christ we start with the fact that in Him—we will make a general statement and then explain it later—we have to do wholly with God and wholly with man, and with both in their complete and utter unity. Not with any god, but with the God who in all the divine freedom of His love, in all His omnipotence and holiness and eternity, is gracious and merciful and long-suffering, who is this not as the One who is self-existent, self-reposing and self-motivated, but in His movement to man. And not with any man, but with the man who in all his creaturely and earthly humanity is converted to God and willing and ready in relation to Him, who is only as he is thankful and therefore obedient. And not with any relationship between them, not with a mere encounter and mutual correspondence, not with a mere being together, but with their unity, with the being of God in and with the human being of man, with the being of man in and with the divine being of God. This is Jesus Christ. We cannot avoid the old formula: very God, very man, very God-man. It is as this One that He is the middle point, and the being of God in His sovereign action of grace and the being of reconciled man are both in Him and are both one in Him. As this One He is the subject of the act of reconciliation between God and all men. As this One He is known in the Christian community: its Lord, the Messiah of Israel, the Saviour of the world, the object of its faith, the basis of its love, the content of its hope.

We hasten to explain that the being of Jesus Christ, the unity of being of the living God and this living man, takes place in the event of the concrete existence of this man. It is a being, but a being in a history. The gracious God is in this history, so is reconciled man, so are both in their unity. And what takes place in this history, and therefore in the being of Jesus Christ as such, is atonement. Jesus Christ is not what He is—very God, very man, very God-man—in order as such to mean and do and accomplish something else which is atonement. But His being as God and man and God-man consists in the completed act of the reconciliation of man with God.

We are again faced with a critical decision in relation to the form of the doctrine of reconciliation.

We have seen that a distinction was and is made between a doctrine of the "person" and a doctrine of the "work" of Christ: *De persona Christi θεανθρώπου* and *De officio Christi mediatorio*. Of the conceptual perspicacity of the two titles and the convenience of the division there can be no question. But, again, we have to consider whether it corresponds to the facts, i.e., whether Jesus Christ is rightly seen if first of all (to follow especially the thinking of the Eastern Church) He is seen in a being which does, of course, rest on an act, the incarnation, but which—introduced and established in this way—is as a *unio* of the person of the Logos and therefore of the divine nature with the human only a static and idle being, not an act or a work—and only then (here we come to the special interest of the Western Church) seen in a work, which does, of course, have its presupposition in that being, but only a formal presupposition, not being identical with it. We have to ask again whether there is in the New Testament any precedent for this division of approach and concept. In the Fourth Gospel does the Son of God exist in any other way than in the doing of the work given Him by the Father? Does the Jesus of the Synoptics exist in any other way than in His addresses and conversations and miracles, and finally His going up to Jerusalem? Does the Christ of Paul exist in any other way than as the Crucified and Risen? Does the New Testament *kyrios* generally ever exist except in the accomplishment and revelation of His ministry and lordship as such? Certainly it is always a matter of His divine and human being and of both in their unity, not yet described in the formulæ of the 4th and 5th centuries, but with no other meaning and intention in relation to the presupposed content. The only thing is that we have to seek the presupposition, the answer to the question "Whom say men that I am?" (Mk. $8^{27}$), not behind but directly within the speech and action and living and suffering and dying (Mt. $11^{4f.}$) of the New Testament Jesus or Christ or Jesus Christ. The consequences of abstraction at this point can never be good. We must not forget that if in the doctrinal decisions of Nicaea and Constantinople and Ephesus and Chalcedon it was a matter of the being of Jesus Christ as such, these decisions had a polemical and critical character, their purpose being to delimit and clarify at a specific point. They are to be regarded as guiding lines for an understanding of His existence and action, not to be used, as they have been used, as stones for the construction of an abstract doctrine of His "person." In Himself and as such the Christ of Nicaea and Chalcedon naturally was and is a being which even if we could consistently and helpfully explain His unique structure conceptually could not possibly be proclaimed and believed as One who acts historically because of the timelessness and historical remoteness of the concepts (person, nature, Godhead, manhood, etc.). He could not possibly be proclaimed and believed as the One whom in actual fact the Christian Church has always and everywhere proclaimed and believed under the name of Jesus Christ. An abstract doctrine of the person of Christ may have its own apparent importance, but it is always an empty form, in which what we have to say concerning Jesus Christ can never be said. Again, it is almost inevitable that a doctrine of the work of Christ separated from that of His person will sooner or later give rise to the question, and perhaps even impose it, whether this work cannot be understood as that of someone other than that divine-human person. Can we not make use of the concept of a created *tertium quid* (as in certain gnostic speculations concerning angels), or more simply of a man specially endowed with divine grace, to help us to understand the subject of this action? Is not such a concept more serviceable than the *vere Deus vere homo* of a doctrine of the person which is merely presupposed? If this is the way of it, an abstract doctrine of the work of Christ will always tend secretly in a direction where some kind of Arianism or Pelagianism lies in wait. What is needed in this matter is nothing more or less than the removal of the distinction between the two basic sections of classical Christology, or positively, the restoration of the hyphen which always connects them and makes them one in the New Testament. Not to the detriment of either the one or the other. Not to sacrifice the Eastern interest to the Western. Not to cause the doctrine of the person of Christ to be absorbed and dissolved in that of His work, or *vice versa*. But to give a proper place to them both, and to establish them both securely in that place.

It is in the particular fact and the particular way that Jesus Christ is very God, very man, and very God-man that He works, and He works in the fact and only in the fact that He is this One and not another. His being as this One is His history, and His history is this His being. This is the truth which must light up the doctrine of reconciliation as Christology. When this is done, it will naturally follow that, as a whole, as a doctrine of the justifying and sanctifying and calling grace of God, as a doctrine of thankfulness, of faith and love and hope, as a doctrine of the community, its human and divine reality, its existence and task, it will be completely dominated and determined by Christology. It will also follow that Christology will not be idle or come under the suspicion that it may be dispensed with. It will take its place without diminution or alteration as the necessary beginning. And it will work itself out in the whole.

## 4. The Three Forms of the Doctrine of Reconciliation

If in this sense and with this understanding we return to the being of Jesus Christ as we have briefly defined it, we find at once that there are three "christological" aspects in the narrower sense—aspects of His active person or His personal work which as such broaden into three perspectives for an understanding of the whole event of the atonement.

The first is that in Jesus Christ we have to do with very God. The reconciliation of man with God takes place as God Himself actively intervenes, Himself taking in hand His cause with and against and for man, the cause of the covenant, and in such a way (this is what distinguishes the event of reconciliation from the general sway of the providence and universal rule of God) that He Himself becomes man. God became man. That is what is, i.e., what has taken place, in Jesus Christ. He is very God acting for us men, God Himself become man. He is the authentic Revealer of God as Himself God. Again, He is the effective proof of the power of God as Himself God. Yet again, He is the fulfiller of the covenant as Himself God. He is nothing less or other than God Himself, but God as man. When we say God we say honour and glory and eternity and power, in short, a regnant freedom as it is proper to Him who is distinct from and superior to everything else that is. When we say God we say the Creator and Lord of all things. And we can say all that without reservation or diminution of Jesus Christ—but in a way in which it can be said in relation to Him, i.e., in which it corresponds to the Godhead of God active and revealed in Him. No general idea of "Godhead" developed abstractly from such concepts must be allowed to intrude at this point. How the freedom of God is constituted, in what character He is the Creator and Lord of all things, distinct from and superior to them, in short, what is to be understood by "Godhead," is something which—watchful against all imported ideas, ready to correct them and perhaps to let them be reversed and renewed in the most astonishing way—we must always learn from Jesus Christ. He defines those concepts: they do not define Him. When we start with the fact that He is very God we are forced to keep strictly to Him in relation to what we mean by true "Godhead."

This means primarily that it is a matter of the Godhead, the honour and glory and eternity and omnipotence and freedom, the being as Creator and Lord, of the Father, Son and Holy Spirit. Jesus Christ is Himself God as the Son of God the Father and with God the Father the source of the Holy Spirit, united in one essence with the Father by the Holy Spirit. That is how He is God. He is God as He takes part in the event which constitutes the divine being.

We must add at once that as this One who takes part in the divine being and event He became and is man. This means that we have to understand the very Godhead, that divine being and event and therefore Himself as the One who takes part in it, in the light of the fact that it pleased God—and this is what corresponds outwardly to and reveals the inward divine being and event—Himself to become man. In this way, in this condescension, He is the eternal Son of the eternal Father. This is the will of this Father, of this Son, and of the Holy Spirit who is the Spirit of the Father and the Son. This is how God is God, this is His freedom, this is His distinctness from and superiority to all other reality. It is with this meaning and purpose that He is the Creator and Lord of all things. It is as the eternal and almighty love, which He is actually and visibly in this action of condescension. This One, the One who loves in this way, is the true God. But this means that He is the One who as the Creator and Lord of all things is able and willing to make Himself equal with the creature, Himself to become a creature; the One whose eternity does not prevent but rather permits and commands Him to be in time and Himself to be temporal, whose omnipotence is so great that He can be weak and indeed impotent, as a man is weak and impotent. He is the One who in His freedom can and does in fact bind Himself, in the same way as we all are bound. And we must go further: He, the true God, is the One whose Godhead is demonstrated and plainly consists in essence in the fact that, seeing He is free in His love, He is capable of and wills this condescension for the very reason that in man of all His creatures He has to do with the one that has fallen away from Him, that has been unfaithful and hostile and antagonistic to Him. He is God in that He takes this creature to Himself, and that in such a way that He sets Himself alongside this creature, making His own its penalty and loss and condemnation to nothingness. He is God in the fact that He can give Himself up and does give Himself up not merely to the creaturely limitation but to the suffering of the human creature, becoming one of these men, Himself bearing the judgment under which they stand, willing to die and, in fact, dying the death which they have deserved. That is the nature and essence of the true God as He has intervened actively and manifestly in Jesus Christ. When we speak of Jesus Christ we mean the true God—He who seeks His divine glory and finds that glory, He whose glory obviously consists, in the fact that because He is free in His love He can be and actually is lowly as well as exalted; He, the Lord, who is for us a servant, the servant of all servants. It is in the light of the fact of His humiliation that on this first aspect all the predicates of His Godhead, which is the true Godhead, must be filled out and interpreted. Their positive meaning is lit up only by this determination and limitation, only by the fact that in this act He is this God and therefore the true God, distinguished from all false gods by the fact that they are not capable of this act, that they have not in fact accomplished it, that their supposed glory and honour and eternity and omnipotence not only do not include but exclude their self-humiliation. False gods are all reflections of a false and all too human self-exaltation. They are all lords who cannot and will not be servants, who are therefore no true lords, whose being is not a truly divine being.

The second christological aspect is that in Jesus Christ we have to do with a true man. The reconciliation of the world with God takes place in the person of a man in whom, because He is also true God, the conversion of all men to God is an actual event. It is the person of a true man, like all other men in every respect, subjected without exception to all the limitations of the human situation. The conditions in which other men exist and their suffering are also His conditions and His suffering. That He is very God does not mean that He is partly God and only partly man. He is altogether man just as He is altogether God—altogether man in virtue of His true Godhead whose glory consists in His humiliation. That is how He is the reconciler between God and man. That is how God accomplishes in

Him the conversion of all men to Himself. He is true man, and altogether man, for in Him we have to do with the manifestation of the glory of the One who is true God and altogether God, and with the conversion to God of the One who is true man and altogether man. Here, too, there is no reservation and no diminution, which would be an immediate denial of the act of atonement made in Him. Jesus Christ is man in a different way from what we are. That is why He is our Mediator with God. But He is so in a complete equality of His manhood with ours. To say man is to say creature and sin, and this means limitation and suffering. Both these have to be said of Jesus Christ. Not, however, according to the standard of general concepts, but only with reference to Him, only in correspondence with His true manhood. As in relation to His Godhead, so also in relation to His manhood, we must not allow any necessary idea of the human situation and its need to intervene. What His manhood is, and therefore true manhood, we cannot read into Him from elsewhere, but must be told by Him. But then we find that it is a matter of the manhood of the eternal Son of God. It is a matter of the real limitation and suffering of the man with whom the high God has ordained and elected and determined to be one, and has therefore humbled Himself. In His limitation and suffering, this is the true man. And that means at once that He is the man exalted by God, lifted above His need and limitation and suffering in and out of His need and limitation and suffering. In virtue of the fact that He is one with God He is free man. He is a creature, but superior to His creatureliness. He is bound by sin, but quite free in relation to it because He is not bound to commit it. He is mortal, and has actually died as we must all die. But in dying He is superior to death, and at once and altogether rescued from it, so that (even as a man like us) He is triumphant and finally alive. As the true God, i.e., the God who humbles Himself, Jesus Christ is this true man, i.e., the man who in all His creatureliness is exalted above His creatureliness. In this He is also exalted above us, because He is different from us, and is given the precedence in the ranks of our common humanity. But He does precede us. As God He was humbled to take our place, and as man He is exalted on our behalf. He is set at the side of God in the humanity which is ours. He is above us and opposed to us, but He is also for us. What has happened in Him as the one true man is the conversion of all of us to God, the realisation of true humanity. It is anticipated in Him, but it is in fact accomplished and revealed. As in Him God became like man, so too in Him man has become like God. As in Him God was bound, so too in Him man is made free. As in Him the Lord became a servant, so too in Him the servant has become a Lord. That is the atonement made in Jesus Christ in its second aspect. In Him humanity is exalted humanity, just as Godhead is humiliated Godhead. And humanity is exalted in Him by the humiliation of Godhead. We cannot regard the human being of Jesus Christ, we cannot—without denying or weakening them—interpret His predicates of liability to sin and suffering and death, in any other way than in the light of the liberation and exaltation accomplished in His unity with God. It is in its impotence that His being as man is omnipotent, in its temporality that it is eternal, in its shame that it is glorious, in its corruptibility that it is incorruptible, in its servitude that it is that of the Lord. In this way, therefore, it is His true being as man—true humanity.

> The Evangelists clung to this in their representation of the human being of Jesus Christ. They left no doubt that it was a human being like others, but even less so that as such it was the human being of the true God, and therefore in spite of its likeness to all others distinguished from all others in its freedom in face of limitation and suffering. From the very first they describe it in the light and clear reference of the final thing they have to report concerning Him: His resurrection from the dead as the event in which His exaltation cannot merely be discerned but is openly manifested—lighting up both that which precedes and that which follows. Therefore they describe the man Jesus as the One who, being tempted and suffering and dying as King, overcomes as King, and therefore passes through the midst of all others as King. That is how we must see Him.

In so far as He was and is and will be very man, the conversion of man to God took place in Him, the turning and therefore the reconciliation of all men, the fulfilment of the covenant. And in the light of Jesus Christ the man who is still not free in relation to limitation and suffering, who is still not exalted, who is still lowly (lowly, as it were, *in abstracto*), can be understood only as false man—just as in the light of Jesus Christ the empty loveless gods which are incapable of condescension and self-humiliation can be understood only as false gods.

> Before we pass on to the third christological aspect, we may at this point interpose another discussion concerning the method of treating the doctrine of reconciliation. In considering the first two aspects we brought together in rather an unusual way two elements in traditional Christology: the doctrine of the two "natures" of Christ, His deity and humanity, and the doctrine of the

two "states" of Christ, His humiliation (*status exinanitionis*) and His exaltation (*status exaltationis*). We must now consider to what extent this presentation involves a change in traditional Christology and soteriology, and how far that change is right and necessary.

In comparison with older dogmatics, our presentation has undoubtedly the advantage that it does far greater justice to the particular doctrine of the two states.

In the older Lutherans this doctrine forms a great excursus in the doctrine of the human nature of Christ, which as they understood it was not merely exalted in the incarnation but actually divinised, i.e., according to their particular doctrine of the communication of the attributes furnished with all the attributes of Godhead. For them the only significance of the doctrine of the two states was that it answered what was for them the very difficult question how far Jesus Christ could have lived and suffered and died as a real man in time and space and under all the other restrictions of human life. For them *exinanitio* meant that for a time, for the period of His life up to and including death, the God-man denies Himself that divinisation of His humanity (either by concealment or by genuine renunciation), but then reassumes it with the *exaltatio* which begins with His triumphant descent into hell.

The older Reformed writers described the two states rather obscurely as the humiliation and exaltation of the divine Logos, and with them the doctrine is simply left in the air, following that of the work of Christ but not organically related to it. It was brought in for the sake of completeness, but on their presuppositions it had only an incidental application. If our presentation is right, then at least the doctrine of the humiliation and exaltation of Christ does acquire a place and function in line with its scriptural and factual importance. But this necessitates certain decisive innovations in relation to the older dogmatics which we must openly admit and for which we must give our reasons.

Now (1) we have not spoken of two "states" (*status*) of Jesus Christ which succeed one another, but of two sides or directions or forms of that which took place in Jesus Christ for the reconciliation of man with God. We used the concepts humiliation and exaltation, and we thought of Jesus Christ as the servant who became Lord and the Lord who became servant. But in so doing we were not describing a being in the particular form of a state, but the twofold action of Jesus Christ, the actuality of His work: His one work, which cannot be divided into different stages or periods of His existence, but which fills out and constitutes His existence in this twofold form. Our question is whether this does not better correspond to the witness of the New Testament concerning Jesus Christ. Where and when is He not both humiliated and exalted, already exalted in His humiliation, and humiliated in His exaltation? Where in Paul, for example, is He the Crucified who has not yet risen, or the Risen who has not been crucified? Would He be the One whom the New Testament attests as the Mediator between God and man if He were only the one and not the other? And if He is the Mediator, which of the two can He be alone and without the other? Both aspects force themselves upon us. We have to do with the being of the one and entire Jesus Christ whose humiliation detracts nothing and whose exaltation adds nothing. And in this His being we have to do with His action, the work and event of atonement. That is the first reason for this alteration of the traditional dogmatic form.

But even more penetrating (2) is the fact that understanding the doctrine of the two states in this way we have tried to interpret it in the light of the doctrine of the two natures, and *vice versa*.

Notice that there can be no question of abandoning the *vere Deus vere homo*. If it is a matter of the reconciliation of man with God in Jesus Christ, i.e., the reconciliation of man with God and by God, then obviously we have to do truly and wholly with God and truly and wholly with man. And the more exact determination of the relationship between God and man in the famous Chalcedonian definition, which has become normative for all subsequent development in this dogma and dogmatics, is one which in our understanding has shown itself to be factually right and necessary. But according to our understanding there can be no question of a doctrine of the two natures which is autonomous, a doctrine of Jesus Christ as God and man which is no longer or not yet related to the divine action which has taken place in Him, which does not have this action and man as its subject matter. There is no such doctrine in the New Testament, although we cannot say that the New Testament envisages the being and relationship of God and man in Jesus Christ in any other way than it became conceptually fixed in the doctrine of the two natures.

Similarly, there can be no autonomous doctrine of the humiliation and exaltation which took place in Jesus Christ, especially without a reference to what took place in Jesus Christ between God as God and man as man. There is a humiliation and exaltation—it hardly needs to be demonstrated that in Phil. 2[6f.] and indeed all the New Testament Jesus Christ is regarded in the light of these two aspects and concepts. But if there is, it is not something incidental to His being. It is the actuality of the being of Jesus Christ as very God and very man. We cannot, therefore, ascribe to Jesus Christ two natures and then quite independently two states. But we have to explain in mutual relationship to one another what Jesus Christ is as very God and very man and what takes place as the divine work of atonement in His humiliation and exaltation.

But this brings us (3) to what is perhaps the greatest objection which might be brought against our presentation from the standpoint of the older dogmatics. To explain in the light of each other the deity and humanity of Jesus Christ on the one hand and His humiliation and exaltation on the other means that in Jesus Christ God—we do not say casts off His Godhead but (as the One who loves in His sovereign freedom) activates and proves it by the fact that He gives Himself to the limitation and suffering of the human creature, that He, the Lord, becomes a servant, that as distinct from all false gods He humbles Himself —and again, that in Jesus Christ man, without any forfeiture or restriction of His humanity, in the power of His deity and therefore in the power of and thanks to the humiliation of God, is the man who is freed from His limitation and suffering, not divinised man, but man sovereign and set at the side of God, in short, man exalted by God. The humiliation, therefore, is the humiliation of God, the exaltation the exaltation of man: the humiliation of God to supreme glory, as the activation and demonstration of His divine being; and the exaltation of man as the work of God's grace which consists in the restoration of his true humanity. Can we really put it in this way? We have to put it in this way if we are really speaking of the deity and humanity of Jesus Christ, of *His* humiliation and exaltation, of *His* being and *His* work.

For who is the God who is present and active in Him? He is the One who, concretely in His being as man, activates and reveals Himself as divinely free, as the One who loves in His freedom, as the One who is capable of and willing for this inconceivable condescension, and the One who can be and wills to be true God not only in the height but also in the depth—in the depth of human creatureliness, sinfulness and mortality.

And who is the man Jesus Christ? He is the One in whom God is man, who is completely bound by the human situation, but who is not crushed by it, who since it is His situation is free in relation to it, who overcomes it, who is its Lord and not its servant.

Conversely, what is the humiliation of Jesus Christ? To say that He is lowly as a man is tautology which does not help us in the least to explain His humiliation. It merely contains the general truth that He exists as a man in the bondage and suffering of the human situation, and is to that extent actually lowly—a general truth which is in fact very forcibly called in question by the humanity of Jesus Christ. But the peculiar thing about the humiliation of Jesus Christ, the significant thing, the effective thing, the redemptive thing, is that it is the work of atonement in its first form. In Him it took place that while maintaining His true deity God became man, in Him to make His own the cause of man. In Him God Himself humiliated Himself—not in any disloyalty but in a supreme loyalty to His divine being (revealing it in a way which marks it off from all other gods). That is the secret of Christmas and Good Friday and the way which leads from the one to the other. Jesus Christ is the Reconciler of all men of all times and places by the fact that in Him God is active and revealed as the One who in His freedom, in His divine majesty, so loves that in Him the Lord became a servant, a servant like all of us, but more than that, the servant of us all, the man who did for us what we ourselves would not and could not do.

Again, what is the exaltation of Jesus Christ? To say that as God He is transcendent, free, sovereign, above the world, and therefore above the limitation and suffering of the human situation is again tautology which does not help us to understand His exaltation. God is always free in His love, transcendent God. He does not cease to be God transcendent when He makes it His glory to be in the depths, in order to make peace on earth to the men of His goodwill. In His Godhead, as the eternal Son of the Father, as the eternal Word, Jesus Christ never ceased to be transcendent, free, and sovereign. He did not stand in need of exaltation, nor was He capable of it. But He did as man—it is here again that we come up against that which is not self-evident in Jesus Christ. The special thing, the new thing about the exaltation of Jesus Christ is that One who is bound as we are is free, who is tempted as we are is without sin, who is a sufferer as we are is able to minister to Himself and others, who is a victim to death is alive even though He was dead, who is a servant (the servant of all servants) is the Lord. This is the secret of His humanity which is revealed in His resurrection and ascension and therefore shown retrospectively by the Evangelists to be the secret of His whole life and death. It is not simply that He is the Son of God at the right hand of the Father, the *Kyrios*, the Lord of His community and the Lord of the cosmos, the bearer and executor of divine authority in the Church and the world, but that He is all this as a man—as a man like we are, but a man exalted in the power of His deity. This is what makes Him the Mediator between God and man, and the One who fulfils the covenant.

If we have correctly related these four considerations concerning the deity, the humanity, the humiliation and the exaltation of Jesus Christ, we not only can but must speak as we have done on this matter. The doctrine of reconciliation in its first two forms will then necessarily begin with a discussion of the God who humbles Himself in Jesus Christ and of the man who in Jesus Christ is exalted.

In the light of this we shall have to consider the whole event of atonement twice over, examining it in detail. The correct titles for these first two sections will be "Jesus Christ, the Lord as Servant" and "Jesus Christ, the Servant as Lord." We shall still follow the traditional path to the extent that in content and meaning this division corresponds exactly to what earlier dogmatics worked out as the doctrine of the high-priestly and kingly office of Christ (in the framework of that doctrine of the threefold office of Christ in which they used to picture His work). I prefer the first two titles as more precise and also more comprehensive (since they also include the earlier doctrine of the person of Christ).

The third christological aspect to which we must now turn is at once the simplest and the highest. It is the source of the two first, and it comprehends them both. As the God who humbles Himself and therefore reconciles man with Himself, and as the man exalted by God and therefore reconciled with Him, as the One who is very God and very man in this concrete sense, Jesus Christ Himself is one. He is the "God-man," that is, the Son of God who as such is this man, this man who as such is the Son of God.

The New Testament obviously speaks of Jesus Christ in both these ways: the one looking and moving, as it were, from above downwards, the other from below upwards. It would be idle to try to conclude which of the two is the more original, authentic and important. Both are necessary. Neither can stand or be understood without the other. A Christ who did not come in the flesh, who was not identical with the Jesus of Nazareth who suffered and died under Pontius Pilate, would not be the Christ Jesus—and a Jesus who was not the eternal Word of God, and who as man was not raised again from the dead, would not be the Jesus Christ—of the New Testament. The New Testament, it is true, knows nothing of the formulæ of later ecclesiastical Christology, which tried to formulate the two aspects with conceptual strictness. But it knows even less of the docetic and ebionite abstractions, the attempts to make absolute either the Godhead or the manhood, which it was the concern of the later Christology to rebut. In fact the one aspect is given the greater prominence at this point, the other at that. But it knows only the one person, Jesus Christ Himself, who without division or distinction is both God and man. We remember: both, not in a general and arbitrarily determined sense of the concepts, but in that sense which has been specifically filled out and made concrete. We must never lose sight of Him in the (often very abstract) content given to the concepts in the fathers and later development. The One who is both in this concrete sense is the Jesus Christ of the New Testament. To understand, we must emphasise the phrase: the One who is both—both, and not a third between God and man or a mixture of the two. The Judaic and Hellenistic environment of the New Testament did know such mixtures. The New Testament speaks the language of this environment, but it does not speak of this kind of third. The concrete views of God and man which it has before it in Jesus Christ cannot be mixed but can only be seen together as the forms of a history: the reconciling God and the man reconciled by Him. In face of the history which took place in Jesus Christ the New Testament says that these two elements of the one grace, the divine and the human, are one in Him, not in one form but in two. For that reason its statements concerning Him always move in either the one direction or the other, from above downwards or from below upwards. The only statement in the New Testament which brings together both in one is properly the name of Jesus Christ, which forbids and makes quite impossible any separation of the one from the other or any fusion of both in a third. When, therefore, the later Christology safeguarded against any confusion or transmutation of the two natures the one into the other and therefore into a third, the innovation was not one of substance but only of theology, and one which the substance itself demanded.

There can be no question of our trying to see a third thing in what we have called the third christological aspect. Everything that can be said materially concerning Jesus Christ and the atonement made in Him has been said exhaustively in the twofold fact—which cannot be further reduced conceptually but only brought together historically—that He is very God and very man, i.e., the Lord who became a servant and the servant who became Lord, the reconciling God and reconciled man. The third aspect can be only the viewing of this history in its unity and completeness, the viewing of Jesus Christ Himself, in whom the two lines cross—in the sense that He Himself is the subject of what takes place on these two lines. To that extent the reconciliation of the world with God and the conversion of the world to God took place in Him. To that extent He Himself, His existence, is this reconciliation. He Himself is the Mediator and pledge of the covenant. He is the Mediator of it in that He fulfils it— from God to man and from man to God. He is the pledge of it in that in His existence He confirms and maintains and reveals it as an authentic witness—attesting Himself, in that its fulfilment is present and shines out and avails and is effective in Him. This is the new thing in the third christological aspect. Jesus Christ is the actuality of the atonement, and as such the truth of it which speaks for itself. If we hear Jesus Christ, then whether we realise it or not we hear this truth. If we say Jesus Christ, then whether we realise it or not we express and repeat this truth: the truth of the grace in which God has turned to the world in Him and which has come to the world in Him; the truth of the living brackets which bring and hold together heaven and earth, God and all men, in Him; the truth that God has bound Himself to man and that man is bound to God. The One who bears this name is Himself this truth in that He is Himself this actuality. He attests what He is. He alone is the pledge of it because He alone is the Mediator of it. He alone is the truth of it. But He is that truth, and therefore it speaks for itself in Him. It is not in us. We cannot produce it of ourselves. We cannot of ourselves attest it to ourselves or to others. But it encounters us majestically in Him—the promise of the truth which avails for us as the atonement—of which it is the truth—took place for us and as ours, the truth which for that reason can and should be heard and accepted and appropriated by us, which we can and should accept as the truth which applies to us. It encounters us in Him as the promise of our own future. It is He, and therefore the actuality of our atonement, who stands before us. It is to Him, and therefore to the revelation of this actuality, that we move. He is the Word of God to men which speaks of God and man and therefore expresses and discloses and reveals God and ourselves—God in His actual relationship to us and us in our actual relationship to God. He is the Word of God by which He calls us in this relationship and therefore calls us to Him and therefore calls us also to ourselves. He was and is the will of God to speak this Word—this Word of His act. And it is our destiny to hear this Word, to live under and with and by this Word. That is the third christological aspect.

Of the doctrine of reconciliation as such we must now say that in the light of this aspect a third and concluding section will be necessary in our presentation: concluding, but at the same time opening up and forming a transition to the doctrine of the redemption or consummation, the "eschatology" in which all dogmatics culminate. It is easy to find a title for this third section: "Jesus Christ the Guarantor." "Jesus Christ the Witness" would also be possible and impressive, but it might be understood too formally, whereas the neutral concept "guarantor" expresses more clearly what we are trying to say—that He who is Himself the material content of the atonement, the Mediator of it, stands security with man as well as God that it is our atonement—He Himself being the form of it as well as the content.

In this section we shall be dealing substantially with what the older dogmatics used to present as the doctrine of the "prophetic" office of Christ. We can only say that as compared with the doctrines of the *munus sacerdotale* and the *munus regium*—which it normally preceded as a kind of unaccented syllable —this doctrine played a rather difficult part and one which did not seem to shed any very great light of its own. It was hardly related, if at all, to the first two offices, and for that reason it had a largely formal character and could be left out altogether by some of the later writers. And it was because its proper role could not be found in the orthodox period that at the time of the *Aufklärung* it emerged from its decline in a form which was fatal. For it now pushed to the forefront as the supposed truth behind all Christology, but in the form of the representation of Jesus as the supreme teacher and example of perfect divine and human love—a representation which has practically nothing in common with the biblical concept of prophecy. The result was that the doctrines of the priestly and kingly office of Christ were now pushed back into the same obscurity of the less important in which this doctrine itself had laboured for so long. The atonement as a work of divine grace for man and to man, which means, the whole actuality of Jesus Christ, was necessarily concealed apart from a few confused and tedious and not very profitable relics. That this may not happen again, we must give due weight to the *munus propheticum* in its proper content and its peculiar significance.

It is not a matter of the content of truth but of the character of truth, of the identity of the divine work of grace with the divine Word of grace, of Jesus Christ who not only is what He is and does what He does but in so doing encounters us, testifying to us, addressing us, promising to us, pledging Himself to us, in all His majesty summoning us—in the right sense as a teacher and example—to come to Him, and in that way His own prophet, the prophet of His future as ours and ours as His.

We have to develop the whole doctrine of reconciliation in accordance with our Christology and the three basic christological aspects. We shall do so in three sections which correspond to the three aspects. The Christology is the key to the whole. From each of the three aspects suggested it will be our starting point and will necessarily control all the detailed developments. But in the light of the Christology there have to be these developments: the three great expositions of the fact and the extent to which the reconciliation of the world with God is actual in Him—in His servitude for us, in the humiliation of God for man which took place in Him, in His lordship over us, in the exaltation of man to God's glory which took place in Him, and all this as truth which He Himself has guaranteed and pledged.

But the christological bases of the doctrine of reconciliation bring us face to face at once and directly with a problem which has met us everywhere in this survey. This problem seems to form, as it were, a second and obscure centre side by side with Jesus Christ. The whole event of atonement seems to be strangely related to it on its negative side just as on its positive side it is grounded and enclosed in Jesus Christ. But so far we have not given it any independent consideration. It is the problem of the sin which has come into the world, or of man as the responsible author but also the poor victim of sin, the one who is blinded by it and closed to the truth. Atonement is the fulfilment by God of the covenant broken by man. Because he sins, and because the world is the world of sin and its consequences, man has need of conversion to God if he is not to perish. And it is in face of this, striving against and overcoming the sin of man, that God in His mercy does what He does, and there happens to man what does happen to him in the divine mercy when Jesus Christ intervenes as the Mediator of the covenant. It is clear that at this heart of its message Christian proclamation must speak very definitely of this hostile element, that therefore there has to be a very clear doctrine of sin in the Church's dogmatics.

But it must not be a doctrine of sin which is autonomous, which considers the matter and investigates and presents it in a vacuum, and therefore again abstractly.

> That is what we find in the older theology and, of course, in most modern theology as well. Between the doctrine of creation and that of the atonement it was and is customary (and logically it is very instructive and didactically most illuminating) to interpose a special section *De peccato*: a doctrine of the fall, of original sin and its consequences, of the state and constitution of sinful man, of individual or actual sins.

It cannot be disputed that this whole sphere—this dark prelude or counterpart to the divine covenant and work of grace—has to be taken very seriously. If there is to be any understanding of the Christian message, we have to investigate it closely and take it into account. There is in fact no page in the Bible in which it does not figure, and many pages in which it seems to do so almost alone. But all the same, we cannot with a good conscience follow the procedure which would give it a treatment which is independent, self-originating and self-contained.

For what is the ontological place of sin in the Bible? Surely not in a realm of its own where it has its own being and can exist in and for itself? In the sphere of Christian thinking at any rate, we cannot seriously and responsibly maintain that it was created by God and belongs, therefore, to the constitution of the world as He willed it. There is no support for any such view in what the Bible itself says. In the Bible sin in all its fearful reality is at a disadvantage compared with even the most modest creature in that it has only "entered into" the world, as we are told in Rom. $5^{12}$. It does not belong to the creation of God. It can be present and active within it only as an alien. It has no appointed place, no place which belongs to it. If it has its place, it is that of an usurpation against the creative will of God, the place of an interloper. It is there where it has no business at all to be as that which God has not willed. It is there where it has nothing either to seek or to tell. And only there can it be sought out and found. And even there, in its nothingness, it does not exist in any way on the basis of its own independent right, or even in its dreadful reality by its own independent power. How could it ever have any such right or power? It has its right, but it is the stolen right of wrong. It has its power, but it is the stealthy power of impotence. It exists and is only in opposition to the will of God and therefore in opposition to the being and destiny of His creature. It can only say No where God says Yes, and where in its own very different fashion the creature of God can also say Yes. When and where has the word and work of sin ever been a solemn Yes? It can only negate, deny, destroy, break down, dissolve. Even where God uses it in His service—and there is no doubt that it is under His lordship and must serve Him, as the Bible makes perfectly plain—it can serve only to fulfil His judgment, which is to shame and oppose and punish itself, or contrary to its own nature to accomplish some positive good in unwilling subservience to His higher control. It is neither a creature nor itself a creator. It is not only incapable of creation, but, being without root or soil in the creaturely world into which it has pushed its alien being, it is quite unproductive. In all its forms it exists and is only as that which negates and therefore as that which is itself negated, on the left hand of God, where God in saying Yes has already said No, where in electing He has rejected, where in willing He has not willed.

*[margin note: Christ is Lord even of that which God does not will]*

But the divine Yes which sin negates and by which it is negated is the Yes of God's covenant with man which is the mystery of creation—the covenant of grace concluded in Jesus Christ from all eternity and fulfilled and revealed in time. What God has determined and done as the Lord of this covenant is His will. The sin of man, being his doing and accomplishing of what God does not will, negates and withstands and rejects it. Sin is therefore not merely an evil, but a breach of the covenant which as such contradicts God and stands under His contradiction. Sin is man's denial of himself in face of the grace of His Creator. It is not directed against a so-called law of nature. There is no law of nature which is both recognisable as such and yet also has divine character and authority. There is no law and commandment of God inherent in the creatureliness of man as such, or written and revealed in the stars as a law of the cosmos, so that the transgression of it makes man a sinner. It is characteristic of the sin of man—and one of its results—that man should think he can know such a law of nature and direct and measure himself and others in accordance with it. But in his creatureliness, in his nature—which is the sum of his possibilities and destiny and nothing more—man is called to hold to the grace of His Creator, to be thankful for it, to bow to it and adapt himself to it, to honour it as the truth. And the essence of sin is that he does not do this. He denies and despises and hates grace and breaks its commandment, the law of the covenant. It is in this opposition that sin takes place, that it has its place and reality: as man's turning aside from God, and therefore as the perversion of his own nature; as the abuse and disturbance and destruction of the possibilities of his creaturely being and the radical compromising of his destiny.

This being the case, sin cannot be recognised and understood and defined and judged as sin in accordance with any general idea of man, or any law which is different from the grace of God and its commandment, the law of the covenant. If it takes place as a breach of the covenant, and not in any other way, it can be known only in the light of the covenant. But since man has broken the covenant, that can mean only in the light of the covenant fulfilled and restored in Jesus Christ and therefore in the light of the atonement made in Him. The Old Testament dispensation with its Law consists in the proclamation of it. But what in the Old Testament Law was meant to be the Law of the covenant of grace moving to its fulfilment has now been revealed by the actual fulfilment of the covenant, by the accomplishment in Jesus Christ of that which was proclaimed in the covenant of God with Israel. God wills what He has done in Jesus Christ. And in so doing He has brought in the Law given to man, the Law against which man as a covenant-breaker has sinned from the very first, the Law in whose transgression all human sin has consisted and does consist and will consist. In the light of Jesus Christ the darkness is revealed as such. It is made plain that man is a sinner. It is shown in what his sin consists. It is that being and acting and thinking and speaking and bearing of man which in Jesus Christ God has met, which in Him He has opposed and overcome and judged, which in Him He has passed over, in spite of which He has converted man to Himself in Him. God is the Lord of the covenant of grace and none else. As such He is revealed in the fulfilment of it and therefore in Jesus Christ, and not otherwise. What He has done in Him is His will with man and therefore that and nothing else is His commandment. But if this is the case, sin is simply that in which man contradicts this will of God, and because of which he for his part is decisively contradicted and opposed by this will of God. The knowledge of sin can relate only to what we are told concerning our being and activity by Jesus Christ as the Mediator and Guarantor of the atonement, to what we have to say after Him, if that knowledge is to be serious. And the confession of sin ("Against thee only have I sinned," Ps. 51[6]) can be accomplished only in the turning to Him and therefore in the knowledge of the conversion of man to God which has taken place in Him. Only in this way is it an actual confessing of real sin as opposed to outbreaks of remorse or depression or bemoaning or despair.

But this means that there can be no place in dogmatics for an autonomous section *De peccato* constructed in a vacuum between the doctrine of creation and that of reconciliation. Who can summon us to keep a law of God which is supposed to be known to man by nature? Who can try to measure the sin of man by such a law? To do that—even in the form of a "doctrine of sin"—is surely to do precisely what we are forbidden to do by the real Law of God revealed by God Himself. To do that is surely to pass by the grace of God, to evolve our own thoughts in relation to the will of God instead of those which He Himself has given us in the commandment held out before us in His grace. And is not this necessarily to sin again— theologically! Or, again, who can summon us in this matter of sin to follow the abstractly considered Law of the covenant of the Old Testament dispensation which is only moving to its fulfilment?—as though we had not yet heard or taken to heart the warnings of Paul against the *nomos* abstractly understood in this way; as though there were even one unconverted Jew who had come to a knowledge of his real sin by following this law; as though it were a good thing to advise Christians first to become such unconverted Jews and to follow this law, in order to push them forward from that point to what will certainly never be a knowledge of their real sin.

If we are not to be guilty of these two errors, we have no option but to consider and answer the question of sin in the light of the Gospel and therefore within the doctrine of reconciliation, to take it up into that doctrine instead of giving it precedence over it as though it were an autonomous question. In this context we shall find the natural place for it immediately after the Christology. It is in the knowledge of Jesus Christ as the revelation of the grace of God that we shall necessarily perceive step by step both the fact that man is a transgressor, and the nature of the transgression in which he contradicts the grace of God and for the sake of which he is decisively contradicted by that grace. Step by step, for if the content of the doctrine of sin—man's active opposition to the God who actively encounters him—is really to be brought out, the complex of the doctrine, like that of the Christology, demands a definite structure in which we will be safest to follow that of the Christology. Necessarily, therefore, it will appear not simply at one point, but at three points corresponding to the three christological bases of the three main sections of the doctrine of reconciliation, and at every point in a corresponding form.

Sin is obviously (1) the negation, the opposite of what God does for us in Jesus Christ in condescending to us, in humbling Himself, in becoming a servant to take to Himself and away from us our guilt and sickness. This is the grace of God in its first form: God gives Himself to us, He makes Himself responsible for our cause, He takes it into His own hand. And the commandment is clear—it is necessarily a matter of our basing our being and activity on the fact that God is ours, that we are the recipients of this gift which is so inconceivably great. Sin in its first form is pride. When God condescends to man, when He makes Himself one with Him in order to be truly his God, man cannot fall way from the work of this mercy of God to him. But what Adam did, what Israel did at all stages in its history, what the world does so long as it does not see itself as the world reconciled in Jesus Christ, what even the Christian does when he forgets that he is a Christian, is the very thing which is forbidden by this first form of grace, the very thing which is made impossible, which is excluded, which is negated because it is itself a negation. It is the fall in the form of presumption, acting as though God had not humbled Himself to man, as though He had not encountered man as the unfathomably merciful One, as though He had not taken to Himself the cause of man. Sin is man's act of defiance. In this first part of the doctrine of reconciliation the doctrine of sin will have to be described and portrayed in the closest connexion with the consideration of Jesus Christ as the Lord who became an obedient servant for us (and therefore with His high-priestly office). It will be characterised, therefore, as the act of pride.

But further, sin is (2) the negation, the opposite of what God did in Jesus Christ, the servant who became Lord, to exalt man—not to deity but to His own right hand in a fellowship of life with Himself. This is the grace of God in its second form: He wills and seeks us as we are, in our creatureliness, as men, that we may be raised to the status of children. That is why He humbled Himself. That is the meaning and force of His mercy. And again the commandment is clear—it is a matter of our being and activity as men in accordance with the exaltation which has come to us. As against that, sin in its second form is sloth. God Himself has not merely shown man the way, but made it for him. God Himself has already exalted him. Therefore man must not wilfully fall. He must not set against the grace of God which is addressed to him, and leads him, and orders his going, his

THE DOCTRINE OF RECONCILIATION

own dark ways of frivolity or melancholy or despair which he seeks and chooses and follows. Adam at the very first fell into this sin too. Israel did it again and again. The world lives and thinks and speaks and seeks and finds on this downward way. Even forgetful Christians are on this way. This is man's disorder—corresponding to the order established by the grace of God. The doctrine of sin will have to treat of this sloth of man in the second part of the doctrine of reconciliation, and therefore in connexion with the consideration of Jesus Christ as the servant who became Lord (the doctrine of His kingly office).

Finally, sin is (3) the negation, the opposite of the fact that God in Jesus Christ has made Himself the Guarantor of the reality of that which has been done by Him as servant and Lord in that movement from above downwards and below upwards, of the fact that in Jesus Christ God has made Himself the witness of the truth of the atonement. This is the grace of God in its third form: God does not act above our heads, He does not ignore us, but He addresses us and calls us. He tells us what He does and He tells us as He does it. His action for us and with us is itself and as such His Word to us. Again the commandment of His grace is clear—it is a matter of hearing and obeying the truth which is told us, a matter of active joy in it. We have to see that that which is told us is true for us: that Jesus Christ is the Lord who became a servant for us, and the servant who became Lord for us, our Lord. As against this, sin in its third form is falsehood. When God Himself is the pledge that He has done all this, man cannot pretend that he knows better. When the truth speaks for itself, man's knowing better is only falsehood, a lie. And, again, this is the sin of Adam, and repeated in many forms it is the sin of Israel, and of the world and of all forgetful Christians. We are all at times, incorrigibly, those who know better—and, therefore, because grace is the truth revealed and known to us, we are all incorrigible liars. The consequences follow. Falsehood is self-destruction. Because man and the world live under the dominion of sin, lying to God and deceiving themselves, they live in self-destruction. At this point it is plain that sin cannot say Yes but only No, that it cannot build up but only pull down, that it can create only suffering and death. Sinful man is as such man without hope. This conflict of sin against the promise and hope given to man in the Word of God will have to be presented in the third part of the doctrine of reconciliation in connexion with the consideration of Jesus Christ as the Guarantor, the doctrine of His prophetic office.

And now we must try to go further. Sin is a reality—as the anti-thesis to

God it is so almost as God Himself is, *sui generis*. But it is not an autonomous reality. As the No which opposes the divine Yes, it is only a reality related to and contradicting that Yes. Therefore it can be known—and all the horror of it can be known—only in the light of that Yes. In all its reality and horror it can never be a first word, nor can it ever be a final word. The atonement made in Jesus Christ teaches us (as nothing else can) to know it and to take it seriously, but we also have to perceive and state that the gracious will and act of God in Jesus Christ are superior to it and overcome it. We ourselves do not look down on it or master it or conquer it or set it aside. We ourselves are not superior to it. But Jesus Christ, against whom sin properly and finally rears itself, is superior to it. In all the forms of the grace of God revealed and active in Him He is superior to sin in all its forms. He looks back on it. He looks down on it. And when we look at Him, for good or evil we, too, can and must look back on it and down on it. He has already effectively contradicted its contradicting. He has already banished the alien and defeated the usurper. In Him, in opposition to this enemy, the kingdom of God has already been victoriously inaugurated, and is present and revealed in power. We should be questioning everything that He is and has done, we should be making ourselves guilty of sin in its last mentioned form of falsehood (and therefore in its other forms as ingratitude and disorder), if we were to try to have it otherwise, if we were to try to think and speak less confidently in relation to Him, with reservations and limitations, and probably at bottom with doubts and denials. The reality of sin cannot be known or described except in relation to the One who has vanquished it. In His light it is darkness, but a darkness which yields. That He is the victor is therefore a Christian axiom which is not only not shaken but actually confirmed by sin. It is He who has the final word.

The fact that He does have the final word, and the extent to which He does, is something which we will have to show in the further development of the doctrine of reconciliation. It will be a matter of perceiving that the atonement made in Him is God's triumphant and effective decision in relation to sin as the great episode. And it will be a matter of understanding this decision concretely and in its context, which is obviously in the light of the Christology and the three christological bases. Therefore we shall have to adduce three propositions, all of which have the same content—that the sinful No of man has been matched and opposed and destroyed by the divine Yes spoken by Jesus Christ even in the sphere of man and the world which we have just considered in the doctrine of sin.

Or positively, we shall have to show what is the divine Yes spoken by God in answer to the human No, in what form it is maintained and fulfilled in the sphere of sinful man and the sinful world, how it is vindicated as the first and final word.

To explain at this point the one and threefold being and work of Jesus Christ in its relevance for the world we shall have to speak first of the three forms of the grace of God which comes to man in Him. We are here dealing with the objective material presented in older dogmatics under the title *De applicatione salutis* (soteriology). On the basis of our presuppositions this complex will work out as follows.

1. In relation to the doctrine of God's self-humiliation for us men accomplished in Jesus Christ, and in direct answer to the doctrine of sin as the human act of pride, the first part of the doctrine of reconciliation will necessarily continue with the doctrine of the divine verdict in Jesus Christ by which man is justified. This justifying sentence of God is His decision in which man's being as the subject of that act is repudiated, his responsibility for that act, his guilt, is pardoned, cancelled and removed, and there is ascribed to him instead a being as the subject of pure acts of thankfulness for this liberation. At this point we have to make it plain that the Gospel is an effective because a well-founded word of consolation resting on the righteousness of God. This is the positive content of the Reformation insight into salvation in the form particularly affected by Luther. And we must weigh it in relation to the Roman (Tridentine) doctrine and also mark it off and confirm it against Protestant misunderstandings and misrepresentations. But all this must be done with the reservation that in spite of the great importance of this insight we are dealing here with only one form of the grace of Jesus Christ. Only Jesus Christ Himself can be the principle of the doctrine of reconciliation, not justification or any other of the true but secondary forms of His grace.

2. In relation to the doctrine of the exaltation of man by God in Jesus Christ, and in direct answer to the doctrine of sin as the sloth of man, the second part of the doctrine of reconciliation will necessarily emphasise the direction given in Jesus Christ in which the sanctification of man is accomplished. This sanctifying direction of man is His decision by which sinful man is addressed and treated as a new subject, so that instead of causing himself to fall he can stand and proceed along the way which God has appointed for him as the way of true freedom, in this way rendering obedience. At this point we have to make it plain that the Gospel is a saving committal and an uplifting obligation, the Reformation insight into

salvation as particularly understood and represented by Calvin. We must do this primarily in its positive content, but also in antithesis especially to the Roman conception of the Christian life and to every form of secular humanism. In some respects we will have to set it even against Lutheranism, marking it off from all kinds of false developments both internal and external, old and new. But, of course, in spite of the rightness and importance of the matter, we shall never do so as though sanctification could or should replace Jesus Christ as the principle, the One and All, of the doctrine of reconciliation.

3. In relation to the doctrine of the unity of God and man introduced in Jesus Christ, and in direct answer to the doctrine of sin as the falsehood of man, the third part of the doctrine of reconciliation will have to set out the promise of God proclaimed in and with His verdict and direction, in which the calling of man takes place. This promise of God, which as the truth overcomes the lie, is God's decision in which He has given to man, quite contrary to the destruction of his existence, an eternal future in fellowship with Himself, that is, in His service, and therefore a teleological direction of his life in time, so that even this life in time acquires a perspective and therefore (small, relative and provisional) ends. In this respect we have to speak of the Gospel as a clarifying directive. And it is here that historically we have to look beyond the circle of vision of the 16th century Reformation, or, rather, to bring to light certain insights into Christian salvation which were then dismissed too summarily or suppressed altogether: life in the present, in expectation of the kingdom of God, in the rest and unrest which this causes, in the discipleship of Jesus Christ, in its eschatological orientation, in its dynamic in this-worldly criticism and construction. In short, this is the place where on the one hand we must find a place for what, since the Reformation, we have surely added to our understanding of the New Testament in respect of its teleological elements, and where, on the other, we may seek agreement between what to-day is felt to be and is, in fact, an antithesis between continental Protestantism and Anglo-Saxon, which was more influenced by the humanistic and enthusiastic movements of the Reformation period. In the light of the particular christological starting-point—and here the doctrine of the prophetic office of Christ will be normative—it will now be a question of bringing together the first two soteriological aspects. All the more carefully, then, we must avoid all appearance of claiming that from this standpoint of calling we are dealing with more than a part of what is the One and All in this matter. It is clear that this, too, can only be one form of the grace of Jesus Christ.

In all three developments we must ensure that Jesus Christ is constantly known and revealed as the One and All that is expounded. He is the One who justifies, sanctifies and calls. He is the High-Priest, King and Prophet. In the measure that He is shown to be the subject of the whole occurrence, the *autor* and *applicator salutis*, the doctrine of His grace, of the mercy of God directed in Him to man, will not in any way obscure by the necessary systematising and sub-dividing of its presentation the unity in which that grace is His grace.

In the whole event of atonement, justification, sanctification and calling, as grounded in the divine verdict, direction and promise, have as it were a central function. In them, in the understanding of grace under these concepts, it is still a matter of expounding the being and work of Jesus Christ as the Reconciler of the sinful world and therefore of sinful man with God. It is still a matter, then, of what took place in Him for the conversion of the world to God. That is how it must be to the very end. When we say justification, sanctification and calling, on the one side we are already expounding the relevance of what was done in Jesus Christ, but, on the other, we are expounding only the objective relevance of it and not its subjective apprehension and acceptance in the world and by us men. We might say, we are dealing with the ascription but not the appropriation of the grace of Jesus Christ, or with what has taken place in Him for the world as such but not for the Christian in particular. In the Christian there is an appropriation of the grace of God ascribed to all men in Jesus Christ, a subjective apprehension of what has been done for the whole world in the happening of atonement. It is absolutely and exclusively in the being and work of Jesus Christ Himself and not in men that this specific form of grace has its basis and power, that it is true and actual that there are amongst other men those who are reconciled with God in Jesus Christ, who recognise and affirm their being as such, who can confess from the heart, with word and deed, that God makes Himself known to the world in the work of atonement, that He faithfully maintains and fulfils His covenant with man in opposition to the fall and sin of man, that He activates and reveals Himself in Jesus Christ as the God of man, that in so doing He has claimed man in all His omnipotence as His man. The doctrine of justification, sanctification and calling must obviously be followed by a discussion of this particular form of grace.

In this connexion the specific point that we have to make is that the being and work of Jesus Christ—for even here we cannot abandon the christological basis—must now be understood as the being and work of

His Holy Spirit, or His own spiritual being and work. The appropriation of the grace of Jesus Christ ascribed to us, the subjective apprehension of the reconciliation of the world with God made in Him, the existence of Christians, presupposes and includes within itself the presence, the gift and the reception, the work and accomplishment of His Holy Spirit. The Holy Spirit is the one eternal God in His particular power and will so to be present to the creature in His being and activity, so to give Himself to it, that it can recognise and embrace and experience Himself and His work and therefore the actuality and truth of its own situation, that its eyes and ears and senses and reason and heart are open to Him and willing and ready for Him. The particular existence of the Son of God as man, and again the particular existence of this man as the Son of God, the existence of Jesus Christ as the Lord who becomes a servant and the servant who becomes Lord, His existence as the Guarantor of truth is itself ultimately grounded in the being and work of the Holy Spirit. He is *conceptus de Spiritu sancto*. And this is the distinctive mark of the existence of the men who perceive and accept and receive Him as the Reconciler of the world and therefore as their Reconciler, who—vicariously for the whole world reconciled by Him—discover that they are His because He is theirs, who on the basis of this discovery and therefore in this special sense exist "in Him," who can be with Him and for Him as He is with them and for them (with and for the whole world). It is the Holy Spirit, the being and work of the one eternal God in this special form, that is still lacking in the world at large. That God did not owe His Son, and in that Son Himself, to the world, is revealed by the fact that He gives His Spirit to whom He will. The hand of God the Reconciler is over all men. Jesus Christ was born and died and rose again for all. The work of atonement, the conversion of man to God, was done for all. The Word of God is spoken to all. God's verdict and direction and promise have been pronounced over all. To that extent, objectively, all are justified, sanctified and called. But the hand of God has not touched all in such a way that they can see and hear, perceive and accept and receive all that God is for all and therefore for them, how therefore they can exist and think and live. To those who have not been touched in this way by the hand of God the axiom that Jesus Christ is the Victor is as such unknown. It is a Christian and not a general axiom; valid generally, but not generally observed and acknowledged. Similarly, they do not know their sin or even what sin is, since it can be known only in the light of that axiom. And naturally they do not know their justification, sanctification and calling as they have already taken place in Jesus Christ.

But the hand of God has touched and seized Christians in this way—which means the presence and activity of the Holy Spirit. In this special sense Christians and only Christians are converted to Him. This is without any merit or co-operation on their part, just as the reconciliation of the whole world in Jesus Christ is without its merit or co-operation. But they are really converted to God in this special sense. The free grace of the sovereign God has in relation to them the special form that they themselves can reach after it. They can understand it as the grace directed to the world and therefore to them. They can live in the light and power of it—under its judgment, but all in all, under the Word, and readily and willingly under the Word, under the divine sentence and direction and promise. Therefore the being and work of Jesus Christ, the One and All of His achievement and the relevance of it has also this—shall we call it for the sake of clarity subjective?—dimension, in which the same One and All is now in the eyes and ears and hearts, in the existence of these men, Christians, who are specially taken and determined by His Holy Spirit. They have over the rest of the world the one inestimable advantage that God the Reconciler and the event of reconciliation can be to them a matter of recognition and confession, until the day when He and it will be the subject of His revelation to all eyes and ears and hearts, and therefore of the recognition and confession of all men. The being and work of Jesus Christ in the form of the being and work of His Holy Spirit is therefore the original and prefigurative existence of Christianity and Christians.

It is of this that we shall have to speak in the two concluding sections of all the three parts of the doctrine of reconciliation. And two things will have to be borne in mind. It is a matter of Christendom and of Christians, of the community ("Church") of Jesus Christ and of its members (individual Christians in their personal relationship to Jesus Christ). There cannot be the one without the other. The Holy Spirit is not a private spirit, but the power by which the Son of God (*Heid. Cat. Qu.* 54) "has from the beginning of the world to the end assembled out of the whole race of man, and preserves and maintains, an elect congregation." But He assembles and preserves and maintains it, not as a pile of grains of sand or as an aggregate of cells, but as a community of those of whom each one can individually recognise and confess by His power "that I am a living member of the same, and will be so for ever." Within this particular group of problems it is clearly a matter of a correspondence, a reflection and a repetition of the relationship between the objective ascription and the subjective appropriation of salvation. Salvation is ascribed to the individual in the existence of the community, and it is appropriated by the community in the existence of the individuals of which it is composed.

In the light of this correspondence it is more fitting to take the question of Christendom before that of the individual Christian.

Traditional dogmatics went to work differently. Logically, and again most instructively from the didactic standpoint, it proceeded at once from the objective demonstration of divine grace to its subjective apprehension in the life of man, i.e., the individual Christian. Or it treated both in the one context, speaking of personal Christian faith, for example, in the same breath as justification, and personal Christian obedience in the same breath as sanctification. We, too, must speak of them in the same breath, so that it is clear that the work of the Holy Spirit is in fact only a particular form of the being and work of Jesus Christ Himself. But we should be making it private in a way which is quite illegitimate if we were to relate it directly to the personal appropriation of salvation by the individual Christian. It was an intolerable truncation of the Christian message when the older Protestantism steered the whole doctrine of the atonement—and with it, ultimately, the whole of theology—into the *cul de sac* of the question of the individual experience of grace, which is always an anxious one when taken in isolation, the question of individual conversion by it and to it, and of its presuppositions and consequences. The almost inevitable result was that the great concepts of justification and sanctification came more and more to be understood and filled out psychologically and biographically, and the doctrine of the Church seemed to be of value only as a description of the means of salvation and grace indispensable to this individual and personal process of salvation. We will only ask in passing whether and to what extent Luther's well-known question in the cloister—which was and will always be useful at its own time and place—contributed if only by way of temptation to this truncation, or whether it is simply an aberration first of orthodoxy and then of the Pietism which began in it and followed it. What is more to the point is to remember (and this, too, is something we can only mention) that we will do well not to allow ourselves to be crowded again into the same *cul de sac* on the detour via Kierkegaard.

Certainly the question of the subjective apprehension of atonement by the individual man is absolutely indispensable. And it belongs properly to the concluding section of the doctrine of reconciliation—yet not in the first place, but in the second, and therefore at the close of this concluding section.

Our theme is the reconciliation of the world with God in Jesus Christ, and only in this greater context the reconciliation of the individual man. This is

THE DOCTRINE OF RECONCILIATION

what was completely overlooked in that truncation. And if it is to be brought to light again, the prior place which the Christian individual has for so long—we might almost say unashamedly—claimed for himself in the dogmatics of the Christian community must be vacated again. We must not cease to stress the individual. We must not throw doubt on the importance of his problem. But!

Only in the proper place. The "pillar and ground of truth" (1 Tim. 3$^{15}$), the salt of the earth, the light of the world, the city set on a hill, is the community of God and not the individual Christian as such, although the latter has within it his assured place, his indispensable function, and his unshakable personal promise. It is not he but the *ecclesia una sancta catholica et apostolica* that stands (in close connexion with the Holy Spirit) in the third article of the Creed. It is the Church which with its perception and experience of the grace of God stands vicariously for the rest of the world which has not yet partaken of the witness of the Holy Spirit. It is the Church which in this particularity is ordained to the ministry of reconciliation and the witness of the grace of God in relation to the rest of the world. It is in its existence, therefore—and only in the sphere of its existence in that of individual Christians—that the salvation ascribed to the world is appropriated by man. It is primarily in it that there is fulfilled in the sphere of sinful man and his world, as the work of the Holy Spirit of Jesus Christ, the subjective apprehension of the atonement objectively made in Him. It is of the Church, then, that in the light of the three christological origins we shall have to speak first in all three parts of the doctrine of reconciliation.

1. The Holy Spirit as the Spirit of Jesus Christ is the awakening power of the Word spoken by the Lord who became a servant and therefore of the divine sentence which judges and justifies sinful man. The work of the Holy Spirit as this awakening power is the historical reality of the community. When that verdict—that verdict of God which, we recall, repudiates and accepts, kills and makes alive—is heard by men, there is in their inner fellowship and there arises in their outward assembly a new humanity within the old. A new history begins within world-history. A new form of fellowship is quietly founded amongst other sociological forms: the apostolate, the disciples, the community, the Church. Its members are those who can believe and understand that sentence, and therefore regard as accomplished the justification of man in Jesus Christ. It is not the faith and understanding of its members which constitute the community, but the Word and verdict of God believed and understood,

Jesus Christ Himself in whose death on the cross that verdict is pronounced. It is not that they know God, but that they are known of God. But these men can know and believe and understand God in that verdict. In the midst of others they are one and conjoined by the fact that they must accept His saying. It is only by that, but actually, visibly and perceptibly by that—and irrevocably—that they are constituted the community. At this point we shall have to speak of the origin and being of the Church in its humanity—of that being which since it is always conditioned by the Holy Spirit as the awakening power of that divine verdict must again and again be an insignificant origin: a continual awaiting of the Holy Spirit as pictured in its constant gatherings, its ever renewed proclamation of the Word, its repeated prayer, its celebration of baptism; but an awaiting in the certainty of receiving, and therefore of its own life in His presence. The community exists in this fruitful expectation which can never cease and never be unrealised. In its humanity it is one historically feeble organism with others, but it is the redeemed community justified by the divine sentence and honoured with the knowledge of the justification of the world.

2. The Holy Spirit of Jesus Christ is the life-giving power of the Word spoken by the servant who became Lord, and therefore of the divine direction which sanctifies sinful man. The work of the Holy Spirit as this life-giving power is the inner upbuilding of the community. When that direction is heard by men, these men are united in a common action, in a common action orientated by a commonly imposed obedience, and, we can and must also say, by a commonly given freedom. The community grows in rendering this obedience, or in this freedom. In it it gains consistency, it acquires order and form, it becomes capable of action. Its members are men who not only regard that direction as given and normative, but who love it for the sake of the One who has given it, who accept it because they see in it the love in which God loved the world and themselves in this special way. The direction of God willingly followed in the power of the Holy Spirit is the life-principle of the Christian Church. Again, it is not by the obedience, the freedom, or even the love of these men that the Church is built up and lives. It lives wholly in the power of its Lord and His Spirit. In His power: the power of its Lord exalted as man to the right hand of God, who summons and draws it onwards and upwards as the community of His brethren, who transforms it into His image (2 Cor. $3^{18}$), by whom it is given to it to seek and to find that which is above, in whom it has already here and now a part in His resurrection and therefore in the

future life of eternity. Because and to the extent that He is mighty in the community by His Spirit, that which it does can and must be done with joy; its worship, its order, the fellowship of Christians, its mutual service, the celebration of the lord's Supper, even its teaching and theology can and must take on the character of a festival; and in it all God can and must be thanked and worshipped. What we have to show is the fact and way in which the Church has never to look after itself, to build up itself, to rule and maintain and defend itself, but simply to live according to the direction of its Lord and His Spirit and in that way to be vigorous and active and truly alive.

3. The Holy Spirit as the Spirit of Jesus Christ is the enlightening power of Him who as very God and very man is the Guarantor of the truth of the atonement made in Him—and therefore the summoning power of the promise given in Him to sinful man. When the promise is heard by men, inwardly and outwardly these men are together ordained to be the community sent out as a witness in the world and to the world. The historical reality and inward upbuilding of this community are not ends in themselves. It is now actually the case that in its particular existence it stands vicariously for the whole world. The Holy Spirit is the enlightening, and as the enlightening the summoning power of the divine promise, which points the community beyond itself, which calls it to transcend itself and in that way to be in truth the community of God—in truth, i.e., as it bears witness to the truth known within it, as it knows itself to be charged with this witness and sent out to establish it. Its members are men who can hope on the basis of the promise. But if they hope seriously, they hope in God, and in God for the world—for themselves, too, but for themselves as those who belong to the world which God has reconciled with Himself in Jesus Christ. They hope to see this the case, i.e., to see the world—and themselves with it—fulfilling its being in the service of God. But, again, it is not the sincerity or drive of this Christian hope which constitutes the light of the community sent out to witness. Only the Holy Spirit of Jesus Christ active within it is this light. But He is the light of the Christian community which shines here in the darkness on earth and in time. And since He is this light, and the community lives by God's promise, necessarily the community itself is bright in the world: a community which proclaims the coming kingdom of God as the substance of the whole future of man; but for that reason a missionary community; a community which is responsible and looks and points forward in face of every development in state or society; an element of prophecy in relation to the world, of greater

and smaller rest and unrest, of soberness and daring confidence in relation to the ultimate, and also and for that reason to penultimate horizons. It is of the community in this ministry of witness that we must speak in the third ecclesiological section of the doctrine of reconciliation.

And then, to conclude, we have to speak in all three parts of the life of individual Christians as such, of their being in Jesus Christ, of their personal knowledge and experience of the atonement, i.e., of the work and witness of the Holy Spirit, by whom in the community, by the service and for the service of the community, but as individuals, they are (1) awakened to faith, (2) quickened in love and (3) enlightened in hope.

It is not necessary to develop this here, since it has already been anticipated under the second heading of this section. We will simply make a general observation on this final theme. In the theology of Schleiermacher and his more or less loyal and consistent followers, this last theme was the first, and it also became the last because on their presupposition there could not be any other. Theology in general and with it the doctrine of the atonement could only be the self-interpretation of the pious Christian self-consciousness as such, of the *homo religiosus incurvatus in se*. In this way Schleiermacher's genius was to bring to its logical conclusion the truncating tendency in the older Protestantism to which we have already alluded. From the very first the present sketch of the doctrine of reconciliation has stood implicitly in the most decided opposition to this conception. We do not intend to avoid the problem of the *homo religiosus* or *christianus*. In the final development of the doctrine of reconciliation we shall have to treat very seriously of this special question of the *homo christianus*, of the Christian and what makes him a Christian, of his understanding of himself. It is, in fact, "self-understood" that he must occupy a special place in dogmatics, and undoubtedly in the analysis of the concepts faith, love and hope we have to do with a *conditio sine qua non* of the whole. Apart from the faith and love and hope of the individual Christian and his understanding of himself as such we cannot see the Christian community, nor can we see the justifying verdict, the sanctifying direction and the summoning promise of God. But faith and love and hope are relative concepts. The being of the Christian indicated by them is a being in relation. Faith lives by its object, love by its basis, hope by its surety. Jesus Christ by the Holy Spirit is this object and basis and surety. And faith and love and hope in this relation to Jesus Christ are all primarily His work, and His work first in the community of God, and only then His work in individual Christians. We must not confuse the *conditio sine qua non* of the knowledge of the atonement with its *ratio essendi*. The doctrine of reconciliation must end where it began. We shall speak correctly of the faith and love and hope of the individual Christian only when it remains clear and constantly becomes clear that, although we are dealing with our existence, we are dealing with our existence in Jesus Christ as our true existence, that we are therefore dealing with Him and not with us, and with us only in so far as absolutely and exclusively with Him.

# Question what you thought before

## Continuum Impacts - books that change the way we think

**AESTHETIC THEORY** - Theodor Adorno 0826476910
**I AND THOU** - Martin Buber 0826476937
**ANTI-OEDIPUS** - Gilles Deleuze & Félix Guattari 0826476953
**A THOUSAND PLATEAUS** - Gilles Deleuze & Félix Guattari 0826476945
**DISSEMINATION** - Jacques Derrida 0826476961
**BERLIN ALEXANDERPLATZ** - Alfred Döblin 0826477895
**PEDAGOGY OF HOPE** - Paolo Freire 0826477909
**MARX'S CONCEPT OF MAN** - Erich Fromm 0826477917
**TRUTH AND METHOD** - Hans-Georg Gadamer 082647697X
**THE ESSENCE OF TRUTH** - Martin Heidegger 0826477046
**JAZZ WRITINGS** - Philip Larkin 0826476996
**LIBIDINAL ECONOMY** - Jean-François Lyotard 0826477003
**DECONSTRUCTION AND CRITICISM** - Harold Bloom et al 0826476929
**DIFFERENCE AND REPETITION** - Gilles Deleuze 0826477151
**THE LOGIC OF SENSE** - Gilles Deleuze 082647716X
**GOD IS NEW EACH MOMENT** - Edward Schillebeeckx 0826477011
**THE DOCTRINE OF RECONCILIATION** - Karl Barth 0826477925
**CRITICISM AND TRUTH** - Roland Barthes 0826477070
**ON NIETZSCHE** - George Bataille 0826477089
**THE CONFLICT OF INTERPRETATIONS** - Paul Ricoeur 0826477097
**POSITIONS** - Jacques Derrida 0826477119
**ECLIPSE OF REASON** - Max Horkheimer 0826477933
**AN ETHICS OF SEXUAL DIFFERENCE** - Luce Irigaray 0826477127
**LITERATURE, POLITICS**
**AND CULTURE IN POSTWAR BRITAIN** - Alan Sinfield 082647702X
**CINEMA 1** - Gilles Deleuze 0826477054
**CINEMA 2** - Gilles Deleuze 0826477062
**AN INTRODUCTION TO PHILOSOPHY** - Jacques Maritain 0826477178
**MORAL MAN AND IMMORAL SOCIETY** - Reinhld Niebuhr 0826477143
**EDUCATION FOR CRITICAL CONSCIOUSNESS** - Paolo Freire 082647795X
**DISCOURSE ON FREE WILL** -
**Desiderius Erasmus & Martin Luther** 0826477941
**VIOLENCE AND THE SACRED** - René Girard 0826477186
**NIETZSCHE AND THE VICIOUS CIRCLE** - Pierre Klossowski 0826477194

## Continuum Impacts
### CHANGING MINDS

www.continuumbooks.com

# Montana's Historical Highway Markers

The cover art is reproduced from Irvin "Shorty" Shope's painting pictured on the cover of *Headin' for the Hills*, a travel booklet published by the Montana State Highway Department [now the Montana Department of Transportation], Helena, in 1937. It is signed "Irvin Shope, '36."

# Montana's Historical Highway Markers

**Revised and Expanded**

Compiled by Glenda Clay Bradshaw,
from original text by Robert H. Fletcher

Updated by Jon Axline

Illustrations by Irvin H. "Shorty" Shope

Montana Historical Society Press, Helena

Montana Historical Society Press
225 North Roberts St.
P. O. Box 201201
Helena, Montana 59620-1201

99 00 01 02 03 04 05      9 8 7 6 5 4 3 2 1

*Library of Congress Cataloging-in-Publication Data*

Fletcher, Robert H., 1885–1972.
    Montana's historical highway markers / compiled by Glenda Clay
Bradshaw : from original text by Robert H. Fletcher : updated by Jon Axline
: illustrations by Irvin H. "Shorty" Shope. – 2nd ed., rev. and expanded.
        p. cm.
    Includes bibliographical references and index.
    ISBN 0-917298-60-8 (sc: alk. paper)
    1. Historical markers–Montana–Guidebooks. 2. Automobile travel–
Montana–Guidebooks. 3. Montana–Guidebooks. 4. Montana–History, Local.
    I. Bradshaw, Glenda Clay, 1949–. II. Shope, Irvin. III. Title.
F732.F56 1999                                               99-18372
917.8604'33–dc21                                                CIP

*Montana's Historical Highway Markers* was made possible in part by funding from the Montana Department of Transportation.

# Contents

# Historical Marker Locations

Each sign's location is indicated by its number. Indian Historical Marker numbers appear in a trapezoid. Markers dealing exclusively with the Lewis and Clark Expedition are denoted by a circle or an oval. All other marker numbers appear in rectangles. Markers denoted by letters are no longer displayed.

The map is divided into "tourism countries," following the organization of the book. A large map of each individual tourism country precedes the chapters in which the signs of that country are described.

Note: Several markers are in rest areas that are accessible only from one side of the freeway.

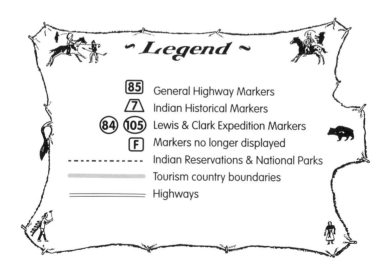

~ *Legend* ~

| | |
|---|---|
| [85] | General Highway Markers |
| [7] | Indian Historical Markers |
| (84) (105) | Lewis & Clark Expedition Markers |
| [F] | Markers no longer displayed |
| - - - - - - - - - | Indian Reservations & National Parks |
| ▬▬▬▬ | Tourism country boundaries |
| ══════ | Highways |

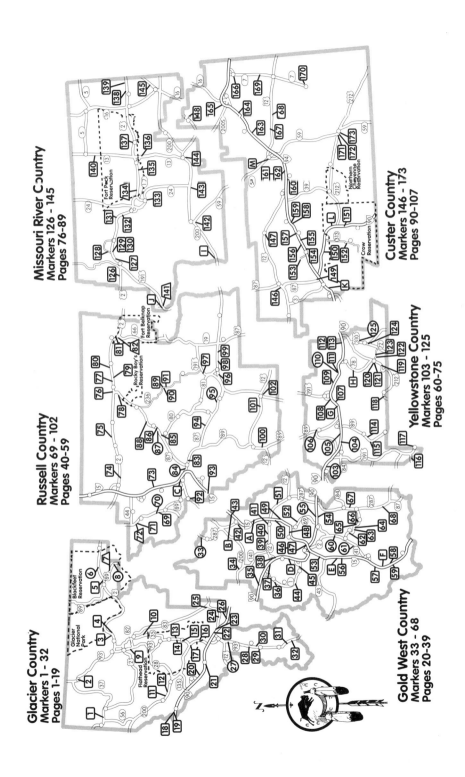

Glacier Country
Markers 1 - 32
Pages 1-19

Russell Country
Markers 69 - 102
Pages 40-59

Missouri River Country
Markers 126 - 145
Pages 76-89

Custer Country
Markers 146 - 173
Pages 90-107

Yellowstone Country
Markers 103 - 125
Pages 60-75

Gold West Country
Markers 33 - 68
Pages 20-39

Glacier National Park

Blackfeet Reservation

Flathead Reservation

Rocky Boy's Reservation

Fort Belknap Reservation

Fort Peck Reservation

Northern Cheyenne Reservation

Crow Reservation

# How to Use this Book

The 1999 edition of *Montana's Historical Highway Markers* includes several changes that will make the book easier to use. In earlier editions, the markers were numbered in the order of their creation; they are now organized geographically by "tourism country," beginning with Glacier Country and moving east. In addition to the statewide map, which shows the boundaries of all five tourism countries, we have included detailed maps of each "country." The Indian Historical Markers, originally listed separately to reflect their status as a special project, have been integrated into the geographical listing. Signs from this project are noted on the maps by a trapezoid. Likewise, historical markers that deal exclusively with the Lewis and Clark Expedition are distinguished on the maps by a circle. All other sign numbers are mapped with rectangular boxes. Signs that are no longer displayed are noted on the map with a letter–as opposed to the numbering system that denotes all of the other signs–and are listed in the last chapter of the book. To find specific events, people, or places referred to on the signs, see the index. The markers are there, too, listed by title.

The quotations from Lewis and Clark's journals have been standardized to conform with the entries found in Gary E. Moulton (through July 27, 1805) and Reuben Gold Thwaites (after July 27, 1805).*

The location of each marker is noted in this book with highway number, nearest mile post marker (MP), and description, such as rest area, city park, or nearest town. Montana's official highway map is the best reference to use with the book. Maps and vacation planning kits are available free of charge by writing Travel Montana, Department of Commerce, P.O. Box 200533, Helena, Montana 59620-0533, or phoning (406) 444-2654 (from Montana) or 1-800-VISIT-MT (from out of state).

* Gary E. Moulton, ed., *The Journals of the Lewis and Clark Expedition*, 8 vols. (Lincoln and London: University of Nebraska Press, 1987); Reuben Gold Thwaites, ed., *Original Journals of the Lewis and Clark Expedition;1804–1806*, 8 vols. (New York: Dodd, Mead & Company, 1904).

# Foreword

Montana's history could never be called dull. Having played a major role in the westward expansion of the 1880s, Montana's heritage is a patchwork quilt of Indian peoples on buffalo plains, raucous mining camps and copper kings, cowboys and grass-fat steers, dry-land homesteaders and sod shanties, loggers and freighters. Montanans have always been proud of that history and of those with the gift to recount it. And the telling of that history has assumed many forms over the years. Legends and winter counts told the tales of Montana's first peoples. Later, journals, diaries, and memoirs described the lives of new people on the land. The first-person telling of history—the storyteller—has forever held a place of honor in this land where the articulate speaker, the good talker, has always found a receptive audience.

In 1935, Bob Fletcher convinced the powers-that-be to place road signs throughout Montana at points of historical significance or interest—or at those places that suggested a good story. Fletcher understood the intimacy of Montana history; after all, in 1935, "back then" was not all that long ago. Fletcher's personal acquaintance with many of the men and women who had helped build the state provided more fuel for his idea and supplied him with the stories and the embroidery for the texts that were cut into the original signs.

Aside from being the first such highway markers in the nation, what made them so remarkable was that Bob Fletcher was able to bring folk history to life. Bob's signs spoke in a distinctly Montana voice, using words like "plub" and "larrup" and phrases like "talk medicine" or "head to the tall and uncut" to tell the story. The folklore and the legendry of the state came alive before readers' eyes at or near the sites where the events had taken place. Using his skills as a storyteller with humor and always an affinity for the land and its peoples, Bob Fletcher told of the dreams, aspirations, successes, failures, and tragedies of Montana. Many Montanans and countless visitors took their first history lessons about the state by reading Bob's signs. Montanans have taken so readily to the road signs that when work was begun in 1986 to refurbish the markers, a hue and cry went out: "Yes, repair the signs and add to them–but don't change the originals!" The signs have become a part of Montana.

Fifty-three years after the historical marker project was completed, Bob Fletcher has found a place in the history of the land he loved most. He was a bit romantic, even nostalgic for "the old days." Yet, his writing and poetry are still a testament to the telling and validation of not just our history but, perhaps more importantly, also the people who made it.

One can only wonder if back in 1935 Bob Fletcher, Shorty Shope, Ace Kindrick, and the Montana Highway Department crew realized what a great contribution they were making to Montana. They might be surprised and pleased to know that we look on their work with the same pride with which they honored other Montanans fifty-three years ago. Bob is gone now, as are Shorty and Ace, but I'd give my best saddle horse if I could see the look on Bob Fletcher's face if he could drive into the Broadus rest stop and see the sign honoring the Montanan who started it all back in 1935.

Michael Korn
Montana Folklife Project

# Acknowledgments

Thanks to all the people who helped track down information on the "old" signs and their creators and on topics for the new markers, including the folks at

The Montana Historical Society

The Montana Department of Transportation (in Helena and at the regional offices)

The Montana Folklife Project

and to all the Montanans around the state who gave their time, talent, and expertise, including Wally McRae, Erva Shope, Richard Shope, Dave Walter, Jim Posewitz, Michael Korn, John Gatchell, Elinor Clack, Betty White, Mick Hager, Tony Incashola and the Flathead Culture Committee, Orville Quick, and Jeff Kindrick. I think of you all each time I drive by one of our signs.

Glenda Bradshaw<br>
Helena, Montana<br>
1989, 1994

Grateful acknowledgment is made for permission to reprint the following:

"The Yellowstone," by Wallace McRae (sign 159), is used with the permission of the author. © 1986 by Wallace McRae.

"Don't Fence Me In," by Robert H. Fletcher (sign 173), is used with permission of Warner Bros. Inc., ©1944 Warner Bros. Inc. (renewed).

Shorty Shope illustrations on pages 19, 54, bottom 61, 75, 77, 79, and 89 are from *Corral Dust* by Bob Fletcher, published by the author, 1934. Used with the permission of Robert K. Fletcher, Missoula, Montana, and Virginia F. MacDonald, Kalispell, Montana.

Shorty Shope illustrations on pages 3, 16, 65, 83, and 105 are from the Western Life Insurance Company booklet on Shope paintings, n.d.

Used with the permission of R. B. Richardson, Helena, Montana.

Shorty Shope illustrations on pages 27, 48, 53, 81, 88, bottom 91, and 103 are from *Local Community History of Valley County, Montana*, published by the Glasgow Women's Club, 1925. Used with the permission of the Montana Federation of Women's Clubs.

Shorty Shope illustrations on pages 11, 31, 43, 46, 50, 67, 70, 97, and 102 are from the Montana Highway Department travel brochure, "Through the Land of the Shining Mountains," by Robert H. Fletcher, n.d.

Shope illustrations on the title page and on pages 1, 6, 14, 21, 35, 36, 41, 59, top 61, 68, 74, 80, 86, 87, top 91, and 92 are from Shope's historical map of Montana produced for the Montana Highway Department.

Illustrations on pages 38, 57, and 98 are from *Historical Markers* by R. H. (Bob) Fletcher, published by the Montana Highway Commission, n.d.

Shorty Shope illustrations on pages 2, 23, 64, 107, and 114 are from a Shope drawing in the collection of the Montana Historical Society Museum, Helena.

The Shope illustration on pages 25 and 30 are from *Gold* by Robert Fletcher, published by the Union Bank and Trust Company, n.d.

The photograph on page xv is used courtesy of the Montana Department of Transportation, Helena.

The photographs on pages xxiii and xxiv are from the Montana Historical Society Photograph Archives, Helena.

The photograph on page xxv is used courtesy of Jeff Kindrick, Helena.

# Introduction to the 1999 Edition

by Jon Axline

THE PRICKLEY PEAR DIGGINGS

Bob Fletcher could hardly have believed the impact his historical highway markers would have on the Montana landscape when he convinced the Montana State Highway Commission to fund the program in 1935. The markers were only part of a much larger tourism-oriented program begun by the commission in 1931. That year, the highway commissioners promoted Fletcher to the position of "Plans Engineer," a title which made him the chief of the publicity department. It was Fletcher's responsibility to develop a statewide and national campaign to promote tourism in the Treasure State during the depths of the country's greatest economic calamity, the Great Depression. By the time the first eleven signs had been installed by the department's maintenance crews in August 1935, Fletcher had already implemented a successful ports-of-entry project and convinced the highway engineers to include turnouts in its designs for use as picnic areas (the precursors to today's interstate rest stops). In 1937, Fletcher oversaw the distribution of the state's official highway maps and produced the first of its first-class promotional brochures, *Headin' for the Hills*. The following year, Fletcher convinced the highway commissioners to buy the Pictograph Cave site near Billings and build a museum there to display the artifacts recovered by archaeologists excavating the site.

Based on a successful program in South Dakota, the ports-of-entry program consisted of rustic-looking log cabins, designed and built by the department, located at each of the main highways on the Montana border. From the cabins, "well-mannered" attendants, nattily dressed in blue jeans, western-style shirts, cowboy boots, and bandannas, distributed promotional literature, answered questions about Montana's history, recreational opportunities, accommodations, restaurants, and other attractions.

In 1938, Fletcher worked out a deal with the Works Progress Administration to construct roadside museums on heavily traveled thoroughfares throughout the state. Although the department was not supposed to be involved in the operation or maintenance of the museums, Fletcher worked tirelessly to scrounge artifacts for exhibit in them, build display cases, and arrange for local people to staff them. Only one of those museums is known to still exist; it sits in Fireman's Park on Main Street in Laurel.

Fletcher's highway historical marker program has, by far, been the most popular of his many pet projects and the only one that still survives. Within six years of the program's initiation in 1935, Fletcher wrote and oversaw the installation of 103 historical markers with topics ranging from the Lewis and Clark Expedition to the oil industry on the High Line near Shelby. As Glenda Bradshaw relates in "Montana History on the Road," the markers received national acclaim as excellent and relevant examples of "regional literature" by such notables as *New Yorker* columnist Lewis Gannett, historian Bernard DeVoto, and newspaper correspondent Ernie Pyle. Fletcher was justifiably proud of his creation since his markers informed and entertained thousands of Montanans and visitors to Big Sky Country. It is also quite possible, moreover, that the markers have been the only exposure many Montanans have had to the state's rich and colorful history. In his 1937 tourism promotional brochure, *Headin' for the Hills*, Fletcher immodestly wrote, "These markers are the best idea I've seen in any state. Each one is placed on a turnout so that you can park and read it without being mortally afraid some one will sneak up behind and telescope you into eternity. The story they tell is pepped up a little for people who are human and don't take themselves . . . too seriously."

It is also important to note that the historical markers were a team effort. Although Fletcher's prose made them famous, part of the charm of the markers also rested on the talents and skills of highway department sign shop foreman Asa "Ace" Kindrick and on the wonderful illustrations provided by the department's graphic artist, Irvin "Shorty" Shope. Unfortunately, many of the contributions to the highway marker program of these two men have disappeared as time, the elements, and changing highway design standards have taken their toll on all but a very few of the original markers.

Today, the Montana Department of Transportation's (MDT) highway historical marker program is still active and vibrant. The markers were upgraded and some of the language was modified in the 1980s. Since 1985, fifty-six highway markers have been added to the system, including nine that describe the contributions of Montana's Native American residents to the state's historical landscape. The language on the new markers is not quite as colorful as that of Fletcher's day, but the intent remains to celebrate Montana's unique history and its people.

Since 1990 I've had the great privilege of overseeing the existing historical markers and adding new ones to the system. Today, most of the markers are installed as mitigation for impacts to historical sites resulting from MDT projects. A few, like the ones in downtown Bearcreek (sign 123) or on Montana Highway 35 along the eastside of Flathead Lake (sign 10), have been installed to commemorate a community or the state's transportation history.

As in the 1930s, the success of the program is still dependent on a number of people, making it truly a team effort. Acknowledgement needs to be given to MDT employees Pat Brannon, Gay Scheibl, Paul Bronson, Jim Cornell, Pam Alderson, and Larry Mad Plume for their time and effort formatting, mapping, and fabricating the markers. Ellen Baumler of the State Historic Preservation Office has reviewed and edited many of the markers for me since 1990. Ellen was also in charge of the Indian Historical Marker program and worked closely with Montana's Indian people to make sure their stories are represented on the state's highways. Finally, Crow Tribal Council Cultural Director Burton Pretty on Top and I worked together in 1998 to revise the Pompeys Pillar (sign 154) and the Crazy Mountains (sign 111) markers to include both the native and nonnative histories of these two significant geographic sites. It is a partnership that will, I hope, lead to new sign projects with Montana's tribal cultural committees.

The Montana Department of Transportation is always looking for new ideas for historical marker topics. If you have one, please contact the department's historian at: Environmental Services, Montana Department of Transportation, 2701 Prospect Avenue, Helena, Montana, 59620-1001. Enjoy your trip through Montana's roadside history!

# Montana History on the Road

by Glenda Clay Bradshaw

"A cowboy leaned over in the saddle of his dusty sorrel to read the roadside sign erected on Highway 34 [now state route 287] near old Nevada City. Next to him a sleek sedan with New York license plates pulled up, and the driver leaned out to study the same sign. The cowboy turned to the driver of the sedan. 'Talks turkey, don't it?' he said. 'I never miss one of 'em when I'm travelin' in Montana.'"

Horseback travel is not so common today, fortysome years after this incident was reported in the *Minneapolis Tribune* on May 11, 1947, but thousands of travelers still stop to enjoy the same signs that flank the highways around Montana. They tell the stories of Montana's past and people—the Native Americans; the earliest non–Indian visitors, such as the members of the Lewis and Clark Expedition; fur trappers and explorers; those who came to strike it rich on gold, livestock, and farming; and some of the significant events that happened in the state during the last two hundred years.

The brainchild of Highway Department traffic engineer Bob Fletcher, Montana's historical markers reflect his love of the history of the West and his conviction that history should be made alive and enjoyable. Fletcher, an outgoing, friendly sort, came to Montana in 1908 and for more than a decade worked across the state as a surveyor before joining the Highway Department. During his travels, he met many old–timers who had experienced firsthand some of Montana's early years and others who knew the stories from parents, relatives, or friends who were here "back when."

Fletcher first conceived the idea for historical signs in the 1920s, but it wasn't until 1935 that he was able to convince the Highway Department that it was a winner. "A fancy historical marker is not necessary—just one that attracts the fancy," he explained. He penned colorful stories about Montana's people, places, and events and made them sound as if an old–timer were leaning against your car, reflecting on days gone by. The Highway Department put up about twenty-five signs in 1935 and then waited for indignant reactions to the liberties that Fletcher had taken interpreting the state's past. But the public responded enthusiastically. Both tourists and residents inundated the Highway Department with praise and requests for copies of the sign texts. Even officials from other states wrote for details so they could incorporate some of the markers' design features in their own roadside signs.

The texts of Montana's historical markers even underwent review outside the state. Lewis Gannet of *New Yorker Magazine* praised them in a 1940 column as regional literature: "In Montana the signs are worth reading. . . . So far as I know, these are the only official road signs in any state of America which dare to be light-hearted or colloquial." Historian and essayist Bernard DeVoto also approved in *Harper's Magazine* in 1946: "Montana does its roadside history exhaustively and well. It marks all the important sites–neatly, in excellent taste. What it says about them is accurate, sufficiently generalized to give the unhistorical tourist the idea but sufficiently full and specific for the expert. And its markers use good prose, lightly written, of a humor and realism that exclude the ancestor-worship of the organized descendants of The Pioneers."

World War II correspondent Ernie Pyle liked them as well: "I wish that every state historical society in America would send a delegation to Montana. They might also invite a few writers of history textbooks to go along. And if they would then practice what they learned, I'll bet that twenty years from now we Americans would know a lot more about American history. Montana makes its history a thing of joy instead of a stodgy sermon."

Then he told this story: "One grave fellow got up in the Malta Lions Club and introduced a resolution asking the state highway department to tear the signs down and replace them with something 'dignified.' Unfortunately, the Lions didn't string him to a tree, but they did shout him down."

People also liked the unique roadway design that provided approach signs to warn drivers to slow down, ample pullouts and parking areas, and signs that could be read from a car.

Fletcher stuck with the Highway Department for over thirteen years, writing more than one hundred signs as well as travel brochures and some free-lance history. A few more signs were added to the collection between the 1940s and the mid-1980s.

Two of Fletcher's colleagues in the Highway Department, Shorty Shope and Ace Kindrick, also played essential roles in designing the historical markers. Shope, a fine artist who was a graphic designer for the department, contributed silhouettes of western subjects to embellish the signs. Shope's illustrations run across the top of some signs; on others they decorate the first letter of the text. Like Fletcher, Shope knew many old-timers; he had drawn them and shared their work, riding roundup, herding cattle, roping at branding time. As Fletcher said, "He has conned nature and models in the raw until he can reproduce the West by means of pen and brush with a faithfulness that makes you smell the sage and feel the warm chinook."

The layout and crafting of the markers fell to Ace Kindrick, ramrod of the Highway Department's sign shop. He hand-lettered the earliest signs on plywood; but after finding that these signs weathered too quickly, Kindrick visited the United States Forest Service sign shop in Missoula to observe the routing technique used on their trail signs. Thereafter, he and his signmen hand-routed the letters into thick wooden boards, spray-painted the panels, and then sanded their surfaces, leaving the recessed letters painted. The rest of the signboard was oiled or otherwise finished to enhance the wood's natural grain. Various woods were tried over the years, but redwood became the wood of choice because it weathers well. Most of the signs were hung from wooden crossbeams and posts and set on fieldstone bases.*

In 1985, the 49th Montana Legislature allocated Federal Revenue Sharing money to refurbish the historical markers. Their plan treated Fletcher's writing as artifact and the signs as an element of Montana's historic landscape. Times have changed, however, and some of Fletcher's colorful language is no longer acceptable. Many of his colloquial terms for Montana's first inhabitants ("Injuns," "squaws," "redskins") carry derogatory connotations. Fletcher seems to have meant no disrespect, as this selection from one of his travel brochures indicates: "Today the Montana Indians are on seven reservations. Our highways pass through or near most of them. These tribes produced some mighty fine characters–orators, statesmen, generals, and philosophers. By the way, don't make any personal remarks about an Indian under the delusion that he doesn't savvy. You may be embarrassed. He might haul off and larrup you with some Harvard English. Also, a blanket Indian's outfit

---

* The fieldstone bases are disappearing as the Department of Transportation replaces them with safer, breakaway sign posts. Not as pretty, but easier on vehicles and people in times of collision.

doesn't look any more locoed to you than yours does to him. The only difference is that he is too polite to let on."

Earlier intentions aside, sign texts that might be misinterpreted have been edited–but rest assured that the vintage "Fletcher" has been kept as pristine as possible.

Women also might have found offense in a couple of the old historical texts. For example, a quote from road–builder Captain John Mullan advises travelers to " . . govern them [pack mules] as you would a woman. . . ." This may seem humorous to some; but more important and exciting events transpired on that heavily traveled route and one of them was substituted for the potentially offensive passage. Montana's historical markers form some of travelers' first and firmest impressions of the state and its people. One of the purposes of the markers is to make those impressions positive ones.

The editing of existing signs and the writing of twenty–three new signs was accomplished during the summer of 1987 as a project shared by the Montana Department of Transportation and the Montana Historical Society. New signs were cut by a "new–fangled," computer–run router and put up the following fall and winter. Montana's historical roadside markers have been rejuvenated and are on duty.

# The Men Who Made The Signs

### Robert H. Fletcher (1885–1972)

Born in Iowa, Bob Fletcher studied mining engineering in Minnesota before coming to Montana in 1908. For several years, surveying work took Fletcher all over the state, enabling him to meet many people and to get an earful of Montana history.

In 1928, Fletcher signed on as plans and traffic engineer for the Montana Highway Department, where he worked for thirteen years. During that time, he wrote creative travel literature, helped establish the port-of-entry stations on arterial highways entering Montana, designed and managed the Montana exhibit at the San Francisco World's Fair, and encouraged the highway department to protect historical and archaeological discoveries, such as Pictograph Caves near Billings.

He also devised and implemented the historical markers program.

Fletcher also became known for his poetry and his freelance historical writing, which included *Free Grass to Fences*, the story of the Montana cattle range. His best-known verse became the basis for Cole Porter's song, "Don't Fence Me In," part of which is reproduced on sign #173, "Big Sky Country."

### Irvin H. "Shorty" Shope (1900–1977)

Born and raised in Boulder, Montana, near his father's small ranch, Shope spent as much time as possible on horseback. After his father's death, the family moved to Missoula where Shope found a mentor in Montana artist Edgar S. Paxson. Shope continued his formal studies in Portland, Oregon, and in New York, finally graduating with a degree in art from the University of Montana in Missoula. He then spent close to ten years working on cattle ranches, studying and drawing scenes of ranch work, western life, and the land.

In 1925, Shope met cowboy artist Charles M. Russell, who looked through Shope's sketches and encouraged the young painter. On the back of one he wrote, "These drawings of Shope's are all good." Russell also told Shope, who was contemplating attending an eastern art school, "Don't do it, the men, horses and country you love and want to study are out here, not back there."

Bob Fletcher met Shope in 1935 and asked him to draw a historical map of Montana for the Montana Highway Department. Shope became the department's advertising illustrator, creating artwork for travel brochures, signs, and other department literature and drawing western scenes and artifacts to ornament the new roadside historical markers.

Shope started doing free-lance work full-time in 1945, completing hundreds of paintings and twenty-two murals. Shope, one of Montana's best-known and most popular artists, also helped found the Cowboy Artists of America.

### Asa T. "Ace" Kindrick (1903–1987)

Born near Seymour, Missouri, Kindrick came to Helena, Montana, with his family in 1914. In 1928, he studied lettering in Detroit, Michigan, and then returned to work in a local automobile and sign shop. The Montana Highway Patrol hired Kindrick to letter their first patrol cars in 1934. The highway department liked his work so well that Kindrick was hired to start a sign shop for them. His employment by the department coincided with the beginning of the historical markers program, and Kindrick put his extraordinary layout and lettering skills to work for Montana history. He directed the highway department sign shop until his retirement in 1969.

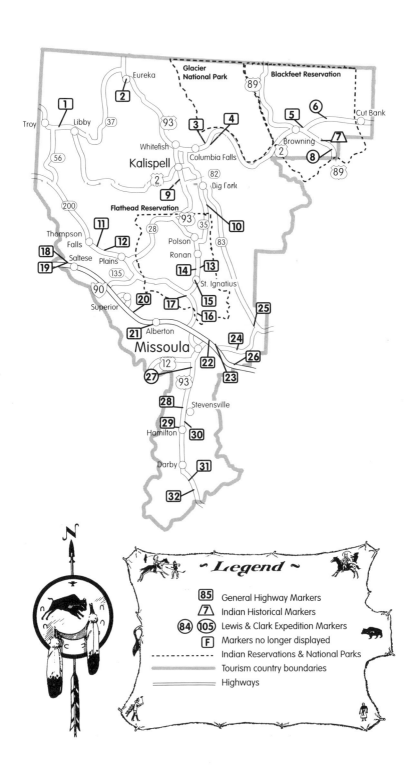

**Glacier National Park**

**Blackfeet Reservation**

Eureka

Troy
Libby
37
56

Whitefish
Kalispell
Columbia Falls
93

Browning
2
Cut Bank

2
82
Big Fork

**Flathead Reservation**

Thompson Falls
200
28
93
35
83

Saltese
Plains
135
Polson
Ronan
St. Ignatius

90
Superior
Alberton
Missoula
12
93
Stevensville

Hamilton
Darby

N

~ Legend ~

85 General Highway Markers
7 Indian Historical Markers
84 105 Lewis & Clark Expedition Markers
F Markers no longer displayed
- - - - Indian Reservations & National Parks
Tourism country boundaries
Highways

# Glacier Country

## 1. Kootenai River
U.S. 2, MP 21, west of Libby

The river is named for the Kootenai tribe that lived and hunted in this part of Montana and adjoining territory in Idaho and Canada. They were settled south of Flathead Lake in 1855 with the Salish on the Flathead Reservation.

They were friendly with neighboring mountain tribes but suffered frequently from the incursions of their bitter enemies, the Blackfeet, who came across the Continental Divide from the plains on horse-stealing and scalp-raising expeditions.

First white men in here were trappers and traders for British fur companies as early as 1809. Placer discoveries were made and mining operations commenced about sixty years later.

## 2. Tobacco Plains
U.S. 93, MP 178, east of Eureka

During the fur trapping and trading days in the early part of the last century this corner of the state was remote and inaccessible from the customary trapping grounds and operating bases of the Americans. Representatives of the British and Canadian companies came in from the north and established posts along the Kootenai River.

The Tobacco Plains were so named by the Indians who planted tobacco for religious uses.

In prehistoric times the valley of the Kootenai was filled with an enormous ice sheet.

## 3.  Badrock Canyon
U.S. 2, MP 140, east of Columbia Falls

The Great Northern Railway was constructed through Badrock Canyon in 1891. Prior to that, in 1890, the railroad contracted with Shepard Sicms & Company to construct a road on the opposite side of the river to carry supplies to the railroad workers. The high canyon walls on the south side of the river were a major obstacle to the contractor, requiring extensive blasting to carve the road high above the canyon's floor. When completed in 1891, the road was so steep in places that wagons had to be lowered down it by ropes tied to trees—thus it was called the "Tote Road" by the local residents. It was not until sometime between 1906 and 1914 that the county built a new highway through the canyon, bypassing the old tote road with a more user-friendly thoroughfare.

Pioneer Billy Berne owned a small homesite at the west entrance to the canyon. Berne and his brother Mike came to Columbia Falls from Butte in 1889. For years the brothers manufactured bricks, which were used to construct many buildings in the area. In 1929, the construction of U.S. Highway 2 destroyed much of the Berne homesite. In 1953, a niece of the Berne Brothers sold a tract of canyon land to the State of Montana for use as a roadside park dedicated to the memory of her uncles.

## 4.  Surrounded by Wilderness
U.S. 2, MP 141, Berne Memorial Park, east of Columbia Falls

You are at the gateway to the upper Flathead River, which drains Glacier National Park, the Bob Marshall Wilderness Complex ("the Bob") and the southeastern corner of British Columbia. Two hundred nineteen miles of the three forks of the Flathead are designated as federal wild and scenic river, which means they are managed to maintain their natural primitive environments and unpolluted waters.

Directly to the south of here is the Swan Mountain Range, which stretches in an unbroken line for 100 miles. No road crosses the top of it. East of the Swan Range is the Bob.

Just around the next corner going toward the Park, you can look east into the Great Bear Wilderness created in 1978 to link vital habitat in the Park and the Bob for the grizzly bear and other wildlife.

## 5. The Blackfeet Nation
U.S. 2, MP 224, east of Browning

The Blackfeet Nation consists of three tribes, the Pikunis or Piegans, the Bloods and the Blackfoot. Each tribe is divided into clans marking blood relationship. The majority of the Indians on this reservation are Piegans.

Many years ago the Blackfeet ranged from north of Edmonton, Alberta to the Yellowstone River. They were quick to resent and avenge insult or wrong, but powerful and loyal allies when their friendship was won.

They were greatly feared by early trappers and settlers because of the vigor with which they defended their hereditary hunting grounds from encroachment.

No tribe ever exceeded them in bravery. Proud of their lineage and history they have jealously preserved their tribal customs and traditions. They have produced great orators, artists, and statesmen.

The Government record of the sign language of all American Indians, started by the late General Hugh L. Scott, was completed by the late Richard Sanderville, who was official interpreter of this reservation.

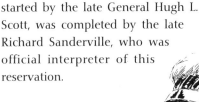

## 6. Camp Disappointment
U.S. 2, MP 233, east of Browning

The monument on the hill above was erected by the Great Northern Railway in 1925 to commemorate the farthest point north reached by the Lewis and Clark Expedition, 1804–06. Captain Meriwether Lewis, with three of his best men, left the main party at the Missouri River and embarked on a side trip to explore the headwaters of the Marias River. He hoped to be able to report to President Jefferson that the headwaters arose north of the 49th parallel, thus extending the boundaries of the newly acquired Louisiana Purchase.

The party camped on the Cut Bank River July 22–25, 1806, in a "beautifull and extensive bottom." Deep in the territory of the dreaded Blackfeet, the men were uneasy. Lewis wrote, "gam[e] of every discription is extreemly wild which induces me to believe that the indians are now, or have been lately in this neighbourhood." Lewis could see from here that the river arose to the west rather than to the north, as he had hoped. Disheartened by this discovery, by the cold, rainy weather, and by the shortage of game, Lewis named this farthest point north Camp Disappointment, the actual site of which is four miles directly north of this monument.

## 7. Old Agency, 1880–1894
U.S. 89, MP 96, south of Browning at Badger Creek turnout

The second Indian Agency on the Blackfeet Reservation was built at Old Agency in 1879. Agent John Young moved the buildings from Upper Badger Creek with help from the Blackfeet Indians. Both men and women dug cellars, hauled stone and mixed mortar. The women covered the exterior with lime from Heart Butte. Built in stockade shape, the Agency had two bastions at diagonal corners to protect against enemy attack. The Indians called it "Old Ration Place" after the government began issuing rations. The "Starvation Winter" of 1883–1884 took the lives of about 500 Blackfeet Indians who had been camping in the vicinity of Old Agency. This tragic event was the result of an inadequate supply of government rations during an exceptionally hard winter. In 1894, after the Great Northern Railway had extended its tracks across the Reservation, the Agency moved to Willow Creek at the present site in Browning. Today, the Museum of the Plains Indian in Browning houses a fine collection of artifacts that illustrate Blackfeet culture before and after the establishment of the Reservation.

## 8.  Captain Meriwether Lewis
U.S. 89, MP 85, north of Dupuyer

Captain Meriwether Lewis of the Lewis and Clark Expedition, accompanied by three of his men, explored this portion of the country upon their return trip from the coast. On July 26, 1806, they met eight Piegans (Blackfeet), who Lewis mistakenly identified as Gros Ventres, and camped with them that night on Two Medicine Creek at a point northeast of here. Next morning the Indians, by attempting to steal the explorers' guns and horses, precipitated a fight in which two of the Indians were killed.

This was the only hostile encounter with Indians that the Expedition encountered in their entire trip from St. Louis to the Pacific and back. Lewis unwittingly dropped a bombshell on the Piegans with the news that their traditional enemies, the Nez Perce, Shoshoni and Kootenai, were uniting in an American-inspired peace and would be getting guns and supplies from Yankee traders. This threatened the Blackfeet's 20-year domination of the Northern Plains made possible by Canadian guns.

## 9.  Kalispell-Somers Railroad Spur Line
U.S. 93, MP 110, between Kalispell and Somers
(scheduled for future installation)

In 1901, Great Northern Railway tycoon James J. Hill and local businessman John O'Brien joined forces to build and operate a 11-mile railroad line to a sawmill on the north shore of Flathead Lake. Hill built this spur line in record time and provided financial assistance for the construction of the sawmill. In return, O'Brien supplied 600,000 railroad ties annually to the Great Northern Railway until 1906 when Hill acquired sole ownership of the sawmill. At Somers, O'Brien built 122 residences and a general store to provide housing and support services to the workers and their families. By 1910, the Somers Lumber Company sawmill was the largest in the Flathead Valley, producing over 30 million board feet of lumber every year. Freight and passenger trains passed over the spur line daily carrying travelers between the Great Northern depot in Kalispell and the steamboat terminal at Somers. The sawmill closed and was dismantled in 1949. The Burlington Northern Railroad used this spur line until 1985.

## 10. A Permanent and Substantial Road
Montana 35, MP 23, south of Big Fork

In the early 20th century, many roads in Montana were constructed by convicts from the state prison in Deer Lodge. The warden believed that manual labor not only taught the men a skill, but also increased their self-esteem and reduced the chances they would later return to prison.

When created in 1913, the Montana Highway Commission had no money to build roads. Instead they funded "demonstration" projects which often used convict labor. The state paid 50¢ a day for each convict, while the counties provided the equipment. About a third of the penitentiary's 600 inmates worked outside the walls building roads and bridges throughout western Montana. This road was constructed by convict labor in 1913 and 1914.

About 111 prisoners worked on the road and lived in two tent camps. They enjoyed a measure of freedom not present in the prison. The food was generally good and the men were treated to evening band concerts performed by their musically inclined comrades. Despite this, thirteen men fled the camps; all were eventually recaptured and returned to prison. Built entirely by hand labor with horse-drawn

scrapers and graders, the road coat $31,825 when completed. This was the longest section of road built by convicts before the program ended in 1927. Although upgraded over the years, the highway retains the same alignment established by Montana's convict laborers before World War I.

## 11. Thompson Falls
Montana 200, MP 52, east of Thompson Falls

Named for David Thompson, geographer and explorer for the North West Co., a British fur trading outfit.

In November 1809 he built a trading post nearly opposite the mouth of Prospect Creek, named it Selish House, and wintered there.

The Flathead Indians called themselves "Selish," meaning "The People." Like most nations they probably figured they were a little finer haired than the foreigners. Thompson was the greatest geographer of his day in British America.

The Clark Fork of the Columbia was named for Capt. Wm. Clark of the Lewis and Clark Expedition.

## 12. Bad Rock Trail
Montana 200, MP 60, between Thompson Falls and Plains

The nearby Bad Rock Trail was an important route for the aboriginal people who inhabited northwest Montana. The first documented account of the trail was by North West Company trader David Thompson in 1809. He reported that it was the scene of many battles between the Kootenai, Salish and the Blackfeet people. Over the ensuing years, the trail became a much cursed obstacle on the road that led up the Clark Fork. It was used by a parade of western notables, including Thomas Francis Meagher, Isaac Stevens, John Mullan, copper king W. A. Clark and mountain man Jedediah Smith.

The best description of the trail was by Father DeSmet in 1841: "I had before seen landscapes of awful grandeur, but this one . . . surpassed all others in horror. My courage failed at the first sight; it was impossible to remain on horseback. My mule was sufficiently kind to allow me to grasp her tail, to which I held on firmly until the good beast conducted me safely to the very top of the mountain. There I breathed freely for a while, and contemplated the magnificent prospect that presented itself to my sight."

In 1883, the Northern Pacific Railway blasted away portions of the trail to complete its transcontinental line. The process was repeated in 1936 when the Montana Department of Transportation completed this segment of the highway. Bad Rock Trail continues to be a commanding presence on this segment of Montana Highway 200.

## 13. The Mission Mountain Wilderness
U.S. 93, MP 40, south of Ronan

The mountains rising to the east lie in the Mission Mountain Wilderness Area and the Mission Mountain Tribal Wilderness. The range is more than a natural wonder; it is the first place in America where an Indian nation has designated tribal lands as a wilderness preserve. The crest of the range forms the eastern boundary of the Flathead Reservation. On the east side, 73,877 acres are managed by the Flathead National Forest; on this side, 89,500 acres are under the purview of the Confederated Salish and Kootenai (Flathead) Tribes. Both wildernesses are managed cooperatively and are open to everyone, though differences in management styles reflect tribal needs and traditions on the west side.

A few tribal elders can still trace the routes of old hunting trails through the Missions. Hunters used them to cross to the eastern Montana plains to hunt buffalo. The mountains hold sacred sites where tribal members go alone to fast and seek spiritual guidance for their lives. Other spots are traditional summer camps where families pick berries, gather medicinal herbs, plants, and roots, and cut tipi poles.

Clarence Woodcock of the Flathead Cultural Committee expressed the tribes's deep-rooted spiritual and cultural ties to the mountains: "They are lands where our people walked and lived. Lands and landmarks carved into the minds of our ancestors through Coyote stories and actual experiences. Lands, landmarks, trees, mountain tops, crevices that we should look up to with respect."

## 14. Fort Connah
U.S. 93, MP 39, north of St. Ignatius

Fort Connah, the last of the Hudson Bay Co. trading posts established within the present borders of the United States, was built about 1/4 mile east of here. Begun by Neil McArthur in fall 1846, his replacement, Angus McDonald, completed it in 1847. It remained an important trading center for the Flatheads until 1871. The old store house is still standing. Mission Valley was thrown open for settlement in 1910. Prior to that time it was almost entirely virgin prairie, unplowed, unfenced and beautiful to see. You rode a saddle horse to get places. Some people wish it were still like that.

## 15. The Mission Valley
U.S. 93, MP 31, St. Ignatius

The Mission Valley, called by the Indians "Place of Encirclement," was occupied by bands of Salish and Kalispel speaking people when the white man came. By treaty with the Government in 1855 it became a part of the reservation of the Confederated Salish and Kootenai Tribes and included some Pend d'Oreille, Kalispel, and Nez Perce.

St. Ignatius Mission, the second built in Montana, was established in 1854 by the Jesuits. The first church was built of whipsawed timber and was held together with wooden pins. Through efforts of the priests the Mission prospered. Four Sisters of Providence from Montreal opened the first school in 1864. The Ursulines arrived in 1890 and opened a school for younger children.

In 1910 the unallotted land on the reservation was thrown open to settlement. The whites and barbed wire moved in.

## 16. The Jocko Valley
U.S. 93, MP 14, south of Arlee

Named for Jacco (Jacques) Raphael Finlay, a fur trader and trapper in the Kootenai and Flathead Indian country, 1806–09.

By treaty of Aug. 27, 1872, the Flathead Indians were supposed to have relinquished claim to their hereditary lands in the Bitter Root Valley, accepting the present reservation in lieu thereof. Charlot, head chief of the Flatheads, always denied signing the treaty although when the papers were filed in Washington his name appeared on them, possibly a forgery.

Arlee (pronounced Ahlee by the Indians) was a war chief and did sign the treaty so the Government recognized him thereafter as head chief. Charlot never spoke to him afterwards.

## 17. Flathead Reservation
Montana 200, MP 116, west of Ravalli

The Native Americans on this reservation belong to the Salish, Kalispel, Spokane, Kootenai and Pend d'Oreille tribes. Lewis and Clark met the Salish in 1805 and described them and their allies, the Nez Perce, as being friendly and exceptional people. "Flathead" was a misnomer applied to the Salish by Lewis and Clark. No one knows for sure where it came from, but like many early names for tribes, it stuck. It seems that the whites almost always had a handle to hang on a tribe before they met anyone who could tell them their own name for themselves.

The Flatheads frequently crossed the mountains to the plains to hunt buffalo and there clash with the Blackfeet, their hereditary enemies. Many of the French and Scotch names amongst them came from marriage with the Hudson Bay Co. trappers and traders in the early fur days.

## 18. The Holacaust*
I-90, MP 4, Dena Mora rest area, west of Saltese

In 1910, this was a remote neck of the woods and hard to reach. Forest fire protection was relatively new. That dry summer many small fires started. Public apathy, together with manpower shortage, lack of organization and good equipment and inaccessibility permitted them to spread and join. Hell broke loose in August. Whipped by 50-mile gales, the combined blaze covered 3,000 square miles in three days. Animals were trapped, 87 human lives were lost, settlements and railroad trestles were destroyed, six billion board feet of timber burned like kindling. The pungent smoke pall stretched to eastern Montana.

Some good came from this costly burnt sacrifice to inadequate organization, funds and public understanding. Legislation was enacted, appropriations were increased, cooperative effort was developed, and the public became forest fire conscious. Now U.S. Forest Service lookouts and aerial patrols discover fires while small, then smoke-chasers by trail and smoke-jumpers by parachute reach and control most of the fires in record time. This devastated area has been restocked with trees that will again produce commercial timber, provide homes for wildlife and recreation for people. Fire protection methods, equipment and organization capable of handling future threats of dry summers will pay off in healthy watersheds and abundant forest products. An uncontrolled forest fire is a terrifying, destructive beast. Please be careful with your matches, cigarettes and campfires, won't you?

*Fletcher may have deliberately misspelled holocaust to reflect local usage.

## 19. Mullan Road

I-90, MP 4, Dena Mora rest area, west of Saltese

During the years 1855–62 Captain John Mullan, 2nd Artillery, U.S.A., located and built what was known as the Mullan Road. Congress authorized the construction of the road under the supervision of the War Department to connect Ft. Benton, the head of navigation on the Missouri, with Ft. Walla Walla, the head of navigation on the Columbia.

In the winter of 1859–60, Capt. Mullan established a winter camp at this point which he called Cantonment Jordan. The Captain had selected this route in preference to the Clark's Fork route because he thought it would have a climatic advantage since it was farther south. However, he later expressed regret for making this choice because investigation showed that the more northerly route was highly favored with chinook winds and the snowfall in consequence was much lighter. The Captain also predicted that both of these routes might eventually be used by transcontinental railroads. His prophesy was correct.

## 20. The Iron Mountain Mine

I-90, MP 58, Quartz Flats rest area, between Superior and Alberton

The Iron Mountain Mine, one of the largest and most successful quartz mines in western Montana, was located about 12 miles north of here. L. T. Jones, a former Northern Pacific Railroad brakeman, discovered the ore body in 1888. Jones and his partners, D. R. Frazier and Frank Hall, located the Iron Mountain and Iron Tower lode claims on upper Hall Gulch. Later they bonded the property for $100,000 to J. K. Pardee, a prominent Montana mining entrepreneur, and Iron Mountain Company was born.

Intensive development began by 1889. Getting the ore to smelters was a major undertaking until 1891 when the Northern Pacific built a rail line from Missoula through Superior, four miles south of the mine.

By 1891 the company had built a concentrator that could reduce 100 tons daily. The concentrates were sent to the American Smelting and Refining Co. at Omaha, Nebraska, or East Helena, Montana, or, later, to Globe Smelter and Reduction Works of Denver, Colorado.

An 1897 state law forced the Iron Mountain Mine to close. It required all mines to have an escape shaft in addition to the main tunnel, and the Iron Mountain had only a main tunnel. From 1889 to 1898, the mine had produced over $1,000,000 and paid out $507,000 in dividends.

Later efforts to reopen the mine had only minor success and all that now remains are several wooden buildings, the railroad grade, many tramway routes, the concrete foundations of the mill, the stone and concrete powder houses, the tailings piles, and the collapsed adits and shafts.

## 21. The Natural Pier Bridge
I-90 Exit #75, 1 mile west of Alberton

This structure is an example of how engineers incorporated a natural feature into the design of a bridge. Designed by Montana Highway Commission bridge engineers, the bridge is a standard riveted Warren through truss. The bridge is unusual in that one of the piers is anchored to a rocky outcrop in the Clark Fork River. The bridge was once a component of the Yellowstone Trail–which traversed Montana from Lookout Pass to North Dakota.

Responding to pressure from the lumber companies and the Yellowstone Trail Association, Mineral County embarked on an ambitious bridge-building program in 1916. Although the county was responsible for the construction of the bridge, fiscal limitations and its location near the Lolo National Forest forced the county commissioners to seek financial aid from the federal government. In early 1917, the county contracted with the Wisconsin-based Wausau Iron Works Company to build the bridge. Work progressed steadily on the bridge for several months when the county ran out of money for its construction. After securing additional federal funds, the county commissioners called a referendum to raise money to complete construction of the bridge. Because of the law, however, the vote could not be held for several months. With the money eventually acquired, the bridge was completed in 1918 at a cost of $100,000.

## 22. Junction of the Hell Gate and Big Blackfoot Rivers
Montana 200, MP 1, west of Milltown

An important Indian road came east through the Hell Gate and turned up the Big Blackfoot. It followed that river almost to its source, then crossed the Continental Divide to the plains country. The Indians called the river the Cokalahishkit, meaning "the river of the road to the buffalo."

Capt. Clark and Capt. Lewis, of the Lewis and Clark Expedition, divided forces near the present site of Missoula on their return trip from the coast. Capt. Lewis and his party followed this Indian road and passed near here July 4th, 1806.

Capt. John Mullan, U.S.A., locator and builder of the Mullan Military Road from Fort Benton to Fort Walla Walla, maintained a construction camp here during the winter of 1861–62 which he named Cantonment Wright. He was the first engineer to bridge the Blackfoot.

## 23. Hell Gate and Missoula
Old U.S. 10, about 1½ miles east of Missoula
on I-90 frontage road

In the Indian days the mountain tribes had a road through here which led across the Continental Divide to the buffalo. The Blackfeet, from the plains, used to consider it very sporting to slip into this country on horse–stealing expeditions and to ambush the Nez Perce and Flathead Indians in this narrow part of the canyon. Funeral arrangements were more or less sketchy in those days even amongst friends, so naturally, enemies got very little consideration. In time the place became so cluttered with skulls and bones that it was gruesome enough to make an Indian exclaim "Isul," expressing surprise and horror. The French trappers elaborated and called it "La Porte d'Enfer" or Gate of Hell.

From these expressions were derived the present–day names Missoula and Hell Gate. If the latter name depresses you it may be encouraging to know that Paradise is just 79 miles northwest of here.

## 24. The Big Blackfoot Railway
Montana 200, MP 6, east of Missoula

The Blackfoot River has been a transportation corridor for hundreds of years, first serving Indian travelers, then later fur trappers, miners, and loggers. The first large–scale timber cutting started in 1885 when the Big Blackfoot Milling Co. located at Bonner. The mill's principal customer was Butte copper magnate, Marcus Daly. The expanding mines created an insatiable appetite for lumber, and in 1898 Daly's Anaconda Copper Mining Co. bought the mill.

The mill started the Big Blackfoot Railway to move timber from outlying cuts to the river. The main line ran from Greenough to McNamara Landing which was on the river about five miles north of here. Logs were skidded by horses to temporary branch lines, then transferred to the main line for the trip to the river. At high water the logs were floated down to Bonner. Once an area was cleared of timber, the temporary rail lines would be moved to the next cut.

The Milwaukee Railroad acquired the Big Blackfoot Railway as a branch line about 1910 and the trains ran until 1916, when logging ceased for ten years. Both resumed in 1926, but the railway's years were numbered. Logging trucks came on the scene in the 1920s and by 1948 had dominated the industry. Hauling by rail had ended by 1957. Trucks also eliminated the need for logging camps, so most of the small communities disappeared too.

One of the locomotives, specially geared for rough track and steep grades, can be seen in the Bonner park.

## 25. Big Blackfoot Railroad
Montana 200, MP 32, at the junction of Montana 200 and Montana 83

Railroad logging was an important facet of the history of Montana's lumber industry. The Big Blackfoot Railroad was one of several logging railroads created to sustain the Anaconda Copper Mining Company's sawmill at Bonner. Built by the Chicago, Milwaukee, St. Paul and Pacific (Milwaukee Road) Railroad between 1911 and 1936, the line was used almost exclusively by the Anaconda Company.

The company acquired 625,000 acres of timber in the Blackfoot River Valley in 1904 to provide lumber and cord wood for its mining and smelting operations in Butte and Anaconda. For twenty-eight years, the company harvested approximately 40 million board feet of lumber annually from its property in the valley—making the Anaconda Company the largest timber producer in Montana.

This section of railroad grade was constructed in 1934. By the early 1940s, however, economic depression, war and the increasing use of trucks to haul lumber caused a sharp decline in the logging industry in the valley.

Although the Anaconda Company ceased logging operations in the Blackfoot Valley in 1949, the line was not abandoned until 1978. Since the line was never intended to be permanent and was often relocated to take advantage of new timber stands, the track was frequently placed directly on the ground without the benefit of ballast or any significant grading. Portions of the old railroad can be seen adjacent to the highway on the south.

## 26. The Welcome Creek Wilderness
I-90, MP 127, about 1 mile east of the Rock Creek exit
(temporarily removed)

Rock Creek, one of the nation's most celebrated blue-ribbon trout streams, is bordered on the west, just a few miles southwest of here, by the Welcome Creek Wilderness Area, established in 1977.

Not a typical wilderness area, Welcome Creek is a small enclave of undisturbed forest designated to protect an important watershed and contains no grand-scale scenic wonders. But to one retired forest ranger it is "a major island in an ocean of roads and logged areas." Welcome Creek is providing a unique opportunity to study long-term changes that logging and management produce on tree growth, soil fertility, wildlife diversity, and watershed protection. It is also a favorite summer home and migration route for about 300 elk that winter in the state's Threemile Game Range in the western foothills of the Sapphire Mountains.

## 27. Traveler's Rest
U.S. 93, MP 82, south of Lolo

The Lewis and Clark Expedition, westward bound, camped at the mouth of Lolo Creek September 9th, 10th, 1805. They had been traveling down the Bitter Root Valley and halted here to secure a supply of venison before crossing the mountains to the west via Lolo Pass. They named the spot Traveler's Rest, and it was at this camp that they first learned of the Indian road up Hell Gate leading to the buffalo country east of the main range of the Rockies.

Returning from the coast they again camped here from June 30th, 1806, to July 3rd. When the party divided, Lewis took the Indian "Road to the Buffalo" and after exploring the Marias River descended the Missouri while Clark went via the Big Hole, Beaver Head, Jefferson and Gallatin Valleys and the Yellowstone River.

They reached their rendezvous near the mouth of the Yellowstone within 9 days of each other.

Considering distance and unexplored terrain, they were tolerably punctual.

## 28. Fort Owen
U.S. 93, MP 67, Stevensville junction

Between 1831 and 1840 the Flathead Indians sent out three delegations, with St. Louis as their objective, to petition that "Black Robes" be sent to teach them. As a result Father De Smet, a Catholic missionary, established the original St. Mary's Mission here in 1841. He and his assistants hewed logs and built a dwelling, carpenter and blacksmith shops, and a chapel. They drove in the first oxen with wagons, carts, and plows that year and in 1842 brought cows from Colville, Washington, and raised a crop of wheat and garden produce, probably the first in Montana.

In 1843, assisted by Father Ravalli and others, he built the first grist mill. The stones were brought from Antwerp, Belgium, via the Columbia River.

The Mission was sold to Major John Owen in 1850. On its site he built a trading post and fort, the north wall of which stands. The Major was a genial and convivial host when travelers came that way, and for many years Fort Owen was an important trading center for whites as well as Indians.

## 29. Rocky Mountain Laboratory
U.S. 93, MP 48, at Hamilton

In earlier days, Rocky Mountain spotted fever was a dreaded malady in the West. The first case of spotted fever was recorded in the Bitterroot Valley in 1873. Neither cause nor cure was known and mortality was high.

Through efforts of the Montana State Board of Health and Entomology, scientists were brought in to solve the mystery. By 1906 they had proved that the bite of a wood tick was the cause of the disease, which was found later to exist throughout the United States. A preventive vaccine was finally developed in this remote laboratory. Yearly vaccination of those who may become exposed to tick bite and effectual treatment methods have solved the problem.

A modern laboratory, now operated by the U.S. Public Health Service, has replaced the tents, log cabins, woodsheds and abandoned schoolhouses that served the first handful of workers. Research has been expanded to include many infectious diseases that are problems in the West.

## 30. Marcus Daly Mansion

Secondary 269 (Eastside Highway), MP 2, north of Hamilton

Hamilton's Daly Mansion was a summer retreat for Butte's "Copper King" Marcus Daly and his wife, Margaret. Daly came to the United States as a poor Irish immigrant at age 15. Attracted to western mining camps, he quickly learned mining skills. Through ingenuity and hard work, he made a fortune from copper and was influential in Montana's politics and economy for many years.

Daly began acquiring land to develop a 22,000 acre stock farm in the late 1880s and platted the town of Hamilton in 1890. His prized thoroughbreds, raised and trained in the Bitterroot Valley, set new records at Eastern tracks. Now open for tours, this 42–room Georgian-revival style mansion contains many exquisite Italian marble fireplaces and an elegant central staircase. Newspapers of that period termed this mansion one of Montana's largest homes, and also one of the West's most pretentious and costly dwellings. Surrounding landscaped grounds include many exotic trees and graceful flowerbeds. Other structures include a greenhouse, playhouse, laundry, servant's quarters and a heated swimming pool.

Daly's mansion is located to your left, just off the Eastside Highway.

## 31. Medicine Tree

U.S. 93, MP 20, south of Darby

This Ponderosa Pine has been standing guard here on the bend of the river for nearly 400 years. Somewhere, imbedded in its trunk, a few feet above the ground, is the horn of a Big Horn ram, the basis of a legend which across the centuries has established the historical significance of the pine as a Medicine Tree.

Once upon a time, when the tree was small, according to Salish Indian lore, a mountain sheep of giant stature and with massive, curling horns, accepting a challenge from his hereditary enemy, Old Man Coyote, attempted to butt it down. The little pine stood firm, but one of the ram's horns caught in the bole, impaling the luckless sheep, causing his death. A Salish war party chased the coyote away from his anticipated feast and then hung offerings of beads, cloth, ribbon and other items on the ram's horns as good medicine tokens to his bravery and to free the scene of evil.

Countless succeeding Indian tribes followed the practice until, less than 100 years ago, the horn disappeared within the tree. But the Indians continue to regard it as a shrine and even the white men honor its sacred legend.

## 32. Ross' Hole
   U.S. 93, MP 13, south of Darby

Alexander Ross, of the Hudson Bay Company, with 55 Indian and white trappers, 89 women and children and 392 horses, camped near here on March 12, 1824, enroute from Spokane House to the Snake River country. Nearly a month was spent here in a desperate attempt to break through the deep snow across the pass to the Big Hole, and from their hardships and tribulations, Ross called this basin "The Valley of Troubles."

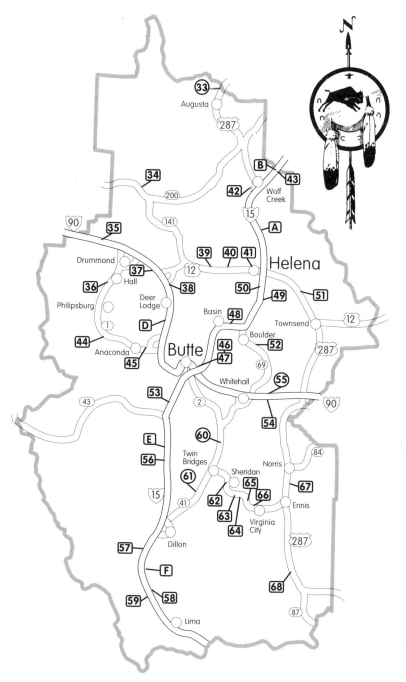

Augusta
33
287
34
200
B
42
43
Wolf Creek
15
141
A
90
35
Drummond
39 40 41
Helena
37
Hall
12
36
38
50
Deer Lodge
49
51
Philipsburg
Basin 48
Townsend
12
D
1
Boulder
287
44
52
Anaconda
Butte
46
45
47
69
53
Whitehall
55
2
90
54
E
60
56
Twin Bridges
84
61
Sheridan
Norris
65
62
66
67
63
Virginia City
Ennis
64
287
57
Dillon
F
68
59 58
87
Lima

For legend, see page 40.

# Gold West Country

## 33. Sun River
U.S. 287, MP 42, north of Augusta

The Sun River was called the Medicine River by the Indians in the days of the Lewis and Clark Expedition (1804–06). The Indian name was probably given because of an unusual mineral deposit possessing marked medicinal properties which exist in a side gulch of the Sun River Canyon west of here.

This country was claimed and occupied by the Blackfeet Nation in the frontier days. After the Indians were relegated to reservations it became cattle range.

In 1913 the U.S. Reclamation Service built a storage and diversion dam near the mouth of the canyon and the water is used for irrigation on the valleys and bench lands east of here.

## 34. The Bob Marshall Wilderness Country ("The Bob")
Montana 200, MP 50.5, 5.5 miles west of junction
with Montana 141

North of here lies the second largest wilderness in the lower 48 states. Made up of the Bob Marshall, Scapegoat, and Great Bear wilderness areas, its north end abuts Glacier National Park, creating a continuous corridor of unspoiled mountains and valleys that harbor grizzly bears, mountain goats, wolverines, elk, moose, deer, and wolves.

Montana first protected part of this country in 1913 when the Sun River Game Preserve was created on the east side of the continental divide. Years of market hunting to supply miners and settlers with meat had decimated the elk herds.

Bob Marshall (1901–1939), pioneer forester and conservationist of the 1930s, was years ahead of his time in recognizing and campaigning for the inherent value of wilderness. His vision helped awaken the U.S. Forest Service to the need to conserve a portion of the vanishing wildlands from which our American heritage had been formed. Before his premature death, he had secured protection for nearly 5.5 million acres, including most of the area that was later to bear his name. Montanans convinced Congress to add the Scapegoat in 1972 and the Great Bear in 1978.

Though wilderness must be balanced with other uses of National Forests, it protects resources for us all, like watersheds, fisheries, and wildlife. Someone once asked Bob Marshall how much wilderness America really needs. In reply he asked, "How many Brahms symphonies do we need?"

## 35. Bearmouth
I-90, MP 143, Bearmouth rest area, west of Drummond

Bearmouth, across the river to the south, was a trading point for the placer camps at Beartown, Garnet and Coloma located in the hills north of here. A pioneer family named Lannen operated the gold exchange and a ferryboat.

The river, officially known as Clark Fork of the Columbia and so named for Capt. Wm. Clark of the Lewis and Clark Expedition, has many local names. Its source is Silver Bow Creek, then it becomes the Deer Lodge River, changes to the Hellgate River, is then called the Missoula and winds up as the Clark Fork.

It had one other name given to it by a white man. In September, 1841, the intrepid Jesuit priest, Pierre Jean De Smet, traveled westward through here on his way from St. Louis to establish a mission for the Flathead Indians in the Bitter Root Valley. He crossed the river at the present site of Garrison and named it the St. Ignatius.

## 36. Southern Flint Creek Valley
U.S. 10A, MP 57, south of Hall

The Flint Creek Valley has, according to archeologists, been the home to humans for around 10,000 years. Fur trappers and traders began frequenting the valley in the early 19th century. Prospectors discovered gold in the Granite Mountains and on Henderson Gulch in the early

1860s. Founded in 1864, Philipsburg became one of the most important mining camps in Montana by the 1880s. In 1865, the Stone stage station was established near here on the road between Philipsburg and the Mullan Road junction south of Drummond. By the early 1880s, the stage stop had grown to include a post office, school, store and boarding house. After the construction of the Drummond–Philipsburg branch of the Northern Pacific Railroad in 1887, this part of the valley became important for the productivity of its farms and ranches.

Named for pioneers Henry and Julia Byrne Hall, the community of Hall was an important agricultural center in the valley and a shipping point for the farm and ranch products raised there. The town thrived until the economic depression following the First World War caused Hall's bank to close. The history and verdant beauty of the Flint Creek Valley is a lasting monument to pioneer vision and enterprise.

## 37. First Discovery of Gold in Montana
I–90, MP 169, Gold Creek rest area, east of Gold Creek

Opposite this point a creek flows into the Clark Fork River from the west. In 1852, a French halfbreed, Francois Finlay, commonly known as "Benetsee," prospected the creek for placer gold. Finlay had some experience in the California goldfields but was inadequately equipped with tools. However, he found colors and in 1858 James and Granville Stuart, Reece Anderson and Thomas Adams, having heard of Benetsee's discovery, prospected the creek. The showing obtained convinced them that there were rich placer mines in Montana. The creek was first called "Benetsee Creek" and afterwards became known as Gold Creek.

The rumors of the strike reached disappointed "Pikes Peakers" as well as the backwash of prospectors from California and resulted in an era of prospecting that uncovered the famous placer deposits of Montana.

## 38. The Valley of a Thousand Haystacks
U.S. 12, MP 0, in Garrison

The Little Blackfoot Valley is filled with lush hay fields. You already may have noticed the rounded haystacks and commented on the strange lodgepole structures standing in many of the fields. This contraption that looks like a cross between a catapult and a cage is a hay-stacker that actually acts like a little of both. It was invented before 1910 by Dade Stephens and H. Armitage in the Big Hole Valley about sixty miles south of here. The device, called a beaverslide, revolutionized haying in Montana. It helped keep the wind from blowing the hay away and cut stacking time considerably.

To work the beaverslide, a large rake piled high with hay is run up the arms of the slide (the sloping portion of the "catapult"). At the top the hay dumps onto the stack. The side gates (the cage part) keep the stack in a neat pile and make it possible to stack higher. The sides were added to the system in the late 1940s. Although the lifting of the rake is usually powered by a takeoff from a tractor, truck or car axle, on some operations horse teams still provide the rpm's to muscle the hay up the slide.

Aside from minor improvements, the beaverslide has remained unchanged since its inception. Once used throughout a good portion of the northern west, modern technology that can shape hay into bales, loaves or huge jelly rolls have replaced it in many areas. The Little Blackfoot is one of several valleys in Montana where you can still see the beaverslide and its distinctive haystacks.

## 39. The Mullan Road
U.S. 12, MP 23, McDonald Pass, west of Helena

From this point west to the Idaho line I-90 follows the route of a military road located and constructed during 1858–62 by Captain John Mullan, 2nd Artillery, U.S. Army. The road was 624 miles long and connected Fort Benton, Montana, with Fort Walla Walla, Washington. An average wagon outfit required a minimum of forty-seven days to travel it.

The Captain, aside from his engineering ability, was a man of considerable acumen as evidenced by the following excerpts from his final report. He prophesied "... the locomotive engine will make passage of the ... wild interior at rates of speed which will startle human credulity."

Mullan himself might have been incredulous had he seen the freight train that crossed this divide in 1865. Seven camels, each laden with 600 pounds of flour, made the trek from Helena to the Deer Lodge mines. One of the less successful experiments in American transportation history, the dromedary carried tremendous loads, was sure footed, and had great stamina, but the horses, mules and oxen of the teamsters and mule train packers stampeded at the sight and smell of them. The camels were gone from Montana by 1867.

## 40. Continental Divide—Elevation 6325
U.S. 12, MP 28, McDonald Pass, west of Helena

MacDonald Pass joins two other Continental Divide crossings as vital links between east and west in Montana. Both Mullan and Priest Passes, just north of this route, had roads as early as the 1850s. In 1870, E. M. "Lige" Dunphy built a toll road over this portion of the Divide making extensive use of log "corduroying" in muddy spots. He hired Alexander "Red" MacDonald to manage the toll gate with charges for all types of transportation except pedestrians and those traveling after dark. During the early 1880s a half dozen six-horse stages a day passed this way to and from Helena and western Montana.

In September of 1911, Cromwell Dixon earned a $10,000 prize when he became the first aviator in America to fly over the Continental Divide not too far from this spot. Today a four-lane highway and an air beacon replace buckboards and biplanes of earlier eras.

## 41. Last Chance Gulch
South Park Street at Cruse Avenue junction, Helena

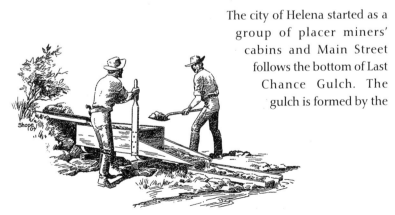

The city of Helena started as a group of placer miners' cabins and Main Street follows the bottom of Last Chance Gulch. The gulch is formed by the convergence of Oro Fino and Grizzly Gulches and its colorful history began when gold was discovered July 14, 1864, by a party returning to Alder Gulch from an unsuccessful prospecting trip. They agreed to camp and give this locality a try as their "last chance." It proved to be a bonanza.

It is estimated that the Gulch produced thirty millions in pay dirt and there is plenty left beneath the present business district. After a cloudburst, colors and nuggets have been found in the gutters.

Main Street is very irregular in width and alignment. Some opine that it was laid out in this matter to restrict the shooting range of impetuous, hot-blooded gents in the roaring days gone by.

## 42. The Mann Gulch Fire

Wolf Creek Bridge Fishing Access northeast of Wolf Creek
on the Frontage Road

At an isolated gulch about three miles northeast of here on August 5, 1949, twelve smokejumpers and a Forest Service employee died when a routine fire unexpectedly turned deadly. The lightning-caused fire at Mann Gulch was spotted by a Forest Ranger about noon on August 5th. Within hours, fourteen of the Forest Service's crack smokejumpers were on the ground in the gulch and moving toward the 55 acre fire. Wind, combined with tinder dry grass and the steep terrain in the gulch, caused a rare and little understood phenomenon called a "blow up." The result was an inferno that quickly enveloped Mann Gulch. The fire jumped the mouth of the gulch and cut off escape to the Missouri River. The men then sought the protection afforded by the ridge line to the north. The raging wall of flame moved faster than the men could climb the steep slope to safety. Realizing they could not outrun the holocaust, the crew's foreman set a back-fire to provide a makeshift shelter for the smokejumpers. Tragically, fear drove the men on and no one sought shelter with the foreman; the last words he recalled hearing before being engulfed by the flames were "To hell with this; I'm getting out of here!" Within minutes, eleven men lay dead on the hillside, killed by the super-heated air generated by the fire. Two other smokejumpers died the following day from severe burns. Three men, including the foreman, survived the fire. Only the 1994 South Canyon Fire in Colorado was deadlier for the National Forest Service's elite smokejumpers.

This marker is dedicated to the thirteen men who died in the Mann Gulch Fire.

## 43. The Montana Central Railroad
I-15, MP 239, Dearborn rest area, north of Wolf Creek

The Montana Central Railroad used to run on the tracks that follow Little Prickly Pear Creek and the highway. It was part of the railroad tycoon James J. Hill's plan to build a vast transcontinental transportation system. As the *Helena Weekly Herald* reported: "The Montana Central was a scheme inaugurated by Col. Broadwater [of Helena] and countenanced by James J. Hill of St. Paul, president of Manitoba Railroad. Its birth was coetaneous with the decision of Mr. Hill to begin the extension of the Manitoba to Montana and the West."

Hill and other railroad magnates took the first through train from St. Paul to Helena on Nov. 18, 1887. At the very hour that locals were dressing the city in flags and bunting to welcome Hill and party, the Northern Pacific Railroad attempted to keep the Montana Central tracklaying crew from building across its line. The blockage attracted much attention and a hot exchange of words, but was settled quickly; and without further incident, the track was completed. The Nov. 21 celebration was held as scheduled.

Helenans had rejoiced five years earlier when the Northern Pacific came to town because it meant competition for the stage companies and bull-team freighters. In turn, arrival of the Montana Central broke the NP's monopoly.

The Manitoba Railway became the Great Northern in 1890 and Montana Central sold out to them in 1907. Burlington Northern now owns these lines as well as most of the others in Montana.

## 44. Atlantic Cable Quartz Lode
Highway 1, MP 20, west of Anaconda

This mining property was located June 15, 1867, the name commemorating the laying of the second transatlantic cable.

The locators were Alexander Aiken, John B. Pearson and Jonas Stough. They were camped on Flint Creek and their horses drifted off. In tracking them to this vicinity the men found float that led to the discovery.

Machinery for the first mill was imported from Swansea, Wales, and freighted by team from Corinne, Utah, the nearest railroad point.

The mine was operated with indifferent success until about 1880 when extremely rich ore was opened up, a 500 ft. piece of ground producing $6,500,000 in gold. W. A. Clark paid $10,000 for one chunk of ore taken from this mine in 1889 and claimed it was the largest gold nugget ever found.

## 45. Anaconda
Montana 1, MP 7, east edge of Anaconda

Selected by Marcus Daly as a smelter site in 1883 because of an abundant supply of good water, Anaconda was the home of the Washoe Smelter of the Anaconda Copper Mining Company until 1980. History has been made here in the science of copper smelting, and the plant is famous throughout the mining and metallurgical world.

From a straggling tent town Anaconda grew to be a modern city, but retained all of the aggressive spirit of the pioneer days. This spirit refused to die with the Anaconda Co. pullout and the town remains a vital community.

## 46. Meaderville
I-15, MP 130, overlook north of Butte

William Allison and G. O. Humphreys had the Butte hill, richest hill on earth, entirely to themselves when they located their first quartz claims there in 1864.

They discovered an abandoned prospect hole which had evidently been dug by unknown miners a number of years before. These mysterious prospectors had used elk horn tines for gads, and broken bits of these primitive tools were found around the shafts. Allison and Humphreys died, their property passed into other hands, and they never knew that they were the potential owners of untold wealth.

Meaderville was named for Charles T. Meader, a forty-niner who went to California via Cape Horn and who came to Butte in 1876.

## 47. Butte
I-15, MP 130, overlook north of Butte

The "greatest mining camp on earth" built on "the richest hill in the world." That hill, which has produced over two billion dollars worth of gold, silver, copper and zinc, is literally honeycombed with drifts, winzes and stopes that extend beneath the city. There are over 3,000 miles of workings, and shafts reach a depth of 4,000 feet.

This immediate country was opened as a placer district in 1864. Later Butte became a quartz mining camp and successively opened silver, copper and zinc deposits.

Butte has a most cosmopolitan population derived from the four corners of the world. She was a bold, unashamed, rootin', tootin', hell-roarin' camp in days gone by and still drinks her liquor straight.

## 48. Mining Country
I-15, Frontage Road, MP 0, north of Basin

This is about the center of a rich mining district extending from Butte to Helena. The mountains are spurs of the Continental Divide.

Ghost and active mining camps are to be found in almost every gulch. The ores yield gold, silver, copper, lead and zinc. The district has been producing since quartz mining came into favor following the first wave of placer mining in the 1860s. In those days placer deposits were the poor man's eldorado. They needed little more than a grub stake, a pick and a shovel to work them. Quartz properties, seldom rich at the surface, required machinery and capital, transportation and smelting facilities.

Before smelters were built in Montana, ore from some of the richest mines in this region was shipped by freight team, boat and rail to Swansea, Wales, and Freiburg, Germany, for treatment.

## 49. Freighters
I-15, MP 178, Jefferson City rest area, south of Helena

Time was when ox and mule teams used to freight along this route. A five-ton truck doesn't look as picturesque but there hasn't been much change in the language of the drivers.

Jerk–line skinners were plumb fluent when addressing their teams. They got right earnest and personal. It was spontaneous, no effort about it. When they got strung out they were worth going a long ways to hear. As a matter of fact you didn't have to go a long ways, providing your hearing was normal. Adjectives came natural to them but they did bog down some on names. They had the same one for each of their string.

Those times have gone forever.

## 50. The Prickly Pear Diggings
I-15, Frontage Road, MP 11, south of Helena

The Fisk or Northern Overland Expedition camped on the future site of Montana City just east of the highway in September, 1862. The outfit consisting of 125 emigrants had left St. Paul June 16, 1862, under the leadership of Capt. James L. Fisk for the purpose of opening a wagon route to connect at Ft. Benton with the eastern terminal of the Mullan Road from Walla Walla.

They found "Gold Tom," one of Montana's first prospectors, holed up in a tepee near here scratching gravel along Prickly Pear Creek in a search for the rainbow's end. The few colors he was panning out wouldn't have made much of a dent in the national debt, but about half of the Fisk outfit got the gold fever and decided to winter here.

Montana City swaggered into existence in September 1864 as a roaring mining town that is only a memory now. Today it is a suburb of metropolitan Helena.

## 51. Thar's Gold in Them Thar Hills
U.S. 12, MP 69, north of Townsend

The mountains to the west are the Elkhorns. Those to the east across the Canyon Ferry Lake are the Big Belts. Both of these ranges are highly mineralized. Confederate Gulch of the Big Belts was famous in the 1860s for its rich placer diggings. Its Montana Bar, at the old boom camp of Diamond City, now a ghost town, has always been known as "the richest acre of ground in the world." The pay streak ran as high as $2,000 to the pan.

Most of the gulches in the Elkhorns were active as placer camps in the early days and this range is dotted with quartz mines still producing lead, zinc, silver and gold. Like most of the mountains in Montana they have been here a long time.

The Lewis and Clark Expedition came up the Missouri River through this valley in July, 1805.

## 52. The Boulder River Bridge
Montana 69, MP 35, at bridge south of Boulder
(scheduled for 2000 installation)

The trusses on this structure were salvaged from the "Hubbard" or "Red" Bridge. The original structure was built by the Gillette–Herzog Manufacturing Company in 1899. The company was one of several Minnesota–based bridge construction firms active in Montana from the late 19th century to the early 1920's. The bridge was one of eight pin–connected Pratt through truss spans built by the company over a ten year period beginning in 1891. It provided access to Boulder from the rich mining and ranching operations located on the west side of the river. The design of this structure represents an accord between local citizens wanting to preserve some aspect of the original bridge, while providing a structure that could accommodate modern traffic needs. The new bridge represents the best of late 19th century and late 20th century technologies.

## 53. The Humbug Spires Primitive Area
I-15, MP 108, Divide rest area, south of Butte

Named for its unique granite peaks, this primitive area is part of a geologic system of large-scale volcanic intrusions known as the Boulder Batholith, which extends north beyond Helena and south into Idaho.

Humbug Spires, which can be seen to the southeast, is part of the Highland Mountains. In 1866, rich gold placers were discovered near the Spires. Most of the mining occurred on the east and south sides of the area and produced large amounts of silver, lead, copper, and gold. Total value of production between 1876 and 1947 is estimated to have been as much as $3 million. Although there currently [1999] is no mining in the Humbug Spires Primitive Area, prospecting is done on surrounding lands.

The Spires offer the finest high quality hard-rock climbing in Montana and are an excellent place to hike, ride horses, sightsee, fish, and hunt.


## 54. Father De Smet
I-90, Frontage Road, MP 3, east of Whitehall

The Lewis and Clark Expedition passed here, westward bound, August 2, 1805. Captain Lewis named the Boulder River "Fields Creek" for one of the party.

In August, 1840, Pierre Jean De Smet, S.J., a Catholic missionary of Belgian birth, camped near the mouth of the Boulder River with the Flathead Indians and celebrated the holy sacrifice of the Mass. Father De Smet left the Indians soon after to go to St. Louis. He returned the following year and established the original St. Mary's Mission in the Bitter Root Valley, hereditary home of the Flatheads. Fearless and zealous, his many experiences during the pioneer days have been chronicled and form a most interesting chapter in the frontier annals of Montana.


## 55. Lewis and Clark Expedition
I-90, Frontage Road, MP 3, east of Whitehall

On August 1, 1805, the Lewis and Clark Expedition camped at a point 200 yards west from this spot, on the south bank of the river facing the mouth of the creek which flows into the river from the north. Meriwether Lewis and three others, on a scouting expedition in the hope of finding Sacajawea's people, had crossed the mountains to the northeast of here and coming down the North Boulder Valley had reached here at 2:00 P.M. They found a herd of elk grazing in the park here and killed two of them. After taking time out for an elk steak lunch, they headed on upstream leaving the two elk on the bank of the river for the expedition's dinner.

Captain Clark with the expedition reached here late in the evening after a strenuous day spent in snaking the boats up the canyon rapids by means of a long rawhide tow line which had broken in the rapids immediately below here with near calamitous results. At sight of the two elk, the hungry men called it a day and pitched camp. Reuben and Jo Fields went on a short hunt up the creek and killed five deer in the willow brakes which caused the stream to be named Field's Creek, now known as North Boulder. A large brown bear was seen on the south side of the river; Clark shot a big horn sheep in the canyon and Lewis shot two antelope a short distance up stream. Near camp was seen the first Maximilan Jay known to science. The temperature at sunrise on August 2 was fifty degrees above zero.

## 56. Browne's Bridge

Old U.S. Highway 91 (adjacent to Interstate 15), 1.5 miles north of Glen at the Montana Department of Fish, Wildlife and Parks Browne's Bridge Fishing Access

Browne's Bridge was constructed as a toll bridge by Fred Burr and James Minesinger in late 1862 and early 1863. The bridge was located on the Bannack to Deer Lodge Road. Joseph Browne, a miner, bought the bridge in 1865. The territorial legislature granted him a charter to maintain the bridge and charge travelers for its use. Within a few years, Browne had acquired about 3,000 acres near the bridge and had developed nearby Browne's Lake for recreational purposes. A post office was located just west of the bridge from 1872 until the early 1880s. Even though most of Montana's counties assumed control of the state's toll facilities by 1892, Browne operated the bridge until his death in 1909. Beaverhead and Madison counties assumed joint ownership of the bridge in 1911.

In 1915 the counties petitioned the Montana State Highway Commission for a new bridge. The Commission designed the bridge in 1915; a Missoula company built it during the autumn and winter of that year. A riveted Warren through truss bridge, it was one of the first structures designed by the Commission's bridge department. In 1920 high water destroyed the old structure, which was located slightly upstream from this bridge.

Beaverhead County rehabilitated this bridge with funds provided by the Montana Department of Transportation.

## 57. Bannack

I 15, MP 55, Barrett's rest area, southbound, south of Dillon

The Lewis and Clark Expedition, westward bound, passed here in August, 1805.

The old mining camp of Bannack is on Grasshopper Creek about twenty miles west of here. The first paying placer discovery in Montana was made in that vicinity by John White, July 28, 1862, and Bannack became the first capital of Montana Territory. They should have built it on wheels. The following spring six prospectors discovered Alder Gulch and practically the entire population of Bannack stampeded to the new diggings where the new camp of Virginia City eventually became the capital until it was changed to Helena.

Henry Plummer, sheriff and secret chief of the road agents, was hanged at Bannack in 1864 by the Vigilantes. It tamed him down considerably.

## 58. The Montana-Utah Road

I-15, MP 37, Red Rocks rest area, north of Lima

Interstate 15 is the latest in a series of roads that have traversed this area since prehistory. Although used for generations by Native Americans, the first recorded use of this route was by the Lewis and Clark Expedition on August 10, 1805. They named cliffs to the north of here after the scores of rattlesnakes they encountered on their trip upriver. With the discovery of gold at nearby Grasshopper Creek and Alder Gulch in the early 1860s, thousands of people came to southwest Montana to mine gold and to "mine the miners." The road originated in Corinne, Utah and traversed a series of high plateaus and narrow canyons on its way north to southwestern Montana. The road was the best route into the territory for the freighters who supplied the mining camps. Drawn by teams of mules or oxen, each wagon carried up to 12,000 pounds of freight. The trip from Utah typically took three weeks and a freighting outfit could usually make three or four round trips each year. Just south of here near Dell, the Montana–Utah Road branched

into three separate trails that led to Bannack, Deer Lodge, Virginia City and Helena. This section of the road terminated at Helena. With the arrival of the Utah & Northern Railroad in 1880, the Montana–Utah Road became obsolete. In the 1920s, however, it again became an important travel corridor first as the Vigilante Trail/Great White Way, then as U.S. Highway 91 and, finally, as Interstate 15.

## 59. Old Trail to the Gold Diggins'
I-15, MP 34, Dell–Red Rock rest area, northbound, north of Lima

Along in the early 1840s the Americans were like they are now, seething to go somewhere. It got around that Oregon was quite a place. The Iowa people hadn't located California yet. A wagon train pulled out across the plains and made it to Oregon. Then everyone broke out into a rash to be going west.

They packed their prairie schooners with their household goods, gods, and garden tools. Outside of Indians, prairie fires, cholera, famine, cyclones, cloud bursts, quick sand, snow slides, and blizzards they had a tolerably blithe and gay trip.

When gold was found in Montana some of them forked off from the main highway and surged along this trail aiming to reach the rainbow's end. It was mostly one-way traffic but if they did meet a backtracking outfit there was plenty of room to turn out.

## 60. Jefferson Valley
Montana 41, MP 47, north of Twin Bridges

The Lewis and Clark Expedition, westward bound, came up the Jefferson River in August, 1805. They were hoping to find the Shoshone Indians, Sacajawea's tribe, and trade for horses to use in crossing the mountains west of here. Just south of here the river forks, the east fork being the Ruby and the west fork the Beaverhead. They followed the latter and met the Shoshones near Armstead, which is now under the Clark Canyon Reservoir 20 miles south of Dillon.

On the return trip from the coast in 1806, Capt. Wm. Clark retraced their former route down this valley to Three Forks, and then crossed the Yellowstone. Capt. Lewis left Clark in the Bitter Root Valley, crossed the Divide via the Big Blackfoot River and thence to Great Falls. They met near the mouth of the Yellowstone, arriving within nine days of each other.

## 61. Beaverhead Rock
Montana 41, north of Dillon

On August 10, 1805, members of the Lewis and Clark expedition pushed their way up the Jefferson River's tributaries toward the Continental Divide and the Pacific Ocean beyond. Toward afternoon they sighted what Clark called a "remarkable Clift" to the west. Sacajawea (or, as Lewis spelled it: Sahcahgarweah), their Indian guide for this portion of the trip, said her tribe called the large promontory "Beaver's head."

Both Lewis and Clark agreed on the rock's likeness to the fur-bearing animal and recorded the name in their journals. They continued south only to encounter a heavy rain and hail storm. "the men defended themselves from the hail by means of the willow bushes but all the party got perfectly wet," Lewis said. They camped upstream from the Beaver's head, enjoyed freshly killed deer meat, then pushed on the next day.

Beaverhead Rock served as an important landmark not only for Lewis and Clark, but also for the trappers, miners, and traders who followed them into the vicinity. It is the namesake for the county in which it is now located, retaining the same appearance that inspired Sacajawea and her people to name it centuries ago.

## 62. Robber's Roost
Montana 287, MP 28, south of Sheridan

In 1863, Pete Daly built a road house on the stage route between Virginia City and Bannack to provide entertainment for man and beast. The main floor was a shrine to Bacchus and Lady Luck. The second floor was dedicated to Terpsichore and bullet holes in the logs attest the fervor of ardent swains for fickle sirens. Occasionally a gent succumbed.

Pete's tavern became a hangout for unwholesome characters who held up stage coaches and robbed lone travellers. One of the road agents is alleged to have left a small fortune in gold cached in the vicinity.

In later years, time and neglect gave the building its present hapless look and it became known as Robbers' Roost. It is in the cottonwood grove just across the railroad tracks. Drive over and pay your respects but please don't dig up the premises trying to locate the cache.

## 63. The Ruby Valley
Montana 287, MP 22, near Alder

The Ruby River was called the Passamari by the Indians and became known as the Stinking Water to the whites in the pioneer days. It joins the Beaverhead to form the Jefferson Fork of the Missouri.

Fur trappers, Indians, prospectors and road agents have ridden the trails through here in days gone by.

The large gravel piles to the west are the tailings resulting from gold dredging operations over about a twenty-year period beginning in 1899. The dredges are reported to have recovered between eight and nine million dollars in gold from the floor of the valley and the lower end of Alder Gulch.

## 64. Adobetown
Montana 287, MP 17, northwest of Virginia City

Placer riches in Alder Gulch spawned many colorful communities. Among them, Adobetown flourished briefly as the center of mining activity in 1864. In that year alone, miners extracted over $350,000 in gold from nearby streams.

Taking its name from the numerous adobe shacks the miners constructed in the vicinity, Adobetown assumed permanence in the fall of 1865 when Nicholas Carey and David O'Brien erected a large log store. The building's central location contributed to the growth of the settlement and the development of other businesses. Stages from Salt Lake City and later the Union Pacific Railroad at Corinne, Utah, made regular stops at the Adobetown store for passengers and mail.

The town received an official post office in 1875 with Carey as postmaster. He, and later his wife Mary, served as the community's only postmasters until her retirement and the subsequent close of the office in the fall of 1907.

Once in lively rivalry with Virginia City for social and political leadership of Alder Gulch, Adobetown's population and importance waned after 1865 as the placer gold gave out in the immediate area.

## 65. Nevada City

Montana 287, MP 16, at Nevada City

A ghost town now, but once one of the hell roarin' mining camps that lined Alder Gulch in the 1860s. It was a trading point where gold dust and nuggets were the medium of exchange: where men were men and women were scarce. A stack of whites cost twenty, the sky was the limit and everyone was heeled.

The first Vigilante execution took place here when George Ives, notorious road agent, was convicted of murder and hanged.

The gulch was once filled with romance, glamour, melodrama, comedy and tragedy. It's plumb peaceful now.

## 66. Virginia City

Montana 287, MP 14, near Virginia City

All of Montana has the deepest pride and affection for Virginia City. No more colorful pioneer mining camp ever existed. Dramatic tales of the early days in this vicinity are legion.

Rich placer diggin's were discovered in Alder Gulch in the spring of

1863 and the stampede of gold-seekers and their parasites was on. Sluices soon lined the gulch and various "cities" blossomed forth as trading and amusement centers for freehanded miners. Virginia City, best known of these and the sole survivor, became the Capital of the Territory. Pioneers, who with their descendants were to mold the destinies of the state, were among its first citizens. If you like true stories more picturesque than fiction, Virginia City and Alder Gulch can furnish them in countless numbers.

## 67. Bozeman Trail
U.S. 287, MP 60, 5 miles south of Norris

In 1840, the Oregon Trail was the primary emigration route across the northern part of the United States. Two decades later, when gold was discovered west of here, a trail called the "Corrine Road" was used to bring supplies north from Salt Lake City to Bannack and Virginia City. John Bozeman, determined to shorten the time and distance to the gold strikes, scouted another route, departing from the Oregon Trail at the North Platte River. The Bozeman Trail, or Montana Cutoff, shown below, crossed here and can be seen on the opposite hillside.

This trail was used from 1863 to 1868. Sioux Indians frequently attacked the wagons and freight trains as they crossed the eastern leg of the trail. Consequently, Fort Reno, Fort Phil Kearney and Fort C. F. Smith were established to protect travelers but were also the target of Indian attacks.

## 68. Raynold's Pass
U.S. 287, MP 16, rest area, south of Ennis

The low gap in the mountains on the sky line south of here is Raynold's Pass over the Continental Divide.

Jim Bridger, famous trapper and scout, guided an expedition of scientists through the pass in June of 1860. The party was led by Capt. W. F. Raynolds of the Corps of Engineers, U.S. Army. They came through from the south and camped that night on the Madison River near this point. Capt. Raynolds wrote "The pass is . . . so level that it is difficult to locate the exact point at which the waters divide. I named it Low Pass and deem it to be one of the most remarkable and important features of the topography of the Rocky Mountains."

Jim Bridger didn't savvy road maps or air route beacons but he sure knew his way around.

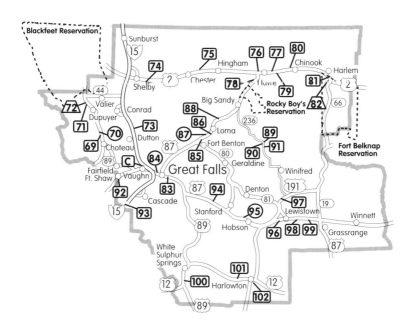

Blackfeet Reservation

Sunburst

15

74 ?

Shelby

Hingham 75 76 77 80

Chester 78 Chinook

Havre 81 Harlem

79 2

Big Sandy 82 66

Valier 88 Rocky Boy's Reservation

72 Conrad 86

71 73 87 Loma 236

70 Dutton 87 89 Fort Belknap Reservation

69 Choteau Fort Benton 89

89 87 80 91

Fairfield Ft. Shaw C 84 85 90

Vaughn Great Falls Geraldine

92 Winifred

Cascade 83 87 94 191

15 93 Denton

Stanford 95 81 97 19

89 Hobson Lewistown Winnett

96 98 99 Grassrange

White Sulphur Springs 87

101

12 100 Harlowton 12

89 102

~ Legend ~

85 General Highway Markers

7 Indian Historical Markers

84 105 Lewis & Clark Expedition Markers

F Markers no longer displayed

- - - - Indian Reservations & National Parks

Tourism country boundaries

Highways

# Russell Country

## 69. Old Agency on the Teton
U.S. 89, MP 45, northwest of Choteau

About ¼ mile SE of this point, a huge native stone marks the site of "Old Agency" of the former Blackfeet Indian Reservation. The agency was established in 1868–69 and with unusual generosity, the whites in authority permitted Blackfeet chiefs to select the location. They chose the spot known to them as "Four Persons" because of the pleasant memories associated with it. Some of their warriors had overtaken and dispatched four furtive Crees there a few years before.

At Old Agency, in 1869, the first government agricultural experiment was conducted. In 1872 the first public school was opened for the benefit of the Blackfeet. Neither project attained notable popularity with the beneficiaries. However, that same year they were impressed by young "Brother Van," a circuit-riding Methodist lay preacher, not so much by the sincere fervor of his oratory as by his courage, skill and stamina during a buffalo hunt staged in his honor.

The Northwest Fur Company and I. G. Baker and Brother operated licensed Indian trading posts near the agency where they pursued the tolerably lucrative business of bartering tobacco, beads, and other essential goods for furs.

At his request, Big Lake, a great chief of the Blackfeet, was buried on a high point overlooking Old Agency so that his spirit could look down on his people as they came to trade.

Reservation boundaries were moved north to Birch Creek by a Congressional Act of April 15, 1874 and in 1876 Old Agency on the Teton was abandoned.

## 70. Blackfeet and Buffalo
U.S. 89, MP 46, north of Choteau

In the days of the fur traders and trappers immediately following the time of the Lewis and Clark Expedition (1804–06) all of this country bordering the Rocky Mountains from here north into Canada and south to the three forks of the Missouri and to the Yellowstone River was buffalo range and the hunting grounds of the Blackfeet Nation. These Indians were fierce and willing fighters who jealously guarded their territory from invasion.

Like all of the Plains Indians they were dependent upon the buffalo for their existence. The herds meant meat, moccasins, robes, leggings and tepees. Board and room on the hoof. Some Indian legends say that the first buffalo came out of a hole in the ground. When the seemingly impossible happened and the buffalo were wiped out there were Indians who claimed the whites found the spot, hazed the herds back into it, and plugged the hole.

## 71. Dupuyer
U.S. 89, MP 76, Dupuyer rest area, north of Dupuyer

Dupuyer, a colorful frontier cattle town and 1880s stop on the Fort Shaw–Fort Macleod Trail, is the oldest town between Fort Benton and the Rocky Mountains. Joe Kipp and Charlie Thomas, whiskey traders, settled here to raise cattle in 1874 and sold their holdings to Jimmy Grant in 1877. Jimmy was killed by an Indian and is buried east of the highway.

To the west, following the base of the mountains, lies one of the oldest trails in the United States. It began when early North American natives used it as a primary north–south route. Jim Bridger and his kind knew it as "The Old Travois Trail." When white men bootlegged

whiskey into Canada, it became known as the "Pondera Trail."

The refugees of the Riel Rebellion came to Dupuyer Creek in 1885 and many remained to make this area their home. The Home Ranch on Dupuyer Creek was headquarters for the famous Seven Block Cattle spread of the Conrads and a frequent stopping place for Montana's noted western artist, Charlie Russell.

## 72. Chief Mountain and Old North Trail
U.S. 89, MP 76, Dupuyer rest area, north of Dupuyer

Chief Mountain, NINASTAQUAY, has always been known to the Blackfeet people. Identified on maps as King Mountain as early as 1796, this outstanding landmark has long been revered for its supernatural powers. Generations of Blackfeet have used Chief Mountain for fasting and prayer. In 1992, the Blackfeet Tribe, by Tribal Resolution, limited public access into the area.

The ancient Old North Trail, well worn by centuries of Indian travois, entered the United States from the north, a few miles west of present day Port of Piegan Customs. It ran along the east slope of the Rocky Mountains from Edmonton, Alberta, to at least as far as Helena, Montana. Perhaps one of the great migration routes of early man, the Trail more recently served the Northwest Plains Indians as the route for war parties and exchanging goods between Canada and the United States. The Museum of the Plains Indian in Browning relates the story of Plains Indian culture including native travel patterns from earliest times to the present.

## 73. The Whoop-Up Trail
I-15, MP 318, Teton River rest area, north of Dutton

During the 1860s and 1870s supplies and trade goods that came up the Missouri River from St. Louis were transferred at Fort Benton from steamboat to wagon freight for inland distribution. In 1868, a freight trail was open from Fort Benton to Fort McLeod, a military post in

Canada located west of Lethbridge. Traders, who eagerly swapped firewater for furs, soon found themselves in need of protection from their patrons who sometimes felt they hadn't been given a square deal. This encouraged the building of "whiskey forts" or trading posts along the trail. The exact origin of the name "Whoop-up" is lost, but one old-timer told this story: "When Johnny LaMotte, one of the traders, returned to [Fort] Benton from across the border, he was asked, 'How's business?' 'Aw, they're just whoopin' 'er up!' was the reply."

The Whoop-up Trail was the precursor in reverse of Alberta–Montana rum-running channels of the noble experiment era. Though its prime traffic furthered the trading of headaches for hides it did gain a modicum of respectability by becoming a supply route for a few legitimate wares consigned to old Fort McLeod. The trail ran near here.

## 74. The Oily Boid Gets the Woim
U.S. 2, MP 282, east of Shelby

A narrow gauge railroad nicknamed the "turkey track" used to connect Great Falls, Montana, and Lethbridge, Alberta. When the main line of the Great Northern crossed it in 1891, Shelby Junction came into existence. The hills and plains around here were cow country. The Junction became an oasis where parched cowpunchers cauterized their tonsils with forty-rod and grew plumb irresponsible and ebullient.

In 1910 the dry-landers began homesteading. They built fences and plowed under the native grass. The days of open range were gone. Shelby quit her swaggering frontier ways and became concrete sidewalk and sewer system conscious.

Dry land farming didn't turn out to be such a profitable endeavor but in 1921 geologists discovered that this country had an ace in the hole. Oil was struck between here and the Canadian line, and the town boomed again.

## 75. The Sweet Grass Hills
U.S. 2, MP 327, east of Chester

You can see the Sweet Grass Hills or the Three Buttes to the north of here on a reasonably clear day. The Indians used them as watch towers from which they could locate buffalo herds. Things sure grow in this country. Some old-timers claim that when they arrived those buttes weren't much bigger than prairie dog mounds.

In 1884 a Blackfoot Indian found gold in them thar hills and the usual stampede followed. The middle peak is called Gold Butte. It was claimed that the placer ground in Two Bits Gulch produced twenty-five cents in colors for every shovel full of gravel.

The pay dirt has been pretty well worked out and the glamour of boom days is gone, but a few old-timers still prospect the gulches, hoping some day to find that elusive pot of gold at the rainbow's end, called the Mother Lode.

## 76. Wahkpa Chu'gn Meat Market
U.S. 2, MP 381, Havre

Just behind this modern shopping center is a market of an earlier vintage. Located on the Milk River (called Wahkpa Chu'gn or "Middle River" by the Assiniboine) is a communal bison kill and meat-processing camp used extensively from about 2000 to 600 years ago. This site contains both a bison jump (where the buffalo would be run over a cliff to their deaths below) and an impoundment (where the animals would be corralled, then killed). The hunter could choose the more efficient method for the situation at hand. The grazing area for the buffalo was southeast of Havre below Saddle Butte Mountain. It is farm land today, but you can visualize the browsing herds and the Indians' drive lanes leading toward the kill site.

The site, listed on the National Historic Register as "Too Close for Comfort" because of its proximity to Havre, is owned by Hill County and administered by the H. Earl Clack Museum. They may be contacted for tours during the summer season.

## 77. Havre
U.S. 2, MP 385, east of Havre

Cowpunchers, miners, and soldiers are tolerably virile persons as a rule. When they went to town in the frontier days seeking surcease from vocational cares and solace in the cup that cheers it was just as well for the urbanites to either brace themselves or take to cover. The citizens of any town willing and able to be host city for a combination of the above diamonds in the rough had to be quick on the draw and used to inhaling powder smoke.

Havre came into existence as a division point when the Great Northern Railroad was built and purveyed pastime to cowboys, doughboys and miners on the side. It is hard to believe now, but as a frontier camp, she was wild and hard to curry.

## 78. Fort Assinniboine
U.S. 87, MP 107, south of Havre

Established in 1879, Fort Assinniboine was one of the most strategically-placed U.S. Army posts in the northwest. Headquarters for the District of Montana, the fort and military reserve encompassed the entire Bears Paw mountain range. The post was constructed by the 18th U.S. Infantry under the command of Colonel Thomas Ruger. When completed, the 51 substantial brick buildings included officers' quarters, barracks, a large hospital, chapel, gymnasium, officers' club, stables, and warehouses. The fort was built to protect settlers to the south from possible raids by Sitting Bull's Hunkpapa Sioux who fled to Canada after Custer's defeat on the Little Big Horn in 1876. The military's fears proved groundless, however, as no serious Indian disturbances occurred in the area.

General John J. Pershing served here in the 1890s, earning his nickname "Black Jack" because of his association with the Afro-American 10th Cavalry–the famed "Buffalo Soldiers." For many years, Fort Assinniboine soldiers worked with the Canadian Mounties to quell smuggling across the border.

In 1911, the War Department abandoned the post. A few years later, the landless Chippewa and Cree Indians found a home on the southern part of the military reserve when it was set aside as Rocky Boy's Reservation. The State of Montana purchased the fort's remaining buildings and 2,000 acres for use as the Northern Agricultural Research Center of Montana State University–Bozeman.

## 79. Hurry, Honyocker, Hurry!
U.S. 2, MP 387, Havre fairgrounds

"Honyocker, scissorbill, nester . . . He was the Joad of a quarter century ago, swarming into hostile land; duped when he started, robbed when he arrived; hopeful, courageous, ambitious: he sought independence

or adventure, comfort and security. Or perhaps he sought wealth; for there were some who did not share the Joad's love of the soil, whose interest was speculative. . . .

"The honyocker was farmer, spinster, deep-sea diver; fiddler, physician, bartender, cook. He lived in Minnesota or Wisconsin, Massachusetts or Maine. There the news sought him out—Jim Hill's news of free land in the Treasure State:

"'More Free Homesteads; Another Big Land Opening; 1,400,000 Acres Comprising Rocky Boy Indian Lands Open to Settlers; MONTANA. . . .

"'By order of the secretary of the interior, the lands shown on the map herein will be opened to homestead settlement March 10, 1910, and to entry at the Glasgow, Montana, land office.'"

Thus Joseph Kinsey Howard described Montana's last frontier of settlement in *Montana High, Wide and Handsome*. Promoted by railway, by government, and by the American dream, train loads of newcomers rolled in and filed homestead entries. They fenced the range and plowed under the native grasses. With the optimism born of inexperience and promoters' propaganda they looked forward to bumper crops on semi-arid bench land, but the benches were never meant for a Garden of Eden. There were a few years of hope, then drought with its endless cycle of borrowing and crop failure. Between 1921 and 1925, one out of every two Montana farmers lost his place to mortgage foreclosure. Those who survived learned the lessons of dryland farming and irrigation.

## 80. The Battle of Bears Paw
U.S. 2, MP 403, Chinook

This battle was fought September 30 to October 5, 1877, on Snake Creek, about 20 miles south of here near the Bears Paw Mountains, where after a five days' siege Chief Joseph, one of five remaining Nez Perce leaders, surrendered to Col. Nelson A. Miles of the U.S. Army.

The usual forked-tongue methods of the whites, which had deprived these Indians of their hereditary lands, caused Joseph and six other primary chiefs to lead their people on a tortuous 2000 mile march from their home in Idaho to evade U.S. troops and gain sanctuary in Canada.

These great Indian generals fought against fearful odds. They and their warriors could have escaped by abandoning their women, children and wounded. They refused to do this.

Joseph's courage and care for his people were admired by Col. Miles who promised him safe return to Idaho. One of the blackest records in our dealings with the Indians was the Government's repudiation of this promise and the subsequent treatment accorded Joseph and his followers.

## 81. Fort Belknap Reservation
U.S. 2, MP 428, rest area, southeast of Harlem

Fort Belknap Reservation was established in 1888 when the Gros Ventres, Blackfeet, and River Crows ceded to the government 17,500,000 acres of their joint reservation that had covered all of northern Montana east of the Rocky Mountains. Home for the Gros Ventres and Assiniboines, who had shared hunting rights on the reservation, it was named for Wm. W. Belknap, secretary of war under President U. S. Grant.

The Gros Ventres (French for "big belly" and pronounced "Grow Von") got the name courtesy of the early French fur trappers. Also known as Atsina, the tribe's own name for themselves is A'a'ninin or "White Clay People." Always a small tribe, they lived in the Red River Valley, North Dakota, from about 1100 to 1400 A.D., then moved west, splitting into two tribes around 1730. One group moved southwest and became the Arapaho, the other northwest, ending up in Montana by the early 1800s. They were close allies to the Blackfeet.

Tradition credits the Assiniboine tribe as separating from the Yanktonai Sioux in the early 1600s. Two of the first ladies of the tribe, wives of leaders, quarreled over an epicurean delicacy, viz. a buffalo heart. The gentlemen chipped in and the tribe split. One faction headed west and became known as the Assiniboine. They call themselves Nakota, meaning "The Peaceful Ones." When the reservation was created, part of the tribe enrolled here and the remainder at Fort Peck, about 180 miles to the east.

## 82. The Vision Quest
Montana 66, near junction with U.S. 2, at MP 428
in view of Snake Butte

High points such as mountain tops and tabletop buttes are considered powerful and sacred areas by many Indian peoples. Snake Butte is one such location, often used as a place for the spiritual rite of vision questing. The individual vision quest is an intensely private ritual in which a man or woman seeks supernatural power, or medicine. The Supreme Being grants this power through an intermediary spirit which can be a living or nonliving entity such as an animal, a spider, a snake, or a rock. The devout quester may acquire powers of war, wealth, love, doctoring, or prophesy which must be used only to good ends; misuse brings very serious consequences, even death. First cleansing the body through a sweatlodge purification ceremony, the quester then withdraws to a secluded location for three to four days. Fasting and praying, the quester seeks contact with a spiritual being. The successful vision quest takes great concentration and courage. Not all quests are successful, but for those so chosen, acceptance of the power offered is a great responsibility, sometimes not without a price. It is said that those who acquire certain powers never live a long life.

## 83. Lewis and Clark Portage Route
U.S. 87/89, MP 91, 10th Avenue South, Great Falls

To avoid the series of waterfalls along the Missouri River north of this point, the Expedition portaged their canoes and several tons of baggage, crossing the highway right here. At the lower camp, some 12 miles NE the crew made crude wagons, the wheels sliced off a cottonwood tree. The upper camp, named after the bears which inhabited the islands, was located some 5 miles SW.

The portage was near man–killing: "the men has to haul with all their strength wate & art," Clark wrote.

## 84. Black Eagle Falls
River Drive, east of 15th Street Bridge, Great Falls

The uppermost of the Great Falls of the Missouri bears west of this point. The name is a modern one derived from an entry for June 14th, 1805 in the journal of Capt. Meriwether Lewis of the Lewis and Clark Expedition. He discovered the falls on that date and wrote, ". . . below this fall at a little distance a beautifull little Island well timbered is situated about the middle of the river. in this Island on a Cottonwood tree an Eagle has placed her nest; a more inaccessable spot I believe she could not have found; for neither man nor beast dare pass those gulphs which separate her little domain from the shores."

After viewing the falls, Capt. Lewis ascended the hill to the former location of the smelter stack and saw ". . . in these plains and more particularly in the valley just below me immence herds of buffaloe. . . ."

## 85. Fort Benton
U.S. 87, MP 41, northeast of Fort Benton

Capt. Clark with members of the Lewis and Clark Expedition camped on the site of Fort Benton June 4, 1805.

Originally a trading post of the American Fur Co., it became head of navigation on the Missouri with the arrival of the first steamboat from St. Louis in 1859. She boomed in the early 1860s as a point of entry to the newly discovered placer mines of western Montana. Supplies were freighted out by means of ox teams and profanity.

An early observer states, "Perhaps nowhere else were ever seen motlier crowds of daubed and feathered Indians, buckskin–arrayed half-breed nobility, moccasined trappers, voyageurs, gold seekers and bull drivers . . . on the opening of the boating season. . . ."

## 86. Great Northern Railway
U.S. 87, MP 51, south of Loma

The railroad grade you see before you was the St. Paul, Minneapolis and Manitoba Railway, a precursor of the Great Northern Railway. James J. Hill, owner and builder, constructed this line in record time in 1887 to serve wealthy mining communities. There he offered more competitive freight rates to take business away from the Northern Pacific and Union Pacific transcontinental railroads.

As railroads competed for ascendancy, Montana's cities vied for transportation facilities. Fort Benton had prospered as the head of steamboat navigation and the hub of freight and stage lines to settlements in Montana, Idaho and Canada. As railroads replaced steamboats as carriers, this line bypassed Fort Benton, ending its economic importance in transportation. This line went directly to Great Falls, enabling that city to grow as an industrial and rail center.

## 87. Marias River
U.S. 87, MP 51, south of Loma

The Lewis and Clark Expedition camped at the mouth of this river just east of here June 3, 1805. Lewis named it Maria's River in honor of his cousin, Miss Maria Wood (over time the apostrophe was dropped). Until exploration proved otherwise, most members of the party believed this river to be the main channel of the Missouri.

On his return trip from the coast in 1806 Capt. Lewis explored the Marias almost to its source.

In the fall of 1831 James Kipp of the American Fur Co. built Fort Piegan at the mouth of the river, as a trading post for the Blackfoot Indians, and acquired 2,400 beaver "plews" or skins by trade during the first 10 days. In 1832 the post was abandoned and the Indians burned it.

## 88. A Montana Crossroads
U.S. 87, MP 55, 3 miles northeast of Loma

The Missouri River once flowed northeasterly through this valley to Hudson Bay. During the Bull Lake Ice Age, an ice dam near Loma diverted the river into its current channel. This channel began filling with glacial sediment, preventing the river from returning to its original course when the dam finally broke about 70,000 to 130,000 years ago. Several sections of the highway between Loma and Havre follow Big Sandy Creek, which is located in the old river channel.

From this point you also have a panoramic view of the drainages of three major Montana river systems: the Teton, Marias and Missouri. To the southwest, the Teton and Marias Rivers merge near Loma before joining the Missouri about a mile downstream. In the background are the Bear's Paw Mountains to the east, Square Butte and Round Butte to the southeast, the Highwood Mountains toward the south, and the Little Belt Mountains in the southwest.

Because of the geography, this area was the crossroads for many events important to Montana history. The Lewis and Clark Expedition passed through here in 1805. They were followed by fur traders, the steamboats, the Great Northern Railway and the homesteaders.

## 89. Fort Chardon

Secondary 236, MP 50, north side of the Missouri River

Captains Meriwether Lewis and William Clark passed through this area (1805) on their expedition to the Pacific Ocean, and the landscape here remains much as they described it. Fur trappers and traders then followed them into the Upper Missouri region. Fort Chardon was erected (1844) on this bank, but local Indian hostilities forced its closure two years later. The north bank also was the site of two important treaty councils. In 1846, Father Pierre Jean De Smet convened the Blackfeet and the Salish here to end their open warfare. In 1855, Governor Isaac I. Stevens organized a meeting of more than 3,000 Blackfeet, Gros Ventres, Nez Perces, and Salish to produce a major treaty between the tribes and the government. This area first was homesteaded in the 1880s. Traces of early homestead irrigation systems can still be seen within the National Historic District.

## 90. The Judith Landing

Secondary 236, MP 49, south of Missouri River

This area, which surrounds the confluence of the Missouri and Judith Rivers, was designated a National Historic District in 1974 because of its historic importance to Montana's transportation system. Missouri River steamboats en route to Fort Benton tied up at Judith Landing to buy fuel from "woodhawks." The rotted stumps of trees cut for fuel can still be seen in the area. At the Judith's mouth, Camp Cooke was built (1866) to protect river travellers from Indian attacks. In 1872, T. C. Power erected the Fort Claggett Trading Post just below the mouth of the Judith. Renamed Judith Landing, the site became a bustling community including (1885) a large stone warehouse, saloon, hotel, stable, blacksmith shop, and store. The PN (Power-Norris) Ferry provided transportation across the Missouri. The Lohse Family started (1923) a new ferry downstream, and it operated until the Winifred Bridge was built in 1982.

## 91. Claggett Hill Trail
Secondary 236, MP 46, northwest of Winifred

In 1866, the U.S. army established Camp Cooke on the west bank of the Judith River near here to protect local settlers from Indian raids. Shortly thereafter, steamboat entrepreneur and trader T. C. Power built a small trading post near the camp to supply goods and services to the soldiers. The post was named Fort Claggett in honor of William Claggett, one of Montana Territory's most respected politicians and capitalists. After Camp Cooke closed in 1870, Power built a second Fort Claggett east of the Judith River about two miles from this marker. Strategically located near a river ford, the fort obtained supplies from steamboats plying the Missouri and shipped out beaver pelts, buffalo hides and cattle. By 1884, this segment of the Claggett Trail was heavily used by freighters, cowboys, businessmen, Indians and miners seeking their fortunes in the nearby Judith Mountains. In the mid–1880s, Power and Gilman Norris formed the Judith Mercantile and Cattle Company with its headquarters at Fort Claggett. At its peak in the late 1880s, Fort Claggett consisted of a store, hotel, saloon, warehouse, mail station, stables and sheep sheds. Although Fergus County has actively maintained portions of the Claggett Trail, this section exists unaltered and is representative of late 19th century freighting roads.

## 92. Fort Shaw

Montana 200, MP 133, west of Fort Shaw

Barring fur trading posts, the first important white settlements in Montana were the mining camps in the western mountains. Everything to the east belonged to the plains Indians and was buffalo range. To protect the miners and settlers from possible incursions of hostile tribes, a series of military posts was established around the eastern border of the mining camps and settlements. Fort Shaw, established in 1867, was one of these. It also protected the stage and freight trail from Fort Benton, head of navigation on the Missouri, to the Last Chance Gulch placer diggings at Helena. Everything north of the Sun River was Blackfeet Indian Territory at that time. The fort was built by the 13th U.S. Infantry, under Major Wm. Clinton.

General Gibbon led his troops from here in 1876 to join General Terry and General Custer on the Yellowstone just prior to the latter's disastrous fight with the Sioux and Cheyenne Indians at the Battle of the Little Big Horn.

## 93. St. Peter's Mission

I-15, MP 245, Missouri River scenic turnout,
southwest of Cascade

Approximately 10 miles northwest of here the Jesuit missionaries to the Blackfeet established their fourth mission near Birdtail stage route on the old Mullan Road. They had abandoned three earlier sites due to Indian attack or inadequacy for subsistence farming. Even this site was left uninhabited for eight years. Ironically, the same year the Jesuits returned (1874), Congress moved the reservation boundary northward, putting the Mission over 60 miles outside Blackfeet country!

To continue operation, the Jesuits converted the Mission into an Indian school for boys. Ten years later, Ursuline nuns opened a girls' school and taught Indian and white children. The Mission flourished until 1895 when the government established its own Indian schools and quit paying tuition. The Ursulines continued to teach white girls there until 1912 when they moved to new quarters in Great Falls.

A small group of Metis (people of Indian and white descent) settled on the Dearborn River near the Mission after the unsuccessful 1870 rebellion in Canada. One of them, Louis Riel, became a lay teacher at St. Peter's until some of his compatriots traveled from Canada in 1884 to ask his help in a second rebellion. Again they failed and Riel was hanged. Metis continued to live near the Mission for years, but their numbers were diminished in a smallpox epidemic in the early 1900s. They are buried in the Mission cemetery.

## 94. "Mining Plays Second Fiddle"
U.S. 87, MP 24, east of Geyser

"MINING PLAYS SECOND FIDDLE – FOR THE FIRST TIME IN MONTANA'S HISTORY AGRICULTURAL PRODUCTS TAKE THE LEAD." Newspaper headlines in 1910 proclaimed the change brought about by settlement of more than one million acres of Montana land. By 1922 over 40% of the entire state would have claims filed on it.

This immediate area got a big influx of homesteaders between 1900 and 1910. Many Finns settled the benchland northeast of here, thereafter called Finn Bench. Many of them got their stake in Montana as coal miners in Sand Coulee, Belt, or Stockett or as silver miners in Neihart.

Once on the freight and stage route between Great Falls and Lewistown, Judith Basin was occupied mainly by a few stockgrowers before that homestead boom. Arrival of the Great Northern Railway in 1908 signaled the end of the isolated range. It advertised "Wheat–Forty Bushels to the Acre" and "Stockmen's Paradise Has Become the Home Builders Garden Spot" to attract farmers to stake their claims here. Great Northern was motivated by its need to fill its box cars for the return trips east. What better way than to promote the government's free land to farmers who would have to ship their crops to eastern markets?

## 95. The Judith River
U.S. 87, MP 58, west of Hobson

When the Lewis and Clark Expedition came up the Missouri River in 1805 Capt. Clark named the Judith River for one of the girls he left behind him.

Southwest of here is the Pig-eye Basin and beyond that, in the Little Belt Mountains, is Yogo Gulch. Yogo sapphires are mined there. They are the deepest colored sapphires found in the world and the only ones mined from a lode. When combined with Montana nuggets they make a mighty pretty and unique combination for rings, cuff links, pins and similar fancy doodads. Oriental, as well as all other Montana sapphires are found in placer ground.

The Judith Basin country was the early-day stomping ground of Charley M. Russell, famous and beloved Montana cowboy artist. Charley is now camped somewhere across the Great Divide where the grass is good and there aren't any fences.

## 96. The Judith Basin Country
U.S. 87, MP 81, west of Lewistown

The first white man to explore this district was Hugh Monroe, called "Rising Wolf" by the Blackfeet Indians. The Judith Basin was favorite hunting ground for this Nation, and Monroe, as an adopted member of the Piegan Tribe, often came here with them during the first half of the last century.

Reed's Fort, a typical Indian trading post, was located near here. Operated by Major Reed and Jim Bowles, the latter a friend of Jim Bridger, the post was going strong during the 1870s.

In the early 1880s cattlemen and prospectors moved in. Rich mines were opened in the Judith Mountains and range stock replaced the vanishing buffalo. This country is rich in frontier history and tales of the pioneers.

## 97. Maiden's Gold
U.S. 191, MP 12, north of Lewistown

The old mining camp of Maiden, now a ghost town, is located about 10 miles east of here. She roared into existence in May, 1880, when gold was discovered by "Skookum Joe" Anderson, David Jones, Frank "Pony" McPartland, J. R. Kemper, C. Snow and others.

"Skookum Joe" and Jones located placer claims in Virgin Gulch and later moved to Alpine Gulch. Several good placer diggings were opened the following month.

The first quartz mine was also located by Anderson and Jones. The Maginnis, the Spotted Horse and the Collar were the best quartz producers. The ore in the Spotted Horse was "high grade" and was found in pockets.

Over three millions in gold were taken from Maiden. Her population was 1,200 at the top of the boom. Ten years later it had dwindled to less than 200. The camp was prosperous for about 15 years.

## 98. Lewistown
U.S. 87, MP 84, east of Lewistown

This area, the final hunting ground for Montana Indians, was the site of battles fought over the buffalo. In 1874 on the Carroll Trail, Reed and Bowles ran a trading post known as "Reed's Fort." Chief Joseph and his band stopped at the post on their retreat across Montana. Camp Lewis was built near the post to guard freight wagons from Indian raiding parties. During the winter, soldiers of the Seventh Infantry relieved boredom by playing cards and that's how two nearby creeks were called Big and Little Casino. Lewistown, named after the camp, was first inhabited by Metis, French Canadian Indians, who migrated into Montana and possibly gave some Montana communities their French names.

## 99. Fort Maginnis
U.S. 87, MP 98, east of Lewistown

Fort Maginnis, the last army post* created in Montana, was built about 8 miles north of here in 1880. This country was great buffalo range

before that time but cattlemen were bringing in stock from the western valleys and the Texas longhorns were being trailed in from the southeast. There wasn't room for both cattle and buffalo, so the latter had to go. The soldiers were to protect the cattle from being mistaken for buffalo by hungry Indians, to encourage settlement of the Judith Basin west of here and to patrol the Carroll Road to keep supplies rolling between Carroll (near the mouth of the Musselshell River) and Helena. By 1890 the post was no longer needed, the threatening Indians having been relegated to reservations, and the fort was abandoned with civilian blessings.

There were also quite a number of palefaced parties who were handy with a running iron and prone to make errors as to brands and ownership. Such careless souls were known as "rustlers." Sometimes the cattlemen called on these pariahs with a posse and intimated that they were unpopular. Usually such a visitation cured a rustler or two permanently.

*The last fort established in Montana was not Fort Maginnis. The army established Fort William Henry Harrison near Helena in 1892.

## 100. The Smith River Valley
U.S. 89, MP 34, south of White Sulphur Springs

The mountains to the west are the Big Belts, and those to the east are the Castle Mountains. The gulches draining the west slope of the Big Belts were famous in the 1860s and 1870s for their gold placer diggings. Montana Bar in Confederate Gulch was called the "richest acre of ground in the world." The Castle Mountains are also well-known for their quartz mines.

Fort Logan, first established as Camp Baker in November, 1869, as a military outpost to protect the mining camps and ranches to the west from possible attack by Indians, was located towards the north end of the valley. The White Sulphur Springs, typical of the many thermal springs in Montana, were discovered in 1866 by Jas. Scott Brewer. Analysis of the water is said to be almost identical with that at the famous spa, Baden Baden, Germany.

## 101. The Crazy Mountains
U.S. 12, MP 95, west of Harlowton

The Crazy Mountains, which you can see to the southwest, are an outlying range. They are far more rugged and beautiful than they appear at a distance. The story goes that a woman traveling across the plains with a wagon train of emigrants went insane. She escaped from the party and was found near these mountains. So they were called the Crazy Woman Mountains, which in time was shortened.

This district was great cow country in the days of the open range, and there are still a number of large cattle ranches in this vicinity, though under fence. The town of Two Dot gets its name from an early day brand.

## 102. E57B The Last Electric Locomotive
U.S. 12, corner U.S. 12 and Central Street, Harlowton park

The Milwaukee Road's 656-mile electrified railroad ended at 11:40 P.M. June 15, 1974, when Engineer Art Morang stopped the E57B & E34C on the Harlowton Roundhouse Track. They were the last operating locomotives of the original 84 locomotives built by General Electric in 1915.

The electric locomotive roster had totaled 116 locomotives of 5 different types operating from Harlowton, Montana, 440 miles to Avery, Idaho, and 216 miles from Othello, Washington, to Tacoma, Washington, over 5 mountain ranges.

The E57B is 57′ 8¾″ long, 16′8″ high (panagraph down), 10′0″ wide and weighs 144 tons. Rated at 1500 H.P. it could develop 2395 H.P. starting effort, a 62% overload. Operated in 1 to 4 unit consists, they were very trouble-free locomotives. The 3000 volt D.C. trolley restricted them to a small portion of the 11,248 mile railroad and they were replaced by the more versatile diesel electric locomotives.

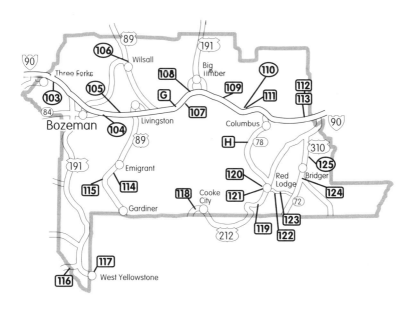

90  89  106  Wilsall  191  108  Big Timber  110  112  113
Three Forks  105  G  109  111  90
103  107  Columbus  310
84  104  Livingston  H  78  125
Bozeman  89  Bridger
191  Emigrant  120  Red Lodge  124
115  114  118  Cooke City  121  72
Gardiner  119  123  122
212
117
116  West Yellowstone

~ Legend ~

| 85 | General Highway Markers |
| 7 | Indian Historical Markers |
| 84 105 | Lewis & Clark Expedition Markers |
| F | Markers no longer displayed |
| - - - - - - - | Indian Reservations & National Parks |
| ════ | Tourism country boundaries |
| ══ | Highways |

# Yellowstone Country

## 103. The Three Forks of the Missouri
Old U.S. 10, MP 1, east of Three Forks

This region was alive with beaver, otter and game before the white man came. It was disputed hunting territory with the Indian tribes. Sacajawea, the Shoshone who guided portions of the Lewis and Clark Expedition, was captured near here when a child, during a battle between her people and the Minnetarees. Her memories of this country were invaluable to the explorers. The Expedition, westward bound, encamped near here for a few days in the latter part of July, 1805. The following year Captain Clark and party came back, July 13, 1806, on their way to explore the Yellowstone River.

In 1808, John Colter, discoverer of Yellowstone Park, and former member of the Lewis and Clark Expedition, was trapping on a stream in this vicinity when captured by a band of Blackfeet. His only companion was killed. Colter was stripped, given a head start, and ordered to run across the flat which was covered with prickly pear. The Indians were hot on his heels but Colter undoubtedly made

Shope

an all-time record that day for sprints as well as distance events. He outran the Indians over a six-mile course and gained the cover of the timber along the Jefferson River. Once in the stream he dove and came up under a jam of driftwood. This hideout saved him from a lot of disappointed and mystified Indians. When night came he headed east, weaponless and outnuding the nudists. He traveled in this condition for seven days to Fort Lisa, his headquarters, at the mouth of the Big Horn River.

In 1810, the Missouri Fur Co. built a fur trading post close by but due to the hostility of the Blackfeet Indians were forced to abandon it that fall.

## 104. Gallatin Valley
Old U.S. 10, 2 miles east of Bozeman

Captain Wm. Clark, of the Lewis and Clark Expedition, with a party of ten men, passed through this valley July 14, 1806, eastward bound, and guided by the Shoshone woman, Sacajawea. They camped that night at the toe of the mountains on the eastern edge of the valley. Captain Clark wrote in his journal: "I saw Elk, deer and Antelopes, and great deel of old signs of buffalow. their roads is in every direction. . . . emence quantities of beaver on this Fork . . . and their dams very much impeed the navigation of it."

In the early 1860s John Bozeman, young adventurer, and Jim Bridger, grand old man of the mountains, guided rival wagon trains of emigrants and gold-seekers through here over the variously called Bonanza Trail, Bridger Cutoff, or Bozeman Road, from Fort Laramie, Wyo., to Virginia City, Mont. The trail crossed Indian country in direct violation of treaty and was a "cut off" used by impatient pioneers who considered the time saving worth the danger. Traffic was not congested.

## 105. Bozeman Pass
I-90, MP 321, Bozeman Pass

Sacajawea, the Shoshone woman who guided portions of the Lewis and Clark Expedition, led Captain Wm. Clark and his party of ten men over an old buffalo road through this pass on July 15, 1806. They were eastward bound and planned to explore the Yellowstone River to its mouth where they were to rejoin Captain Lewis and party who were returning via the Missouri River.

In the 1860s John M. Bozeman, an adventurous young Georgian, opened a trail from Fort Laramie, Wyoming, to Virginia City, Montana, across the hostile Indian country east of here. He brought his first party through in 1863 and the next year guided a large wagon train of emigrants and gold-seekers over this pass, racing with an outfit in charge of Jim Bridger. Bridger used a pass north of here. These pioneer speed demons made as much as fifteen to twenty miles a day–some days. The outfits reached Virginia City within a few hours of each other.

## 106. Shields River Valley
U.S. 89, MP 24, north of Wilsall

This river was named by Capt. Wm. Clark of the Lewis and Clark Expedition in honor of John Shields, a member of the party. Capt. Clark and his men, guided by Sacajawea, the Shoshone woman, camped at the mouth of the river July 15, 1806, while exploring the Yellowstone on their return trip from the coast.

Jim Bridger, famous trapper, trader and scout, guided emigrant wagon trains from Fort Laramie, Wyoming, to Virginia City, Montana, in the 1860s, crossing hostile Indian country via the Bonanza Trail. Bridger's route came up this valley from the Yellowstone, followed up Brackett Creek, crossed the divide west of here to strike Bridger Creek and thence down the latter to the Gallatin Valley.

## 107. The Original Voges Bridge
Grey Bear Fishing Access, off I–90 Exit #362, west of Big Timber

In late 1913, Sweet Grass County residents petitioned the County Commissioners to build a bridge across the Yellowstone River west of Big Timber. The petition was submitted to the commissioners by New York millionaire oil man and part-time Montana rancher, W. Dixon Ellis of the Briggs–Ellis Cattle Company. Dixon offered to donate $5,000 toward the construction of the bridge if the commissioners agreed to build it the following year. In April, 1914, the county contracted with the Security Bridge Company to construct a 2–span pin–connected Pratt through truss bridge at this site for $14,995. Designed by Sweet Grass County Surveyor J. B. Kleinhesselink and County Assessor D. J. Walvoord, the 378-foot long bridge included an experimental floor system that allowed use of the bridge by the new 20-ton tractors of the time. The Security Bridge Company completed the structure in June, 1914 and it eventually became known as the Voges Bridge by area residents. Charles

Voges owned a nearby sheep ranch and donated the land for the existing one-room school on the north bank of the river in 1920. When completed, the Voges Bridge provided access to the transportation systems on the south side of the river to the farmers and ranchers living north of the Yellowstone. The bridge was also the last pin-connected bridge built across the Yellowstone River.

## 108. The Bonanza or Bozeman Trail
U.S. 191, MP 1, west of Big Timber

In the early 1860s there wasn't a ranch in this country from Bismarck to Bozeman and from the Platte River to Canada. To whites it was land considered "fit only to raise Indians" and while some of them were hoping for a crop failure, the majority were indifferent. They didn't care how much the tribes fought amongst themselves. They were like the old-timer whose wife was battling a grizzly bear. He said he never had seen a fight where he took so little interest in the outcome.

Then the white man's greed asserted itself and he looked for a shortcut from the Oregon Trail at Laramie, Wyoming, to the gold diggin's of western Montana. The Bonanza or Bozeman Trail across Indian hunting grounds was the result. It forded the Yellowstone near here, coming from the southeast. It was a trail soaked with the blood of warriors, soldiers, and immigrants. Thousands of Sioux warriors, primarily under Red Cloud, bolstered by hundreds of Cheyennes and some Arapahos, fought the trail for six years and forced its closure by the Government in 1868.

## 109. The Thomas Party
I-90, Frontage Road, MP 381, east of Greycliff

In 1866, William Thomas, his son Charles, and a driver named Schultz left southern Illinois bound for the Gallatin Valley, Montana. Travelling by covered wagon, they joined a prairie schooner outfit at Fort Laramie, Wyoming, and started over the Bridger Trail.* The train was escorted by troops detailed to build a fort (C. F. Smith) on the Big Horn River.

From the site of this fort the Thomas party pushed on alone. A few days later they were killed at this spot by hostile Indians. Emigrants found the bodies and buried them in one grave.

The meager details which sifted back greatly impressed William Thomas's seven-year-old nephew. Seventy-one years later (1937), this nephew closely followed the Bridger Trail by car and succeeded in locating the almost forgotten grave.

*The Thomas party actually traveled on the Bozeman Trail.

## 110. Captain Wm. Clark
I-90, MP 381, Greycliff rest area, east of Big Timber

You are now following the historic trail of the Lewis and Clark Expedition. On his return from the Pacific in July 1806, Captain Clark camped for six days about forty miles downstream, near Park City. The Expedition had been looking for timber suitable for building canoes ever since striking the river near Livingston. They found a couple of large cottonwoods here that would serve. They fitted their axes with handles made from chokecherry and went to work making two canoes. When finished they laced them together with a deck of buffalo hides between. Seven men, Sacajawea and her child went curving down the river on this makeshift yacht, arriving at the mouth of the Yellowstone August 3rd. Captain Lewis split off north on the return trip and explored the Marias River and returned via the Missouri, joining them on August 12th.

## 111. The Crazy Mountains
I-90, MP 381, Greycliff rest area, east of Big Timber

Called Awaxaawippiia by the Apsaalooka (Crow) Indians, the Crazy Mountains, which you can see to the northwest, are an igneous formation forged about 50 million years ago. For the Apsaalooka, they are the most sacred and revered mountains on the northern Great Plains. Awaxaawippiia was a place of refuge and protection. The Apsaalooka's enemies would not follow them into the mountains. Because of their great spiritual power, Awaxaawippiia continues to be an important vision quest site for the tribe. Famed Chief Plenty Coups had a vision there in 1857 in which, he said, the end of the plains Indian way-of-life was shown to him.

There are several stories about how the mountains got their current name. The most popular story goes that a woman traveling across the plains with a wagon train went insane. She escaped from the party and was found near these mountains. So they were called the Crazy Woman Mountains, a name which was eventually shortened. Perhaps the mountains were named, as others have claimed, because of their crazy appearance. The Crazy Mountains were an important landmark for Bozeman Trail emigrants in the Yellowstone Valley. This district was great cow and sheep country in the days of the open range, and there are still a number of large ranches in this vicinity, though now under fence.

## 112. Columbus
I-90, MP 419, Columbus rest area, west of Park City

The town of Columbus is located about 9 miles west of here. There is probably no town (or city) in Montana that had a more spectacular career, or more hectic embarrassment in finally "lighting" on an incorporated name than did the county seat of Stillwater. From 1875, when the Countryman stage station was known as Stillwater, until its incorporation in 1907, its name was changed every time the whims of a merchant moved his stock of merchandise, or a new business appeared. First it was "Eagle's Nest," about two miles west of town; then an Indian trading post was listed as "Sheep Dip," and it was not until the Northern Pacific built a station here in 1882 and named it Stillwater that the town's location attained permanence. Even this name didn't last long, however, as the N.P. had already listed a Stillwater, Minnesota, on their main line and the similarity of Minnesota and Montana led to misdirected shipments, so the name of Columbus replaced Stillwater on January 1, 1894.

There was just reason, perhaps, that this part of the Yellowstone was slow in getting settled. It was borderland on the north side of the Crow Reservation, and there were constant raids on the area by Sioux and Cheyenne war parties who would just as soon attack the white invaders. This ever-present danger didn't appeal to many prospective home-seekers, who hightailed it over to the Gallatin or other points farther west.

## 113.  Park City
I-90, MP 419, Columbus rest area, west of Park City

The town of Park City is located about seven miles east of here. In 1882, a colony from Ripon, Wisconsin, making the trip in the prairie schooners, settled in this region. It was to be their future home, so they planted trees and made what improvements they could to ultimately beautify the little city. A section of land was donated to them, and things started off in a prosperous pleasant manner. The railroad soon came through and established a station. The bare, sandstone bluffs north of town inspired the officials to christen the place Rimrock, but not so with the persons who had planted sprigs and started a city of trees. Bravely they clung to the name Park City, and Rimrock finally disappeared with the list of unused titles. This was unfortunate inasmuch as the general manager of the N.P. resented this stubbornness on the part of the homesteaders, and in retaliation he changed the location of the proposed railroad yards and shops from this townsite to Laurel.

## 114.  Emigrant Gulch
U.S. 89, MP 28, north of Gardiner

A party of emigrants who had traveled with a wagon train across the plains via the Bozeman or Bonanza Trail arrived in this gulch August

28, 1864. Two days later three of these men explored the upper and more inaccessible portion of the gulch and struck good pay. A mining boom followed.

When cold weather froze the sluices the miners moved down to the valley, built cabins and "Yellowstone City" began its brief career. Provisions were scarce that winter. Flour sold for $28 per 96 lb. sack, while smoking tobacco was literally worth its weight in gold.

The strike was not a fabulous one, but snug stakes rewarded many of the pioneers for their energy and hardships.

## 115. The Absaroka-Beartooth Wilderness
U.S. 89, MP 24, Emigrant rest area, north of Gardiner

The Absaroka–Beartooth Wilderness, which lies to the east, contains the largest single expanse of land above 10,000 feet in elevation in the United States. The U.S. Forest Service set aside portions of the region as primitive areas in 1932, and Congress voted it a wilderness area in 1978. Visitors spent 392,000 collective days here in 1983, making it the fourth most visited wilderness in America.

Artifacts and pictographs indicate that people have hunted in these mountains for thousands of years, but it has always been country for people to visit, not live in. Reserved by treaty for the Crow in the early 1800s, the tribe shared with the less-rugged mountains on the west side of the wilderness (that you can see from here) their name for themselves, Absaroka (Absoarkey). The rugged mountains on the east side they named Beartooth, after one tooth-shaped peak. Gold discoveries in the 1860s attracted prospectors to Emigrant Gulch, and an 1880 treaty moved the reservation boundary eastward to allow

previously clandestine mining claims to be developed.

The entire wilderness is a watershed for the Yellowstone, the longest undammed river left in the United States. It flows over 670 miles from its sources out of Yellowstone National Park and is the lifeblood of about one-third of Montana and much of northern Wyoming.

## 116. Targhee Pass
U.S. 20, MP 0, west of West Yellowstone

This pass across the Continental Divide takes its name from an early-day Bannack Chief. Free trappers and fur brigades of the Missouri River and Rocky Mountain Fur companies were familiar with the surrounding country in the early part of the last century.

Chief Joseph led his band of Nez Perce Indians through this pass in 1877 while making his famous 2,000-mile march from the central Idaho country in an effort to evade U.S. troops and find sanctuary in Canada. He was closely followed through the pass by the pursuing forces of General Howard. Joseph repulsed or outdistanced all the commands sent against him until finally forced to surrender to Col. Nelson A. Miles at the Battle of the Bear's Paw, when within a comparatively few miles of the Canadian line.

## 117. The 1959 Earthquake
City park at West Yellowstone

On August 17, 1959, at 11:37 P.M., this spectacularly scenic section of Montana became the focus of worldwide attention and made modern history. A heavy shock smashed the soft summer night, earth and rock buckled, lifted and dropped. In several mighty heaves Mother Earth reshaped her mountains in violent response to an agony of deep-seated tensions no longer bearable. A mountain moved, a new lake was formed, another lake was fantastically tilted, sections of highway were dropped into a lake, the earth's surface was ripped by miles of faults, and 28 persons were missing or dead. The area is now safe and much of it has been preserved and marked by the Forest Service for all to see. The Madison River Canyon Earthquake area, located a few miles northwest of here, is an awesome testimonial to Nature's might.

## 118.  Cooke City

U.S. 212, MP 3, west of Cooke City

In 1868 a party of prospectors came into this country by way of Soda
Butte Creek. They found rich float but were set afoot by Indians. Caching
their surplus supplies on the stream now called Cache Creek, they made
it back to the Yellowstone and reported their find. In the next few years
many prospectors combed these mountains; the first real development
began about 1880 with Jay Cooke's infusion of eastern capital.

Chief Joseph's band of fugitive Nez Perce Indians came through here
in 1877. In 1883 there were 135 log cabins in the settlement, two general
stores and thirteen saloons.

Cooke City had been waiting years for reasonable transportation
connections to the outside world so that her promising ore deposits
could be profitably mined. She's no blushing maiden, but this highway
was the answer to her prayers.

## 119.  The Beartooth Highway

U.S. 212, MP 61, south of Red Lodge

Although these mountains were criss-crossed by trails used by Native
Americans since prehistory, it was not until the early 20th century that
many sought a permanent route over the mountains to Cooke City
and Yellowstone National Park.

Beginning in 1924, a group of Red Lodge businessmen, led by Dr. J.
C. F. Siegfriedt and newspaper publisher O. H. P. Shelley, lobbied
Montana's congressional delegation to construct a road between their
community and Cooke City. Because of their efforts, President Herbert
Hoover signed the Park Approach Act into law in 1931. The Act funded
the construction of scenic routes to the country's national parks through
federally-owned land. The Beartooth Highway was the only road
constructed under the Act. Construction on the $2.5 million project
began in 1932.

The Beartooth Highway is an excellent example of "Seat-of-Your-Pants" construction with many of the engineering decisions made in the field. Some 100 workers employed by five companies blasted their way up the side of the 11,000-foot plateau. The workmen gave names to many features of the road that are still used today, including Lunch Meadow, Mae West Curve and High Lonesome Ridge. The road officially opened on June 14, 1936. The spectacular Beartooth Highway is a testimonial to the vision of those who fought for its construction and a tribute to those who carved it over the mountains.

## 120. Red Lodge
U.S. 212, MP 69, in Red Lodge

Coal was discovered in the Rock Creek Valley nearly two decades before Red Lodge was established as a mail stop on the Meeteetse Trail in 1884. In 1887, the Rocky Fork Coal Company opened the first large-scale mine at Red Lodge sparking the community's first building boom, consisting mostly of "hastily constructed shacks and log huts." The completion of the Northern Pacific Railway branch line to Red Lodge in 1890 resulted in the construction of many brick and sandstone buildings that now line the city's main street.

Like all mining camps, Red Lodge had a large population of single men and an abundance of saloons. For many years, the notorious "Liver-eating" Johnston kept the peace as the town's first constable. Red Lodge also boasted several churches and social clubs for those not inclined toward the city's more earthier entertainment.

Hundreds of people came to Red Lodge in the 1890s and early 1900s. Immigrants from all over Europe worked shoulder-to-shoulder in the coal mines, but settled in neighborhoods called Finn Town, Little Italy and Hi Bug. Their cultural traditions endured and are celebrated at the city's annual Festival of Nations.

Production in the coal mines declined after World War I, eventually leading to their closure by 1932. The completion of the scenic Beartooth Highway in 1936 revitalized Red Lodge by linking it directly to Yellowstone National Park. Today, Red Lodge's past is represented by its historic buildings and by the pride its citizens take in its history and traditions.

## 121. The Red Lodge Country
U.S. 212, MP 69, in Red Lodge

According to tradition, a band of Crow Indians left the main tribe and moved west into the foothills of the Beartooth Range many years ago. They painted their council tepee with red clay and this old-time artistry resulted in the name Red Lodge.

This region is a bonanza for scientists. It is highly fossilized and Nature has opened a book on Beartooth Butte covering about a quarter of a billion years of geological history. It makes pretty snappy reading for parties interested in some of the ologies, paleontology for example.

Some students opine that prehistoric men existed here several million years earlier than heretofore believed. Personally we don't know, but if there were people prowling around that long ago, of course they would pick Montana as the best place to live.

## 122. Smith Mine Disaster
Secondary 308, MP 5, east of Red Lodge

Smoke pouring from the mine entrance about 10 o'clock the morning of February 27, 1943, was the first indication of trouble. "There's something wrong down here. I'm getting out," the hoist operator called up. He and two nearby miners were the last men to leave the mine alive.

Rescue crews from as far away as Butte and Cascade County worked around the clock in six-hour shifts to clear debris and search for possible survivors. There were none. The night of March 4, workers reached the first bodies. More followed until the toll mounted to 74. Some died as a result of a violent explosion in No. 3 vein, the remainder fell victim to the deadly methane gasses released by the blast.

The tragedy at Smith Mine became Montana's worst coal mine disaster, sparking investigations at the state and national level. Montana Governor Sam C. Ford visited the scene, offered state assistance and pushed a thorough inquiry into the incident.

Today's marker of the Smith Mine Disaster follows a simpler one left by two of the miners trapped underground after the explosion, waiting for the poisonous gas they knew would come.

"Walter & Johnny. Goodbye. Wives and daughters. We died an easy death. Love from us both. Be good."

## 123. Bearcreek
Secondary 308, in Bearcreek

Platted in 1905 by George Lamport and Robert Leavens, Bearcreek was the center of an extensive underground coal mining district. At its height during World War I, Bearcreek boasted a population of nearly 2,000 people. The community was ethnically diverse and included Serbians, Scotsmen, Montenegrans, Germans, Italians and Americans. They were served by seven mercantiles, a bank, two hotels, two billiard halls, a brickyard and numerous saloons. The town also boasted concrete sidewalks and an extensive water system. No church was ever built in Bearcreek. Foundations of many of the town's buildings, in addition to some structures themselves, consisted of sandstone quarried in the nearby hill. The local railway, the Montana Wyoming and Southern, carried coal from the mines through Bearcreek where it was distributed to communities across Montana.

The Lamport Hotel was once located on the foundation to the right of this marker. Built in 1907, it was described as "well furnished . . . the beds being especially soft and sleep producing. [The] meals are served with a desire to please the guests and no one leaves without a good impression and kindly feelings for the management." The hotel was razed about 1945.

In 1943, Montana's worst coal mining disaster at the nearby Smith mine took the lives of 74 men, many of whom lived in Bearcreek. The tragedy hastened the decline of the town. Many buildings in Bearcreek were moved to other communities or demolished, leaving haunting reminders of their presence along Main Street. The railroad tracks were removed in 1953 and the last mining operation closed in the 1970s. Today, Bearcreek is the smallest incorporated city in the state.

## 124. Jim Bridger, Mountain Man
U.S. 310, MP 26, south of Bridger

Jim Bridger arrived in Montana in 1822 as a member of a Rocky Mountain Fur Co. brigade. For years he had no more permanent home than a poker chip. He roamed the entire Rocky Mountain region and often came through this part of the country. A keen observer, a natural geographer and with years of experience amongst the Indians, he became invaluable as a guide and scout for wagon trains and Federal troops following the opening of the Oregon Trail.

He shares honors with John Colter for first discoveries in the Yellowstone Park country. He was prone to elaborate a trifle for the benefit of pilgrims, and it was Jim who embroidered his story of the petrified forest by asserting that he had seen "a peetrified bird sitting in a peetrified tree, singing a peetrified song."

The Clarks Fork of the Yellowstone was named for Capt. Wm. Clark of the Lewis and Clark Expedition. Chief Joseph led his band of Nez Perce Indians down this river when he made his famous retreat in the summer of 1877.

## 125. The Pryor Mountains
U.S. 310, MP 29, Bridger rest area, north of Bridger

The Pryor Mountains to the east cover roughly 300,000 acres. Once entirely Crow Indian territory, now only the north end of the range is on the Crow Reservation. The south end is in the Custer National Forest. The range is bound on the east by Bighorn Reservoir and on the south by the Pryor Mountain National Wild Horse Range. The mountains came by their name indirectly from Pryor Creek, which Captain William Clark named for Lewis and Clark Expedition member Sergeant Nathaniel Pryor.

The Pryors hold many intriguing features, including ice caves, sinks, and caverns, and archeological finds, such as Clovis Points indicating human occupation as long as 10,000 years ago. In the south end of the range, remains of log and frame houses and barns attest to the homesteads staked after passage of the Forest Homestead Act in 1906. Most of the settlers came from this area. Though they cultivated some crops, for many homesteading was a pretense for mountain grazing on adjacent forest and reservation ranges. One forest ranger observed that some claimants had applied for places where it would be impossible to winter over, though to hear them talk "one would think that Pryor Mountain contained the biggest part of the Banana Belt and that pineapples grew wild."

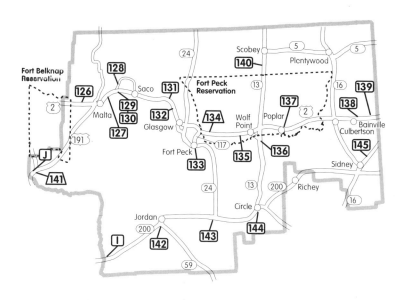

~ Legend ~

[85]  General Highway Markers
[7]   Indian Historical Markers
(84) (105) Lewis & Clark Expedition Markers
[F]   Markers no longer displayed
------ Indian Reservations & National Parks
━━━  Tourism country boundaries
═══  Highways

## 126. Early Day Outlaws
U.S. 2, MP 467, west of Malta

Take it by and large, the old West produced some tolerably lurid gun toters.

Their hole card was a single-action frontier model .45 Colt, and their long suit was fanning it a split second quicker than similarly inclined gents. This talent sometimes postponed their obsequies quite a while, providing they weren't pushed into taking up rope spinning from the loop end of a lariat by a wearied public. Through choice or force of circumstances these parties sometimes threw in with the "wild bunch" rough riding, shooting hombres, prone to disregard customary respect accorded other people's brands.

Kid Curry's stomping ground in the 1880s was the Little Rockies country about forty miles southwest of here. July 3, 1901, he pulled off a premature Independence Day celebration by holding up the Great Northern No. 3 passenger train and blowing the express car safe near this point. His departure was plumb abrupt. The Great Northern would still probably like to know where he is holed up.

## 127. Cattle Brands
U.S. 2, MP 474, 1.6 miles east of Malta

# CATTLE  BRANDS

*M*any a dogie #(not "doggie"- dudes please note) has been decorated with one of these famous Montana Irons.

| | | | |
|---|---|---|---|
| CA *Running CA* | ☆ *Bug* | ꝡM *Seven VM* | A *Square & Compass* |
| 79 *Seventy nine* | © *Circle C* | ⚵ *Shaving mug* | ᴜ *Quarter circle U* |
| D-S *DHS* | SH *Monogram SH* | 40 *Forty* | ⊐ *Lazy H hanging 2* |
| o8 *Three circle* | R *Bar R* | LU *LU bar* | 32 *Reversed E2 bar* |
| N-N *N bar N* | D *Flying D* | T *Umbrella* | P *Lazy P swinging 9* |
| Y *Turkey track* | X *Long X* | ⚘ *Spearhead* | Two *pole pumpkin* |
| ⌐X *Hat X* | ∇ *Bull head* | ⚔ *Rocking Chair* | 7-7 *Seven bar seven* |
| 777 *Three sevens* | oo *Two dot* | U *Antler* | UF *Monogram FUF* |
| Ν *N bar* | 1X *Inverted TX* | VVV *Three V's* | = *Railroad track* |
| Ψ *Pitch fork* | ⌂ *Hash knife* | X *Hourglass* | E *Monogram PLE* |
| ʃ *Fish hook* | 2A *Two A bar* | ⌂ *Rafter circle* | Ω *Horseshoe bar* |
| Q *Piece of pie* | ⚐ *Mill Iron* | W *W bar* | ⊕ *Circle diamond* |
| CK | O *Circle* | U *U Lazy J* | ✠ *Maltese cross* |
| IX | LO | 707 | SL |
| JO | OW | XIT | WM |

#A dogie is a little calf who has lost its mammy and whose daddy has ran off with another cow.

## 128. The Cree Crossing
U.S. 2, MP 490, east of Malta

The Milk River, which flows through this prehistoric valley of the Missouri now filled with glacial debris, is crooked as a dog's hind leg. At certain times of the year it may appear to be somewhat trivial and even dusty. But during the spring thaws it gets right down to business and runs bank full.

One of the best fords across the river in this part of Montana lies a few miles northeast of here. It was used by the Indians to reach favorite buffalo range in the Big Bend country. Although used by other tribes it became known to the whites as the Cree Crossing.

There are many glacial boulders in this vicinity on which ancient Indian carvings are found.

## 129. Milk River Ford
### Secondary 243, MP 2, north of Saco

Cree Crossing was an important ford across the Milk River for generations. It was first used by Native Americans and, later, by local ranchers and homesteaders. In July, 1934, the Public Works Administration and the Army Corps of Engineers began work on the Fort Peck Dam southeast of here. The massive earth–filled structure required tons of rock and gravel fill. One of the most important quarry sites for the project was located near Cole, several miles north of Cree Crossing. Dump trucks hauling rocks and gravel to the dam site were

forced to cross the river here. In November, 1934, Phillips County announced plans to construct a reinforced concrete box culvert to improve Cree Crossing.

County work crews began construction of the structure in the spring of 1935. The simple structure was described as "reinforced concrete with a base that goes below the bed of the river and extends upwards several feet above the normal low water mark." The county funded the construction of the $1,000 culvert, while the Malta Commercial Club provided $600 to grade the road between U.S. Highway 2 and Cole. Completed in late June, 1935, the commercial club sponsored a picnic at the Milk River Ford on July 4, 1935 to celebrate its completion. For over sixty years, the Milk River Ford carried traffic over the river– except during high water when it was often submerged below the water line.

## 130. Sleeping Buffalo Rock
### U.S. 2, MP 490, east of Malta

On the crest of a ridge near the Cree Crossing of the Milk River is a group of glacial boulders which from a distance resemble a herd of sleeping buffalo.

They were held sacred by the Indians and one in particular was thought to be the leader. It is now a part of this monument. Some prehistoric sculptor tried to further the resemblance with crude carvings on the boulder.

The tribes have legends of the herd's origin, and long before the white men came sacrificed possessions to the Sleeping Buffalo Rock.

## 131. Liquid Gold
### U.S. 2, MP 527, Vandalia rest area, east of Hinsdale

Water is the life blood of Montana. During the state's early settlement, the rivers provided transportation and trading routes; later they sustained the livestock and crops of ranchers and homesteaders; and they still provide Montana's base for agriculture, industry, and tourism. The Milk River that parallels Highway 2 from Glasgow to Hinsdale is one of the most important rivers in the north-central part of the state.

One of the earliest Milk River users was Augustin Armel (AKA Hamel) who arrived about 1820. He worked at all the major American Fur Co. posts on the Missouri River until the 1850s. In 1855, he opened Hammell's House, the first trading post on the Milk River, located about 7 miles southwest of here (near Vandalia). Tom Campbell's House followed, built near the same site in 1870. Neither lasted very long, and no physical remains of them have been found.

Later comers to this region raised mostly cattle, sheep, and wheat. They needed water on more of the land than was blessed with it and today you can see the irrigation system along Highway 2. The Lower Milk River Valley Water Users Association promoted the construction of the Vandalia Dam and Canal in the early 1900s. Area rancher, H. H. Nelson, interested in attracting settlers, became  involved in irrigation after establishing Vandalia in 1904. Nelson was director and superintendent for construction of the dam at Vandalia and the canal that runs from there east to Nashua. The dam was completed in 1917. Nelson's hopes for a sizable settlement at Vandalia never materialized.

## 132. Buffalo Country

U.S. 2, MP 535, west of Glasgow

Buffalo meant life to the Plains Indians, and the mountain Indians used to slip down from the hills for their share, too. Some tribes would toll buffalo into a concealed corral and then down them; another system was to stampede a herd over a cliff; but the sporting way was to use bows and arrows and ride them down on a trained buffalo horse.

Fat cow was the choice meat. The Indians preserved their meat long before the whites ever had any embalmed beef scandals. They made pemmican by drying and pulverizing the meat, pouring marrow bone grease and oil over it, and packing it away in skin bags. It kept indefinitely, and in food value one pound was worth ten of fresh meat.

Tanned robes and rawhide were used for bedding, tepees, clothes, war shields, stretchers, travois, canoes, and bags. Horns and bones made tools and utensils. The buffalo played a prominent part in many of their religious rites and jealousy of hereditary hunting grounds brought on most of the intertribal wars.

## 133. Old Fort Peck

Montana 24, MP 59, at Fort Peck

On the west bank of the Missouri River about 1 mile from the Dam was located Old Fort Peck.

The stockade was about 300 feet square with walls 12 feet high of cottonwood logs set vertically, 3 bastions and 3 gateways on the front, and 2 bastions on the rear, enclosed quarters for men, store houses, blacksmith shops, stables and corral. Built in 1867 by the firm of Durfee & Peck as a trading post, the fort was named for Colonel Campbell K. Peck. Although not an Army post, it often served as temporary headquarters for military men and commissioners sent out by the Government to negotiate with the Indians.

To peaceful Indians it was an important trading post, to trappers and rivermen a safe shelter from warlike Indians. Stern-wheel steamers loaded and unloaded here and took on wood for steam for their journeys.

Old Fort Peck is history. Its site lies peacefully, with its memories, covered by a man-made lake which is formed by the largest earth-filled dam ever built by man.

## 134. In Memoriam
U.S. 2, MP 590, one half mile east of Frazer,
across from dance grounds

In the summer of 1837 an American Fur Trading Company steamboat laden with trade goods made its way from St. Louis to Fort Union. Smallpox broke out among the crew, but the boat continued to its destination. Contact with the steamboat's crew during the distribution of trade goods exposed the Wichiyabina or Little Girls' Band of Assiniboine, starting a terrible epidemic which eventually affected all the tribes of what is now northeastern Montana. Many of the tribes had never been exposed to this virulent European disease and were extremely susceptible. The disease seemed to strike the young, vigorous and most able-bodied family members with such swiftness that burial in many cases was impossible. Ninety-four percent of the Wichiyabina or Little Girls' Band of Assiniboine died. By the winter of 1838, when the disease had run its course, the Wichiyabina or Little Girls' Band of Assiniboine were no more. The 80 remaining Band members banded with other smallpox survivors and formed the Redbottom Band (Hudesabina) of Assiniboines. Today the Assiniboine people still mourn the untimely passing of so many of their ancestors, innocent victims of this dreadful pestilence.

## 135. Wolf Point
U.S. 2, MP 590, west of Wolf Point

The Lewis and Clark Expedition passed here, westward bound in 1805. Fur trappers and traders followed a few years later. Steamboats began making it from St. Louis up the Missouri as far as Fort Benton in the early 1860s and this was considered the halfway point between Bismarck and Fort Benton. Wood choppers supplied cord wood for boats stopping to refuel. An American Fur Company packet burned and blew up in 1861 not far from here. A deck hand tapped a barrel of alcohol by candle light with a gimlet. The fumes, the candle, and 25 kegs of powder did the rest.

This district was favorite buffalo country for the Assiniboines and Sioux.

A party of trappers poisoned several hundred wolves one winter, hauled the frozen carcasses in and stacked them until spring for skinning. It taught the varmints a lesson. No one in Wolf Point has been bothered by a wolf at the door since then.

## 136. The Wolf Point Bridge
Montana 13, MP 46, southeast of Wolf Point

The Wolf Point Bridge was the result of many years of lobbying by Roosevelt and McCone county citizens led by Wolf Point businessman William Young. In 1927, the Montana Highway Commission and Bureau of Public Roads approved the project. The Missouri Valley Bridge and Iron Company of Leavenworth, Kansas began construction of the bridge in 1929.

The company's construction camp on the north bank of the river included a powerhouse, workshops, office, a dance hall, bunkhouse and several small cottages to house the workers' families. For most of 1929 and 1930, the site was the most popular tourist attraction in northeastern Montana.

The Wolf Point Bridge was dedicated on July 9, 1930. The celebration included speeches, bands, a float, cowboys, and a daylight fireworks show. The bridge was blessed by tribal elders from the Fort Peck Reservation. A crowd of perhaps 15,000 people attended the festivities.

The Wolf Point Bridge is the longest and most massive through truss in Montana. The structure is 1,074-feet long and contains 1,150 tons of steel. The 400-foot span is the longest in the state. When dedicated in 1930, the bridge was called "A memorial to those whose lives have been lost in the Missouri and a monument to those whose cooperation made possible its erection."

## 137. Fort Peck Indian Reservation
U.S. 2, MP 612, city of Poplar

Fort Peck Indian Reservation is the home of two tribes, the Assiniboines, whose forefathers were living in this vicinity when Lewis and Clark came up the Missouri in 1805, and the Dakota (Sioux), descendants of the "hostiles" who fiercely resisted the white invasion of their homelands. Some of the Dakotas took part in the Minnesota uprising of 1862 and moved west when the Army tried to round them up. Others took part in Custer's demise at the Battle of the Little Big Horn in 1876. The Assiniboines, also of Dakota descent, split from the Yanktonai band in the early 1600s and migrated west. They shared the vast Blackfeet hunting territory set aside by the Treaty of 1855 from which Fort Peck Reservation was created in 1888 when 17,500,000 acres were ceded to the government. Part of the tribe resides on the Fort Belknap Reservation, 160 miles west of here.

Named for Campbell Kennedy Peck, Fort Peck was originally a fur trading post established near the mouth of the Milk River by Abel Farwell for the Durfee and Peck Co. in 1866–67. In 1873, the Bureau of Indian Affairs began using part of the post as Fort Peck Indian Agency. Flooded out by an ice jam on the Missouri in 1877, the agency was moved to the present site at the mouth of the Poplar River. The earlier site now rests under the waters behind Fort Peck Dam.

## 138. Fort Union
U.S. 2, MP 666, east of Bainville

Fort Union, one of the largest and best known trading posts of the fur days, was located on the Missouri near the mouth of the Yellowstone, about 14 miles southeast of here. Built by the American Fur Company in 1828 for trade with the Assiniboine Indians, its importance increased with the arrival of the first steamboat from St. Louis, the "Yellowstone," about June 17, 1832.

The Blackfeet, influenced by British fur companies, had refused to trade with Americans until Kenneth McKenzie, in charge of Ft. Union, succeeded in having a band of this nation brought to the fort in 1831.

## 139. Snowden Bridge
U.S. 2, MP 666, east of Bainville

The only vertical lift bridge in Montana is located 10 miles south of here on the Missouri River. Built for Great Northern Railway by the Union Bridge and Construction Co. of Kansas City in 1913, it consists of three 275-foot fixed spans and one 296-foot lift span that raised to allow passage of river traffic. All of the spans are Parker riveted through trusses. When completed, it was the longest vertical lift bridge in existence and had the second largest clear opening of all movable bridges in the world.

In 1926, the one-track bridge was modified by the addition of timber approach ramps and a plank deck to accommodate local vehicular traffic. A signal system regulated direction of flow and tolls were collected from motorized and horse-drawn vehicles.

No record exists of the number of times the lift span was operated, but it was rare due to declining navigation on the Missouri. The last time there was need for it, when Fort Peck Dam was being built in the 1930s and barges loaded with construction materials needed the bridge raised to pass upstream, the mechanism no longer worked. The original hoist mechanism is still in place, but the operating machinery was retired in 1943.

Snowden Bridge was closed to auto traffic in 1985 when a new bridge was built three miles downstream.

## 140. Wood Mountain Trail
Montana 13, MP 47, south of Scobey

This Indian trail extended from the Yellowstone River past this point to the Wood Mountains in Canada. It was used for decades by the Sioux and the Assiniboine tribes in pursuit of the migrating buffalo. Also stalking this meat staple on the hoof were the Metis, a French Canadian band of Indians who used the trail. In the 1800s fur hunters and trappers made continual use of the passage and at the turn of the century, settlers and homesteaders followed. It was over this trail in July of 1891 that Sitting Bull and his Sioux warriors were escorted from Canada by Canadian Mounties and Jean Louis Le Gare, the man responsible for Sitting Bull's surrender at Fort Buford.

Scobey, Montana, was named for Major Scobey who served at Fort Buford and later worked with the Indian Bureau on the Fort Peck Reservation.

## 141. The Little Rocky Mountains
U.S. 191, MP 102, south of Malta. Tribal association:
Fort Belknap

Many Indian people believe that spirits dwell in north central Montana's "island" mountains: the Sweet Grass Hills and the Bears Paw and Little Rocky ranges. Their rugged peaks, clustered like tepees in a camp, offer access to the supernatural and provide a nesting place for eagles, the messengers of the spirits who live there. Generations of Blackfeet, Gros Ventre, Assiniboine, and Chippewa–Cree have used these isolated areas for fasting, prayer and vision questing. Here are the precious gifts of water, plants, animals, and solitude from the Great Spirit. Stories describing the supernatural powers of the Little Rocky Mountains abound. One such story, handed down in many variations, tells of a terrible water–monster called Bax'aa that inhabited the spring on Eagle Child Mountain, frightening or even slaying some who attempted to fast there. Another well known site at the western end of the Little Rockies is a battleground remembered among northern Montana tribes for its spiritual significance. The great Gros Ventre warrior Red Whip won victory there over the Sioux against incredible odds. His success is attributed to a powerful war charm and a vision that foretold the battle.

## 142. Indian Country
Montana 59, MP 83, south of Jordan

Until the early 1880s this portion of Montana was wild unsettled country where roving parties of Sioux, Crow and Assiniboine Indians hunted buffalo and clashed in tribal warfare. Sitting Bull's band of Hunkpapa Sioux frequently ranged through here and except for a few nomadic trappers there were no white men.

With the coming of the Texas trail herds the buffalo were slaughtered to clear the range for beef critters and the cattle kings held sway for many years.

In 1910 the first wave of homesteaders surged in and the open range dwindled before their fences and plowed fields. The glamour of the frontier days is gone.

## 143. Dinosaurs
Montana 200, MP 248, Flowing Wells rest area, east of Jordan

Difficult to believe now, but 80 million years ago the middle of our continent was a shallow sea. This area, when not underwater, was part of a hot, humid tropical coastline of marshes, river deltas, and swamps, bearing dense vegetation probably similar to that found on the southern coast of Louisiana today.

Fossils tell us that turtles, crocodiles, lizards, toads, fishes, small primitive mammals, and dinosaurs lived on this coastal plain. Many of the most complete dinosaurs on display in the world were gathered here in Garfield County. The first Tyrannosaurus rex skeleton came out of its hills in 1902. In fact, four of the six* tyrannosaurs found in the world are from Garfield County and five of the six are from Montana. The Garfield County Museum in Jordan holds replicas of a tyrannosaur skull, a duckbill dinosaur skull, and a triceratops skeleton.

Paleontologists were puzzled by the scarcity of young dinosaurs and eggs in this rich fossil area. One explanation was discovered in 1978 on the eastern front of the Rocky Mountains about 300 miles west of here. Hundreds of eggs from at least three different dinosaur species and thousands of whole and partial dinosaur skeletons were found. This new evidence indicates that the dinosaurs migrated from the coast to the mountains to lay their eggs and raise their young. One may see fossils from this site at the Museum of the Rockies in Bozeman, Montana.

* As of 1999 twenty tyrannosaurs have been found in North America; about half of them were discovered in Montana.

## 144. Circle
Montana 200, MP 268, McCone County Museum, Circle

Major Seth Mabry, a Confederate Army officer, came to the Redwater Valley about 1883, driving a herd of longhorns from Texas. President of the Mabry Cattle Co., he branded with a plain circle iron. From the brand, the operation became known as the Circle Ranch. They sold three to four thousand beeves each fall for about 13 years.

Other cattlemen ran the ranch until about 1900 when Peter Dreyer and Hans Grue bought it and used it as a summer camp for sheep and as a stopover for themselves and other ranchers going to and from Glendive. Two bachelors ostensibly cared for the ranch, but actually they started a saloon there. Since strong drink spoiled the sheepherders' work habits, Dreyer and Grue offered the place to Dreyer's brother-in-law, Peter Rorvik, in 1903. During an absence of the saloonkeepers, the Rorviks and their six children moved in. The next summer saw 100,000 sheep on the Redwater River. The herders and ranchers needed a supply source, so Rorvik opened a store on the ranch.

So began the town of Circle about one-half mile southeast of here. In 1907, the surrounding lands were opened to homesteading and the area has been producing grain as well as livestock ever since.

## 145. Old Fort Gilbert
Montana 200, MP 58, north of Sidney

"Old Fort Gilbert" was situated directly east of this point on the west bank of the Yellowstone River. The Fort was named after Colonel Gilbert, onetime commanding officer at Fort Buford, and existed between the years 1864 and 1867. It was used as a trading center in the lower Yellowstone Valley. This point also marks the south boundary of the Fort Buford Military Reservation, which post operated for many years on the north bank of the Missouri River at the mouth of the Yellowstone.

By taking the side road just north of here and going west a short distance to Fort Gilbert Lookout Point, on the bluffs, you have an excellent view of the Yellowstone Valley. Well worth the drive.

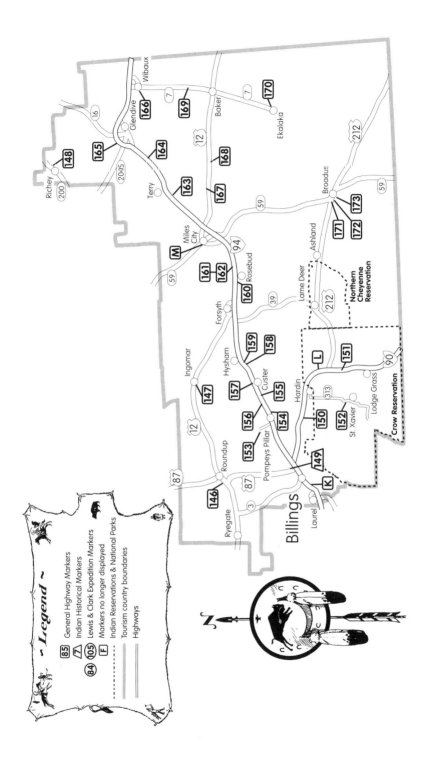

~ *Legend* ~

85 General Highway Markers

⚐ Indian Historical Markers

84 105 Lewis & Clark Expedition Markers

F Markers no longer displayed

----- Indian Reservations & National Parks

--- Tourism country boundaries

=== Highways

Richey
200
148
165
16
200S
Glendive
Wibaux
166
7
169
7
170
Baker
Ekalaka
164
12
168
Terry
163
167
212
59
Broadus
173
171
172
Miles City
M
94
161
162
Rosebud
160
59
Ashland
Lame Deer
212
Northern Cheyenne Reservation
59
Forsyth
39
Ingomar
Hysham
159
158
L
151
147
157
Custer
155
Hardin
Lodge Grass
90
156
154
313
Crow Reservation
Roundup
153
Pompeys Pillar
150
St. Xavier
152
12
87
87
149
146
3
K
Ryegate
Laurel
Billings

# Custer Country

## 146. Cow Country

U.S. 12, MP 167, west of Roundup

In the 1880s, days of the open range, many a roundup outfit worked this country. The spring roundup gathered the cattle in order to brand and tally the calf crop. The fall roundup gathered beef critters for shipping.

An outfit consisted of the captain, the riders, the "reps" from neighboring ranges, the cavvy or horse herd in charge of the day herder and night hawk, the four horse chuck wagon piloted by the cook and the bed wagon driven by his flunkey. Camp moved each day.

The cowboys rode circle in the morning, combing the breaks and coulees for cattle and heading them toward the central point to form a herd. In the afternoons of spring roundup the guards kept the herd together, the cutters split out the cows with calves, the ropers dabbed their loops on the calves, took a couple of dally welts around the saddle horn and dragged 'em to the fire. There the calf wrestlers

flanked and flopped them and the brander decorated them with ear notches, or dew laps, and a hot iron. It wasn't all sunshine and roses.

## 147. Ingomar
U.S. 12, MP 229, at Ingomar

Upon completion of the Milwaukee Railroad in 1910, Ingomar became a hub of commerce in the area bounded by the Missouri, Musselshell and Yellowstone Rivers. From Ingomar, horses and wagons carried supplies to the settlers and brought produce back to the community. The railroad promoted the growth of the area by encouraging settlers to use the 1909 Homestead Act to stake 320 acre claims. There were an average of 2500 homestead filings per year in this area between 1911 and 1917.

Ingomar claimed the title of "Sheep Shearing Capital of North America." Shearing at Ingomar was advantageous because of its vital location on the route between the winter pastures and the free summer grass. From Ingomar, the wool was loaded directly onto the railroad cars without risk of weather damage or delayed delivery to the buyers. Two million pounds of wool a year were shipped from Ingomar during the peak years of the 1910s.

A devastating fire in 1921, drought and depression have taken their toll on the area but the original frame school building, Bookman's store and the Jersey Lilly Saloon are recognized by the National Register of Historic Places.

## 148. Richey
Montana 200, MP 27, Richey rest area, between Billings and Hardin

In the fall of 1909, a Great Northern survey crew came through here and by 1912 all the surrounding area had been homesteaded except the badlands. Those early years were hard on the settlers. In spite of the survey, there were no roads, no railroad, no market, no grain elevators and some years no crops!

In 1911 one of the homesteaders, Clyde Richey, applied for a post office to serve the area, and the town has borne his name ever since. As the railroad built in this direction, a squatter town sprouted up on the prairie and the farmers sold stock to build an elevator. In 1916, Great Northern surveyed a townsite and sold lots. The "old town" merchants quickly moved to be near the depot and the first newspaper began publication. The entire community celebrated Steel Day, Dec. 2, 1916, when the first train arrived on the tracks, laying the last ties before it as it came.

Great Northern Railway had intended to extend the line across central Montana into Lewistown, but World War I interrupted those plans and the line terminated at Richey. As in so many areas, the other small towns nearby died out as the railroad town became the trade center. In February, 1986, the tracks were removed and once again Richey was without a railroad.

## 149. The Place Where the White Horse Went Down
Boot Hill Cemetery near junction of Montana 3
and U.S. 87 in Billings Heights

In 1837–38 a smallpox epidemic spread from the American Fur Trading Company steamboat St. Peter which had docked at Fort Union. The terrible disease for which the Indians had no immunity eventually affected all Montana tribes. A story is told among the Crow of two young warriors returning from a war expedition who found their village stricken. One discovered his sweetheart among the dying, and both warriors, grieving over loss of friends and family, were despondent and frustrated because nothing could alter the course of events. The young warriors dressed in their finest clothing and mounted a snow-white horse. Riding double and singing their death-songs, they drove the blindfolded horse over a cliff and landed at what is now the eastern end of the Yellowstone County Exhibition grounds. Six teenage boys and six teenage girls who were not afflicted with the disease witnessed the drama; they buried the dead warriors and left the camp. Great loss of life among the tribe followed in the wake of the epidemic. Although time has reduced the height of the cliff, the location is remembered even today as The Place Where the White Horse Went Down.

## 150. Buffalo Country
I-90, MP 476, Hardin rest area, between Billings and Hardin

Buffalo meant life to the Plains Indians, and the mountain Indians used to slip down from the hills for their share, too. Some tribes would toll buffalo into a concealed corral and then down them; another system was to stampede a herd over a cliff; but the sporting way was to use bows and arrows and ride them down on a trained buffalo horse.

Fat cow was the choice meat. The Indians preserved their meat long before the whites ever had any embalmed beef scandals. They made pemmican by drying and pulverizing the meat, pouring marrow bone grease and oil over it, and packing it away in skin bags. It kept indefinitely, and in food value one pound was worth ten of fresh meat.

Tanned robes and rawhide were used for bedding, tepees, clothes, war shields, stretchers, travois, canoes, and bags. Horns and bones made tools and utensils. The buffalo played a prominent part in many of their religious rites and jealousy of hereditary hunting grounds brought on most of the intertribal wars.

## 151. Garryowen
I-90, MP 514, Garryowen, south of Hardin

Garryowen, the old Irish tune, was the regimental marching song of the 7th Cavalry, General Custer's command.

The Battle of the Little Big Horn commenced in the valley just east of here June 25, 1876, after Custer had ordered Major Marcus A. Reno to move his battalion into action against the hostile Sioux and Cheyennes, led by Gall, Crazy Horse, Two Moons and Sitting Bull.

Reno, with 112 men, came out of the hills about 2 1/2 miles southeast of here and rode within 1/4 mile of the Indian camp where he was met by the hostiles who outnumbered the soldiers ten to one. Dismounting his men, Reno formed a thin skirmish line west across the valley from the timber along the river. After severe losses he was forced to retreat to high ground east of the Little Big Horn where he was joined by Major Benteen's Command. The combined force stood off the Indians until the approach of Gibbon's column from the north on the following day caused the hostiles to pull out. Reno and Benteen were not aware of Custer's fate until the morning of the 27th.

## 152. Fort C. F. Smith
Secondary 313, MP 23, at Old Fort C. F. Smith turnoff,
west of Lodge Grass

The ruins of this military post are about 25 miles west of here. In August 1866, two companies of soldiers guided by Jim Bridger established the fort on a plain overlooking the Big Horn River between Spring Gulch and Warrior Creek. It was built of logs and adobe, the third, last and most northerly of three posts built to protect emigrants and freighters on the Bozeman or Bonanza Trail from the Sioux and Cheyennes defending their hunting grounds.

The "Hayfield Fight" occurred August 1st, 1867, three miles east of the fort when a handful of soldiers in a log corral stood off an attacking band of Cheyennes estimated at several hundred strong. The Cheyenne had not anticipated the soldiers' new repeating rifles which were quickly reloadable.

The Sioux under Red Cloud forced the closing of the trail and abandonment of the fort under the Fort Laramie Treaty in 1868. The Indians lost the battle but won the war, though their victory would be short-lived given the ever-increasing encroachment by the settlers.

## 153. Camp #44 of the 1873 Yellowstone Expedition
Secondary 568, MP 2 (just north of the Yellowstone
River bridge)

In June, 1873, a Northern Pacific Railroad surveying party escorted by 1,500 soldiers, including the 7th Cavalry under the command of George Armstrong Custer, and 326 civilians, left Dakota Territory for the Yellowstone Valley to survey a route for the second transcontinental railroad.

The Lakota Sioux and Cheyenne were opposed to the railroad and clashed with the soldiers on several occasions throughout July. On August 11th, the expedition camped for a well-earned rest at this site. Five days later, shots were fired at them by six Lakota warriors hiding near Pompeys Pillar. One man later humorously reported that in the "ensuing scramble for cover, nude bodies [scattered] in all directions on the north bank. Shirts, pants and boots decorated the area along the north bank for a hundred yards." The soldiers returned fire and eventually drove the Indians away; no one was killed in the skirmish. Perhaps figuring that discretion was the better part of valor, the soldiers thereafter chose to "bear the heat rather than risk another swim in the

Yellowstone." It was not reported if Custer was among those caught with his pants down by the Lakota on that hot August day in 1873.

## 154. Pompey's Pillar
I-94, Frontage Road, MP 25, east of Pompey's Pillar

Called Iishbiia Anaache or "Place Where the Mountain Lion Dwells" by the Apsaalooka (Crow) people, Pompey's Pillar was a well known landmark to the Plains Indians. It was here, at a strategic natural crossing of the Yellowstone, or Elk River as it was known to the Apsaalooka, that the Indian people met to trade and exchange information. They painted pictographs and etched petroglyphs onto the sheer cliffs of the feature. Apsaalooka legend reports that Pompey's Pillar was once attached to the sandstone bluffs on the north side of the river. At one point, however, the rock detached itself from the cliffs and rolled across the river to it present site.

Pompey's Pillar was also a significant landmark for Euro-American explorers, fur trappers, soldiers and emigrants. It was discovered by Canadian North West Company employee Francois Larocque in 1805. A little less than a year later, on July 25, 1806, it was visited by a 12-man detachment under the command of William Clark that included Sacajawea and her infant son. Clark carved his name and the date on the rock and named it in honor of Sacajawea's son. He was just one of hundreds of individuals who have left their marks on the rock for generations.

Pompey's Pillar is now a National Historic Landmark administered by the Bureau of Land Management and is once again a meeting place for people on the northern Great Plains.

## 155. Buffalo Country
I-94, MP 42, Custer rest area, west of Custer

Buffalo meant life to the Plains Indians, and the mountain Indians used to slip down from the hills for their share, too. Some tribes would toll buffalo into a concealed corral and then down them; another system was to stampede a herd over a cliff; but the sporting way was to use bows and arrows and ride them down on a trained buffalo horse.

Fat cow was the choice meat. The Indians preserved their meat long before the whites ever had any embalmed beef scandals. They made pemmican by drying and pulverizing the meat, pouring marrow bone grease and oil over it, and packing it away in skin bags. It kept indefinitely, and in food value one pound was worth ten of fresh meat.

Tanned robes and rawhide were used for bedding, tepees, clothes, war shields, stretchers, travois, canoes, and bags. Horns and bones made tools and utensils. The buffalo played a prominent part in many of their religious rites and jealousy of hereditary hunting grounds brought on most of the intertribal wars.

## 156. Junction of Big Horn and Yellowstone Rivers
I-94, MPs 38 & 42, Custer rest area, west of Custer

The area which surrounds the mouth of the Big Horn River as it enters the Yellowstone 13 miles east of here is one of the most significant areas in the early history of Montana.

The Yellowstone was known universally to the Indians as Elk River, early French explorers called it Riviere Roche Jaune. The Big Horn was called Le Corne.

Captain William Clark of the Lewis and Clark Expedition, on his return trip from their journey to the Pacific Ocean, camped on the east bank of the Big Horn River, Saturday, July 26th, 1806.

The following year, on November 21st, 1807, an expedition led by Manuel Lisa, a St. Louis fur trader, arrived at the mouth of the Big Horn River. He built a fur trading post which he named Fort Remon in honor of his two-year-old son. This was the first building erected in what is now the State of Montana. From here Lisa sent John Colter to make contact with the Indians who were in winter camp to induce them to come to his post and trade their furs for goods. On this journey Colter discovered the wonders of present-day Yellowstone National Park.

In 1876 during the Sioux and Cheyenne Indian campaign of that year, General Terry and Colonel Gibbon marched up the Big Horn River to the site of Custer's defeat at the Battle of the Little Big Horn. They arrived two days after the battle. The steamer *Far West*, carrying supplies, plied the waters of both rivers and brought the wounded from that encounter back to Fort Abraham Lincoln, Dakota Territory.

## 157. Junction
Old U.S. Highway 10, in Custer, Junction City Memorial Park

The frontier town of Junction was just across the Yellowstone River. It was a stage station for outfits heading for old Fort Custer which used to be twenty-five or thirty miles south of here on the Crow Reservation. The original Reservation took in everything in Montana west of the Tongue River and south of the Yellowstone.

There isn't anything left of Junction except a few unkept graves along the hillside but she was lurid in her days. Calamity Jane sojourned there awhile and helped whoop things up. Calamity was born in Missouri, raised in Virginia City, Montana, and wound up at Deadwood, South Dakota. She had quite a dazzling social career.

Several years ago they found a skeleton of a three-horned dinosaur in the formation which makes the bluffs on the north side of the river. It must have bogged down some time before Junction did, probably a couple of million years.

## 158. Yellowstone River Trading Posts
I-94, MP 65, Hysham rest area, south of Hysham

Even before the Lewis and Clark Expedition returned to St. Louis in 1806, enterprising fur traders looked to the upper Missouri and Yellowstone rivers as a source of profit. At various times between 1807 and 1876, eight trading posts were located between the mouths of the Big Horn and Tongue rivers. Most were owned and operated by the American Fur Company–a firm organized in 1808 by John Jacob Astor. Rather than rely on the rendezvous system and the mountain men, the "Company" built a series of fixed posts designed to encourage the local tribes to trade at the forts. American Fur Company forts were virtual duplicates–each was about 100 square feet with cottonwood palisades and block houses at opposite corners. The forts included Fort Remon or Manuel Lisa (1807–1809), the first Fort Benton (1821), the second Big Horn Post (1824), Fort Cass (1832–1835), Fort Van Buren (1835–1843), Fort Alexander (1842–1850) and two Fort Sarpys.

Nearly all the existing accounts of the forts tell stories of a lively trade that was often filled with danger for both trader and Native American. By 1876, the fur trade was no longer profitable and the trading post was abandoned. While their presence was fleeting, they significantly impacted the lives of Native Americans and those who chose to garrison these isolated places. The trading posts represented a colorful era in Montana's history.

## 159. "The Yellowstone," by Wallace McRae
I-94, MP 65, Hysham rest area, south of Hysham

Millions of buffalo curried her flanks
as she shed winter's ice in the spring.
In the smoke of ten thousand campfires
she heard drumbeats and war dances ring.
On the crest of her bosom she sped Captain Clark
and Sacajawea as well.
She bisected the prairie, the plains and the mountains
from her birthplace in "John Colter's Hell."
To the traveler she whispered, "Come, follow me,"
with a wink and a toss of her head.
She tempted the trapper, gold miner and gambler
to lie down by her sinuous bed.
"Safe passage," she murmured provocatively,
"safe passage and riches as well."
She smiled as the thread of Custer's blue line
followed her trails and then fell.
She carved out the grade for the railroads;
She took settlers to their new home.
Watered their stock, watered their fields
and let them grow crops on their loam.
Her banks were the goal of the trail herds;
her grass was the prize that they sought.
'Till the blizzard of '86 and seven,
nearly killed off the whole lot.
Don't boss her, don't cross her, let her run free
and damn you, don't dam her at all.
She's a wild old girl, let her looks not deceive you . . .
But we love her in spite of it all.
—*copyright 1986 Wallace McRae*

## 160. The Rosebud River

Secondary 446, MP 2, Far West Park, north of Rosebud

This stream was noted by Captain Wm. Clark, July 28th, 1806, when he was descending the Yellowstone River.

In June, 1876, the columns of General Gibbon and General Custer, both under command of General Terry, met here, the former coming from the west and the latter from the east. They were under orders to campaign against the Sioux and Cheyenne Indians.

The Generals held a conference aboard the supply steamer "Far West" and it was decided that Custer take his column up the Rosebud on a fresh Indian trail which had been found by a scouting party under Major Reno. He started June 22nd. Terry and Gibbon were to proceed to the mouth of the Big Horn and follow that stream up to the valley of the Little Big Horn where they believed the hostiles would be found. Custer was expected to contact Gibbon June 26th and the two columns would cooperate in an attack.

Custer reached and attacked the Indian camp June 25th and his entire command was all but wiped out.

## 161. Cattle Brands

I-94, MP 112, Hathaway rest area, between Forsyth and Miles City

# CATTLE BRANDS

*M*any a dogie #(not "doggie"- dudes please note) has been decorated with one of these famous Montana Irons.

| | | | |
|---|---|---|---|
| CA *Running CA* | ☆ *Bug* | W *Seven VM* | A *Square & Compass* |
| 79 *Seventy nine* | © *Circle C* | ⏄ *Shaving mug* | ᴜ *Quarter circle U* |
| DS *DHS* | SH *Monogram SH* | 40 *Forty* | ᵈ₂ *Lazy H hanging 2* |
| ₀8 *Three circle* | R *Bar R* | LU *LU bar* | 32 *Reversed E2 bar* |
| N-N *N bar N* | D *Flying D* | T *Umbrella* | ᑯ *Lazy P swinging 9* |
| Y *Turkey track* | X *Long X* | 4 *Spearhead* | ⊕ *Two pole pumpkin* |
| ₐX *Hat X* | ▽ *Bull head* | ₰ *Rocking Chair* | 7-7 *Seven bar seven* |
| 777 *Three sevens* | oo *Two dot* | W *Antler* | ꓵF *Monogram FUF* |
| N *N bar* | ⊥X *Inverted TX* | VVV *Three V's* | = *Railroad track* |
| Ψ *Pitch fork* | ⌒ *Hash knife* | X *Hourglass* | PLE *Monogram PLE* |
| ᶴ *Fish hook* | 2A *Two A bar* | ⌂ *Rafter circle* | ⌒ *Horseshoe bar* |
| ⌒ *Piece of pie* | ⊰ *Mill Iron* | W *W bar* | ⑥ *Circle diamond* |
| CK | O *Circle* | U *U Lazy J* | SL |
| 1X | LO | 707 | WM |
| JO | OW | XIT | |

#A dogie is a little calf who has lost its mammy and whose daddy has ran off with another cow.

## 162. Rosebud

I-94, MP 112, Hathaway rest area,
between Forsyth and Miles City

From July 28, 1806, when Wm. Clark passed Rosebud Creek on his way down the Yellowstone, this river valley has served as one of the major avenues for development and trade in eastern Montana. Innumerable trappers and traders followed Clark's route, including the American Fur Co. which constructed Ft. Van Buren at the juncture of the Rosebud and Yellowstone in 1835. The fort proved unprofitable and was abandoned in 1843.

Buffalo hunters took over 40,000 robes from this area alone during the 1860s and 1870s, shipping them out by river boat. The slaughter disrupted eastern Montana's Indian culture and precipitated several years of bloody confrontation culminating in the Battle of the Rosebud on June 17, 1876, and the Battle of the Little Big Horn eight days later.

In late 1882, the Northern Pacific R.R. established a siding in the Rosebud vicinity as it pushed westward. Soon a town sprang up as a livestock shipping center with Butte Creek and the Rosebud forming a natural corral. Rail and auto transportation quickly replaced wagon and river traffic. As Rosebud grew it even acquired its own car dealership, the Otis Davis Agency featuring the E.M.F. line. Many an old-timer assumed the initials meant "Every Morning Fix 'em."

## 163. Powder River

Old U.S. 10, MP 14, southwest of Terry

This is the river that exuberant parties claim is a mile wide, an inch deep, and runs uphill. The statement is exaggerated. Captain Clark, of the Lewis and Clark Expedition, named it the Redstone in 1806 and afterwards found out that the Indians called it the same thing but they pronounced it "Wahasah." He camped just across the Yellowstone from the mouth of the Powder on the night of July 30th, 1806.

Generals Terry and Custer, moving from the east to take part in a campaign against the Sioux and Cheyenne Indians, camped on the Yellowstone about 25 miles west of here June 10, 1876. From that point Major Reno was sent with six troops of the 7th Cavalry to scout the Powder and Tongue valleys for Indian sign. He swung further west and picked up a fresh trail on the Rosebud. It was this trail that led Custer into contact with the hostiles resulting in the Battle of the Little Big Horn.

## 164. The Yellowstone River
I-94, MP 192, Bad Route rest area, northeast of Fallon

Interstate 90 generally follows the Yellowstone River from Glendive to Livingston, Montana. This river originates south of Yellowstone National Park and terminates when it joins the Missouri River north of here. It is the longest undammed river in the lower 48 states.

When the West was won, most rivers were lost to damming and dewatering. This river is the exception; it remains wet, wild and dam-free over its entire length. The Yellowstone flows free for over 650 miles, draining a watershed greater in area than all of the New England states combined.

In the 1970s Montanans held a great debate over this mighty river's future. When the dust settled, the state reserved a substantial amount of water to remain instream so that the Yellowstone might never be depleted and might forever remain free-flowing.

Other uses of the river–municipal, agricultural and industrial–are also provided for. Today, this waterway is in balance with all its users, including nature's creatures. Few American rivers can still make that claim.

## 165. Glendive
Old U.S. 10, MP 326, west of Glendive

A yachting party consisting of Capt. Wm. Clark, of the Lewis and Clark Expedition, six of his men, Sacajawea and her child floated by here August 1, 1806, navigating a craft made by lashing together two hollowed-out cottonwood logs. It was Clark's birthday and the outfit had to land that afternoon to let a herd of buffalo swim the river ahead of them.

Sir George Gore, a "sporting" Irish nobleman, arrived on the scene to hunt in 1855 with Jim Bridger as a guide. Gore's harvest during an eleven-month stay in the Yellowstone Valley included 105 bears, over 2,000 buffalo, and 1,600 elk and deer. He hunted for the thrill of the chase and

trophies, only infrequently using the meat. The Crows, who occupied this country, hotly protested the devastation of their food supply.

It was Sir George who named the local tributary to the Yellowstone River "Glendive," and the town assumed the same name 25 years later. During the cattle boom of the 1880s Glendive became the "Queen City of the Cow Land." In 1884, 12,800 "pilgrims" or eastern cattle were unloaded here in one week to help stock the range. They may have been "barnyard stock" but their progeny grew up rough, tough and hard to curry.

## 166. Pierre Wibaux
### Montana 7, MP 80, Wibaux Park, Wibaux

In 1876, this was strictly buffalo and Indian country. There wasn't a ranch between Bismarck, North Dakota, and Bozeman, Montana. But the U.S. Cavalry rounded up the hostile Indians from 1876 to 1881 and forced them onto reservations while the buffalo hunters were busy clearing the range for the cattle boom of the Eighties.

Pierre Wibaux ran one of the biggest cattle spreads around here in the early days. His will provided a fund to erect a statue of himself "overlooking the land I love so well." It stands a mile west of the town of Wibaux.

From this end of Montana to the west end is just about the same distance as from New York to Chicago. You have to push a lot of ground behind you to get places in this state.

## 167. Powder River
### U.S. 12, MP 32, east of Miles City

When a top rider from this part of the country is forking the hurricane deck of a sun-fishing, fuzztail, some of his pals are prone to sit on the rope rail of the corral, emitting advice and hollering "Powder River! Let 'er buck!!" by way of encouragement. The 91st Division adopted that war cry during the first

World War and spread it far and wide. Well, this is the famous Powder River, that enthusiasts allege is a "mile wide, an inch deep, and runs up hill."

The entire Powder River country was favorite buffalo hunting range for the Sioux and Cheyenne Indians before the day of cattle men. Many intertribal battles were fought in this region as well as frequent skirmishes between Indians and the U.S. troops. The country is rich in Indian lore and tales of the subsequent reign of the cattle kings.

## 168. After The Roundup
U.S. 12, MP 43, east of Miles City

D. J. O'Malley grew up living at frontier forts because his stepfather served in the 19th Infantry. He lived at Fort Keogh, near Miles City, for five years before going to work in 1882 at age 16 for the Home Land and Cattle Co. (N–Bar–N) for $45 a month. His 14-year tenure with the outfit included three trail drives from Texas.

In O'Malley's day, writing verse about life on the range was a common cowboy pastime, and O'Malley was one of the best. His poem, "After the Roundup," appeared in the Miles City *Stockmens' Journal* in 1893. Thirty years later, it had become the classic, "When the Work's All Done This Fall." Here is the refrain from the original poem:

> After the round up's over,
> After the shipping's done,
> I'm going straight back home, boys,
> Ere all my money's gone.
> My mother's dear heart is breaking,
> Breaking for me, that's all;
> But, with God's help I'll see her,
> When work is done this fall.

## 169. Wagon Road
Montana 7, MP 44, north of Baker

Around these gumbo buttes and across these ridges and valleys, the old trail wended its way between Ft. Lincoln on the Missouri River in Dakota Territory and Ft. Keogh on the Yellowstone River in Montana. Government mail stages, covered wagons, soldiers, people searching for homes, wealth, or adventure–with horses, ox teams, and mules– plunged or plodded along this undulating trail. In 1887, one freight train of 95 wagons, each drawn by 4 to 6 horses or mules, and each loaded with civilian goods of all kinds made up the largest train to make the trip. All were constantly watched and harassed by the Indians, whose lands and way of life were, by trick and treaty, being forever forced from them. With the building of the Northern Pacific Railroad, and also the fences by homesteaders, the trail was abandoned. A few grassy ruts may be seen on the ridge to the southwest.

## 170. Ekalaka
Montana 7, MP 1, north of Ekalaka

Some people claim an old buffalo hunter figured that starting a thirst emporium for parched cowpunchers on this end of the range would furnish him a more lucrative and interesting vocation than downing buffalo. He picked a location and was hauling a load of logs to erect this proposed edifice for the eradication of ennui when he bogged down in a snowdrift. "Hell," he exclaimed, "Any place in Montana is a good place for a saloon," so he unloaded and built her right there. That was the traditional start of Ekalaka in the 1860s and the old undaunted pioneer spirit of the West still lingers here.

When it became a town it was named after an Indian girl, born on the Powder River, who was the daughter of Eagle Man, an Ogalala Sioux. She was a niece of the War Chief, Red Cloud, and was also related to Sitting Bull. She became the wife of David H. Russell, the first white man to settle permanently in this locality.

## 171. Southeastern Montana
U.S. 212, MP 79, Broadus

The first white man to enter Montana was Pierre de La Verendrye, a French explorer, who arrived in this corner of the state on New Year's Day, 1743. His party had traveled southwest from a Canadian fur trading post to investigate Indian tales of the Land of the Shining Mountains.

Next came the trappers, following the Lewis and Clark Expedition of 1804-06. Like the rest of Montana east of the mountains this portion remained unsettled Indian and buffalo country until the Texas trail herds overran the range in the 1880s. Up to that time it was a favorite hunting ground for roving bands of Cheyenne Indians and the various Sioux tribes.

With the coming of the cowman the buffalo gave way to the beef critter and high-heeled boots replaced buckskin moccasins.

## 172. The Powder River Country
U.S. 212, MP 79, Broadus rest area, southern edge of Broadus

From its source in central Wyoming to its union with the Yellowstone River, the Powder River is 250 miles long, "A mile wide and an inch deep; too thick to drink and too thin to plow." During World War I, Montana's 91st Division gained national notoriety for the river with its war cry of "Powder River let' er buck!" The origin of the river's name, however, is obscure.

In July, 1806, Captain William Clark christened it the "Red Stone" river. Later renamed the Powder River, historians supposed it took its name from the dark gunpowder-colored soil and sand along its banks. But army scout William Drannan maintained that the river was inadvertently named by Vierres Roubidoux, a French guide, who shouted "Cache la Powder!" (Hide the Powder!) when a group of soldiers he was escorting was attacked by Indians.

Located in the center of Powder River County, Broadus was once situated 20 miles upstream on the Powder River in 1900. Named for a pioneer family, Broadus was relocated to this site at the beginning of the Homestead Boom in 1907. The community's strategic location at the junction of two important highways made Broadus an important trade center despite its great distance from any railroads. Designated the county seat of the newly created Powder River County in 1919, Broadus was once described as one of the "Biggest Little Towns in the West."

## 173. Big Sky Country
U.S. 212, MP 79, Broadus rest area, southern edge of Broadus

Don't fence me in,
Gimme land, lotso' land
Stretching miles across the West.
Don't fence me in,
Let me ride where it's wide
And that's how I like it best.
I want to see the stars,
I want to feel the breeze,
I want to smell the sage
And hear those cottonwood trees.
Just turn me loose,
Let me straddle my old saddle
Where the Rocky Mountains rise.
On my cayuse,
I'll go siftin', I'll go driftin'
Underneath those Western skies.
I gotta get where the West commences,
I can't stand hobbles;
I can't stand fences.
Don't fence me in.

Montana's big sky has inspired many poets. The verses above were penned by Bob Fletcher, father of the state's historical highway markers, which were first erected in the 1930s. In 1934, Cole Porter bought this poem from Fletcher, and it became one of Porter's greatest hits. It was not until 1954 that Fletcher got credit for composing the famous lyrics that inspired the hit song, "Don't Fence Me In."

# Markers No Longer Displayed

The following markers were removed for a variety of reasons, most having to do with the changing shape of the highway. Still, their text is interesting and relevant, and you may enjoy referring to them as you pass the areas where they used to stand.

## A. Gates of the Mountains and the Bear Tooth
I-15, MP 209, north of Helena, Exit 29

Friday, July 19, 1805.

"this evening we entered much the most remarkable clifts that we have yet seen. these clifts rise from the waters edge on either side perpendicularly to the hight of [about] 1200 feet. . . . the tow[er]ing and projecting rocks in many places seem ready to tumble on us. the river appears to have forced its way through this immence body of solid rock for the distance of 5¾ Miles and where it makes it's exit below has the[r]own on either side vast collumns of rocks mountains high. . . . it is deep from side to side nor is ther in the 1st 3 miles of this distance a spot except one of a few yards in extent on which a man could rest the soal of his foot. . . . from the singular appearance of this place I called it the gates of the rocky mountains" (Extract from Capt. Meriwether Lewis' Diary, Lewis and Clark Expedition).

## B. Missouri River Canyon
I-15, MP 239, Dearborn rest area

The Lewis and Clark Expedition, westward bound, camped just across the river on the night of July 17, 1805. Their equipment was packed in eight canoes. These were rowed, poled, or towed as conditions demanded. Some of the party walked, following an old Indian road through this portion of the canyon. The following morning, as Capt. Lewis recorded in his diary, they ". . . saw a large herd of the Bighorned anamals* on the immencely high and nearly perpendicular clift opposite to us; on the fase of this clift they walked about and bounded from

rock to rock with apparent unconcern where it appl[e]ared to me that no quadruped could have stood. . . ."
  *Mountain sheep

## C.   The Sun River
  U.S. 89, MP 0, Vaughn weigh station

This river was called "The Medicine" by the Indians. On the return trip from the coast Capt. Lewis, of the Lewis and Clark Expedition, struck this river approximately fifty miles west of here. He followed it down to the Missouri passing near this point, July 11, 1806. In his journal under that date he said, "when I arrived in sight of the whitebear Islands the missouri bottoms on both sides of the river were crouded with buffaloe[.] I sincerely beleif that there were not less than 10 thousand buffaloe within a circle of 2 miles arround that place."

The city of Great Falls covers a portion of the plain across which the Expedition made their difficult eighteen–mile portage around the falls of the Missouri in June, 1805.

## D.   Deer Lodge Valley
  U.S. 10, 5 miles south of Deer Lodge

At the mouth of Rattlesnake Creek, south of Dillon, a phonetic speller erected a road sign in 1862. One side reads

Tu Grass Hop Per digins
30 myle
Kepe the Trale nex the Bluffe

The directions on the other side were a trifle sketchy. They read

Tu JONNI GRANTS
One Hundred and Twenti myle

The placer diggings were at Bannack and the city of Deer Lodge is built on a part of Johnny Grant's ranch. The miners considered Johnny a tolerably close neighbor.

This valley has been a great stock country since the 1850s when said Johnny Grant and friends used to pick up worn–down, footsore cattle along the Oregon Trail and haze them up to Montana to rest and fatten.

The mountains to the east are the Continental Divide. Those to the west are the Flint Creek Range.

## E. The Big Hole River
I-15, 2 miles north of Melrose

This stream was named the Wisdom River by Captains Lewis and Clark. Their expedition, westward bound, passed its mouth Aug. 4, 1805. "Hole" was a term frequently used by the fur trappers in the early part of the last century to designate a mountain valley. An extensive valley west of here drained by this river became known as "The Big Hole" and the name of the river was changed accordingly.

The Battle of the Big Hole was fought Aug. 9, 1877, in the valley just mentioned. Chief Joseph's band of fugitive Nez Perce Indians repulsed U.S. troops under command of General Gibbon.

## F. Camp Fortunate
I-15, 20 miles south of Dillon

In August, 1805, Capt. Lewis, of the Lewis and Clark Expedition, while scouting to the west of here, found a camp of the Shoshone Indians. He had hoped to meet them ever since leaving the Three Forks of the Missouri.

He persuaded their chief and some of the tribe to return to this point with him to meet Capt. Clark, who, with the main body of the Expedition, was coming up the creek with canoes. Clark arrived August 17, 1805.

Sacajawea, who guided portions of the Expedition, had been captured at Three Forks by an enemy tribe when a child. She recognized the Shoshone chief, Cameahwah, as her brother. This furthered the friendly relations started by Lewis, and he and Clark were able to secure horses for their outfit from the Indians. They cached their canoes and part of their supplies near here and pulled out towards the West August 24th to cross the Continental Divide.

## G. John M. Bozeman
I-90, 14 miles east of Livingston

John M. Bozeman, the Georgian who pioneered the "cutoff" trail from Fort Laramie, Wyoming to the gold diggin's at Virginia City, Montana, in the early Sixties, was killed up this draw by Blackfeet Indians in April, 1867. He and Tom Coover were on their way to Fort C. F. Smith on the Big Horn River. They had camped on the Yellowstone and Indians stole some of their horses that night. The next day, while Bozeman and

Coover were eating, five Indians came into camp with these stolen horses and professed to be friendly Crows. Not until too late were they recognized as Blackfeet by the white men. Without warning they shot and killed Bozeman.* Coover was wounded but escaped. Bozeman is buried in the town west of here that bears his name.

> *Historians doubt the veracity of this version of John Bozeman's death. Some now believe that white men disguised as Indians committed the murder.

## H. Jorgen Elesius Madson
### Montana 78, MP 28, south of Absarokee

Jorgen Elesius Madson, Pioneer Lutheran pastor, began his ministry in the foothills of the Crazy Mountains during 1895. His circuit riding included the open range and mountain valleys from Hardin to the Snowies near Lewistown to the Belts and Beartooth Mountains. From Melville he served a wide area, traveling great distances, ministering to scattered families and communities. He organized the numerous churches of the southern Montana district.

On the opening of the Crow Reservation he homesteaded across the highway from this marker. This home he named "fagerheim" (Beautiful Home) because of the surrounding natural beauty. From here he continued his work among the homesteaders and ranchers and in the growing communities of the Billings and Yellowstone areas until his demise January 6, 1928.

For a time he was the only Lutheran minister in Montana; under rugged pioneering conditions and at great personal sacrifices he devoted his lifelong ministry to the Land of the Shining Mountains.

## I. Fort Musselshell
### Montana 200, 1.5 miles east of Mosby

Fort Musselshell was located on the Missouri River about 35 miles north of here. It was a trading post in the 1860s and 1870s and as such had a brief but colorful career. The only whites in that part of the state were woodchoppers for the Missouri River steamboats, wolfers, trappers and Indian traders.

The River Crows and Gros Ventre Indians traded there. A buffalo robe brought them 3 cups of coffee, or 6 cups of sugar, or 10 cups of flour. It was tolerably profitable business from the trader's standpoint.

The Assiniboines and Sioux regarded this post as an amusement center where bands of ambitious warriors could lie in ambush and get target practice on careless whites.

During the cattle days of the 1880s the mouth of the Musselshell became a cattle rustler's hangout but after a Vigilance Committee stretched a few of them they seemed to lose interest.

## J The Little Rocky Mountains
U.S. 191, MP 102, south of Malta

The Little Rocky Mountains are rich in Indian lore, tales of gold strikes and the fortunes made, stories of the days when cowpunchers from nearby cattle outfits made Zortman and Landusky their off-time headquarters, of the Kid Curry Outlaw Gang and a hundred others of the days when these towns were booming, thriving, typical western mining camps.

The future, as well as the past, of the Little Rocky Mountains, may lie underground. Since the discovery of gold in Alder Gulch in 1864, $25 million in gold has been taken from the mines at Ruby Gulch, Landusky and Beaver Creek. The names of Charles Whitcomb, Robert Coburn, Louis Goslin and B. D. Phillips are synonymous with the gold-mining days. The second largest cyanide mill in the world was at one time located in Ruby Gulch.

For the future, the Azure Caves which honeycomb Saddle Butte with crystalline rooms and passages of grandeur and beauty, are expected to make the Little Rockies one of the West's most awe-inspiring wonders.

But, in the opinion of mining experts, there is still gold in these hills. Once again Zortman and Landusky will be thriving camps, they believe.

## K. Indian Caves
U.S. 87/212, Pictograph Cave State Monument
southeast of Billings

These two rock caves in the sandstone rimrock of Bitter Creek, provided air-conditioned housing for some of Montana's early families even before Pharaoh's daughter found Moses adrift on the Nile, as long ago as 2500 B.C. The cave, right, is called "Pictograph." "Ghost" Cave is to the left.

This was an ideal primitive campground, with water in a nearby spring, fuel along the coulee bottom, shelter overhead. A lookout posted on the cliff could spot the enemy or game herds miles away.

Prehistoric tribes squatted in these rock shelters and on the slopes in front, roasting buffalo meat and cracking the marrow bones with stone hammers. The earliest artists decorated Pictograph Cave walls with enduring dark pigment. Later painters, possibly the early Crow Indians, added pictures of guns and coups sticks in red, indicating more recent occupancy.

The site was excavated as a WPA archaeological project in the late 1930s. The dotted lines in the caves indicate the floor levels when the excavations began. Four buried layers give evidence of major periods of occupation. Thousands of bones and artifacts were recovered and classified.

Since no sites of this type have been found on the Great Plains, this one is of national significance. Please help preserve it for those who follow.

## L.   The Crow Indians
I-90, Crow Agency

"Crow" is the white man's mistaken interpretation of the Indian name Absaroka, meaning "bird" or "thing that flies." The nation divided into two tribes, the River and the Mountain Crows. In frontier days they warred with the Sioux and Blackfeet on the north and east and were usually friendly with the Nez Perce and Flatheads from the west. They were accomplished horse thieves and kept themselves well provided with ponies. Horse stealing was a highly honorable and adventurous practice amongst the western Indians.

Never bitterly opposed to the whites, many of their warriors served as scouts for the U.S. Army in their campaigns against hostile tribes.

Their great chief, Plenty Coups, was chosen as the representative of all the American Indians to place their wreath on the tomb of the Unknown Soldier at Arlington.

## M.  The Tongue River
U.S. 12, MP 2, west of Miles City

Captain Wm. Clark, of the Lewis and Clark Expedition, camped with his party on an island in the Yellowstone, opposite the mouth of the Tongue, July 29th, 1806. The Indian name for the river is "Lazeka."

Construction of Fort Keogh, named for one of Custer's captains killed at the Battle of the Little Big Horn in 1876, was started in 1877. That knob off to the south is Signal Butte. During the Indian troubles the army used to flash sun mirror messages to a post in the Black Hills 175 miles away. A cloudy day sure threw a lot of static into that pioneer wireless system.

Miles City, named after General Nelson A. Miles, started in 1877 as a shack and tent town with a population running largely to prospectors and miners from the Black Hills, buffalo hunters, traders and gamblers. She was wild for a while. When the cattle days of the 1880s arrived many a Texas trail herd came through here and the city soon acquired a national reputation as a cattle and horse market which it has never relinquished.

# Recommended Reading

Alberta–Montana Heritage Partnership. *Alberta-Montana Discovery Guide: Museums, Parks and Historic Sites*. Edmonton: Alberta Montana Heritage Partnership, 1997.

Ambrose, Stephen E. *Undaunted Courage: Meriwether Lewis, Thomas Jefferson and the Opening of the West*. New York: Simon and Schuster, 1996.

Arlee, Johnny. *Over a Century of Moving to the Drum: Salish Indian Celebrations on the Flathead Reservation*. Helena: Montana Historical Society Press, 1998.

Baker, Don. *Next Year Country: The Story of Eastern Montana*. Boulder, Colorado: Fred Pruett Books, 1992.

Blew, Mary Clearman. *All but the Waltz: Essays on a Montana Family*. New York: Penguin, 1992.

Brown, Mark H. *The Plainsmen of the Yellowstone: A History of the Yellowstone Basin*. Lincoln: University of Nebraska Press, 1969.

Bryan, William L., and Michael Crummitt. *Montana's Indians: Yesterday and Today*. 2d ed. Helena, Mont.: American and World Geographic Publishing, 1996.

Bullchild, Percy. *American Indian Genesis: The Blackfeet Story of Creation*. Berkeley: Ulysses Press, 1998.

Cheney, Roberta Carkeek. *Names on the Face of Montana*. Missoula, Montana: Mountain Press, 1983.

De Voto, Bernard. *Across the Wide Missouri*. Boston: Houghton Mifflin, 1947.

———. *The Journals of Lewis and Clark*. Boston: Houghton Mifflin, 1953.

Dimsdale, Thomas J. *The Vigilantes of Montana*. Norman: University of Oklahoma Press, 1953.

Dippie, Brian W. ed. *Charlie Russell Roundup: Essays on America's Favorite Cowboy Artist*. Helena: Montana Historical Society Press, 1999.

Doig, Ivan. *This House of Sky: Landscapes of a Western Mind.* New York: Harcourt Brace Jovanovich, 1978.

Ewers, John C. *The Blackfeet: Raiders on the Northwestern Plains.* Norman: University of Oklahoma Press, 1958.

Federal Writers' Project. *The WPA Guide to 1930s Montana.* Forward by William Kittredge. Tucson: University of Arizona Press, 1994.

Grant, Marilyn. *Montana Mainstreets Volume 1: A Guide to Historic Virginia City.* Helena: Montana Historical Society Press, 1998.

Graves, Lee. *Montana's Fur Trade Era.* Helena, Mont.: American and World Geographic Publishing, 1994.

———. *Bannack: Cradle of Montana.* Helena, Mont.: American and World Geographic Publishing, 1991.

Guthrie, A. B., Jr. *The Big Sky.* Boston: Houghton Mifflin Co., 1974.

Hart, Jeff. *Montana Native Plants and Early Peoples.* rev. ed. Helena: Montana Historical Society Press, 1996.

Hedren, Paul L. *Traveler's Guide to the Great Sioux War: The Battlefields, Forts and Related Sites of America's Greatest Indian War.* Helena: Montana Historical Society Press, 1996.

Horner, John R., and James Gorman. *Digging Dinosaurs: The Search That Unraveled the Mystery of Baby Dinosaurs.* New York: Harper Collins, 1988.

Horner, John R., and Edwin Dobbs. *Dinosaur Lives: Unearthing an Evolutionary Saga.* New York: Harper Collins, 1997.

Howard, Joseph Kinsey. *Montana, High, Wide and Handsome.* Lincoln: University of Nebraska Press, 1983.

Hunter, James. *Scottish Highlanders, Indian Peoples: Thirty Generations of a Montana Family.* Helena: Montana Historical Society Press, 1997.

Kittredge, William, and Annick Smith, eds. *The Last Best Place: A Montana Anthology.* Helena: Montana Historical Society Press, 1988.

Langford, Nathaniel P. *Vigilante Days and Ways.* rev. ed. Helena: American and World Geographic Publishing, 1996.

Lowie, Robert H. *The Crow Indians.* Lincoln: University of Nebraska Press, 1983.

Maclean, Norman. *A River Runs Through It and Other Stories*. Chicago: University of Chicago Press, 1976.

———. *Young Men and Fire*. Chicago: University of Chicago Press, 1992.

Malone, Michael P. *The Battle for Butte: Mining and Politics on the Northern Frontier, 1864–1906*. Helena: Montana Historical Society Press, 1995.

Malone, Michael P., Richard B. Roeder, and William L. Lang. *Montana: A History of Two Centuries*. rev. ed. Seattle: University of Washington Press, 1991.

McCarter, Steve. *Guide to the Milwaukee Road in Montana*. Helena: Montana Historical Society Press, 1992.

Merrill, Andrea, and Judy Jacobson. *Montana Almanac*. Helena, Mont.: Falcon Press, 1997.

Montana Historical Society. Montana Mainstreets Volume 2: *A Guide to Historic Glendive*. Helena: Montana Historical Society Press, 1998.

Moulton, Gary E. ed. *The Journals of the Lewis and Clark Expedition*. 11 vols. Lincoln: University of Nebraska Press, 1983–97.

Murphy, Mary. *Mining Cultures: Men, Women, and Leisure in Butte, 1914–1941*. Urbana: University of Illinois, 1997.

Purple, Edwin R. *Perilous Passage: A Narrative of the Montana Gold Rush, 1862–1863*, ed. Kenneth N. Owens. Helena: Montana Historical Society Press, 1995.

Raban, Jonathan. *Bad Land: An American Romance*. New York: Pantheon Books, 1996.

Rankin, Charles E. ed. *Legacy: New Perspectives on the Battle of the Little Bighorn*. Helena: Montana Historical Society Press, 1996.

Ronda, James P. ed. *Voyages of Discovery: Essays on the Lewis and Clark Expedition*. Helena: Montana Historical Society Press, 1998.

Russell, Charles M. *Trails Plowed Under: Stories of the Old West*. Lincoln: University of Nebraska Press, 1996.

Sievert, Ken, and Ellen Sievert. *Virginia City and Alder Gulch*. Helena, Mont.: American and World Geographic Publishing, 1993.

———. Montana Mainstreets Volume 3: *A Guide to Historic Lewistown*. Helena: Montana Historical Society Press, 1999.

Smith, Phyllis. *Bozeman and the Gallatin Valley: A History*. Helena: Falcon Press, 1997.

Swartout, Robert, and Harry Fritz, ed. *The Montana Heritage: An Anthology of Historical Essays*. Helena: Montana Historical Society Press, 1992.

Toole, K. Ross. *Montana: An Uncommon Land*. Norman: University of Oklahoma Press, 1984.

———. *Twentieth Century Montana: A State of Extremes*. Norman: University of Oklahoma Press, 1983.

Vichorek, Daniel N. *The Hi-Line: Profiles of a Montana Land*. Helena, Mont.: American and World Geographic Publishing, 1993.

Walter, Dave. *Montana Campfire Tales: Fourteen Historical Essays*. Helena, Mont.: Falcon Press, 1997.

Welch, James. *Fools Crow*. New York: Viking Penguin, 1986.

———. *Killing Custer: The Battle of the Little Big Horn and the Fate of the Plains Indians*. New York: W. W. Norton, 1994.

———. *Winter in the Blood*. New York: Viking Penguin, 1986.

West, Carroll Van. *A Traveler's Companion to Montana History*. Helena: Montana Historical Society Press, 1986.

Wilfong, Cheryl. *Following the Nez Perce Trail*. Corvallis: Oregon State University Press, 1990.

Wollaston, Percy. *Homesteading: A Montana Family Album*. New York: Lyons Press, 1997.

Wolle, Muriel. *Montana Pay Dirt: A Guide to the Mining Camps of the Treasure State*. Athens: Swallow Press/Ohio University Press, 1982.

Zimmer, William F. *Frontier Soldier: An Enlisted Man's Journal of the Sioux and Nez Perce Campaigns, 1877*, ed. Jerome A. Greene. Helena: Montana Historical Society Press, 1998.

# Index to the Sign Text

Sign names are listed in quotation marks.